Covenant Theo

Contemporary Approaches

Covenant Theology

Contemporary Approaches

Edited by Mark J. Cartledge and David Mills

University of Liverpool Anglican Chaplaincy Lectures
1997 – 2000

paternoster
press

Contents

List of Contributors

Editors

The Revd Dr Mark J. Cartledge is Chaplain and Tutor at St John's College, University of Durham. His teaching and research interests are in the areas of practical theology, Pentecostal/ charismatic theology and church-based community and youth work. His doctoral dissertation is to be published as *Charismatic Glossolalia: An Empirical-Theological Study* (Ashgate, 2001). He was formerly Anglican Chaplain to the University of Liverpool (1993–98).

Professor David Mills has a Personal Chair in the department of English Language and Literature at the University of Liverpool. His research interests are in the area of medieval English literature and especially medieval drama. He has co-edited the *Chester Mystery Cycle* for the Early English Text Society. His most recent monograph, *Recycling the Cycle: The City of Chester and its Plays*, was published by the University of Toronto Press (1999). An article on covenant theology and the cycle is currently at press for Leeds Studies in English. He is a member of the Executive Board of the Records of Early English Drama, a member of the Editorial Board of Medieval English Theatre and a trustee of St Deiniol's Library, Hawarden, North Wales.

Contributors

Professor Gary D. Badcock is Professor of Systematic Theology at Huron University College in London, Ontario, Canada. He is a Canadian by birth and formerly taught systematic theology at the Universities of Aberdeen and Edinburgh. His books include *Light of Truth and Fire of Love: A Theology of the Holy Spirit* (Eerdmans, 1997) and *The Way of Life: A Theology of Christian Vocation* (Eerdmans, 1998). He is writing a major study of the doctrine of the church.

Dr Mark Bonnington is a Tutor in New Testament studies at Cranmer Hall, St John's College, University of Durham. His doctoral research was on Paul's letter to the Galatians, due to be published by Paternoster Press; he is writing a commentary on Paul's first epistle to the Corinthians in the *Between Two Horizons* series (Eerdmans).

Professor Stephen R.L. Clark is Professor of Philosophy at the University of Liverpool. He describes himself as an Anglican and a Neoplatonist. His books include *How to Think about the Earth* (Mowbrays, 1993), *Animals and their Moral Standing* (Routledge, 1997), *God, Religion and Reality* (SPCK, 1998), and *The Political Animal* (Routledge, 1999). He is a member of the Farm Animal Welfare Council and the Animal Procedures Committee.

Professor James D.G. Dunn is Lightfoot Professor of Divinity at the University of Durham. Formerly he was a Lecturer and Reader at the University of Nottingham. He has supervised many doctoral students and written extensively on New Testament subjects, most recently *The Theology of Paul the Apostle* (Eerdmans / T. & T. Clark, 1998). He is working on the first volume of a trilogy to be entitled *Christianity in the Making*. The first volume, *Jesus Remembered*, is due to be published in 2002.

Professor Robin Gill is the Michael Ramsey Professor of Modern Theology in the University of Kent at Canterbury and an honorary Canon of Canterbury Cathedral. Among his recent books are *Churchgoing and Christian Ethics* (Cambridge University Press, 1999) and *A Textbook of Christian Ethics* (T. & T. Clark, rev. edn, 1995).

He is also the series editor of *New Studies in Christian Ethics* and an editor of *The Cambridge Companion to Christian Ethics* (2001), both published by Cambridge University Press.

Professor John Goldingay is David Allan Hubbard Professor of Old Testament at Fuller Theological Seminary, Pasadena, California. He was formerly Principal of St John's Theological College, Nottingham. He has written a number of books on Old Testament interpretation, which include *Models for Scripture* (Eerdmans, 1994) and *Models for Interpreting Scripture* (Eerdmans, 1995).

Professor Trevor Hart is Professor of Divinity at the University of St Andrews. He has teaching and research interests in Christian doctrine and systematic theology. His publications include *Justice, the True and Only Mercy: Essays on the Life and Theology of Peter Taylor Forsyth* (T. & T. Clark, 1995), *Faith Thinking* (SPCK, 1995) and *Regarding Karl Barth* (Paternoster, 2000). He is the project director for the 'Theology and Imagination' project in the Institute for Theology, Imagination and the Arts at the University of St Andrews.

The Revd Dr Margaret Whipp is a doctor and priest in the Church of England. She is a consultant in oncology and palliative medicine and is the Director of Patient Care for Hartlepool and District Hospice. She is interested in theological ethics and practical theology and is the Director of Academic Development for the North East Ecumenical Course.

Introduction

This book contains the texts of four Chaplaincy lectures delivered at the University of Liverpool between 1997 and 2000. After each main chapter, which contains the text of the lecture itself, a response follows. Unfortunately space does not permit any further response by those scholars who agreed to deliver the lectures in the first place. The progression from Old to New Testament, then to systematic theology and pastoral theology in the form of Christian ethics is intentional. We hope that the range of biblical, historical, theological and pastoral/ethical material will enable readers to make connections across the theological subdisciplines. Such connections are important in viewing theology as an integrative discipline rather than a series of fragmented specialisms with little or no relation to one another. In order to enable the reader to understand the project, we shall briefly describe how the project evolved and introduce the contributors in turn.

The lecture series contained in this book grew out of the ongoing work of the Anglican Chaplaincy in the University of Liverpool. The Chaplaincy had for a number of years organised a series of Open Meetings where students and staff could gather in order to listen and respond to a well-known speaker. These speakers were committed Christians who wished to engage with subjects relevant to higher education, intellectual enquiry and the Christian life. Out of this existing vision, with the encouragement and the support of the university, the idea for a new and more formal project emerged. We are extremely grateful to the University of Liverpool for its support.

In developing the series from its less formal beginnings, we were fortunate to have within the university an eminent philosopher with particular interests in the philosophy of religion and theology. We therefore invited Professor Stephen Clark, holder of the Philosophy Chair in the University of Liverpool, to deliver the first lecture. Professor Clark chose as his subject the topic of vegetarianism in the Old Testament material concerning covenant and life. Therefore in the text of the lecture contained in this book, Professor Clark deals with the areas of creation, future eschatological hope, the bargains we make and the things that 'are God's Love'. Contemporary questions are given a fresh dimension by a creative engagement with the text of the Old Testament.

Professor John Goldingay responds to Professor Clark, using the metaphors of a mirror and a window to introduce the hermeneutical issues that arise from the lecture. In so doing he summarises the meaning of the Old Testament concept of covenant and engages with the relevance of covenantal attitudes to animals. He thus provides an important and scholarly counter to the contemporary perspective of Professor Clark.

Professor Clark had set us running with the subject of covenant. It now seemed appropriate and important to continue on this path. Professor James D.G. Dunn agreed to deliver our second lecture on the subject of biblical covenants. He suggests that the way we speak of two covenants, the old and the new, is divisive. He asks why Christians use the Old Testament when they regard the Old Covenant (synonymous with Testament) as largely obsolete. He suggests, from a Jewish perspective, that it could be asked: why should Christianity take the Scriptures of another religion? Professor Dunn reviews closely the evidence, in both Old and New Testaments, and suggests a way forward that unites the evidence within one rather than two covenants.

Dr Mark Bonnington responds to Professor Dunn's lecture. Dr Bonnington agrees with much of what Professor Dunn argues, but suggests that the evidence is problematic for him in some respects. While there is clearly some continuity between the old and new covenants, there is also some serious discontinuity. This response explores the nuances of Mosaic and Abrahamic covenants in these terms before answering Professor Dunn's question directly.

With the project of contemporary approaches to covenant theology well established, we invited Professor Gary D. Badcock to deliver the third lecture in the series. Professor Badcock discusses the notion of covenant in relation to the doctrine of God, focusing upon and elucidating the covenant theology of seventeenth-century scholastic Calvinism (Reformed theology). This particular point of entry is subsequently compared to the theology of Karl Barth. What emerges is a revolutionary doctrine of God and a plea for theological humility.

In his response to Professor Badcock, Professor Trevor Hart explores the relation between the covenant metaphor and the concept of transcendence as mapped out by Professor Badcock. He also suggests further engagement with the political context of the seventeenth century. He continues by relating the notions of covenant and kingship together before exploring Christology and the theology of Karl Barth. Professor Hart proposes the integration of heart, imagination and head (as well as will) as being important for the theological task.

Finally, to draw the series to a close, we invited Professor Robin Gill to deliver the fourth lecture. Professor Gill considers the ethical dilemma of withholding and withdrawing treatment in the context of health care and asks how the theological notion of covenant can assist. Behind the lecture lie questions to do with how Christian ethical stances relate to secular and other religious traditions. Professor Gill describes the debate regarding this dilemma and suggests a way forward by using the related concepts of contract and covenant in contemporary heath care.

The Revd Dr Margaret Whipp responds to Robin Gill. She focuses upon the concept of 'care' by arguing that the relational notion of 'loving-kindness' associated with the Hebrew word *hesed* is significant to the contemporary discussion. It is this relational approach to ethics that needs to complement the informed rationality usually associated with decision-making in contemporary Western medical ethics.

We would like to express our deep appreciation to all those involved in this project. We are grateful to the lecturers, some of whom travelled a good distance to Liverpool, not only for giving a lecture but also for preparing a text for publication. This book would have been impossible without the respondents. We are grateful for those willing to engage in public conversation through the pages of this book. Tony Graham, from Paternoster Press, deserves to be thanked for his interest and enthusiasm, as well as his patience!

We trust that these essays will provide much food for theological thought. We also trust that they will enable the reader to learn more of the God of the covenant who revealed himself supremely in the person and work of Jesus Christ, and renews us in our covenant relations by means of his gracious Holy Spirit.

Mark J. Cartledge
David Mills

The Covenant with All Living Creatures[1]

Chaplaincy Lecture 1997

Stephen R.L. Clark

The Scriptures

Philosophers are usually expected to argue only from premises acceptable to a secular audience, in ways that require no special commitment beyond that to the value of argument itself. As a philosopher, I see no particular reason to deny myself the opportunity to argue from other, more 'sectarian', premises, in ways now unfamiliar to an unbelieving nation. In so doing I may (as theistical philosophers often do) sound more traditional than many theologians.

Covenant theology is normally concerned with the Mosaic covenant, and the 'new covenant' promised by the prophets: theologians usually give these a humanitarian reading. It is certainly worth reading them like that. Consider the Ten Commandments, in view of recent commentary by poorly educated reporters (and clergy). These commandments (popularly so called) prohibit acts that would make life within a decent society more difficult. Do not steal, or seek to kill; do not cause marital troubles; do not envy others; do not claim that God requires what God does not; do not always treat everything as if it were a tool or stuff for your own purposes (allow all things their space); honour those from whom you take your life. Above all, never let another ideal or goal take precedence over those divine requirements. In brief, let nothing matter more to you than leaving everything the space ordained by God: remember, you were slaves in Egypt. Atheistical commentators, or spokespersons of the Secular Society (and other similarly nineteenth-century holdouts), will often complain about the 'absolutist' or 'authoritarian' or 'joyless' character of the commandments. In doing so, they prove that they have never truly read them. Theistic tradition, ever since Abraham, has been concerned to identify the practical and theoretical conditions under which we have some chance of being just. The truth is, probably, that we will not succeed. It does not follow that we should not try, nor that it is impossible to win.

We can learn from Ezekiel what it is to turn one's back on the laws: the man of violence 'obeys none of them, he feasts at mountain-shrines, he dishonours another man's wife, he oppresses the unfortunate and the poor, he is a robber, he does not return the debtor's pledge, he lifts his eyes to idols and joins in abominable rites; he lends both at discount and at interest. Such a man shall not live' (Ezek. 18:10–13 NEB). Consider also the offence (2 Kgs. 23:10) of passing children through the fire 'to Molech' (or 'as a burnt offering'). Consider the iniquity of Sodom (not what people now suppose): 'This was the iniquity of your sister Sodom: she and her daughters had pride of wealth and food in plenty, comfort and ease, and yet she never helped the poor and wretched' (Ezek. 16:49 NEB).

The Bible's claim is that our possession of the land (and anything else we think we own) is conditional on our keeping to the covenant, whose conditions are listed in Deuteronomy 28 (29:1 says this Moab covenant is in addition to the one at Horeb). So also the Psalms (132:12): the covenant with David's line is conditional.

Those conditions are regularly ignored. We easily believe that we can avoid all consequences for our sin:

> You keep saying, 'This place is the temple of the LORD, the temple of the LORD, the temple of the LORD!' This catchword of yours is a lie; put no trust in it. Mend your ways and your doings, deal fairly with one another, do not oppress the alien, the orphan, and the widow, shed no innocent blood in this place, do not run after other gods to your own ruin. (Jer. 7:4–6 NEB)

There have been many attacks on the scriptures as being 'anti-environmentalist'. On the contrary, so I contend, the scriptures emphasise our duties – not as 'stewards', but as neighbours. It is true that Baal, in some sense a Nature-god, is not approved (see 2 Kgs. 11:17–18, Jehoiada's covenant against Baal) and some critics suspect – not entirely without reason – that modern pantheistic environmentalism, and New Age ideas, are exactly that sort of Baal- worship.

Beginning from the Beginning

From the very first chapter of Genesis it is affirmed that Being itself is good. 'God could not have created a thing had he hated it, as the Wisdom of Solomon says (11:24–5) and the mere fact that he keeps it in being is the proof that he loves it.'[2] After the flood God makes a covenant with all living: there shall never again be a flood to destroy all living creatures (Gen. 9:8ff.). The Lord rejoices in his works (Ps. 104).

Some modernist theologians[3] explain the apparent failings of our present world as God's chosen way of creating rational individuals. Everything, by their account, exists for us to use. The God of orthodoxy has no need of secondary causes of this sort. Whatever he creates, he creates for its own sake, because he chooses to. Some have held that he created every possible creature; others that he actualises only some real possibilities; others again that even God the Omniscient cannot inspect all possible, so-far non-existent, beings (because there can be no criteria for their identity beyond what he makes real in creating some 'of them'). Whatever the truth of this, we can be confident that he creates exactly what he wants, for its own sake or 'for His glory'.[4] Nor does the God of orthodoxy need to make particular creatures co-existent: as far as we can see he may have randomised creation, since his chosen must, in any case, relate to anyone at all who is their neighbour, irrespective of their nature or their merits. Nor does he select for special treatment just those creatures that a finite observer might expect: nothing in the long ago determined him to raise up mammals, hominids, or Abram.[5] So orthodox theocentrism is far less committed to the notion of a Visible Plan than atheistic critics have supposed.

Granted that things exist 'for their own sake', because God wishes just those things to be, then they aren't simply 'for us'. From this beginning we can see that the commandments have a wider message than simple social solidarity.

Consider the sabbath rules (Exod. 16:23ff.: no gathering of food on the sabbath; Exod. 20:8–9: keep the sabbath holy): the sabbath is not just the seventh day; it is also the tenth day of the seventh month; and in the seventh year land is left for the poor and the wild things (Lev. 25:6). Amos (8:5) links the sabbath requirement explicitly to a ban on the commercial exploitation of the poor. Jeremiah (11:3) makes possession of the land conditional on obedience.

There are related commandments about Jubilee, and about the rules of war: Leviticus 25:23 says that no land is to be sold outright (lest land accumulate in the hands of the rich); Deuteronomy 20:19–20 requires us not to burn fruit-bearing trees in war; Isaiah 24:5 makes it clear that violation of the eternal covenant leads to disaster (as does Jer. 4:23; and 5:25: 'your wrongdoing has upset nature's order').

When Babylon has fallen,

> there no Arab shall pitch his tent,
> no shepherds fold their flocks.
> There marmots shall have their lairs,
> and porcupines shall overrun her houses;
> there desert owls shall dwell,
> and there he-goats shall gambol. (Is. 13:20–1 NEB)

> The whole world has rest and is at peace;
> it breaks into cries of joy.
> The pines themselves and the cedars of Lebanon exult over you:
> Since you have been laid low, they say,
> no man comes up to fell us. (Is. 14:7–8 NEB).

The land shall have the sabbaths we denied to it (Lev. 26:34). If we want a share in the sabbath, we must not seek to deny it to others. As I remarked some years ago:

> The natural historian of a future age may be able to point to the particular follies that brought ruin – chopping down the tropical rain forests,

meditating nuclear war, introducing hybrid monocultures, spreading poisons, financing grain-mountains, and rearing cattle in conditions that clearly breach the spirit of the commandment not to muzzle the ox that treads out the corn (Deuteronomy 25:4). The historian whose eyes are opened to the acts of God will have no doubt we brought our ruin on ourselves, that it is God's answer to the arrogant.[6]

Or as another said:

> These were the words of the LORD to me: Prophesy, man, against the shepherds of Israel; prophesy and say to them, You shepherds, these are the words of the Lord GOD: How I hate the shepherds of Israel who care only for themselves! Should not the shepherd care for the sheep? You consume the milk, wear the wool, and slaughter the fat beasts, but you do not feed the sheep. You have not encouraged the weary, tended the sick, bandaged the hurt, recovered the straggler, or searched for the lost; and even the strong you have driven with ruthless severity ... I will dismiss those shepherds: they shall care only for themselves no longer; I will rescue my sheep from their jaws, and they shall feed on them no longer. (Ezek. 34:1–4, 10 NEB)

Ezekiel, or the Lord, here takes it for granted that true shepherds care for sheep.

> A righteous man cares for his beast,
> but a wicked man is cruel at heart. (Prov. 12:10 NEB; cf. 27:23ff.)

Literally, of course, shepherds care for sheep only that they may profit from them in the end, but perhaps this was not so in the beginning, and need not be wholly so even now.

> For any man who is just and good loves the brute creatures which serve him, and he takes care of them so that they have food and rest and the other things they need. He does not do this only for his own good but out of a principle of true justice; and if he is so cruel toward them that he requires work from them and nevertheless does not provide the necessary food, then he has surely broken the law which God inscribed in his heart. And if he kills any of his beasts only to satisfy his own

pleasure, then he acts unjustly, and the same measure will be measured
out to him.[7]

Hope for the Future

God's oracle to Isaiah:

> The wolf shall live with the lamb,
> the leopard shall lie down with the kid,
> the calf and the lion and the fatling together,
> and a little child shall lead them.
> The cow and the bear shall graze,
> their young shall lie down together;
> and the lion shall eat straw like the ox.
> The nursing child shall play over the hole of the asp,
> and the weaned child shall put its hand on the adder's den.
> They will not hurt or destroy
> on all my holy mountain;
> for the earth will be full of the knowledge of the LORD
> as the waters cover the sea. (Is. 11:6–9 NRSV)[8]

The covenant of peace lies on the far side of a transformation, for
God will 'create new heavens and a new earth; the former things
shall not be remembered or come to mind' (Is. 65:17; see Rev.
21:1).

So what is the effect of this belief that 'the whole creation has
been groaning in labour pains until now' (Rom. 8:22 NRSV; see Is.
26:17ff.)? In the new world none will hurt or harm; here, it often
seems, we – all sentient creation – are condemned to hurt and harm
each other:

> You make darkness, and it is night,
> when all the animals of the forest come creeping out.
> The young lions roar for their prey,
> seeking their food from God.
>   (Ps. 104:20–1 NRSV; see Job 38:39ff.)

If, as so many people hasten to insist, 'animals were *given* to us', it is only because we have all been 'given' to each other: given, in part, that we may care for, and respect, each other. We should care for the weak and helpless, 'champion the widow, defend the cause of the fatherless, give to the poor, protect the orphan, clothe the naked' (2 Esd. 2:20ff.; see Is. 1:16ff.). Even when we have done that, we shall be in the wrong, and need forgiveness: but maybe we need not trouble ourselves to do much more. In the new world, there will be no marriages, no temples and no courts of law. There, we shall call no man 'father'. There, we shall be naked and unashamed.[9] But it does not wholly follow that we should try to live by those laws here and now. Vegetarians, according to Karl Barth,[10] are trying, like conscientious nudists, to anticipate the kingdom – though the case would be more convincing if it were not so easy for us (I say nothing about lions, nor yet the Inuit) to be vegetarian.

Some of those who live in expectation of an imminent *parousia* have seemed to conclude that, being in the image of God, we are now entitled to do as we please with things. After all, some say, if this-world-here is due for demolition, then God himself must think it is garbage. But 'those who boast of the dignity of their nature and the advantages of their station and thence infer their right of oppression of their inferiors, exhibit their folly as well as their malice'.[11] Nebuchadnezzar learnt the hard way that God 'is able to bring low those who walk in pride' (Dan. 4:37). And:

> Let the same mind be in you that was in Christ Jesus,
> who, though he was in the form of God,
> did not regard equality with God
> as something to be exploited ... (Phil. 2:5–6)

A few of us may manage to make appropriate vows of poverty, chastity, non-violence, obedience, and to greet each other – which again is all of us[12] – as the children of God we hope to be considered. We may strive to see that 'garbage' is only in the eye of the beholder, that to *be* at all is to be something, to be informed, illuminated, by a real form, an aspect of God's Grandeur.[13] Because this is indeed a radical alternative, which few of us adopt, we usually console ourselves by thinking of it, rather than attempting it. As Orwell commented, 'we all live by robbing Asiatic coolies, and those of us who are "enlightened" all maintain that those coolies ought to be set free; but our standard of living, and hence our "enlightenment", demands that the robbery shall continue'[14] – so we are satisfied with saying that we *wish* to stop. The world we actually inhabit is not that real world we say we believe in, but one constructed around the life we actually live.

Pigs, according to Chrysippus, should be reckoned locomotive meals, with souls instead of salt to keep them fresh.[15] Trees, according to a recent, astonishingly ignorant columnist, are only bits of wood. The bloated turkeys bred for Christmas tables are incapable of natural reproduction, so they must be artefacts. 'There is a price to be paid for fabricating around us a society which is as artificial and as mechanised as our own; and this is that we can exist in it only on condition that we adapt ourselves to it. This is our punishment.'[16] Once we have abandoned anthropocentric fantasies of this sort we should ask instead how God, the transforming God, would have us think of pigs, of trees, of Nature, and how, in expectation of the Coming, we should treat them. Nothing is 'just garbage'; nothing is 'just a pig'; even of a fish it is blasphemy to say it is *only* a fish, or of a flower that it is 'only a growth like any other'.[17]

The Noahic covenant permits us to make use of other creatures, in a ruined world, so long as we do not use their blood, which is their life (Gen. 9:3ff; see also Lev. 17:13–14; Deut. 12:15–16). The Mosaic law lays down further, explicit principles: we may not, for example, muzzle the oxen that tread out the corn (Deut. 25:4), nor take mother and young from any nest (Deut. 22:6–7; see Lev. 22:28), nor take a calf, lamb or kid from its mother till seven days after its birth (Lev. 22:26–7), nor boil a kid in its own mother's milk (Deut. 14:21), nor leave a beast trapped in a well on the pretext that today is holy (Deut. 22:4; see Luke 14:5), nor yoke ox and ass together (Deut. 22:10), nor plough up all the fields, in every year, and so deprive the wild things of their livelihood (Lev. 19:9–10; 23:22; 25:6–7).

I am aware, before you tell me so, that many of these laws may once have had a ritual or anagogical significance. 'Does God care for oxen? Or is the reference clearly to ourselves?' (1 Cor. 9:9). I see no reason not to answer, 'Both.' 'Thou hatest nothing that thou hast created – why else wouldst thou have made it? How could anything have continued in existence, had it not been thy will?'

(Wis. 11:25ff.). That is certainly how the commands have been taken, in rabbinic, Christian and Islamic commentary. They may indeed have their beginnings in religion rather than human morals, in the vision of what shall be rather than the plan to do as well as we can here and now. But maybe that is where the love even of humanity begins: not in the bargains struck by desperate brigands modern moralists sometimes identify as the real form of morals, but in the revelation that we may yet be gods.

All these laws are regularly broken now, and all the laws that echo or put fences round them. Later prophets make it clear that even permitted sacrifices, which are the only source of lawful meat, are not approved:

> I have had enough of burnt-offerings of rams
> and the fat of fed beasts;
> I do not delight in the blood of bulls,
> or of lambs, or of goats. (Is. 1:11)

Once again, I am aware that these condemnations are sometimes said to be merely provisional, and that Isaiah, or the Lord, was only objecting to sacrifices made 'with unclean hands': are our hands clean? But in any case, all such sacrifices ended, for those who follow Christ, at the crucifixion.

Paul accepted that Christians need not fear to eat the meat of beasts sacrificed to idols, but only on the assumption that by doing so they did not worship demons, and on condition that this 'liberty' did not become a pitfall for the weak (1 Cor. 8:12–13; cf. Rev. 2:14; 2:20). Those tempted to continue eating meat – and doing all the other things that amount to that – should perhaps now wonder what it is they worship, and refrain. Everything God made is good, no doubt (1 Tim. 4:4; see 1 Cor. 10:25): but that is a very strange reason to treat it just as 'useful', or to suppose that everything it does, or has done to it, must be perfectly all right. I am told that Islamic commentators have also argued that animal sacrifice, and meat-eating, is permitted, or even required – but the assumption is still made that the animals have really been treated justly. If (as I suppose) they have not, then the sacrifice is unclean.

Turning aside from the mechanised, anthropocentric world to
the world promised by the prophets (even if we cannot get there by
ourselves, or swiftly) is a wakening.

> We live in a world of unreality and dreams. To give up our imaginary
> position as the centre, to renounce it, not only intellectually but in the
> imaginative part of our soul, that means to awaken to what is real and
> eternal, to see the true light and hear the true silence. A transformation
> then takes place at the very roots of our sensibility, in our immediate
> reception of sense impressions and psychological impressions. It is a
> transformation analogous to that which takes place in the dusk of
> evening on a road, where we suddenly discern as a tree what we had at
> first seen as a stooping man; or where we suddenly recognise as a
> rustling of leaves what we thought at first was whispering voices. We
> see the same colours, we hear the same sounds, but not in the same
> way. To empty ourselves of our false divinity, to deny ourselves, to
> give up being the centre of the world in imagination, to discern that all
> points in the world are equally centres and that the true centre is
> outside the world, this is to consent to the rule of mechanical necessity
> in matter and of free choice at the centre of each soul. Such consent is
> love. The face of this love which is turned towards thinking persons is
> the love of our neighbour: the face turned towards matter is love of the
> order of the world, or love of the beauty of the world which is the same
> thing.[18]

Weil here draws too rigid, too Cartesian a distinction between
thinking persons and matter: there are innumerable grades of
being, tradition tells us, 'below' and 'above' the thinking person.
'The moral consequence of faith in God', so Niebuhr tells us,
'is the universal love of all being in Him ... This is [faith's]
requirement: that all beings, not only our friends, but also our
enemies, not only men but also animals and the inanimate, be met
with reverence, for all are friends in the friendship of the one to
whom we are reconciled in faith.'[19] How can we be reconciled to
God, if we show no mercy to our neighbour? 'If a man nurses
anger against another, can he then demand compassion from the
LORD?' (Ecclus 28:2–3).

Bargains within the Covenant

But is this possible? Is the argument against any attempt to 'immanentise the eschaton' simply that it is quite beyond our power, and therefore that the rules we live by must indeed be different? Is it (as hosts of moralists have held) impossible to reach an agreement with non-humans of a kind that give a sense to talk of 'justice between man and beast'?

The real oddity of the Stoic (Augustinian, Thomist, Cartesian and modern) claim that we can make no bargains with the animals, and that they therefore (?) lie beyond the sphere of justice,[20] is that we have been making bargains with them for millennia. If human beings are, specifically, talking animals, it is worth noting that we have also talked *to* animals, and understood their answers. By this I mean nothing fabulous or sentimental. We communicate with non-humans (and with humans) at a non-verbal level, understanding each others' moods and intentions. Most of our alliances have been exploitative – either of the non-humans we persuade into our keeping, or of those we prey on in the wild. Domestication is a process employed on humans as well as non-humans, and as open to manipulation, on both sides. Dogs manipulate their humans, thereby displaying their grasp of their own and their humans' status in the pack. Domestic animals, human and non-human, are bred and reared to know their limits: philosophers and political theorists, meditating on those limits, construct imaginary compacts to explain, and to constrain, what happened 'naturally'. It is even possible – although the great age of innovative domestication was the Neolithic – for human beings to come to tacit agreements with wild creatures: Jane Goodall lived among the Gombe chimpanzees more equably than Colin Turnbull did among the human ilk.[21] Understanding our limits, and what motivates creatures of different kinds in social situations, is vital to the construction of enduring communities.

There are indeed limits to our understanding, and to the possibilities for friendly association, though they are not necessarily the ones we commonly imagine. Language does not always unite us, but divides. Even Augustine acknowledged that it was easier for dumb animals of different species to get on together than two humans who did not know each other's language, and easier to get

on with one's dog than with a foreigner![22] Our ethical relationship
to creatures that we *can* be friends with will be different from that to
those we cannot: but it does not follow that we should think of the
latter only as unfriends or enemies or mere material.

Among the loyalties we actually and historically form are ones
toward domestic or working animals. A child's affection for a cat or
dog or horse is not much different from her affection for her human
friends and family. She values its company and reciprocal affection,
demands that others care for it, and could easily resent occasional
bids for solitude or independence. Those who work with 'animals'
are usually, and naturally, attached to them even when they have
put 'childish things' away. They come to see, more or less knowl-
edgeably, with the others' eyes, and allow them more or less of
liberty to go their own way when it suits them. Dogs, cats and
horses are the commonest non-human creatures to elicit, and partly
reciprocate, affection, in the settled West. But cows, pigs, hawks,
snakes, spiders all have their admirers, here and elsewhere. It seems
indeed to be a species characteristic that we readily adopt small
(smallish) creatures and rear them in our midst, expecting them to
learn enough of our ways to be called 'tame'. It is no contradiction
to add that we frequently betray what trust they have in us.[23]

So the claim that we cannot make bargains with non-human
animals is simply false. How detailed the bargains that we make can
be, and what motivates us all (human and non-human) to keep
them, will vary. Many such bargains will be marginal to the central
interests of each of the bargaining tribes; others will be so significant
as to change the natures of those who enter them, or are brought up
in them. Most, as I remarked, are exploitative: even the bargain
with dogs, which was once almost of equals, has long since been
rewritten to allow 'us' civilised humans liberty to do very much as
we please with them – while at the same time reserving the right to
sneer at other human tribes who have a different use for them, as
food. That the bargain was, or is, exploitative does not mark it off as
any different from the social compacts that political theorists more
usually debate. The 'sort-of-contracts' that lie, in historical reality,
behind the modern state are just as forced. Some of the peoples that
the people of Israel encountered when they invaded Palestine chose
to bind themselves and their descendants to be hewers of wood and
drawers of water, rather than be destroyed (Josh. 9:3ff.). A similar

choice, or something like a choice, was made, back in the Neolithic Age, by several species (and, perhaps significantly, by hardly any since). Dogs, horses, cattle, sheep and camels 'chose' to be domestic, and have paid a savage price since then. Creatures that 'chose' freedom (including people who turned their back on 'civilised' society[24]) risk extinction in a world controlled by 'civilised' people.

The original 'sort-of-compact' that was made guarantees their species' survival, and better medical care than they would have as wild things:[25] the price is that they are available for use, as food, amusement or laboratory material. That there were literal, individual, informed choices, way back then, is not required – any more than such actual choices are required by social contract theorists. It is, some say, quite reasonable to agree to give up natural, risky liberties, for the state's care and protection: maybe our ancestors did not do this of their own volition (and we have had no choice), but state authority is thereby justified, because we *could* have consented.[26] So could domestic animals – though we may surely have some doubts that they would, that anyone would – consent to the conditions under which they live at present? Might there not be a better, fairer bargain? Is it not already obvious that whatever contract of care and protection we, perhaps, proposed, has long been broken?

That the bargain is broken when, for example, we ship living cattle over many miles and hours to be slaughtered among strangers for meat that no one needs, has seemed obvious to many who had not previously worried about the plight of cattle, and who might still think nothing wrong, as such, in killing 'animals' for food. Similar incidents during the slave trade began to awaken a suspicion that it was not the passing incidents, but the trade itself, that should be banned – despite the obvious truth that every civilised society till then had licensed slavery. Breeding, rearing, mutilating, imprisoning, torturing and killing non-human animals are all questionable practices, even if those animals are not themselves in any position to rebel (any more than serfs have been for most of human history). The growing perception that serfs and slaves and foreigners are *human*, and the corresponding thought that there are other social forms that could accommodate our friendship, has changed our moral consciousness: we can no longer comfort ourselves with the thought that people who are poor, casteless or 'primitive' are so unlike 'us' that we need not fear that we are doing them wrong.

A similarly changing perception of non-human animals makes it impossible, in good faith, to think that an impartial judge would vindicate our conduct towards them.[27]

The thought at which some humane commentators stop (as I already hinted) is that it is wrong to hurt non-humans, but not wrong to kill them. Ending their lives does them no harm, because they have – it is said – no general plan of life, nor any expectation of their ends. That much the same can be said of many *human* animals is either accepted (and the ban on killing infants, imbeciles, the ordinarily feckless, or the elderly, judged less significant than the ban on 'real murder') or hurriedly disguised. Killing such *human* 'marginals' is judged wrong because of its effect on general morale, or as an offence of the same order as demeaning even unconscious human bodies. It might as well be argued that killing non-humans is also a desecration: an open declaration that their lives are not valued. If the principle on which liberal zoophiles depend (that hurting, but not killing, is wrong) were as obvious as some suppose, we would not disapprove of people who have their pets 'put down' for trivial reasons. Instead, we think such 'pet-lovers' have betrayed their trust and shown most clearly that they did not love at all. Even utilitarians, who place the value of an entity in its utility, may reasonably say that a living animal has more utility, more value, than a dead one: the value its flesh adds to the lives of others is rarely as great as the value it adds to its own. Non-utilitarians, who reckon that an entity may be valued 'in itself' and irrespective of the quality of life dependent on it, will have more reason to think that killing things requires a defence.

One argument against allowing murder is, of course, simply the self-interested one: that I am likely to live more safely among people who condemn homicide, and even defend each other against offenders. 'Animals', it is said, will not be affected either way by our forebearance, and may therefore be safely killed. The claim is dubious, since a non-aggressive lifestyle is as effective in avoiding most aggression in the case of animals as well as humans. But it is even more doubtful that the ethical argument against killing really depends on bargains of that sort. Those who are bound only by the laws of brigandage are not generally well regarded. Even or especially liberals will think it wrong to kill off Amazonian tribes to get their land, even if there is not the slightest risk that the tribesmen could kill us instead (and if there is, the sooner – I suppose – they are killed, the better). The same good reason not to kill non-human tribes is just that they have lives of their own to live, that we have no God-given privilege to take away what God has given them. What is astonishing is that good liberals, at this point in the argument, so often fall back on ideologies that are otherwise associated with paradigmatic enemies of liberal values. Non-aggression is all very well, they say, but we are living in the jungle, and at war with every other kind of creature. Radical zoophiles, so it seems, are traitors.

Like other patriots, humanists assume far too easily that all good people agree, but it is not quite out of place to emphasise the arrangements that 'we' and our ancestors have actually made. There is a difference between creatures bred and reared to be a part of 'our' community, and those outside. The rights that radical zoophiles demand for domestic and other 'cultured' animals need not be ones that every wild thing has, or can be assumed to have. It is for this reason, among others, that the suggestion that such zoophiles don't 'really' believe that animals have rights, or they would be out defending blackbirds against foxes, and worms against blackbirds, as well as foxes against hunters, is misplaced. The truth is that we do not feel ourselves obliged to defend even all *human* beings against assault. In most cases it is enough that we do not ourselves assault them, and defend and nurture only our own dependents. Domesticated creatures (including us) have been, hamfistedly and hypocritically, creating a community that sometimes serves as a model for a larger, global order – but that is an order that we cannot ourselves create. They will not hurt or destroy on all God's holy mountain – but the best that we can manage here and now is to care for our own, and not attack the others.

'Things are God's Love'

Awakening to realise the real beings of the creatures among whom we live, we have the opportunity to forge new images, new ways of living, that accommodate the interests of all. In attempting this, we have all art and literature to draw upon. For the mistake too often made has been to think that we should dispense with all such historical or mythological or personal associations if we are to realise the truth.

'Enlightenment' has been equated with a decently modern emancipation from superstitious reverence or compassion – but even Spinoza (who followed Stoic argument in holding that only a 'womanish and sentimental pity'[28] stood in the way of using everything non-human as we pleased, would have drawn the line at irreverence. It is true enough that an amorous adolescent would do well to distinguish the real being of his inamorata from the dramatic and emotional fictions in which he cloaks her. It is quite untrue that he should therefore think of her as no more than bare, forked animal: that would itself be a dramatic and emotional fiction. What matters is that he, that they, should wake up to the possibility of friendship. That friendship is incompatible with the 'knowingness' that is too often inculcated. A foolish work of elementary English criticism, examined by Lewis, sought to 'debunk ... a silly piece of writing on horses, where these animals are praised as the "willing servants" of the early colonists in Australia' (on the plea that horses are not much interested in colonial expansion). Lewis comments that its actual effect on pupils will have little to do with writing decent prose: 'some pleasure in their own ponies and dogs they will have lost: some incentive to cruelty or neglect they will have received: some pleasure in their own knowingness will have entered their minds' – but 'of Ruksh and Sleipnir and the weeping horses of Achilles and the war-horse in the Book of Job – nay, even of Brer Rabbit and of Peter Rabbit – of man's prehistoric piety to "our brother the ox" they will have learnt nothing.'[29]

Treating our friends, or our potential friends, as merely flesh – which is, merely material – is no advance at all on treating them as characters, even if the characters and parts that we impute to them are faulty.

> Don't you see that that dreadful dry light shed on things must at last wither up the moral mysteries as illusions, respect for age, respect for property, and that the sanctity of life will be a superstition? The men in the street are only organisms, with their organs more or less displayed. For such a one there is no longer any terror in the touch of human flesh, nor does he see God watching him out of the eyes of a man.[30]

Even of a fish it is blasphemous to say that it is only a fish.[31] We do not know what fish are meant to be, nor what, in the restoration, they will be – except that God will reckon they are 'good'. We can go further: 'Picasso was right when he said that we do not know what a tree or a window is. All things are very mysterious and strange and we only overlook their strangeness and their mystery because we are so used to them. We only understand things very obscurely. But what are things? Things are God's love become things.'[32]

So we should live as non-violently as we can manage, building up our friendships and respecting the limits that are needed to allow each kind its place. Let us live according to those rules that will allow as many creatures as possible, of as many kinds, their best chance of living a satisfactory life according to their kind. Let us acknowledge our particular duties of care and forebearance to those creatures who have been part of our society for millennia. Let us acknowledge that, as the Qu'ran told us, there are other nations in the world, with whom we should not expect to be at war. Until the nineteenth century every civilised society kept slaves. Until the twentieth every civilised society believed that property could be acquired by military conquest (brigandage). There are still brigands, and slave-runners, in the world, but no one else acknowledges their claims.

In the twenty-first (I live in hope) we might begin to acknowledge that we have no *right*, no general entitlement, to treat our kindred as no more than means. The robbery will, no doubt, continue. Particular legislation, in particular times and places, may be required to identify some acts as crimes. The global commonwealth may need to lay down minimal conditions of common decency in the treatment of non-humans. It is one thing to recognise that 'animals' have feelings, and lives of their own to live, and so to include their interests in any impartial calculation of the greater good. It is another to acknowledge that this recognition demands of us that we not think them merely means to an end, even so benign an end as that same 'greater good'. It is yet another to seek to live in ways that we can bear to remember when we meet our kindred in the eschaton.

The covenant God made, we are told, in the beginning and affirmed since then, is to grant all things their space. 'The mere fact that we exist proves his infinite and eternal love, for from all eternity he chose us from among an infinite number of possible beings.'[33]

Every thing we meet is also chosen: that is a good enough reason not to despise or hurt it. Whether it will be a strong enough reason to prevent us, I do not know. God knows.

Endnotes

1   This Chapter is based on material published in S.R.L. Clark, *Biology and Christian Ethics*, 283–300. Copyright © 2000 by Cambridge University Press. Used with the permission of the publisher

2   E. Cardenal, *Love*, tr. D. Livingstone (London: Search, 1974), 43.

3   John Hick, e.g. *Evil and the God of Love* (London: Fontana, 1968).

4   I suspect that this, conjoined with the equally necessary thought that God cannot be supposed to want what happens to those creatures, requires us to adopt a substance rather than an event ontology (thereby offending other postmodern thinkers).

5   Which is why Stephen Jay Gould is wrong to think that the apparently stochastic nature of evolutionary history somehow counts against the existence of a Creator (*Wonderful Life* [London: Hutchinson Radius, 1989]): see my 'Does the Burgess Shale Have Moral Implications?' *Inquiry* 36 (1993), 357–80.

6   S.R.L. Clark, *Civil Peace and Sacred Order* (Oxford: Clarendon, 1989), 150.

7   Anne Conway, *Principles of the Most Ancient and Modern Philosophy*, ed. A.P. Courdert and T. Corse (Cambridge: Cambridge University Press, 1996), 35. The book was originally published posthumously in 1690.

8   I do not doubt that the words were originally meant as exaggerated praise for some newborn, mortal prince. But such praise, if it is not to be merely idolatrous sentimentality, utters an eschatological hope.

9   Eldo Barkhuizen, the copy-editor, has pointed out to me that scripture always suggests that the redeemed will be clothed (e.g. in white linen: see Rev. 7:9), but I doubt if this is intended so literally (see, e.g., Rev. 19:8). Exactly what it means would be the topic of another chapter entirely. Here the point is only to provide an example of something that may be ordinary in the world to come, without being proper in the present.

10 Karl Barth, *Church Dogmatics*, 4 vols., ed. G.W. Bromiley and T.F. Torrance (Edinburgh: T. & T. Clark, 1936), 3/4, 350ff.

11 Humphrey Primatt, *The Duty of Humanity to Inferior Creatures* (2nd edn ed. A. Broome 1831; Fontwell: Centaur, 1990), 22.

12 For there is no reason to draw one clear line around 'the human species': see my 'Is Humanity a Natural Kind?' in T. Ingold (ed.), *What Is an Animal?* (London: Routledge, 1994), republished in *The Political Animal* (London: Routledge, 1999).

13　See G.M. Hopkins, 'God's Grandeur', in *Poems of Gerard Manley Hopkins*, ed. W.H. Gardner and N.H. Mackenzie (London: Oxford University Press, 1970), 66.

14　Orwell, cited by W. Berry, *What Are People For?* (London: Rider, 1990), 201.

15　Chrysippus, according to Porphyry, *On Abstinence* 3.20.1, in A.A. Long and D. Sedley (eds.), *Hellenistic Philosophers* (Cambridge: Cambridge University Press, 1987), 54P, 1:329.

16　P. Sherrard, *The Eclipse of Man and Nature* (West Stockbridge: Lindisfarne, 1987), 71–2.

17　G.K. Chesterton, *The Poet and the Lunatics* (London: Darwen Finlayson, 1962; first published 1929), 54, 58; see also 68–9.

18　Simone Weil, *Notebooks*, tr. A. Wills (London: Routledge & Kegan Paul, 1956), 1:115.

19　H. Richard Niebuhr, *Radical Monotheism and Western Culture* (New York: Harper & Row, 1960), 126.

20　An inference for which I have yet to see a single decent argument.

21　Jane van Lawick-Goodall, *In the Shadow of Man* (London: Collins, 1971); Colin Turnbull, *The Mountain People* (London: Cape, 1973).

22　Augustine, *City of God* 19.7: 'linguarum diversitas hominem alienat ab homine … ita ut libentius homo sit cum cane suo quam cum homine alieno.'

23　See further my 'Enlarging the Community', in Brenda Almond (ed.), *Introducing Applied Ethics* (Oxford: Blackwell, 1995), 318–30, republished in *The Political Animal*.

24　See Pierre Clastres, *Society Against the State*, tr. R. Hurley (New York: Urizen, 1977).

25　Stephen Budiansky, *The Covenant of the Wild: Why Animals Chose Domestication* (London: Weidenfeld & Nicolson, 1994), uses this, unconvincingly, to excuse almost all present treatment of the non-human.

26　See my 'Slaves and Citizens', *Philosophy* 60 (1985), 27–46, republished in *The Political Animal*.

27　'Ask it for once without presupposing the answer of the egotism of our species, as God might ask it about his creatures: Why should a dog or a guinea pig die an agonizing death in a laboratory experiment so that some human need not suffer just that fate?' (Erazim Kohak, *The Embers and the Stars* [Chicago: University of Chicago Press, 1984], 92).

28　Benedict Spinoza, *Ethics and Selected Letters*, tr. S. Shirley (Indianapolis: Hackett, 1982), 4p37s.

29　C.S. Lewis, *The Abolition of Man* (London: Bles, 1946), 12–13. See my *Animals and their Moral Standing* (London: Routledge, 1997), for a further exploration of this passage.

30　Chesterton, *The Poet and the Lunatics*, 70.

[31]   Ibid. 58.

[32]   Cardenal, *Love*, 43; see also my *God, Religion and Reality* (London: SPCK, 1998).

[33]   Cardenal, *Love*, 40.

2

Covenants and Nature

A Response to Stephen Clark

John Goldingay

The most interesting, creative, illuminating, dangerous and misleading exercises in reading the Old Testament happen when people study it in the light of some new question or conviction they bring to the text. That question or conviction may open a new window that enables us to see aspects of the text we had missed, and/or may constitute a mirror, which means we do not see the text but only ourselves reflected. One can watch this kind of study happening in Matthew's reading of Isaiah, or St Bernard's reading of the Song of Songs, or Luther's reading of Romans, or Wellhausen's reading of the Pentateuch, or feminism's reading of Genesis. In practice, I imagine that all ventures in interpretation create both windows and mirrors.

A further exercise in interpretation is to look at this process to try to discern where a question or conviction is functioning as a mirror and where as a window. This second exercise ideally requires the participation of readers who are open-minded but a little less committed than the first set of readers. They need to be people who are open to seeing through new windows but are not so committed that they may fail to recognise mirrors. Professor Clark's chapter reads the Old Testament and the idea of covenant in the light of the conviction that God and the human world are all in covenant relationship with the animal world, and that we ought to live accordingly. Does that open up a window on the Old Testament itself, or is it an idea alien to the Old Testament? My conclusion is that it lies somewhere in between.

Covenant

In English we use the word 'covenant' to denote a moral commitment made in the context of a relationship and undertaken with some formality, which reflects the seriousness with which we intend to take the commitment. A covenant is thus like a contract in implying a commitment, but this commitment is a moral, not a legal one, lacking the legal framework and the legal protection of a contract; you do not usually think of suing someone for failing to keep a covenant. A covenant involves a relationship, but no ordinary relationship: it presupposes a level of commitment not required of most relationships, and a formalising of that commitment, which shows that we really mean it.

In British English a covenant can be two-sided or mainly one-sided. Marriage is a two-sided covenant; a commitment to giving a certain amount of money to a charity is a one-sided covenant. American English uses the word 'pledge' for the latter, and thus the word 'covenant' refers more exclusively to mutual commitments. This in fact keeps closer to the etymology of the word 'covenant', which suggests a coming together or an agreement. American English thus compares (though a little paradoxically) with the Greek of the Septuagint and the New Testament, which prefers the word *diathēkē* to the regular Greek *synthēkē*. The latter could perhaps suggest too mutual, too contractual an understanding of the relationship between God and Israel or the church. German *Bund* also essentially denotes a mutual relationship, often a contractual one; it covers both 'covenant' and 'federation'.

In Hebrew, *bᵉrîṭ* covers the ground of (one-sided) pledge, (two-sided) covenant, and (legal) contract or federation or treaty or alliance. For instance, God makes a one-sided covenant commitment to Noah and later to the rest of the human and animal world, and another to Abraham, while Josiah and Ezra lead their people in making one-sided covenant commitments to God. Such one-sided covenants presuppose that the other party accepts the commitment (as happens when British people covenant their giving), and in that sense they presuppose an element of reciprocity. But no reciprocal commitment on the same scale is required; all the other party has to do is accept the commitment. The point is highlighted by the nature of the sign that guarantees the Noah covenant, the appearing of the rainbow, which is a fact whether anyone sees it or not. It is highlighted in another way by the nature of the sign that guarantees the Abraham covenant, for accepting circumcision is the only condition for the fulfilment of Yhwh's very far-reaching promises to Abraham; nothing like the detailed commitment of the Mosaic covenant is required.

God is also involved in that more integrally two-sided covenant relationship with Israel as a people, formalised at Sinai and renewed in the Plains of Moab. Deuteronomy, indeed, is the most systematically expressed mutual covenant document in the Old Testament. Interestingly, Deuteronomy is also the covenant document that most systematically reflects the nature of the treaty relationship between a major power and a minor power. If the one-sided covenants are more like a pledge or a *diathēkē*, this covenant is more like a contract, more of a *synthēkē* or *Bund* (though the Greek translations still usually use *diathēkē*). Israel can be (and is) sued for failing to keep its side of the contract. Human beings such as Abraham and Abimelech, and David and Jonathan, also make reciprocal covenants, the former at least being more like a treaty.

Theologians have sometimes spoken of the original relationship between God and humanity (and/or God and creation) portrayed in Genesis 1–2 as having the nature of a covenant. As happens with many other biblical terms, their use in theological discussion thus comes to be different from their use in scripture itself. This is not so much wrong as something we need to keep our wits about; we need to notice it happening if we are to try to avoid reading our categories into scripture. The fact that Genesis does not use the word 'covenant' until after the flood is unlikely to mean nothing. I suspect it suggests that there is no need for the formalising or legalising of the relationship between God and the world when the relationship is in its unspoiled state. It is when humanity is discovered to be wrong-minded from youth (8:21) and God has acted so destructively towards the world that God comes to make the kind of irrational promise that Noah receives, and to seal it with a covenant commitment.

Commenting on the Moses covenant and the new covenant envisaged by Jeremiah, Professor Clark says that 'theologians usually give these a humanitarian reading', which I presume denotes a reading that takes them as concerned with human beings and not animals. This might imply that this 'reading' is an act of interpretation on the exegetes' part of the kind that might have gone another way, as if the texts are ambiguous and it is a matter of choice how one reads them. I suggest that an examination of the text of Exodus—Deuteronomy and Jeremiah 31:31–4 establishes beyond reasonable doubt that their own wholly dominant, where not exclusive, concern is with human beings.

The covenant with Noah is indeed different in its explicit inclusion of all the beings created on the sixth day. This makes the Noah story paradoxical, because it also explicitly legitimates the eating of meat; which raises the question whether even the inclusion of animals in this covenant is for humanity's sake.

Animals

Among the Old Testament passages that have most to say about animals are the following.

Genesis 1—4

Genesis 1—4 includes two creation stories that characteristically both raise searching questions within themselves and suggest contrasting perspectives when we read them alongside each other. They do this in their treatment of the animal world. In Genesis 1 the created world apart from humanity, including the animal world, has great prominence in its own right and is wholly good. Human beings are put in control of the animal world, including birds, sea-creatures, reptiles, and wild animals (1:26–8). The control does not imply a gentle pastoral picture. The verb *rādâh* (NRSV 'have dominion') always denotes hard-won dominance or domination like that of an emperor or an oppressor; it presupposes resistance rather than co-operation (e.g. Lev. 26:17; Is. 14:6; Ps. 110:2; Neh. 9:28). The same is true of the verb *kābaš* (NRSV 'subdue': e.g. Josh. 18:1; Jer. 34:11; Zech. 9:15; 2 Chr. 28:10). It denotes rape in Esther 7:28.

All this suggests that on the basis of words alone there was plausibility in the claim that Genesis 1 encouraged human spoiling of the earth, though the fact that serious spoiling of this kind began only in the modern period suggests that it was not the key factor. After the giving of control to human beings, we are surprised to discover that by implication they are not supposed to eat animals (nor are animals to eat animals). What kind of control do animals need if they are not to be eaten? Or is the question, what kind of control would be needed to stop them eating each other?

My suspicion is that the apparent tensions within Genesis 1 reflect the fact that its concerns lie elsewhere than ours. The chapter is the beginning of a 'Priestly' account of Israel's history. It thus has a direct relationship with the material in Leviticus enjoining which animals may be eaten and which may not, detailing the sacrifices that involve their being cooked and eaten, and describing the festivals at which they are eaten with particular celebration.

A major point about Genesis 1 is to establish the framework for these aspects of Israel's religious life. The emphasis on the structuring of life by the sun and moon and the seasons relates to its significance for Israel's worship life. Similarly, the emphasis on the animals multiplying 'according to their kinds' relates to the Priestly emphasis on orderliness in nature, which reflects and encourages orderliness within Israel and between Israel and the world. The patterning of what may be eaten at the Beginning, after Noah, and after Sinai is part of the patterning of the Torah as a whole. It may be simply a patterning. It is no more offering historical information or instructional norm than is the picture of God's doing the work of creation over six days. To require vegetarianism on the basis of Genesis 1 is a similar mistake to the requiring of belief in a seven-day creation or to the opposing of evolution because it conflicts with belief in God's creating animals 'according to their kinds'.

The same conclusion emerges from the fact that other creation stories than Genesis also describe humanity as originally vegetarian. An Egyptian hymn hundreds of years older than the time of Moses addresses Amon-Re as 'the one who made grass for the cattle and the fruit-tree for humankind'.[1] Nor is that understanding only a Middle Eastern phenomenon.[2] This may indeed reflect a human unease about killing and eating animals (to which traditional cultures lived closer than people in modern cultures), a feeling now reviving in Europe and America. But if there was an unease, it did not affect people's lives. The texts associate vegetarianism with a long-gone time to which people cannot return. Vegetarians are like naturists (though we may be glad of some people who insist on witnessing in this way to that unease and be able to live with them more easily than we could with people who insisted on naturism!).

In Genesis 2—3 the animals are formed as potential helpers and partners for the sake of the first human being. The exercising of the power to name them then suggests a controlling relationship that limits the sense in which they can be helpers and partners. They are thus explicitly distinct from and subordinate to human beings and not adequate as companions for the man. They are not described as good, and one of them leads Adam and Eve astray. In Genesis 4, furthermore, one of Adam and Eve's sons wins God's acceptance for killing one of the sheep he looks after and burning part of it as an offering to God, while the son who offers a non-animal sacrifice does not please God. By the time of the flood, the eating of animals is accepted, for God tells Noah to take with him seven pairs of animals that can be eaten in Israel, but only one pair of animals that cannot be eaten.

Exodus, Leviticus and Deuteronomy

Exodus, Leviticus and Deuteronomy include exhortations that require a number of actions serving the interests of animals, as Professor Clark notes. The question is, why is this? It is surely for God's sake that livestock, like human beings, observe the sabbath (Exod. 20:10). Notwithstanding Mark 2:27, the Old Testament does not imply that the sabbath was made for human beings or animals (e.g. because we need rest), except in the sense that it acts as a reminder for them that the week belongs to God. The sabbath was made for God. It is also thus incidental that wild animals benefit from the sabbath year's fallowing (Exod. 23:10–11): that is simply a fortunate consequence of this way of recognising that the years and the produce of the land belong to God. The rules in Exodus 21:33—22:4, in turn, relate to animals purely as human property. Even the requirement to have mercy on your enemy's ox or donkey may have as its main concern the limiting of the human enmity that destroys community life. It is a way of loving your enemy by being concerned about your enemy's property, at least as much as a way of loving animals.

Looking back to the exhortation not to muzzle the ox when it is treading out the grain (Deut. 25:4), Paul asks whether God is concerned about oxen or whether Deuteronomy is speaking entirely for the sake of human readers of Deuteronomy like himself (1 Cor. 9:9). Professor Clark comments, 'I see no reason not to answer, "Both."' Many readers have seen a very good reason not to give this answer: Paul's rhetorical question is designed to elicit the answer 'No, God is entirely concerned about us.' But preachers sometimes find that the trouble with rhetorical questions is that people may answer them, and that they are susceptible to the answer the questioner did not intend. This may apply even to inspired rhetorical questions. Paul gives a hostage to fortune by his question.

Many readers have been inclined to reckon that Paul indeed assumes that the answer to his question is not 'both', and have agreed with him so far, but have disagreed with him regarding the self-evident meaning of Deuteronomy 25:4. They may be glad to take the opportunity he unintentionally gives them to disagree with him. On the other hand, ironically, one of the most creative (which is not the same as being compelling or right) contemporary inter- preters of Old Testament law also argues that the answer is not 'both'. In Calum Carmichael's view, the context in Deuteronomy 25 shows that verse 4 is not really about animals at all. It indeed expresses God's concern for human beings. The ox stands for an Israelite, for the context suggests that the prohibition relates not to the support of the ministry (the topic to which Paul relates it) but to the need not to deny an Israelite his portion in the land. That is the aim of the requirement about brothers-in-law that follows. In 22:10, the argument also suggests, the ox again stands for the Israelite, who should not marry a non-Israelite.[3] Howard Eilberg-Schwartz makes the argument more broadly, noting how widely animals symbolise or represent humanity in the Old Testament: they provide 'food for thought'. The point about refer- ences to animals lies in the varied senses in which they are relevant to human beings. Israel appears 'in the mirror of nature'; animals are never referred to in their own right but only because of their usefulness in this connection. Christianity's abandonment of animal sacrifice is then a sign of its moving to a new root metaphor (that of the human body) in an urban rather than an agricultural culture.[4]

Leviticus 1—7

Leviticus 1—7 is dominated by accounts of how to kill animals so that they can be burnt and/or eaten in the course of worship. Whereas the Old Testament disapproves of human sacrifice, though recognising that it was practised from time to time in Israel as elsewhere, it shows no sign of disapproving of animal sacrifice. Andrew Linzey has taken up the argument that animal sacrifice might have been acceptable because it was a way of enabling a creature to find its end in its return to its maker, and thus find its happiness in God and for God's glory.[5] The same might be argued with regard to killing human beings for God's glory. It does not provide a rationale for killing animals and not killing human beings in worship.

Professor Clark comments that some prophets indicate that animal sacrifices are 'not approved', but these prophets give no hint that this relates to a concern for the animals involved. Whether or not the prophets imply a root-and-branch opposition to sacrifice, they make it quite explicit that disapproval derives from the fact that the people's worship is not accompanied by right behaviour in relation to other human beings. God's disapproval applies to the whole of worship, including prayer, praise, and offerings of other things than animals (e.g. bread). And in the last of the books in the prophetic canon, God's disapproval concerns the fact that the animals are blind, lame or sick, and that people fail to bring the best of their flocks for sacrifice (see Mal. 1).

The vision for a New Day expressed in Zechariah 14:21 includes continuing animal sacrifice. Isaiah 25:6 similarly envisages a feast on this New Day that will include rich, well-marrowed food. And if animal sacrifice becomes redundant after Christ's death, this in itself constitutes no comment on whether it is disapproved of for the animals' sake. The New Testament contains no pointers in this direction; indeed the death of Christ and the giving of the Spirit explicitly means that more meat-eating is now required (see Acts 10).

As in many traditional societies, the eating of meat was much less common in Israel than is the case in modern Western societies; one may note the prevalence of reference to grain and fruit in passages such as Deuteronomy 8:7–10; Hosea 2:22; Amos 9:13–14. One implication of the rules about sacrifice is that eating meat regularly takes place in a religious context; it is not a domestic affair. Paradoxically, the practice of sacrifice may have the effect of constraining meat-eating. But this is hardly its design. On the other hand, Deuteronomy 12 permits people to kill animals for meat in a non-religious setting, because they live a long distance from the shrine. The King James Version speaks here and elsewhere of the people 'lusting after' meat, but the word in question applies elsewhere to God's 'desire' and should surely be understood more neutrally. It denotes illicit desire in Numbers 11, but this illicit desire is for fish, cucumbers, melons, leeks, onions and garlic, as well as meat; though I would go a long way with anyone who recognised that onions and garlic are key to cooking. Israelites enjoyed eating meat; that is treated as a morally neutral fact. What is important is that they should not eat meat in an apostate way.

Psalm 104

Psalm 104 rejoices in the way God established the earth securely and provides for it day by day. This includes giving drink to wild animals and making grass grow for cattle, providing trees for birds to nest in and remote mountains for wild goats and coneys, making the night as a time for lions to seek their food from God, and providing the creatures of the sea with their food. Animals, like human beings, are inbreathed by God's spirit/breath. God's address to Job in Job 38—39 also emphasises the independent significance of the animal world, along with many other aspects of the creation such as desert areas, which are empty of even animal life. The wild ass, the wild ox, the ostrich, the horse and the hawk show that the world does not circulate around a human being like Job. These things indeed 'exist "for their own sake", because God wishes just those things to be'; 'they aren't simply "for us"'. In 38:39–41 God implicitly provides the lion with its prey, and explicitly does so for the raven. Of course God does that by enabling lion and raven to catch, kill and eat other creatures. The same point will be implicit in Psalm 104 (cf. Ps. 147:9).

Isaiah 11:6–8

Isaiah 11:6–8, in contrast, pictures wolf and lamb, leopard and kid-goat lying down together, and lion becoming vegetarian. We might ask of this passage an equivalent to Paul's question, 'is it for lambs and goats that God is concerned?' First, God apparently needs to turn some of these animals into something other than themselves: wolves, leopards, and lions who live like this have ceased to be wolves, leopards and lions. It might be that Isaiah 11 is thus picturing God as involved in an act of new creation that improves on the first creation or implements its original design. But the general context in Isaiah does not make one expect discussion of the destiny of the animal world. Further, the narrow context in Isaiah 11:1–5 and 9 suggests that verses 6–8 use talk of 'unnatural' harmony in the animal world as a metaphor for harmony in the human world. Strong and powerful people will live together with the weak and powerless because the latter can believe that the former are no longer seeking to devour them. The book called Isaiah indeed opened by using animals to stand for human beings (1:3), in connection with the question of knowledge, as in 11:9. So they do in verses 6–8.

Whether that is correct or not, it provides a parable for the allusions to the animal world in the Old Testament as a whole. It is not a topic of interest in its own right; it is of interest only in so far as it relates to the human world. This is paradoxically so even in Job 38—39, which refers to the animal world only to make a point about the human world. The independent significance of the animal world is mentioned only because of its significance for the human world. As Paul puts it, 'is it for oxen that God is concerned? Or does he not speak entirely for our sake?' The answer is, yes, God speaks entirely for our sake. This would cohere with the fact that the vision of a New Day in Ezekiel 34:25–8 assumes that wild animals retain their instincts to eat living things and promises the community's protection by devices other than changing the animals' nature. The same assumption may underlie Hosea 2:18, where the arrangements for 'that day' include a covenant whereby humanity will be protected from the varying threats posed by the animal world.[6]

Feedback

I began by noting that people who read the Old Testament in the light of modern questions often see things there that have previously been missed, even if they also run the risk of reading modern concerns into the text. The Old Testament does not directly assert that women and men have equal status in the world, or that all races are equal before God and must treat each other on equal terms, or that all human beings are equal before God and therefore must not enslave one another, or that human beings must not make war on each other because they are all made in God's image, or that humanity is to look after the earth rather than exploit it. Indeed the Old Testament contains material that can be read either way on each question.

Professor Clark begins by noting that he does not write as a philosopher starting from secular premises; but in practice new insight on scripture often comes through people starting from secular premises rather than from traditional Christian ones that have made Christians read scripture according to a certain slant. In recent years the process can be seen most clearly with regard to the position of women. New premises have enabled people to see things that were always there but were invisible. They then may enable people to read scripture in a way that produces a picture that does better justice to the whole. It will not be surprising if unbelievers spot God's truths that everyone needs to take note of. As Professor Clark puts it, if we ill-treat animals, we have surely broken the law God inscribed in our hearts. Unbelievers have that law written in their hearts as much as believers do, and sometimes seem to have less inhibition about recognising it.

This works in the following ways with regard to animals. I have suggested that the author of Job was unconcerned about animals in their own right. Yet by a feedback mechanism, the fact that the book appeals to the significance of animals in their own right means it is implying that they are important in their own right. If the care of shepherds for sheep can be used as a theological illustration, as Professor Clark notes it is, then Ezekiel implicitly recognises the appropriateness of a caring rather than an exploitative stance in relation to animals, which would exclude their being treated as if they were machines, or their being reared in inhumane conditions (I write midway between the two great turkey-slaughter festivals, Thanksgiving and Christmas). So a secularly derived insight may help us to see implications in scripture that we would not otherwise have seen. We need to carry on having the discussion over whether (for instance) the acceptance of the sacrifice of animals in the Old Testament and of meat-eating in the New is a point at which the Bible has not worked out the logic of its own presuppositions or whether (as I rather think) they put a question mark by the claim that the Bible points towards universal vegetarianism.

Endnotes

[1]   Col. 6; see James B. Pritchard (ed.), *Ancient Near Eastern Texts Relating to the Old Testament* (Princeton: Princeton University Press, 1969), 366.

[2]   See Claus Westermann, *Genesis 1–11* (ET Minneapolis: Augsburg/ London: SPCK, 1984), 162–5.

[3]   Calum M. Carmichael, *The Laws of Deuteronomy* (Ithaca: Cornell University Press, 1974), 238–40, 159–63.

[4]   Howard Eilberg-Schwartz, *The Savage in Judaism* (Bloomington: Indiana University Press, 1990), 115–40.

[5]   Andrew Linzey, *Animal Theology* (Urbana: University of Illinois, 1995), 103–4. He attributes the argument to Eugene Masure as cited by Eric Mascall in his *Corpus Christi: Essays on the Church and the Eucharist* (London: Longmans, 1965), 92.

[6]   See Francis I. Andersen and David Noel Freedman, *Hosea* (Anchor Bible; New York: Doubleday, 1980), 279–81.

3

Judaism and Christianity: One Covenant or Two?

Chaplaincy Lecture 1998

James D.G. Dunn

Posing the Problem

Fundamental to Christianity is the concept of two covenants – an old covenant and a new covenant. Christianity's foundation documents, its holy writings, are structured according to this scheme: the Christian Bible consists of two parts, the Old Testament and the New Testament. And since 'Testament' and 'Covenant' are synonymous, two different translations of the same Greek term, we can restate the point: the Christian Bible consists of two covenants, the Old Covenant and the New Covenant. However, this so-familiar formulation, this structuring principle within Christian self-understanding, both masks and poses two important problems.

One problem is the traditional Christian assumption that 'the old covenant' is *passé*. Paul uses the term *katargeo* in talking about it: the old covenant is 'ineffective, abolished, set aside, rendered defunct' (2 Cor. 3:7, 11, 13–14). Hebrews speaks of it as 'rendered obsolete' and 'growing old, close to disappearing' (Heb. 8:13, my translation). And yet – but the irony is rarely appreciated – Christians continue to count the Old Testament (Covenant) as part of *Christian* scripture. In other words, since the Old Testament is roughly three-quarters of the Christian Bible, three-quarters of

Christian scripture consists of a religious system Christianity regards
as defunct. Despite the comments of Paul and Hebrews, the old
covenant is still part of Christianity! To pose the same problem from
the other side: what right has Christianity to take over the scriptures
of what is a different religion?

The second problem posed by talk of old covenant and new is
that Christians have traditionally identified the old covenant with
Judaism; the new covenant they identify, of course, with
Christianity. The corollary from the same disparagement of the old
covenant – and one again too little consciously grappled with by
Christians – is that *Judaism itself* is also *passé*. If 'old covenant' is *passé*,
and old covenant = Judaism, then Judaism is presumably equally
'defunct', at least as seen from that Christian perspective. From this
perspective the traditional anti-Jewish polemic that has so seriously
besmirched Christian history emerged. Already in the second
century the theme of supersessionism was well established. For
example, according to Barnabas 4:6–8, the people of Moses have
forfeited the covenant; it is 'ours' and not 'theirs' (Barn. 13—14).
And according to Melito of Sardis, 'the people [Israel] was a model',
but 'the church' is 'the reality', and now the people has been made
void and the model abolished; what was once precious (Jerusalem
and its sacrificial cult) is now worthless (*Peri Pascha* 39–45). In short,
Christianity had superseded Judaism; Christianity had sucked out all
that had been good in the religion of early Judaism, and the empty
shell of rabbinic Judaism could be cast aside.

In the modern period the attitude was expressed more subtly:
Second Temple Judaism was referred to as *Spätjudentum*, 'late
Judaism'. Such a formulation could be used precisely because it was
assumed that the role of Judaism had been primarily to prepare for
the coming of Christianity; therefore the Judaism of the time of
Jesus was the last phase of Judaism; once Jesus came, once
Christianity came, Judaism was finished![1] What such writers
thought about contemporary Judaism is less clear: if first-century
Judaism was 'late Judaism', what on earth should the next nineteen
centuries of Judaism be called?

Can this any more be defended? The fact that such corollaries to an
old/new covenant schema lay so close to the surface, and yet were
rarely faced, can no longer be tolerated. The importance of the issue
should be obvious. First, as became clear in outlining the first problem,

the identity of Christianity itself is at stake: in what sense are the scriptures of the old covenant part of Christian scripture? what is the relation of old covenant to new *within* Christian identity? And second, as the second problem reminds us, the question of Christianity's continuing relation to Judaism is posed with fresh sharpness: if the old covenant is to be more closely identified with Judaism, then Christianity's claims also upon the scriptures of the old covenant means that the relation of Christianity to Judaism has more the character of an *ecumenical* than an *interfaith* issue.

The Covenants

To tackle such questions we need to step back: first, to remind ourselves what 'covenant' means; and then to outline what are the key covenants within the biblical traditions.

'Covenant' means simply 'agreement', or, more formally, 'treaty' or 'contract'. It is this range of meaning on which Paul plays when he links talk of the covenant with Abraham with the idea of a last will and testament; the word itself permits this transition in thought (Gal. 3:15–17). In terms of the present discussion, the covenants in view are those the Jewish scriptures refer to as made by God with human beings – agreements God entered into and by which he bound himself.[2]

These covenants within the Jewish scriptures (the 'Old Testament') can be classified into four groups.

1. The covenant(s) with Abraham and the patriarchs

The singular (or plural) can be used since what seems to be in view in the later covenants is a reaffirmation or renewal of the (same) covenant given earlier.[3] The covenant with Abraham was first enunciated in Genesis 12:2–3:

> I will make of you a great nation, and I will bless you, and make your name great, so that you will be a blessing. I will bless those who bless you, and the one who curses you I will curse; and in you all the families of the earth shall be blessed.

After further and obviously related promises in 13:14–17 and 15:4–5, what seems to be the formal ratification of the covenant with Abraham is described in 15:17–19:

> When the sun had gone down and it was dark, a smoking fire-pot and a flaming torch passed between these pieces [of the sacrificed animals and birds cut in two]. On that day the LORD made a covenant with Abram, saying, 'To your descendants I give this land, from the river of Egypt to the great river, the river Euphrates ...'

A further important restatement or re-establishment of the covenant is given in Genesis 17:1–21. It is at this point that Abram is renamed Abraham ('ancestor of a multitude'), the covenant's eternal validity is stressed, circumcision of all male members of Abraham's household is made a requisite of covenant membership, and the line of promise is specified as descending through Isaac rather than Ishmael. There are still two more reaffirmations of the covenant in Genesis 18:18 and 22:16–18, the latter after Abraham had 'passed the test' and proved his unconditional loyalty by demonstrating his readiness to sacrifice Isaac his son, the son of promise, if commanded to do so by God.

Essentially the same covenant is made with Isaac in Genesis 26:2–4:

> The LORD appeared to Isaac and said, 'Do not go down to Egypt; settle in the land that I shall show you. Reside in this land as an alien, and I will be with you, and will bless you; for to you and to your descendants I will give all these lands, and I will fulfil the oath that I swore to your father Abraham. I will make your offspring as numerous as the stars of heaven, and will give to your offspring all these lands; and all the nations of the earth shall gain blessing for themselves through your offspring ...'

And again with Jacob in 28:13–15:

> And the LORD stood beside him and said, 'I am the LORD, the God of Abraham your father and the God of Isaac; the land on which you lie I will give to you and to your offspring; and your offspring shall be like

the dust of the earth … and all the families of the earth shall be blessed in you and in your offpsring.'

The covenant is reaffirmed to Jacob again in 35:11–12.

2. The covenant with Israel

Here again we can probably speak of what are essentially the same covenant. In the Pentateuchal/Hexateuchal history as now constituted, the covenant with Israel is made first at Mount Sinai in Exodus 19:5–6:

> Now therefore, if you obey my voice and keep my covenant, you shall be my treasured possession out of all the peoples. Indeed, the whole earth is mine, but you shall be for me a priestly kingdom and a holy nation.

Next in the plains of Moab, in the Deuteronomic version of events – particularly Deuteronomy 29–31:

> These are the words of the covenant that the LORD commanded Moses to make with the Israelites in the land of Moab, in addition to the covenant that he had made with them at Horeb. (29:1)

Then follows the famous threat of curse implemented in Israel's dispersion from the land and promise of restoration to the land of promise and subsequent prosperity (Deut. 30).

The same covenant is solemnly reaffirmed at Mounts Ebal and Gerizim in Joshua 8:30–5.

3. Special covenants

We read also of a number of special covenants made with individuals. *Phinehas*'s zeal in stamping out sexual relations with Midianite women (the sin of Baal-Peor), and thus maintaining Israel's purity, is rewarded by his being granted a 'covenant of peace … for him and for his descendants after him a covenant of perpetual priesthood' (Num. 25:12–13). This sequence of events had special significance in Jewish history (Sir. 45:23–4), with Phinehas portrayed as the archetypal zealous Jew to be emulated by Maccabean resistance fighters (1 Macc. 2:54; 4 Macc. 18:12) and subsequently by Zealots in the build-up to the Jewish revolt in 66 CE.[4]

More significant for Christians has been the special covenant made with *David*, that David's son would build a house for God's name (the Temple), that God would establish the throne of his kingdom forever, and that God would be a father to him and he a son to God: 'Your house and your kingdom shall be made sure forever before me; your throne shall be established forever' (2 Sam. 7:16) – another 'everlasting covenant' (2 Sam. 23:5).

4. The new covenant

Talk of a 'new covenant' appears explicitly in the still more famous (for Christians) Jeremiah 31:31–4:

> The days are surely coming, says the LORD, when I will make a new covenant with the house of Israel and the house of Judah. It will not be like the covenant that I made with their ancestors when I took them by the hand to bring them out of the land of Egypt – a covenant that they broke, though I was their husband, says the LORD. But this is the covenant that I will make with the house of Israel after those days, says the LORD: I will put my law within them, and I will write it on their hearts; and I will be their God, and they shall be my people. No longer shall they teach one another, or say to each other, 'Know the LORD', for they shall all know me, from the least of them to the greatest, says the LORD; for I will forgive their iniquity, and remember their sin no more.

There is some dispute as to whether other similar-sounding prophecies should be seen as variations on the same theme (rather like the repeated promises to Abraham and the patriarchs, or the different versions of the covenant with Israel), or as quite different hopes. The two most relevant of these other prophecies are Isaiah 59:20–1 and Ezekiel 36:24–7.

> And he will come to Zion as Redeemer, to those in Jacob who turn from transgression, says the LORD. And as for me, this is my covenant with them, says the LORD: my spirit that is upon you, and my words

that I have put in your mouth, shall not depart out of your mouth, or out of the mouths of your children, or out of the mouths of your children's children, says the LORD, from now on and forever. (Is. 59:20–1)

I will take you from the nations, and gather you from all the countries, and bring you into your own land. I will sprinkle clean water upon you, and you shall be clean from all your uncleannesses, and from all your idols I will cleanse you. A new heart I will give you, and a new spirit I will put within you; and I will remove from your body the heart of stone and give you a heart of flesh. I will put my spirit within you, and make you follow my statutes and be careful to observe my ordinances. (Ezek. 36:24–7)

In fact, these two should probably best be regarded as variant forms of what was essentially the same hope for a more effective version of the original covenant that had been made with Israel. Most noticeably, the promises of forgiveness of iniquity (Jeremiah), removal of transgression (Isaiah), and cleansing from uncleanness (Ezekiel) are all closely linked; and the Isaiah prophecy demonstrates that the hope of God's (new) covenant (Jeremiah) went quite naturally hand in hand with hope of God's spirit within them (Ezekiel). But we will return to these matters shortly.

If the above texts and classification provide the basic data for any discussion of covenants within Israel's history, then the obvious question to be posed is, how should these covenants be seen to relate to each other? To simplify matters, we can leave aside the special covenants (3). However important they are for Jews and Christians, they do not bear so directly on the question of old covenant and new. But the question is still complex enough: how are the other covenants (1, 2 and 4) to be correlated? And how does their correlation illuminate the issues posed in the opening section?

The traditional Christian view is, of course, that the covenant with Israel (2) represents the old covenant of which Jeremiah speaks – the old covenant therefore typifying Israel, and subsequently Judaism. In contrast, the new covenant (4) denotes Christianity: this new covenant is referred to in the words of the Lord's Supper, as recorded in 1 Corinthians 11:25 ('This cup is the new covenant in my blood'); and again in Paul's own taking up of the contrast between old and new covenants in 2 Corinthians 3:6, where the new covenant 'of spirit' clearly is seen to supersede the old (3:14). But will this do? Is it quite so straightforward as this summary might suggest?

The New Covenant

Let us first ask how the covenant with Israel (2) may be related to the new covenant (4). Several points immediately call for comment.

First, as already noted briefly, Jeremiah seems to have had in mind not so much a *different* covenant as a *more effective* covenant, a *renewed* rather than a *new* covenant – Jeremiah 31:33:

> But this is the covenant that I will make with the house of Israel after those days, says the LORD: I will put my law within them, and I will write it on their hearts; and I will be their God, and they shall be my people.

And this new covenant is *still in terms of the law*. The covenant is still made by God with his people; the law still functions as the terms of that covenant – what God demands and expects of his covenant people. The only difference is that this law, the same law, will be written in their hearts, thus, obviously, ensuring greater obedience through greater motivation and more instinctive or spontaneous obedience.

This hope and prophecy thus echo what had always been recognised, particularly within the Deuteronomy–Jeremiah tradition,[5] namely, that mere instruction in the law (as in the fundamental text, Deut. 6:4–9) would in itself never be sufficient to ensure obedience to the law. Israel's stubbornness would result in disobedience, abandoning the covenant and following other gods, and bring the calamity of the curses of the covenant on Israel's head (particularly Deut. 29:17–29). They needed, in Deuteronomy's unforgettable metaphor, to circumcise the 'foreskin' of their *hearts*, and be no longer stubborn (Deut. 10:16). Or in Jeremiah's taking up of the same metaphor:

> Circumcise yourselves to the LORD, remove the foreskin of your hearts, O people of Judah and inhabitants of Jerusalem. (Jer. 4:4)

Jeremiah probably had this in mind when he spoke of the new covenant: the new (or renewed) covenant would be assured of success where the old covenant had failed, precisely because the law would be written in their hearts; or, in other terms, circumcision would be of the heart and not just 'in the flesh'. Consequently, they would not need to be instructed in the meaning of the covenant and in the maintenance of the covenant relationship, because they would know God with immediacy for themselves (Jer. 31:33–4).

Also, the first Christians evidently believed that this hope had been realised in their case. This is clear from Paul who speaks of his Corinthian converts as

> a letter of Christ, prepared [or delivered] by us, written not with ink but with the Spirit of the living God, not on tablets of stone but on tablets of human hearts. (2 Cor. 3:3)

And he speaks of his ministry as that of 'a new covenant, not of letter but of spirit' three verses later (2 Cor. 3:6). The echo of the complex of prophecies outlined under the new covenant (4) would be hard to ignore: the same contrast between the law (written on tablets of stone)[6] and writing on the heart, linked with talk of the new covenant (Jer. 31:32–3); and the same contrast between the 'stone heart' and the 'fleshly heart' = 'new spirit'/'my (God's) Spirit' of Ezekiel 36:26–7 (and 11:19). Equally striking is Paul's claim in Philippians 3:3, 'For it is we who are the circumcision, who worship by the Spirit of God' (cf. Rom. 2:28–9). Here again the thought is of an inward work of God in the heart achieving a reality closer to what God looked for through the covenant and the law than anything achieved by external instruction or outward circumcision in the flesh. The fact that Paul expresses himself with such deliberate echo of the older terms of covenant relationship ('tablets of human hearts', 'we are the circumcision') confirms that he did not think of the new covenant as wholly new in its terms, only in its effectiveness. The new covenant, for Paul as well as for Jeremiah, is but the more effective achievement of the old by further divine initiative.

Second, what then of Paul's criticism of the law, a well-known, even infamous feature of Paul's theology? In the texts being discussed Paul's criticism of the law is primarily a criticism of its ineffectiveness – still in echo of the old Deuteronomistic complaint on the subject. Here it is important to observe that this criticism is focused on the stress the law seems to put on the outward and visible, as distinct from the inward and spiritual (Rom. 2:29; 2 Cor. 3:6; Phil. 3:3). This criticism he sums up in the word *gramma*, 'letter' (Rom. 2:29; 7:6; 2 Cor. 3:6); not to be ignored is the fact that Paul never refers to 'the law' as such in 2 Corinthians 3, but only to the *gramma*.

The point is that *gramma* denotes the visible letter on the page or scroll, the law as written, visible to sight in the written letter. If the law is being summed up in this 'letter', then it is the law reduced to the letter, the visible regulation, the outward act of compliance, circumcision in the flesh. Paul makes the point explicitly in Romans 2:28–9:

> For the true Jew is not the one visibly marked as such, nor circumcision that which is performed visibly in the flesh, but one who is so in a hidden way, and circumcision is of the heart, in Spirit not in letter [*gramma*]. (my translation)

Hence also Paul's claim that Christians experience the inward reality of the Spirit, which is the antithesis of the *gramma*: 'we are slaves not under the old written code [*gramma*] but in the new life of the Spirit' (Rom. 7:6); 'ministers of a new covenant, not of letter [*gramma*] but of spirit; for the letter kills, but the Spirit gives life' (2 Cor. 3:6).

In short, both old covenant and new focus on the law. But the old covenant is typified, in both Jeremiah's and Paul's eyes, by its ineffectiveness; and this ineffectiveness Paul attributes to a misplaced emphasis on the outward and visible, on what is done in the flesh. I note in passing, but do not have space to elaborate, that the letter to the Hebrews makes an equivalent criticism of the old covenant as too much focused on the cult, that is, on the outward and visible cult.

Third, for Paul a more effective keeping of the law is possible within the new covenant. Paul expresses this thought in different ways in his letter to the Romans: through faith, through the Spirit, through love: 'Do we make the law invalid by faith? Not at all! On the contrary, we establish the law' (Rom. 3:31; my translation).

In the same context Paul can even talk of 'the law of faith' (Rom. 3:27), where he evidently had in mind that the real requirement of the law is actually fulfilled through faith (Rom. 9:32), that is, by 'the obedience of faith' (Rom. 1:5).

> What the law was unable to do in that it was weak through the flesh, God sent his own Son in the very likeness of sinful flesh, and as a sin-offering, and condemned sin in the flesh, in order that the requirement of the law might be fulfilled in us, who walk not in accordance with the flesh but in accordance with the Spirit. (Rom. 8:3–4; my translation)

Here Paul is explicit: the ineffectiveness of the law is remedied by the Spirit. Those who walk according to the Spirit presumably, therefore, meet Jeremiah's old expectations, that one day the law would be obeyed from the circumcised heart (cf. Gal. 5:16–25; and again Phil. 3:3).

> Owe nothing to anyone, except to love one another; for the one who loves the other has fulfilled the law. For the commandment 'You shall not commit adultery; You shall not kill; You shall not steal; You shall not covet', and any other commandment, is summed up in this word, in the command 'You shall love your neighbour as yourself'. Love does no wrong to the neighbour; therefore, the fulfilment of the law is love. (Rom. 13:8–10; my translation)

However we should interpret and draw out the full meaning of these passages, the basic point for us is clear: Paul saw the establishing and fulfilling of the law as still an important goal for members of the new covenant. The law still functioned to indicate God's requirements; the new covenant was simply a more effective enabling for its members to meet those requirements.

An important corollary immediately comes to the fore: that any attempt to set old covenant against new covenant by identifying the old covenant exclusively with the law, is badly mistaken. The long-established tradition that identifies the old covenant with the

law and the new covenant with the gospel, thus making the
law/gospel antithesis the heart of its theologising, or the heart of the
antithesis between Judaism and Christianity, is profoundly
mistaken. A too simple law/gospel antithesis has seriously mistaken
Paul's theology and gospel. For *both* covenants the objective is the
same: how may the law best be fulfilled, how best may the will of
God be done? The issue is the law's implementation, not its
abrogation.

The Covenant with Abraham

If that clarifies, at least to some extent, the relation between the old
Sinai covenant with Israel (2) and the new covenant of Jeremiah
(4), how then is the covenant with Abraham (1) to be correlated
with the old and new covenants? The issue here is focused by the
fact that Paul's argument in Galatians 3 and Romans 4 seems to go
behind the covenant with Israel (2) and to root Christian claims in
the covenant/promise made to Abraham (1). Moreover, Paul seems
to argue from the promise to Abraham (1) directly to the new
covenant (4), bypassing the Sinai covenant (2). In Galatians 3:19–29
Paul's argument is that the covenant with Abraham was first and
provides the primary model for God's dealings with human beings –
that is, as a direct act of God to human faith. The law came later and
does not change the terms of that original covenant and promise; on
the contrary, the law's role in protecting Israel was a temporary one
and has in effect ended with the coming of Christ and of the
possibility of faith directly in and through him.[7] Romans 4 likewise
argues directly from the faith of Abraham to faith in Christ, and
seems to cut out any role for the law at this point. What are we to
make of this? Does this line of Pauline argument not cut across the
conclusions already drawn?

Here again the matter is not so simple, and we need to examine
the data more closely – in this case, the covenant with Abraham.

Under closer examination it becomes clear that the promise to
Abraham always had three strands: (1) the promise of seed; (2) the
promise of land; and (3) the promise of blessing to the (other)
nations.

1. The promise of seed

I will make of you a great nation ... (Gen. 12:2)

I will make your offspring like the dust of the earth; so that if one can count the dust of the earth, your offspring also can be counted. (Gen. 13:16)

Look towards heaven and count the stars, if you are able to count them ... So shall your descendants be. (Gen. 15:5)

As for me, this is my covenant with you: You shall be the ancestor of a multitude of nations. (Gen. 17:4)

I will bless you, and I will make your offspring as numerous as the stars of heaven and as the sand that is on the seashore. (Gen. 22:17)

2. The promise of land

To your offspring I will give this land. (Gen. 12:7)

All the land that you see I will give to you and to your offspring forever. (Gen. 13:15)

To your descendants I give this land, from the river of Egypt to the great river, the river Euphrates ... (Gen. 15:18)

I will give to you, and to your offspring after you, the land where you are now an alien, all the land of Canaan, for a perpetual holding. (Gen. 17:8)

3. The promise of blessing to the nations

In you all the families of the earth shall be blessed. (Gen. 12:3)

Abraham shall become a great and mighty nation, and all the nations of the earth shall be blessed in him ... (Gen. 18:18)

By your offspring shall all the nations of the earth gain blessing for themselves ... (Gen. 22:18)

Particularly notable is the way in which, when the promise is repeated, the covenant renewed with Isaac and Jacob, all three strands are woven firmly together:

> to you and to your descendants I will give all these lands ... I will make your offspring as numerous as the stars of heaven, and will give to your offspring all these lands; and all the nations of the earth shall gain blessing for themselves through your offspring ... (Gen. 26:3–4)

> The land on which you lie I will give to you and to your offspring; and your offspring shall be like the dust of the earth ... and all the families of the earth shall be blesed in you and in your offspring. (Gen. 28:13–15)

In the light of this, two further points of clarification call for comment. First, despite the closeness of the interweaving of these strands, it is evident that the first two strands have been regarded as the more important in Israel's self-understanding over the centuries. The promise of seed to Abraham through Isaac, and of land for Abraham's descendants (through Isaac!) became fundamental to Israel's identity. The echo of these two strands elsewhere in scripture (Old Testament) is worth at least sampling. Note, for example, the following texts.

> See, I have set the land before you; go in and take possession of the land that I swore to your ancestors, to Abraham, to Isaac, and to Jacob, to give to them and to their descendants after them. (Deut. 1:8, 11)

> My servant Moses is dead. Now proceed to cross the Jordan, you and all this people, into the land that I am giving to them, to the Israelites ... From the wilderness and the Lebanon as far as the great river, the river Euphrates, all the land of the Hittites, to the Great Sea in the west shall be your territory. (Josh. 1:2–4)

> He is mindful of his covenant forever,
>   of the word that he commanded, for a thousand
>   generations,
> the covenant that he made with Abraham,
>   his sworn promise to Isaac,
> which he confirmed to Jacob as a statute,
>   to Israel as an everlasting covenant,

saying, 'To you I will give the land of Canaan
    as your portion for an inheritance.' (Ps. 105:8–11)

In those days the house of Judah shall join the house of Israel, and together they shall come from the land of the north to the land that I gave your ancestors for a heritage. (Jer. 3:18)

Somewhat unnerving, however, is the recognition that the same remains true today: the restoration of the nation of Israel (1948) is predicated on the same two promises; and the promise of the land ('from the river of Egypt to the great river, the river Euphrates'?) remains at the root of right-wing policy and West Bank settlement within the present nation of Israel. Nowhere else is the text of scripture treated so much as a twentieth-century political manifesto!

Second, in contrast to the emphasis given to the first two strands of the Abraham covenant (the promise of seed and of land), the third strand features very little. It is alluded to in Psalm 72:17 – a prayer on behalf of the king:

May his name endure forever,
    his fame continue as long as the sun.
May all nations be blessed in him;
    may they pronounce him happy.

And it is clearly in view in Jeremiah 4:1–2:

If you return, O Israel, says the LORD,
if you return to me,
if you remove your abominations from my presence,
    and do not waver,
and if you swear, 'As the LORD lives!'
    in truth, in justice, and in uprightness,
then nations shall be blessed by him,
    and by him they shall boast.

But the only explicit reference to this third strand of promise as part of the covenant with Abraham comes in the deutero-canonical ben Sira (Ecclesiasticus):

Abraham was the great father of a multitude of nations,
  and no one has been found like him in glory;
he kept the law of the Most High,
  and was taken into covenant with him;
he established the covenant in his flesh,
  and when he was tested he was found faithful.
Therefore the LORD assured him by an oath
  that the nations would be blessed through his posterity;
that he would multiply him like the dust of the earth,
  and exalt his posterity like the stars,
and cause them to inherit from sea to sea
  and from the River to the ends of the earth. (Sir. 44:19–21)

Should we assume, however, that the third strand lies behind the occasional stress within the prophets that Israel has an obligation towards the (other) nations? Thus in Isaiah 49:1–6 the Servant of Yahweh (= Israel – 49:3) is commissioned to be 'a light to the nations, that my [God's] salvation may reach to the end of the earth' (49:6). Jeremiah's prophetic commissioning similarly includes the charge to be 'a prophet to the nations' (Jer. 1:5). Moreover, the Isaiah prophecies in particular envisaged a time when the nations would flock to Mount Zion to learn of God: 'For out of Zion shall go forth instruction, and the word of the LORD from Jerusalem' (Is. 2:3). Or again, 56:6–7 envisages 'foreigners who join themselves to the LORD ... and hold fast my covenant' coming to God's holy mountain, 'for my house shall be called a house of prayer for all peoples.' The openness of God to repentant Gentiles is the fundamental message of the prophecy of Jonah, and reflects the same strand within Israelite thought.

Whether all these texts (with others) should be simply grouped together is a fair question. Do the passages cited two paragraphs earlier (Ps. 72:17; Jer. 4:1–2; Sir. 44:21) indicate a hope of Israel's success and prosperity, and of blessing for the nations as simply a reflection of that success (a kind of 'trickle-down' theory of divine blessing)? Notable in the case of ben Sira 44 is the fact that the promise of blessing for the nations seems to be tied into a heightened aggrandisement of the promise of land ('to inherit from sea to sea and from the River to the ends of the earth'); that is to say, the promised blessing to the nations is probably envisaged as a reflection of Israel's success and prosperity. In some contrast, do the texts in the paragraph previous to this one imply a greater openness to the thought of what we might call a more even-handed concept of divine blessing? – that is, the thought of Israel as a channel of divine blessing/salvation 'to the end of the earth' (Is. 49:6), and not so much as its focus (with blessing to the nations as secondary, a reflection of the primary blessing)?

In short, the fact that there are different strands within the covenant made with Abraham injects a further complication into the discussion of old and new covenant. In asking how early Christianity, Paul in particular, correlated old covenant and new, we have to examine more closely the influence of the promises to Abraham on both early Jewish and early Christian thinking.

Contrasting Interpretations of the Abrahamic Covenant

What difference, then, is made to our principal question (the relation of old to new covenant) by the fact that the covenant with Abraham had several strands? The answers of Israel's tradition, on the one hand, and of Paul and his fellow Christians, on the other, are strikingly different.

In the former case the answer is, in effect, none. No difference. Here it is important to note how Abraham's acceptance of the covenant was already tied into his observance of the obligations of the law within the accounts of Abraham's own lifetime. In Genesis 17:9–14 the repetition/renewal of the covenant with Abraham and his descendants becomes dependent on his male heirs being circumcised. And in Genesis 22:1–19 the further renewal of the covenant follows upon Abraham's successfully passing the test of his faithfulness to God in being willing to sacrifice his son (the son of promise) to God. Indeed, the renewal of the covenant with Isaac can even report God as making this renewed covenant 'because Abraham obeyed my voice and kept my charge, my commandments, my statutes, and my laws' (Gen. 26:5).

In other words, here already emerges the image of Abraham as the perfect lawkeeper. And here too we see the root of a Jewish rejoinder, indeed of a scriptural rejoinder to Paul. Paul's attempt to

separate the Abrahamic covenant from the Sinai covenant would
seem to be already undermined more or less from the beginning:
obedience and faithfulness to God's commandments were already
bound into the covenant with Abraham and the patriarchs;
Abraham as the model member of the covenant was as one who had
been circumcised and remained faithful to the law.

This, in fact, was the current exposition of Abraham's righteousness at the time of Paul – as we can see from contemporary Jewish
writings:

> Abraham ... kept the law of the Most High,
>   and was taken into covenant with him;
> he established the covenant in his flesh,
>   and when he was tested he was found faithful.
> Therefore the Lord assured him by an oath ... (Sir. 44:19–21)

> Was not Abraham found faithful when tested, and it was reckoned to
> him as righteousness? (1 Macc. 2:52)

> Was not our ancestor Abraham justified by works when he offered his
> son Isaac on the altar? ... Thus the scripture was fulfilled that says,
> 'Abraham believed God, and it was reckoned to him as righteousness.'
> (Jas 2:21–3)

It seems therefore to have been a consistent line within early Jewish
thought to treat the Abrahamic covenant as a whole, and as a whole
to correlate it with obedience and faithfulness to the law. There was
evidently already in place a well-thought-through theological
rationale, which in effect indicated the predominant way in which
Paul's Jewish contemporaries saw the relation between the three
strands of the Abrahamic promise. In particular, the promise of
blessing to the nations was simply subsumed within a covenant
validated by Abraham's obedience and faithfulness.

How then did Paul react to that contemporary interpretation of
the Abrahamic covenant and its relation to the law? And would
Paul's response have appeared as an outrageous departure from
the more traditional interpretation, even as an anti-Jewish
interpretation? Does Paul's interpretation after all give ground for

the subsequent Christian antithesis between law and gospel, old covenant and new?

When we turn to Paul it quite quickly becomes clear that he gives the third strand of the Abrahamic covenant much more prominence than his contemporaries, particularly in his own self-understanding as an apostle and in his exposition of the gospel. We see this in his earliest statement regarding his apostleship, in Galatians 1:15–16:

> When it pleased the one who set me apart from my mother's womb, and called me through his grace, to reveal his Son in me, in order that I might preach him among the Gentiles … (my translation)

The echo of two of the passages cited above can hardly be accidental:

> Before I formed you in the womb I knew you,
> and before you were born I consecrated you;
> I appointed you a prophet to the nations. (Jer. 1:5)

> The LORD called me before I was born,
> while I was in my mother's womb he named me …

> I will give you as a light to the nations,
> that my salvation may reach to the end of the earth. (Is. 49:1–6)

Paul evidently regarded his apostolic commissioning as a prophetic calling to continue Israel's role, to carry out Israel's obligation to bring light to the nations. Paul in effect sides with that strand of Israel's theology which showed itself as more open to the Gentiles.

Given that the Acts account of Paul is often at odds with the apostle's self-portrayal, it is of interest to note that on this point the Acts portrayal is wholly at one with Paul himself. In all three accounts of Paul's conversion there is an emphasis on his calling to the Gentiles – summed up in the final version:

> the Gentiles – to whom I am sending you to open their eyes so that they may turn from darkness to light and from the power of Satan to God, so that they may receive forgiveness of sins and a place among

those who are sanctified by faith in me. (Acts 26:17–18; cf. 9:15; 22:21)

And in Paul's sermon in Pisidian Antioch he is portrayed as citing the very Isaiah 49:6 he echoes in Galatians 1:15–16:

> The Lord has commanded us, saying,
> 'I have set you to be a light for the Gentiles,
>   so that you may bring salvation to the ends of the earth.' (Acts 13:47)

The Paul of Acts is as open to the Gentiles as the autobiographical Paul. This was a consistent and fundamental trait of his character and of his theology.

Even more striking is the fact that Paul actually cites the third strand of the Abrahamic covenant as the first statement of the gospel – Galatians 3:8:

> Scripture, foreseeing that God would justify the Gentiles from faith, preached the gospel beforehand to Abraham, 'In you shall all the nations be blessed.' (my translation)

The quotation is a mixture of the two first statements of the third strand – Genesis 12:3 ('In you all the families of the earth shall be blessed') and Genesis 18:18 ('all the nations of the earth shall be blessed in him'). In other words, Paul regarded the gospel of Christ as the fulfilment of Abraham's covenant, as the fulfilment of the promise (and commission) given to Israel as Abraham's heirs. That is, he both reminds his Jewish contemporaries of the relatively neglected third strand of the covenant with Abraham; and he indicates that he understands that third strand more as a commission to bring benefit to Gentiles than simply a promise that they will benefit from Israel's success.

Equally noteworthy is the way Paul interprets the other two strands of the promise to Abraham (seed and land) in the light of this understanding of the blessing to the nations. In Galatians 3 he immediately follows his exposition of the blessing to the nations, in terms of the Spirit received through faith (3:14), with the (to us) surprising interpretation of Abraham's promised *seed* as summed up in Christ (3:16). In fact the interpretation was thoroughly Jewish in character.[8] The point, however, is that he was able to produce a quite acceptable interpretation (the seed is Christ) to counter the traditional Jewish interpretation, which tied the promised blessing to the nations too closely to the physical descendants of Abraham: ethnic Israel. In contrast, if the seed is Christ, then those who are Christ's (Gentiles as well as Jews) are Abraham's seed, heirs according to the promise (3:29).

Similarly in his other exposition of the promise to Abraham, Paul was able to interpret the other strand of promise (promise of *land*) in an equivalently universal way. The promise was 'that he should be heir of the world' (Rom. 4:13). Again this is not an arbitrary or idiosyncratic interpretation introduced by Paul. As Sirach 44:21 indicates, the promise of land had been already elaborated to embrace the whole earth; and, a few decades after Paul, Abraham's inheritance is understood as the world to come (2 Bar. 14:13; 51:3). So, once again, Paul was able to take a perfectly acceptable elaboration of the promise to Abraham and thereby to open out the interpretation of the Abrahamic covenant in conformity with his understanding of Abraham's blessing to the nations.

What all this means is that the debate between Paul and his fellow Jews on the interpretation of the covenant with Abraham is to be conceived as a debate *within* Second Temple Judaism and not as a debate between Christianity and Judaism.

Conclusion: One Covenant

To sum up an overlong exposition, then, the antithesis between old covenant and new, which we find particularly in Paul, should not be interpreted as an antithesis between the law and the gospel, far less as an antithesis between Judaism and Christianity. For Paul, as for the Judaism of his day, the new covenant is best understood as a renewal of the old, and as a more effective version of the old. Not least of importance is the fact that Paul continued to insist that the covenants are Israel's (Rom. 9:4), that believing Gentiles are given part in the olive tree that is Israel (11:17–24), and that the new covenant is also and still *Israel's* hope (11:26–7). In the face of such emphases, it is simply not possible, or at least not credible, to argue

from Paul that Christianity has taken over from Israel, as though
Judaism no longer had any right to exist!

Moreover, the criticism Paul makes of the law is a criticism not
of the law as such, but of the current emphases within Second
Temple Judaism, which in his view reinforced the weakness of the
law (particularly, too strong emphasis on circumcision in the flesh).
And in emphasising the priority of the covenant with Abraham,
Paul was reminding his Jewish contemporaries that the third strand
of that covenant had to be given due emphasis and that the other
two strands could quite properly be interpreted in conformity with
the more open tradition of Israel's thinking about the nations. In
other words, Paul was engaged in an internal Jewish debate about
how the promise to Abraham should be related to the covenant on
Sinai and pressing a line of interpretation that had good precedent
within Jewish scripture and tradition.

In short, the old and new covenants should be seen not so much
as two quite different covenants, but as two interpretations of the
first covenant: the promise to Abraham. The new covenant, for
Paul as well as his Jewish predecessors, is not a rejection of the old so
much as a more effective implementation of the old. And
Christianity is not so much an antithesis to Judaism as the means
by which Gentiles were drawn into Israel (together with Jews) in
fulfilment of Israel's historic mission to the nations.

Endnotes

1   E.g. even W. Pannenberg, *Jesus – God and Man* (London: SCM,
    1968), can pose the alternative with regard to Jesus' 'conflict with the
    law': 'either Jesus had been a blasphemer or the law of the Jews – and
    with it Judaism itself as a religion – is done away with' (255)!

2   For a summary but full treatment of 'covenant' see G.E. Mendenhall
    and G.A. Heron, 'Covenant', *Anchor Bible Dictionary*, ed. David Noel
    Freedman (New York: Doubleday, 1992), 1:1179–1202.

3   This ambiguity may well explain the plural used by Paul in Rom. 9:4.
    See my *Romans* (Word Biblical Commentary, 38; Dallas: Word,
    1988), 527.

4   See particularly M. Hengel, *The Zealots: Investigations into the
    Jewish Freedom Movement in the Period from Herod I until 70 AD*
    (ET Edinburgh: T. & T. Clark, 1989), 146–228.

5   Jeremiah is generally attributed to the Deuteronomic school; see, e.g., M. Weinfeld, *Deuteronomy and the Deuteronomic School* (Oxford: Clarendon, 1972), 27–32.

6   The more explicit allusion is to Exod. 34, where the covenant is repeatedly identified with 'stone tablets' (34:1, 4, 28–9).

7   For details of the argument in Gal. 3 see my *Epistle to the Galatians* (Black's New Testament Commentary; London: A. & C. Black, 1993); also *Theology of Paul the Apostle* (Grand Rapids: Eerdmans, 1998), §6.4.

8   Dunn, *Galatians*, 184–5.

Is the Old Covenant Renewed in the New?

A Response to James D.G. Dunn

Mark Bonnington

Introduction: Mapping Covenantal Relationships

Covenantal thinking is woven deeply into the fabric of Christian theologising about its development out of Judaism. It is intrinsic to the way Christianity recognises and interprets the Hebrew Bible as Christian Scripture and is one of the major theological currencies in which understandings of Christianity's historic relations with Judaism are transacted. Yet the language of *new* covenant can leave us uncomfortable: what are the implications for the 'old' covenant? And what are the implications for how we construct our understanding of Judaism, ancient and modern?

Throughout his chapter Professor Dunn stresses the continuity between the covenants of the 'Old Testament' and covenantal thinking of the New Testament. His argument proceeds by relating the Pauline thinking about covenant first to the Mosaic covenant and then the covenant with Abraham.

In relation to Sinai covenant Dunn's central appeal is to the idea of covenant 'renewal'. Jeremiah's new covenant is really a covenant renewal – a promise to render effective the Sinai covenant. This too is the presupposition of the New Testament language of new covenant and it is of a piece with this that, like the Mosaic covenant, Paul teaches the fulfilment of the law. It is best to acknowledge the centrality of these fundamental continuities and articulate the distinctions between old and new covenants not as a contrast between an old, past, failed covenant and a new 'successful' one, but as a single covenant renewed and rendered effective in Christ: 'the new covenant is best understood as a renewal of the old, and as a more effective version of the old.'

In dealing with the promises to Abraham, Paul is at home in the Judaism of his day. It is true that Paul presses the covenant promises of seed, land and blessing to the nations in new and distinctive directions. But these directions cohere with existing theological trajectories within contemporary Judaism, and set Paul within that Judaism not against it. So 'Paul was engaged in an internal Jewish debate' and was 'pressing a line of interpretation that had good precedent within Jewish scripture and tradition.'

Dunn's practical intent is irenic. The cash value of his analysis for the relations between Christianity and Judaism is clear: 'the relation of Christianity to Judaism has more the character of an *ecumenical* than an *interfaith* issue.'[1]

New Covenant and Old in Jeremiah

How adequate is Dunn's formulation that new covenant language is really about covenant renewal? We may agree that the background to the New Testament language of 'new' covenant is to be found in the famous prophecy of Jeremiah 31.[2] But is this covenant 'renewal' rather than a 'new' and therefore 'different' or 'second' covenant? Is the new covenant simply a more effective form of the old? Suggesting that 'new covenant' language is essentially 'renewal' language compresses the distance between 'new' and 'old' and allows Dunn to present both as different versions of the same.

For Jeremiah the covenant is not seen principally in legal terms but in historical and relational ones. This is the 'Deuteronomic' reading of Israel's history interwoven with relational imagery. In her idolatry Israel has been faithless to YHWH, gone after other gods and broken the covenant. Jeremiah's central metaphors are relational – the sexual imagery of marriage, unfaithfulness and prostitution and the family imagery of a father with his rebellious children:

> I thought
>> how I would set you among my children,
> and give you a pleasant land,
>> the most beautiful heritage of all the nations.
> And I thought you would call me, My Father,
>> and would not turn from following me.
> Instead, as a faithless wife leaves her husband,
>> so have you been faithless to me, O house of Israel, says the
>> LORD. (3:19–20)

YHWH is jealous in his love for Israel. Despite his faithfulness to her, YHWH has divorced Israel because of her idolatry in going after other gods:

> Have you seen what she did, that faithless one, Israel, how she went up on every high hill and under every green tree, and played the whore there? And I thought, 'After she has done all this she will return to me'; but she did not return, and her false sister Judah saw it. She saw that for all the adulteries of that faithless one, Israel, I had sent her away with a decree of divorce; yet her false sister Judah did not fear, but she too went and played the whore. Because she took her whoredom so lightly, she polluted the land, committing adultery with stone and tree. (3:6–9)

As in Mosaic law (Deut 24:1–4) there can be no return to the first husband after divorce (3:1). Israel and Judah have broken the covenant and God will send the disaster of exile upon them (e.g. 11:1–17).

This historical and relational covenantal thinking remains in view when YHWH promises a return from exile and a new covenant (31:31–4). The covenant that follows the exile is to be different from that which followed the exodus – for the problem throughout has been Israel's idolatry (so Jer. 11:1–17). God does not simply forgive his people and patch up the relationship. This is no renewal of marriage vows nor a remarriage to a former partner, but a whole new relationship. The last covenant broke down over Israel's endemic unfaithfulness so that the Mosaic covenant had ended in divorce. Yet YHWH remained faithful – out of that faithfulness he offers not to renew the old but rather offers a new start where Israel

will have the law internalised and own YHWH as her God. The
post-exilic relationship is to be dissimilar in kind to the post-exodus
one: 'It will not be like the covenant that I made with their ancestors
... a covenant that they broke, though I was their husband, says the
LORD' (31:32). Her former sinful ways are to be forgiven and
forgotten in a vital new beginning (31:34–5). A whole new way of
relating to YHWH, rendered necessary by former failure, will be
made possible in the new covenant (31:4, 21).

Jeremiah does not specifically characterise the relationship of the
new covenant as a marriage. This may be deliberate: precisely to
avoid the suggestion that the new covenant relationship is of the
same kind as the old. In any case, what marital language there is in
the immediate context points in the same direction: Israel is
addressed as a virgin (31:4, 21). If we are to make anything of this we
should note that there is to be no return to the former husband, no
remarriage, no renewal of marriage vows. All these would carry the
past history of the relationship into the future. God will give Israel
the new start of taking her as his virgin bride, 'remembering her sin
no more' and giving her a new start – a possibility without parallel in
the less figurative world of human relationships. Such imagery
demands the language of newness not of renewal.

All this is the logic of covenantal relationship and of trust rather than
simply of legal obligation more or less effectively performed.
The problem with the Sinai covenant was not the ineffectiveness of the
covenant but the broken trust and flawed character of God's people
that left Israel's relationship with YHWH with a recurring history of
failure. That failure is so closely associated with the Sinai covenant that
Jeremiah cannot offer hope to Israel without a new start that deals with
the character issue. To describe the 'new covenant' of Jeremiah 31 as a
'renewal' of the covenant would be a substantial diminution of the
depth and radicality of the disjunction that Jeremiah envisions. If we
ask, 'Does Jeremiah intend two covenants or one?' the answer is,
emphatically, 'Two.' Anything less would be to condemn God's
people to the endless spiral of failure endemic in the history of God's
people in the post-Sinai period.[3]

To say that renewal is not the principal theme within Jeremiah's
treatment of the covenant is not of course to deny the real existence
of renewal themes in the prophetic expectation of Israel. Undoubtedly the appeals to circumcise the heart (Jer. 4:4; cf. Deut. 10:16)

call upon God's people to renew their obedience and return to him in order to avoid calamity. But Jeremiah 4:4 is an appeal for potential renewal *within the existing 'old' covenant structure*. Jeremiah goes on to give an extensive exposition of the unpreparedness and inability of the people of Judah to respond to the warning and exhortation to mend their ways despite impending doom (chs. 4–5). Thus it is precisely the failure of covenant renewal that makes the plight of Judah so desperate and leads to the offer of a new covenant in Jeremiah 31.

The other prophets Dunn quotes do not help with the covenant renewal theme either. Ezekiel's language of washing from uncleanness and replacing the heart of stone with a heart of flesh clearly envisages a spiritual renewal for effective obedience – but there is no language of covenant here, let alone of new covenant. Isaiah 59:20–1 does speak of covenant and of God giving his spirit, but the text merely says that God promises not to take his prophetic word from Israel – there is nothing here about effective obedience to the Sinai covenant. When we look for a precedent for new covenant language, Jeremiah 31 is our guide, with its unique and radical promise of a *new* covenant. Within biblical theology the background of the New Testament language of new covenant must therefore take seriously the radical disjunction inherent in Jeremiah's covenantal language.

Of course, to understand Jeremiah in this way is hardly foreign to the New Testament. After an extensive quote from Jeremiah 31 the writer to the Hebrews comments, 'In speaking of a new covenant he treats the first as obsolete. And what is becoming obsolete and growing old is ready to vanish away' (Heb. 8:13).[4] Thus the writer both recognises the *de facto* continuing existence of the old covenant and denies its continuing validity.

Covenant and Law in Paul

Dunn moves directly from these Old Testament prophetic texts to Paul. He advances three arguments to lead to the conclusion that 'Paul saw the establishing and fulfilling of the law as still an important goal for members of the new covenant. The law still functioned to indicate God's requirements; the new covenant was simply a more effective enabling for its members to meet those requirements.' We have already considered his first argument, that 'new covenant' language in Paul emerges from this Old Testament complex of prophecies and focuses on covenant renewal: 'the new covenant, for Paul as well as for Jeremiah, is but the more effective achievement of the old by further divine initiative.' Secondly, he argues that Paul's stress on the inward rather than external 'letter' of the law indicates that 'Paul's criticism of the law is primarily a criticism of its ineffectiveness.' Thirdly, on the basis of Romans, he suggests that 'for Paul a more effective keeping of the law is possible within the new covenant.'

How adequate is it to claim that for Paul the new covenant is the making effective of the old? Central to Dunn's answer are his claims that 'both old covenant and new focus on the law', that 'Paul saw the establishing and fulfilling of the law as still an important goal for members of the new covenant. The law still functioned to indicate God's requirements; the new covenant was simply a more effective enabling for its members to meet those requirements', and that 'For *both* covenants the objective is the same: how may the law best be fulfilled, how best may the will of God be done?' (emphasis Dunn's)

The fundamental datum with which we must come to terms is Paul's rejection of observance of Torah as the essential covenantal obligation under the new covenant in Christ. This was to break entirely with the Jewish tradition of what E. Sanders has taught us to call 'covenantal nomism' – the conviction that those obligations required to maintain righteousness within the covenant are the 613 commandments of the Mosaic Torah. For Paul both Jews and Gentiles could be righteous before God without the requirement to be circumcised and keep Torah. It was the implications for Jews that made Paul's law-free gospel to the Gentiles so dangerous (so Gal. 2:11–14; cf. Acts 21:27–36).

Paul does, of course, say many positive things about the law: 'the law is holy, and the commandment is holy, just and good' and 'the law is spiritual' (Rom. 7:14). The 'just requirement of the law' is to be fulfilled in believers (Rom. 8:4), Paul claims to establish/uphold the law (Rom. 3:31) and he uses the Decalogue and other Mosaic commandments to inform his ethics (Rom. 13:8–10; 1 Cor. 5–7).[5] All this is an important corrective to an overly negative view of the law and promotes Paul's claim to continuity between the old and the new.[6]

Nevertheless three sets of considerations count against Dunn's reading of this material. First Paul has rather obviously redefined what 'law' means. His use of the word law (*nomos*) includes as its basic meaning the Mosaic Torah, but it can also cover among other things the Pentateuch, law more generally and something much broader like 'principle' (Rom. 3:27; 7:21). In particular Paul can speak of the 'law of Christ', which he is under even though he is not under 'the law' (1 Cor. 9:20–1; Gal. 6:2). The content of the ethical injunctions to be laid upon members of the new covenant people is much less specific than the Torah. Moreover the Torah obligations are as a whole no longer in force. Paul can go as far as to say that neither circumcision nor uncircumcision counts for anything, but keeping the commandments of God (1 Cor. 7:19). Clearly the logic of such a statement is that circumcision is not one of God's commandments – what God requires is no longer 'the law'.

Secondly, when Paul writes of the uncircumcised who 'do instinctively what the law requires' (Rom. 2:14, 25–7) he clearly does not envisage perfect Torah observance – for circumcision is clearly excluded. Paul comes close to this idea again in Romans 7:22 ('I delight in the law of God in my inmost self'). Here the internalisation of the law goes not with more effective law-keeping but with the opposite, Paul's most powerful exposition of the radical nature of human sin – his inability to do as he knows he ought.

Thirdly, Paul's use of verbs like 'fulfilling' (Rom. 8:4) and 'establishing' (Rom. 3:31), which Dunn picks up, is notoriously imprecise – as Dunn himself recognises elsewhere.[7] Fitzmyer, for example, says that in claiming to 'establish the law' in Romans 3:31 Paul 'affirms the *basic message* of the Old Testament, and in particular that of the Mosaic law itself, *rightly understood*.'[8] Thus he recognises that it is not the law as legal requirement that is 'established' but something like the 'thrust', 'essence' or 'true meaning' of the law that Paul has in view.

Although Paul's attitude to the Abrahamic covenant is more positive, it reinforces the same basic point. Paul handles the Abrahamic material principally by means of a promise-fulfilment schema, taking up the various strands of the Abrahamic promises and pressing them in new directions. He interprets the promise of seed Christologically and universalises the promises of land and of blessing to the nations. Because of this stress on the nations/Gentiles, the Abraham material is ripe for Paul's exposition of his law-free gospel to the Gentiles. Much of his interpretation *can* be seen as a more-or-less understandable development, albeit in a distinctively Christian direction, of the Jewish Abraham traditions. But at one crucial point Paul diverges from that tradition significantly in a way that coheres with what we have seen above: he plays the covenant with Abraham off against the Sinai covenant of law.

Not only does Paul emphasise the promise of the Abrahamic covenant to the nations; he also sees the implications of this for Jews. If righteousness before God is possible without Torah obedience for Gentiles, then the implications for Jews are immediately clear: they do not need to keep Torah either. It is not the inclusion of Gentiles *per se* that is the great danger to Judaism in the early churches, but the implications for Jews that make the law-free gospel such a problem.

This is the central logic of the Abraham material in the argument of Romans: 'God is one; and he will justify the circumcised on the ground of faith and the uncircumcised through that same faith' (Rom. 3:30). If people are righteous before God by faith, Jews and Gentiles alike, then Torah need no longer be kept. Indeed this is the obvious implication to which Paul responds: the law is then overthrown, the Mosaic obligations are no longer binding. Paul's response to this suggestion is one Dunn picks up – 'On the contrary, we uphold [Dunn: 'establish'] the law' (Rom. 3:31). The exposition of the Abraham theme in chapter 4 justifies this claim. What follows is not an explanation of how the law is upheld in the sense that believers really keep the Torah after all. Rather Paul argues that the law is upheld in the sense that the promise it held out is inherited by those who have faith. The Torah *is* being claimed as authority – but an authority whose promises relativise its claim to act as the authoritative standard of ethical behaviour for those righteous before God. In arguing in this way Paul makes an excellent historical point. To assert that Abraham kept all the law before it was explicitly revealed in Sinai was wishful thinking historically, and to reject such wishfulness raised the important question of what exactly made Abraham righteous. Paul's answer is faith, not law.

The argument of Galatians is different but shares the same basic shape: the Abrahamic covenant relativises the Mosaic law. The law was a Johnny-come-lately and as such could not invalidate the promise of 430 years earlier (Gal. 3:17).[9] The law was temporary – the promise was sublimated until the time for the revelation of faith. Torah acted as a good but temporary guardian – one to which believers are therefore no longer subject (Gal. 3:23–6). In the context of Galatians the message is clear – the Mosaic obligations are no longer binding because of the fulfilment of the promise to Abraham in Christ and in the Spirit. Here undoubtedly we are right to speak of one covenant. There is fundamental continuity between the covenant promise to Abraham and its fulfilment in Christ. But the problem of Mosaic covenant will not go away – the continuity of the Abrahamic covenant highlights rather than ameliorates the discontinuity with Mosaic legal obligations. Essentially the same point is made in the only passage where Paul speaks in his own terms of 'new covenant'. In speaking of the old covenant as the dispensation of fading splendour he relativises the old covenant under Moses as impermanent and overshadowed by the glory of the new (2 Cor. 3).[10]

To say with Dunn that 'The law still functioned to indicate God's requirements; the new covenant was simply a more effective enabling for its members to meet those requirements' is, at best, to say what Paul says without saying what Paul means. It disguises the fact that for Paul the law (as ethical norm) has been redefined. If Paul does expect believers to be under a law, then that law is not Mosaic Torah but the 'law of Christ' fulfilled in the bearing of one another's burdens (Gal 6:2). Most commentators would not, I think, accept without qualification Dunn's emphasis that the new covenant *focuses* on the law, nor that it was *simply* a more effective enabling of law-keeping.

Conclusion: One Covenant or Two?

Dunn has set out a powerful argument for a sympathetic reading of the continuity between old and new covenants in Paul. Dunn's answer to his own question 'One covenant or two?' is clearly 'one' – the new is but the old renewed. Old covenant and new stand not in contrast but in continuity. They are both about the same thing – keeping the law. By contrast I have argued that the answer is more complex. The covenant of promise to Abraham is fulfilled in Christ. But the old covenant of Torah in Moses is surpassed in the new covenant – more contrast than continuity. One covenant or two? Both.

Endnotes

1   To suggest that we can draw Christian conclusions for interfaith relations on the basis of Paul alone (e.g. without taking into consideration Hebrews) is to open another discussion. I take it that the heart of Dunn's discussion is over the new covenant in Paul rather than in Hebrews or the Last Supper accounts.

2   The idea of a new covenant is absent from Second Temple Judaism outside Qumran where it occurs in the Pesher on Habakkuk from Qumran Cave 1 (1QpHab) 2:3 and in various passages in the Cairo (Genizeh text of the) Damascus (Document) (CD), where the references 'new covenant' are to the Qumran community itself.

3   So S. Lehne, 'once the Lord's judgement has been carried out to the full by the Babylonians the only way forward is to begin in a completely different way' (*The New Covenant in Hebrews* [Sheffield: Sheffield Academic Press, 1990], 34).

4   Cf. the similar principle in Philo, *Quis Rerum Divinarum Heres sit* 278.

5   See, e.g., B.S. Rosner, *Paul, Scripture and Ethics: A Study of 1 Corinthians 5–7* (Leiden: E.J. Brill, 1994).

6   Seeing the law as essentially good is, of course, much more prominent in the Calvinist tradition than the Lutheran tradition, against which so much of the polemic of the New Perspective on Paul has been directed.

7   J.D.G. Dunn, *Romans 1–8* (Word Biblical Commentary; Dallas: Word, 1988), 423.

8   J.A. Fitzmyer, *Romans* (Anchor Bible; London: Geoffrey Chapman), 367, my emphasis.

9   Note the similar argument in Rom. 7:1–4 expressed in more personal terms: believers 'have died to the law' and are thus free of its obligations.

10   'In the light of the surpassing glory of Christ the old and new covenants are viewed as mutually exclusive opposites' (Lehne, *New Covenant*, 69).

5

The God of the Covenant

Chaplaincy Lecture 1999

Gary D. Badcock

Theology and the Covenant

The idea of covenant is generally recognised to be something basic to the message of the Bible. Not only does the covenant structure the basic division between Old and New Testament in the Christian scriptures, but covenants between God and select individuals or groups of people appear and reappear at regular intervals through the length and breadth of biblical narrative. The covenant is an especially important concept in the foundation stories of the people of God. God speaks to Abraham, for example, in the following terms: 'I will establish my covenant between me and you, and your offspring after you throughout their generations, for an everlasting covenant, to be God to you and to your offspring after you' (Gen. 17:7). Or again, 'The LORD said to Moses: Write these words; in accordance with these words I have made a covenant with you and with Israel ... And he wrote on the tablets the words of the covenant, the ten commandments' (Exod. 34:27–8). That the God of the Bible is a God of covenant thus stands in the biblical tradition as a kind of irreducible datum, as something with which we simply have to do.

Not only is covenant a foundational concept in the Bible; it is also a flexible, adaptable notion, doing service repeatedly in a variety of key biblical contexts. The following words from the book of Jeremiah, for example, show that whatever we might be tempted to think – even on the basis of the Exodus passage just cited – God's covenant is anything but written in stone: 'The days are surely coming, says the LORD, when I will make a new covenant with the house of Israel and the house of Judah ... I will put my law within them, and I will write it on their hearts; and I will be their God, and they shall be my people' (Jer. 31:31, 33). Jesus' words at the institution of the Lord's Supper also give new meaning and importance to the concept of the covenant: 'he took a cup, and after giving thanks he gave it to them, saying, "Drink from it, all of you; for this is my blood of the covenant, which is poured out for many for the forgiveness of sins"' (Matt. 26:27–8).

The political and cultural background of the biblical concept of covenant has been well rehearsed in the literature. Covenants were a commonplace of ancient Near Eastern societies. A covenant was an agreement between two parties, generally legal in character, which imposed specified conditions and obligations on signatories. These parties needed not to be of equal social status or political power. A covenant, for example, could have the effect of formalising the superior–inferior relationship between a dominant nation and its client. From the point of view of historical scholarship, it is something of a historical accident that this already existing political and legal concept was taken up into the language of scripture. From the point of view of theology, it would generally be said that the already existing concept of the covenant was used analogically by biblical writers to refer to the relationship between God and the people of God – though one important gloss on such interpretation would be that humans can exhibit covenant faithfulness only because of the prior covenant faithfulness of the God who created them.

In scripture, however, none of this is explicit. The wider cultural context in which covenant operated is not alluded to, nor is a theory of religious language ever so much as mentioned. Indeed, nothing remotely approaching a theological theory of 'covenant' is to be found in scripture. In the Bible, the covenant is not a doctrinal or theological construction so much as a relational or practical one, the meaning of which is possibly assumed, but the implications of which must be worked out across time in moral and religious struggle. The primary point at stake, then, is faithfulness to the covenantal promise, which has its issue in behaviour and action. Jeremiah's proclamation 'I will be their God and they shall be my people' is a kind of summary presentation of this aspect of the covenant, bringing the relational and practical dimension of the biblical covenant to the fore. What is envisaged is that people will keep their covenantal obligations because of the particular quality of their relationship with God.

But suppose we were to press the kinds of theological questions raised by the idea of the covenant in scripture. What would be the result? What implications, in particular, would the concept of covenant have for our understanding of God? At this point, a surprising fact emerges, for the adaptation of the covenant in systems of Christian theology has at best been fragmentary, while what there has been in the way of systematic expositions of 'covenant theology' is neither widely nor sufficiently well known. The result is that in Christian theology, treatments of the doctrines of God, Trinity and Christ, for example, only infrequently draw on the theology of the covenant. The mainstream doctrine of God in the tradition as infinite, eternal, unchanging, and so on, developed in a way that almost entirely by-passes the biblical understanding of the God who keeps covenant with his people. Theology, in consequence, can sometimes seem to be profoundly out of step with the message of scripture at this point.

The Covenant in Reformed Theology

I suggested above that while the concept of the covenant has not been generally developed in a strictly theological sense in the mainstream Christian tradition, there might well be minority theological voices in which the language of covenant can be heard. In fact, it turns out that there is a fulsome development of the theology of the covenant in a certain type of Christian systematic theology. It is, however, found in a tradition of thought that has come to be widely seen as discredited: Reformed (or Calvinist) theology in the scholastic period.[1] For this reason, I wish in this chapter to do something that has come to be rather unfashionable, but which I believe will be illuminating, and spend a short time exploring the concept of the covenant in scholastic Reformed thought. In particular, I propose to examine the relationship between the idea of the covenant and the doctrine of God in this tradition, since this is a point of considerable interest to me, and, I wish to suggest, of contemporary theological relevance as well.

Scholastic Calvinism in the seventeenth century developed an elaborate argument according to which the whole of God's engagement with the world occurs solely by way of covenant. The greatest confessional exposition of scholastic Reformed theology, the mid-seventeenth-century Westminster Confession of Faith, sets out the grounds for this in an admirably concise way: 'The distance between God and the creature is so great, that although reasonable creatures do owe obedience unto Him as their Creator, yet they could never have any fruition of Him as their blessedness and reward but by some voluntary condescension on God's part, which He hath been pleased to express by way of covenant' (*West. Conf.* 7.1). In speaking in this way, the Westminster Assembly formally adopted (albeit in a moderate form) a set of ideas that had circulated in both Zwinglian and Calvinist circles from the time of the Reformation, but which came to be further refined only in post-Reformation theological developments. While the ultimate basis for such use of the concept of covenant is always said to be the teaching of Holy Scripture, the argument used suggests something more than bare reliance on the pure milk of the Word. In short, metaphysical grounds are discerned in Holy Scripture for the necessity of the covenant. The Westminster Confession puts the point particularly succinctly: unless God so wills, and so commits himself, there can be no relationship between creaturely obedience and divine reward, for God is so transcendent that he cannot otherwise be engaged by the creature. Though we owe God everything, God owes us nothing, unless he somehow condescends to 'owe' us what he promises.

On the basis of such presuppositions, successive Reformed theologians in the scholastic period sought to demonstrate, often in the logico-deductive methods characteristic of philosophy at the time, that the biblical idea of the covenant of God is properly basic to the whole of the Christian understanding of God. The covenant, therefore, while having temporal application and implication, is rooted ultimately in the eternal purpose, will, and even *being* of

God. The primary route by which this was established was by way of the argument that the covenant is rooted ultimately in the divine 'decrees'. An astonishing development of this 'decretal theology' can be witnessed both in the Continental Protestantism of the seventeenth century, and in the English Puritanism of the Civil War era. In this theology the decrees of God are not treated as something theologically secondary, something to be rigidly distinguished, for example, from the doctrine of the divine substance or that of the Trinity. The doctrine of the decrees rather belongs in the strictest possible sense to the doctrine of God. According to the Continental Calvinist Johannes Wollebius (1586–1629), for example, a divine decree is to be understood as an 'internal' or 'immanent' work of God, while whatever is 'in God' in this sense quite simply 'is God'.[2] Like God, the decrees are eternal and absolute, existing before any created thing, and of a radically different character than any creature. Though the precise language to be used at this point was disputed, it would appear that, in general, the covenant amounts to the temporal expression or realisation of this pre-temporal decree or act of will, that is to say, its actual application to particular people and to their relationship with God in space and time.[3]

A number of points can be made by way of clarification. To begin with, we should note that it is not altogether anomalous to find Christian theologians speaking of something other than the divine substance, or attributes, or for that matter of the persons of the Trinity, in their treatments of the doctrine of God. The theologians of the Christian East, for example, have an established doctrine of the divine 'energies', which are understood to be as eternal and absolute and in their own way as basic to the doctrine of God as are our concepts of divine substance, attributes and persons. On the whole, Western theologians have worked with these categories alone in their treatments of God, but the Reformed, as we can see, introduced this further notion of the decrees to supplement the more familiar Western theological conceptuality. 'Following the consideration of the essence of God ... and of the persons', writes Francis Turretin (1623–87), 'comes the discussion of the essential internal acts of God, commonly called the decrees.'[4] The decrees of the Reformed are in fact surprisingly akin to the doctrine of the divine energies in Eastern Christianity. Both doctrines are susceptible to trinitarian explication; for example, both have an application to the divine life of the three persons *ad intra*, or from all eternity, and also *ad extra*, or in relation to the created order (though these are always rooted in the relations *ad intra*). We might add as well that neither view is commonly understood within mainstream Western theology.

One crucial point that needs to be noted, and that is distinctive of the doctrine of the decrees among the Reformed, is that the decrees are seen as products of divine *will*.[5] They exist, in other words, only because they are eternally *willed* by God, or are *chosen* by God as the basis for his activity in relation to the created world. If we ask why there are divine decrees, the only answer that can be provided is that they exist for the sake of God's glory. They are in this sense utterly basic, basic in the sense that there is nothing other than the sheer fact of their being willed by God that can explain their existence. In other words, the Reformed doctrine of God at this point is consistently *voluntarist*. We might summarise by saying that what God *is*, is to be discerned not only by reference to the concept of God's essence, or by way of the doctrine of the Trinity, but also by way of explicit reference to what God *wills*. What God *wills* is primarily his own glory, but this, by virtue of the gracious condescension of God's will, is attained in his relation to creation through the divine decrees, and the covenantal causality that flows from them in time.

The best-known features of the Reformed doctrine of the decrees relate to the question of the doctrine of salvation. In itself, this is not surprising, for the whole of Christian theology has a fundamental soteriological orientation. But scholastic Reformed theologians took this principle to surprising lengths in their theologies. Not only are the decrees the basis for the doctrine of predestination, according to which God ordains from all eternity that the glory of his grace and justice should jointly be revealed in the election and reprobation of fixed numbers of rational creatures (usually both angelic and human), but the event of salvation itself has its basis in a very particular decree, called by many of the most influential sources the 'covenant of grace'. According to this theory, God's good purpose in creating the world could not be frustrated by the intervention of sin in the fall, for this too was foreordained. With the fall, there was also equally decreed from all eternity that atonement for sin would be provided. According to the Reformed scholastics, God the Father and God the Son entered into a 'pact' or 'mutual agreement' before all time, by the terms of which the whole story of our redemption was in a sense told before it ever happened. To quote one source,

> God the Father exacted from the Son perfect obedience to the law unto the death which he must face on behalf of chosen seed to be given him; and promised him, if he gave the obedience, the seed in question as his own … inheritance; and in return the Son, in promising this obedience to God the Father and producing it in the literal act, demanded of Him in turn the right to demand this seed for himself as an inheritance.[6]

Psalm 2 is frequently cited in this connection, as referring to the eternal pact between the Father and the anointed Son:

> I will tell of the decree of the LORD:
> He said to me, 'You are my son;
>   today I have begotten you.
> Ask of me, and I will make the nations your heritage,
>   and the ends of the earth your possession.' (Ps. 2:7–8)

By virtue of the presupposed immutability of God, this pact must be deemed to be eternal and irrevocable. Thus our faith is assured: God has bound himself, in his own trinitarian will, to stand by those whom he predestines to salvation. And this trinitarian will, as has already been observed, is in the strict sense something internal to the Godhead. Thus the whole question of the covenant is conceived as a function of the doctrine of God.

Karl Barth on the Covenant

The voluntarism implicit in the classical Calvinist doctrine of the covenant is perhaps its most important feature, and this is something to which I will return shortly. For the present, I would like to turn to the question of the continuing influence of this theology. For it might well be asked why the Calvinism of the seventeenth century, which was, after all, a religiously barbarous time, the age of the Civil War in Britain and of the Thirty Years' War in Europe, has been resurrected in this chapter. When set over against the achievements of the scientists and philosophers of the day, Reformed scholasticism seems antiquated even by the standards of its own time. The answer is twofold. First, it represents what can only be described as the boldest treatment of the idea of the covenant to be found anywhere in the Christian tradition. And second, I wish to suggest, a variety of broadly similar themes reappear in what is arguably the most influential of the many streams of twentieth-century theology. I refer, of course, to the theology of Karl Barth. Barth's theology, I wish to argue, is rather closer to these scholastic sources than many care to admit. Furthermore, one of the interesting and important things about Barth's theology in this respect is that his influence extends well beyond the narrow confines of classical Calvinism (indeed, his influence is scarcely felt at all there) to much modern Presbyterian, Lutheran, Anglican, Congregationalist, and even Roman Catholic theological thought. What has taken place in Christian theology in the twentieth century through the work of Karl Barth, I wish to suggest, is a kind of translation of the classical Reformed doctrine of the covenant into contemporary terms, and with this, a remarkably widespread adoption of certain of its central features into the work of many of the theologians who have laboured in these other traditions.

This is likely to prove a controversial assertion, not least because many of the most ardent disciples of Barth, especially in the English-speaking world, would prefer to reject any dependence upon the classical Reformed doctrine of the covenant on Barth's part. Some of them, indeed, tend to begin their expositions of Barth's theology with just this point.[7] Let me, therefore, offer an _apologia_ of sorts in advance of what follows. My claim is not that Barth develops a position consistent in all respects with scholastic Calvinism, but rather that in his theology, he achieves a _translation_ of themes deriving from scholastic Calvinist thought into his own theological idiom. As in other Barthian 'translation' exercises, such as his adaptation of the Chalcedonian dogma, much is lost in the process – but equally, much is also preserved. Barth so thoroughly 'translates' the classical Reformed conceptuality into his own distinctive parlance that the resemblance between the two positions is readily overlooked. The upshot, I believe, is that there is a much stronger connection between the Barthian position at this point and that of his scholastic forebears than many Barthian commentators seem prepared to countenance, and accordingly, a clearer line relating the seventeenth century to our own time than is generally recognised.

Let me begin with Barth's rather curious but key assertion that God's being is 'event'. He writes:

> We are dealing with the being of God: but with regard to the being of God, the word 'event' is *final*, and cannot be surpassed or compromised. To its very deepest depths God's Godhead consists in the fact that it is an event – not any event, not events in general, but the event of his action, in which we have a share in God's revelation.[8]

This is a less-than-obvious statement by any measure, but the real clue to understanding it is found in the fact that the language of 'event' emerges in Barth's theology as an alternative to the substance language of classical theism. Barth's intention is to avoid any implication that God is lifeless, such as one finds, as he sees things, in the notions of God as 'supreme substance' or as 'absolute being'. What we might call the *livingness* of God is a postulate of prime importance in Barth's theology. On this basis he can claim that God's being cannot be marked off ontologically or even abstracted from what God *does*. Since what God does is seen in the Christian revelation, we are obliged to say that God is who he is, not only for us but also *in himself*, precisely in his outreach to the world in Jesus Christ. Thus God is not so much a substance with attributes for Barth as he is a deed, that is to say, an event.

I submit that we can take this further, and say that for Barth all conceptions of divine being have what can only be described in the technical philosophical sense as an 'existential' content. In effect, God for Barth becomes a kind of cosmic existentialist, who constitutes his being by way of his own actions. This too is likely to be a controversial suggestion, so let me elaborate. The fact is that in Barth's theology, as soon as we begin to probe how it might be conceivable to think of God as event, or to try to flesh it out, as it were, we are directly led to a second concept, that of 'decision'. Barth writes, 'The fact that God's being is event, the event of God's act, necessarily ... means that it is His own conscious, willed and executed decision ... It is His conscious decision, and therefore not the mechanical outcome of a process of rationality ...'[9] The existential language of decision thus assumes a central role in the Barthian conception of God. We could go further, in fact, and say that in Barth's theology, God is the purest existentialist, an existentialist in a way that you or I could never be: 'No other being exists absolutely in its act. No other being is absolutely its own, conscious, willed and executed decision.'[10]

These are not isolated or unimportant statements in the Barthian corpus. Furthermore, the language used here, which is found in the context of Barth's doctrine of God in the second volume of the *Church Dogmatics*, has wider support in the warp and woof of the Barthian system. In his development of the doctrine of the Trinity in the first volume of *Church Dogmatics*, for example, Barth argues that God is who he is in his act of revelation. Revelation is not, therefore, something secondary to God's 'Godness' in its proper sense, something somehow removed from what God the Father, Son and Holy Spirit are from all eternity. Instead, the triune God *is*, in Barth's formulation, the singular act in which he comes to us as the Revealer, the Revelation and its Revealedness. In the doctrine of God in the second volume of *Church Dogmatics* this act is understood with total logical consistency to be God's free decision of love to be God in Jesus Christ, and thus to be the God who chooses a definite relationship to the creature for himself.[11] For Barth, God must be conceived both in himself and in his relation to the world as the living God of the Bible. This seems an obvious enough point, but what this obvious point demonstrates, in Barth's mind, is that God's life is to be seen as something 'expressed and attested in concrete decision ...'[12]

The Barthian theologian has thus to reject all positions that do not allow there to be movement, life, or, in particular, *decision* in God in himself, on the grounds that this decision is actually revealed in Jesus Christ. We might put this another way, by saying that God 'is' in Barth's conception a very particular kind of action; his 'essence', in fact, is to 'exist' in this action, the action by which he chooses from all eternity and in every instant of our time to make room in himself for the human creature. Significantly, we can put this another way using Barth's own shorthand theological vocabulary, and say that God is none other than the God of the 'covenant'.

A Revolutionary Doctrine of God

We have seen that in classical Calvinism, the doctrine of the decrees underlies and provides the speculative theological basis for the fearsome Calvinist doctrine of election. Much the same, however, must be said of the notions of event and decision in Barth's doctrine of God. Again, these lay the theoretical basis for the manner in which the Barthian doctrine of election develops. At this point, however, the differences between classical Calvinism and Barth are at least as great as the similarities, for in his doctrine of election, Barth breaks with the Reformed dogmatic tradition, which understands election more generally as God's determination of the salvific fate of specific human beings on the basis of his absolute decree, to understand election as the eternal choice of God to be our God in Jesus Christ.[13] According to Barth, it is *Jesus Christ* who in the biblical witness is the true chosen one from among the chosen people of Israel. It is *he* who is the covenant partner of God, by virtue of God's own eternal choice to be God in him. We too are elect, but only in what is a strictly derivative and secondary and almost unimportant sense, in that our humanity is chosen *in him*, that is, as God chooses to be himself in the incarnate one, the God-man Jesus, and so to be himself only in fellowship with us.

This approach to the doctrine of election has a number of interesting features. Firstly, it shows God to be relational. Election involves both the concrete relation between the Father and the Son, and also God's relation to humankind, since from all eternity he has chosen to be related to us in the incarnate one, Jesus Christ. Both relations are encompassed in the doctrine of election, while in this way, God's own self-relatedness is understood to involve his relation to the world in general, and to humanity in particular. Secondly, Barth's doctrine of election has clear implications for trinitarian theology. The key point Barth will make at this point is that there is no 'discarnate Word', no Word of the Father other than Jesus Christ, in the sense that by the eternal divine election, Jesus Christ is in the beginning with God.[14] Thirdly, all of this has clear connections with the doctrine of salvation. In one especially revealing passage, Barth writes:

In the beginning it was the choice of the Father Himself to establish this covenant with man by giving up His Son for him, that He Himself might become man in the fulfilment of His grace. In the beginning it was the choice of the Son to be obedient to grace, and therefore to offer up Himself and to become man in order that this covenant might be made a reality. In the beginning it was the resolve of the Holy Spirit that the unity of God, of Father and Son, should not be disturbed or rent by this covenant with man, but that it should be made the more glorious, the deity of God, the divinity of His love and freedom, being confirmed and demonstrated by this offering of the Father and His self-offering of the Son.[15]

There are obvious resonances here of the classical Reformed idea of the 'pact' between the Father and the Son that is found at the heart of the 'covenant of grace' in scholastic Reformed dogmatics.[16] There is also something common to the two heavily voluntarist emphases found in the two doctrines of God. But Barth's position is much more radical. The idea of the covenant, which in Barth's mind is reducible to the formula God for us and us for God, is taken to extraordinary lengths in his hands. On the one side it entails universalism, or at least something difficult to distinguish from it, as all men and women are 'in Christ' solely by virtue of the Son's assumption of human nature in the incarnation. It is sometimes said in criticism of Barth that the only thing a person needs to do to be saved in his theology is to be born; believing in Jesus can only add to the brute *fact* of salvation the *knowledge* of salvation, nothing more. This is something of a caricature, no doubt, but like many a caricature, it represents in its way a fair enough point. More interesting and important is that on the other side, revolutionary implications follow for Barth's whole conception of God. For Barth, God is from eternity to eternity the one who chooses to be who and what he is in Jesus Christ. In short, there is literally no God without us.

I have used strong words here, words such as 'radical' and 'revolutionary', to describe the character of Barth's theology. My own view would certainly be that Barth is best understood from beginning to end as a revolutionary theologian, a thinker who departs at almost every turn from classical Christian conceptions of God. The clearest illustrations of this fact are to be found in Barth's treatment of what are classically normative theological themes. Typically, Barth will turn the tradition on its head while in dialogue with older Christian thinkers. In his Christology, for example, Barth will employ the formulae of the Council of Chalcedon, and speak of Jesus Christ as perfect in Godhood and as perfect in humanity. Yet the perfect Godhood of Christ means his lowliness, his abasement, even his *sinfulness*, whereas his perfect humanity means his glory, his exaltation, his utter righteousness. Barth consistently defies traditional expectations in this way. Yet at the same time, Chalcedonian orthodoxy is consciously reasserted in this new way, a way Barth and his disciples, at least, see as completely consistent with what we might call the 'real intention' of the Fathers of Chalcedon.

The same thing has also to be said of Barth's treatment of the covenant. Barth certainly knew the classical Reformed doctrine of the decrees, for in his early years as a scholar, he worked extensively and enthusiastically on the theology of the Reformed scholastics (unlike, it has to be said, the vast majority of his commentators). It would not be too much to say, in fact, that in a certain sense he takes the classical doctrine as his starting point. But in his theology, the abstract decree of God as the absolute Lord of all creation becomes instead something known from revelation as a concrete decision of love. A sovereign act of will ordaining 'whatsoever comes to pass', and ultimately determining the eternal salvation or damnation of countless millions of rational creatures becomes instead the rather more generous (and certainly no less divine) decision of God to be who he is in Jesus Christ. As theological claims go, this one undoubtedly has something to be said for it. Were we to have to choose between them, many of us would understandably prefer Barth's revision of the theology of the covenant to the older alternative.

Concluding Assessment

Several points can be made by way of a conclusion. Firstly, it might be said that Barth's many theological disciples ought to be more aware of his intellectual lineage. His doctrine of the covenant is directly related to a strong tradition of theological voluntarism in the Reformed tradition, according to which God is conceived in terms of the concept of will, so that even the truth and goodness of God can appear to be

functions of the absolute power of God. Though this might appear to
be a barren soil on which to grow a theology, it is interesting that
through its Barthian adaptation much new life has in fact been breathed
into the bones of Christian theology in our time, and that this has been
accomplished in theologies making their homes well beyond the
confines of the Reformed tradition.

Secondly, however, there is a more pertinent question
concerning how the biblical idea of the covenant is to be theologically appropriated and, in particular, how this might affect our
understanding of God. We have now seen two major examples of
this, two readings, as it were, of the God of the covenant, both of
which are committed to the view that the concept of the covenant
is of central and even of pivotal importance for the whole of
theology. Now one of the questions that has to be asked about this is
just how it is that any of us can know so much about the will of God.
Can we indeed probe the divine councils, and understand what is
decreed? The standard answer given, of course, is that the will of
God is something revealed. In the gospel itself, and in the distinction it makes at the point of reception between the elect and the
reprobate, between those who believe and obey and those who do
not, the eternal decrees of God are expressed in time in a form that is
essentially knowable, though perhaps not knowable from start to
finish. Or, in the Barthian adaptation, God's primal decision to be
God in Jesus Christ, and so not to be God in isolation but only *with
us* — to be the God of the covenant, in other words — gives us
nothing less than access to the being of God. What is generally overlooked by the practitioners of this theology is how utterly remarkable a position it is. Many of Barth's more ardent disciples today go
so far as to speak of how God literally 'defines his deity' both for
himself and for us in the Christ-event. God defines it, in fact, in a
way essentially knowable and known, by defining it in a human life
in time. The upshot of this, however, is that Barth himself, and
especially his less careful disciples after him, would appear to claim
more knowledge of God than any other theologians in the prior
history of Christian thought. Though this does not amount to a
criticism so much as an observation, I believe that it ought at least to
give pause for thought, and reason to evaluate carefully what we
read and hear.

This leads naturally and necessarily to the third point, which is a consideration in this context of the traditional doctrine of the ultimately 'apophatic' character of theology in general, and of the doctrine of God in particular. It is assumed almost universally in the older theological tradition that God is strictly 'beyond speech', and not only beyond speech but also beyond any human or even angelic conception. It seems to me that there are very few classical theological themes more worth recovery in the contemporary context than this one. What this would mean in relation to the theology of the covenant and in connection with the theme of the God of the covenant is that all our talk must be consciously recognised to be severely limited. In the final analysis, we must embrace a certain agnosticism in thinking the Christian faith. The God of the covenant is therefore beyond all understanding, and even beyond all concept of covenant.

To my mind at least, this suggests that the attempt to make the theology of the covenant truly basic in theology can be a misguided venture – so long, at least, as we do not take a stand for theological modesty, and recognise the limitations of our speech and concepts in our treatments of God. To say too much at this point, in other words, is a powerful temptation that needs to be resisted. Yet, at the same time, there is no question that the idea of the covenant is integral to the Christian view of God. At the beginning of this chapter, I made what at the time seemed a small point, but which in the end seems a rather large one: the Bible, for all its use of the language of covenant, stops well short of making great claims concerning divine being and the eternal will of God. It insists instead on a basically practical, ethical – one might even say 'religious' – orientation at this point, through the idea of covenantal faithfulness. The thrust of biblical language about the covenant is precisely this question of faithfulness: the point is to say that the God of the covenant is faithful. Covenants are about promises and obligations, nothing more or less. The language of covenant is thus a language of faith and trust. In employing the language of covenant, I wish to suggest, the Bible signals something arguably of much greater importance than can be found in any of the theological constructions that have preoccupied us in this chapter. What it signals is that true knowledge of God, of the God of the covenant, is knowledge that – as Calvin puts it – neither flits about in the head, nor penetrates to God's essence, but instead makes a humbler home in the heart and in the lives of those who live trustingly under the promises of God.[17]

In what sense, therefore, is our God the 'God of the covenant?' Not, I have suggested, in the sense that God's being can literally be defined by reference to covenantal conceptuality, for in the strict sense, God cannot be conceived or defined at all. But this does not necessarily mean that all talk of covenant is merely talk of appearance, talk of how God 'seems' to us rather than how or what God 'is' in himself. The final point I wish to make is that the appeal for theological modesty that has just been made does not commit us to the view that all theology is purely subjective, in the sense that nothing whatever can be said positively of God. The reality is rather more subtle: God *is* the God of the covenant, but the length, height and depth of his covenant is ultimately beyond measure. Undoubtedly, there must be something common between divine faithfulness and our own, between God's promises and our promises. If this were not so, then we would be unable to understand anything at all of God or of his ways. Yet we are also told that

> as the heavens are higher than the earth,
> > so are my ways higher than your ways,
> > and my thoughts than your thoughts. (Is. 55:9)

Our theology, then, must be developed somewhere between these two poles of affirmation and negation. The classical answer to our dilemma is to say that our affirmations are accordingly contained in God 'eminently', or in a higher sense than we can grasp – which is to say, both our affirmations and their negation have a place in theology. It is this, I have suggested, that is missing from the theology of the covenant in the Reformed scholastics and in Karl Barth, and that most needs to be recovered in our own.

Endnotes

1   William Klempa, 'The Concept of the Covenant in Sixteenth- and Seventeenth-Century Continental and British Reformed Theology', in Donald K. McKim (ed.), *Major Themes in the Reformed Tradition* (Grand Rapids: Eerdmans, 1992), 94–107.

2 Johannes Wollebius, *Compendium Theologiae Christianae*, 1.3.2–3, tr. John W. Beardslee III, in idem (ed.), *Reformed Dogmatics* (New York: Oxford University Press, 1965).

3 John Coccejus, e.g., speaks of the covenant of grace as being rooted in the life of the Triune God himself, involving a pre-temporal 'pact' on the part of the Father and the Son. This, in turn, grounds the historical execution of covenant in time, through revelation. See Klèmpa, 'Concept of the Covenant', 101–2.

4 Francis Turretin, *Institutio Theologiae Elencticae*, Locus 4, q.1.1, in Beardslee, *Reformed Dogmatics*.

5 See, e.g., Heinrich Heppe, *Reformed Dogmatics*, tr. G.T. Thomson (Edinburgh: T. & T. Clark, 1950), 139.

6 Heidegger, cited in Heppe, *Reformed Dogmatics*, 376.

7 Klempa, 'Concept of the Covenant', 95, is a notable exception: 'the theology of Karl Barth displays remarkable similarities to the covenant theology of John Coccejus', adding, 'though not without corrections of some important emphases'.

8 Karl Barth, *Church Dogmatics*, 4 vols., ed. G.W. Bromiley and T.F. Torrance (Edinburgh: T. & T. Clark, 1936–69), 2/1, 263.

9 Barth, *Church Dogmatics* 2/1, 271.

10 Ibid.

11 Barth, *Church Dogmatics* 2/2, 6–7, 76–7.

12 Ibid. 79.

13 Ibid. 51–8.

14 Ibid. 94–9, 104.

15 Ibid. 101–2.

16 Cf., however, Barth, *Church Dogmatics* 4/1, 65, where Barth went on to reject the classical Reformed theory of the 'pact' between the Father and the Son on the grounds that there is only one will in God, so that the partners in the covenant of grace are not the Father and the Son, but God and humankind.

17 John Calvin, *Institutes of the Christian Religion*, ed. John T. McNeill and tr. Ford Lewis Battles (Philadelphia: Westminster Press, 1960), 1.5.9.

6

Poetry and Praxis

A Response to Gary Badcock

Trevor Hart

In what sense is the God of Christians the 'God of the covenant'? Gary Badcock's approach to this question is wide-ranging in scope, touching on issues in biblical, historical and modern theology, and framing his discussion with an important claim about the nature and logical status of language about God in general and the covenant metaphor in particular. A response cannot hope to address every salient point. In what follows, therefore, I propose to pick up on just a few of the core issues Badcock's chapter raises, and to explore them in relation to one another.

Metaphor and Transcendence

Badcock begins by recognising the centrality of the covenant metaphor in Scripture. In connection with God, he suggests, this image stands as an 'irreducible datum' that can hardly be ignored and must presumably be made sense of by any serious attempt to generate a theology from these sources. He also acknowledges, though, the inherently analogical or metaphorical status of this datum.[1] Covenant language in the Bible is borrowed from the political and legal discourse of ancient Near Eastern societies and, as is the case with all metaphor, this compels the recognition of both similarities and differences

between the two terms. There are, in other words, some things proper
to the human 'covenants' familiar to the Old Testament world that are
genuinely analogous to and may helpfully serve as models for the
relationship between the Lord and Israel, and there are other aspects
that are unhelpful and perhaps even threaten to obscure or distort the
nature of that relationship. This is the nature of all metaphor. As Sallie
McFague reminds us, metaphorical statements 'always contain the
whisper, "it is *and it is not*"'.[2] To overlook this vital qualification of
metaphorical assertion is to misunderstand it, and to fall into a wooden
literalism that, by erasing the poetic qualities of the language, traps us
within the horizons of the familiar. The whisper '*and it is not*', in other
words, leads us out beyond what we suppose we already know, and
opens the world up to us in all its complex difference and diversity.
Where there is no analogy there can be no speech about the new, and
hence no meaningful knowing of it. But if the genuine newness of the
new is to be known, we must respect the levels of dissimilarity, and
must allow our familiar language to be opened up for us in new
ways beyond its established range of meanings, modified now by its
application to a discrete circumstance.

In the case of language applied to God, of course, this same qualification is raised to a different pitch by the demand for due recognition of God's transcendence with respect to the created order.
Here, the levels of dissimilarity expressed in such phrases as the
'wholly otherness' of God threaten to all but eclipse levels of simi-
larity, and thereby undercut meaningful speech about God altogether. This basic doctrinal tenet and its possible implications haunt
Badcock's consideration from the outset, and come to the fore in its
final section where he urges upon us a theology 'developed somewhere between [the] two poles of affirmation and negation.' That
may simply mean a theology that admits of its most prized assertions
'it is *and it is not*'. Or it may mean something different and more
problematic. I shall return to this in my penultimate section.

Badcock reminds us that the model of covenant in Scripture is
not uniform, but 'a flexible, adaptable notion, doing service repeatedly in a variety of key biblical contexts'. So another relevant question might well be 'which or what sort(s) of covenant' should we
associate with the God known in Scripture? The metaphor is one
that lends itself readily to typological or figural treatment. Such
adaptability might be supposed to augur well for the subsequent

theological development of the motif within the history of the tradition. In fact, though, as Badcock indicates, there has been a relative dearth of systematic treatments of the theme, not least in relation to the core doctrines of God, Christ and redemption. In electing to consider the notable exception of Reformed orthodoxy he unearths more issues than his discussion is able reasonably to accommodate within its allotted scope. There are, though, other features of Reformed covenant theology that deserve exploration, because they bear significantly on Badcock's own proposed classification of the model as essentially a relational or practical construction that informs and shapes personal religious disposition with respect to God:

> The thrust of biblical language about the covenant is ... to say that the God of the covenant is faithful. Covenants are about promises and obligations, nothing more or less. The language of covenant is thus a language of faith and trust ... What it signals is that true knowledge of God ... is knowledge that ... neither flits about in the head, nor penetrates to God's essence, but instead makes a humbler home in the heart and in the lives of those who live trustingly under the promises of God.

As we may see, though, this essentially ethical accounting of the metaphor's role makes it more rather than less important to interrogate it, and to specify quite precisely in what sense the whisper '*and it is not*' may need to be amplified for those lacking ears to hear.

Figuration and Political Theology

One consideration Badcock passes over entirely is the political background that rendered this perennial biblical theme theologically attractive in the post-Reformation era. Figuration, like metaphor, depends on the discernment of genuine similarities of circumstance between two times, places, figures, institutions or sets of events. The appropriation of the biblical theme of covenant as an organising principle for Christian theology in the sixteenth and seventeenth centuries was certainly no accident, but was in effect a figural application of the biblical text to the political realities of the

church's life in the newly emerging democracies of Europe; and
while, as Badcock observes, the covenant theme was certainly taken
up into complex doctrinal accountings of the 'orders of salvation', it
was also possessed of an ecclesial and political dimension easily overlooked in our own more individualistic age. The church, like Israel
of old, was pictured as a 'nation' in covenant with God (sometimes,
as in Scotland, ecclesial and political boundaries came close enough
to overlapping for figure and reality to blur together in this vision),
and the practical issues arising from attempts to maintain this bold
claim in the face of broader political realities were anything but
individualistic or restricted to the soul's communion with God.
The circumstances, for example, in which the Westminster
Confession of Faith was drafted make this quite clear.

Covenant theology predates the meeting of the Westminster
Assembly by more than a century,[3] but the specific circumstances
that led to the English Parliament convening an Assembly at all lent
to this particular biblical metaphor a sharper than average bite. In his
book *The Covenants of Scotland* J. Lumsden traces no less than
thirty-one covenants in the political life of the nation between the
Dun Covenant of 1536 and the Children's Covenant of 1683.[4] A
complex relationship can be traced between extant political
conceptuality and the reading of the Bible during this period. On
the one hand, renewed familiarity with the classic themes of the
biblical narrative certainly influenced the political applications of
the concept, the covenantal relations between Israel, her king and
her God being appealed to by various groups craving scriptural
warrant for their preferred socio-political models. On the other
hand, though, familiarity with the established tradition of 'pacts',
'bands' and 'covenants' that may be traced back into medieval
feudal polity had a reciprocal impact upon the ways in which
Scripture was read, not least in the systematic appropriation of the
covenant metaphor within Puritan theology.[5] As I have already
indicated, the use of any metaphor entails careful discernment of the
sense in which the two realities are unlike as well as like, and all
the more so when God is one of the realities with which we are
concerned. Ironically, the very political context that rendered
biblical covenant language so relevant to theologians in the Puritan
era also posed some significant risks of hermeneutical slippage.
More precisely, there was a manifest tendency to interpret biblical

narratives in the light of familiar political and social mechanisms in such a way as to introduce elements inappropriate to the unique relationship between the Lord and his people.

This may account in part for the willingness among covenant theologians (including those at Westminster) to embrace a model of the relationship between God and the elect in which it was openly and unashamedly admitted that there were 'conditions' to be met on both sides. Political agreements were inevitably of just such a sort, and not least the Solemn League and Covenant of 1643, which was in large measure responsible for the Assembly being convened at all. But the language of 'conditions' attaching to salvation and sharing in the covenant relation with God seems, at least at first sight and without further careful theological explication, to reach back behind the Reformation to the very sort of medieval 'works righteousness' against which Martin Luther (1483–1546) had rebelled as a source of eventual despair. His agonised question 'How can I get a gracious God?' is easily recast in the form 'How can I be sure that I have adequately fulfilled the relevant conditions of the covenant?' or 'How can I be sure that I am among the number of the elect?'

Ironically, questions of a similar sort crop up again and again in the annals of pastoral care attaching to the 'covenant' tradition in theology. The great Puritan theologian William Perkins (1558–1602) is alleged to have gone to his deathbed in an agony of doubt concerning his identity as one of the elect, and the security of his place within the 'covenant of grace'. The so-called 'practical syllogism' beloved of some Reformed theologians[6] was designed to allay such fears, but often served only to reinforce them as, like Luther, many of those who looked to the quality of their own lives (seeking the relevant 'signs' or conditions of faith and obedience) found there only grounds for doubt and despair. Luther's answer to this existential angst was boldly to proclaim what he took to be the message of Paul's epistle to the Romans, that salvation is 'by grace alone', by which Luther understood something entirely unmerited and unconditionally bestowed. Deliberately to reintroduce the language of conditions to be fulfilled by human participants in the so-called 'covenant of grace' risks seriously compromising the simplicity of Luther's appeal to grace thus understood. Grace that, as an unconditional openness to and unmerited acceptance of the sinner into relationship, nonetheless looks for (one might even say *demands*) an equally unconditional response of gratitude, love and obedience from its object as the appropriate mode of reception and indwelling, is one thing. But it is a thing to which the contractual language of 'conditions' seems peculiarly inappropriate. Grace that has 'conditions' attached to it (which is conditional upon some satisfactory performance on our part) is not 'grace' in this same radical sense.

Covenant and Kingship: The Doctrine of God

Ironically, far from provoking insecurity, the appeal to the conditionality of the covenant model was intended to do the opposite. As we have said, the conditions were held to exist on both sides of the agreement. Here again the impact of political thought may be traced in the covenant scheme's practical effect on the doctrine of God, the doctrine Badcock's chapter focuses upon most directly. The Westminster Confession, as Badcock notes, resounds with a deep sense of God's sovereign majesty, a sovereignty manifest, as the Confession's early chapters remind us, in his complete self-sufficiency, his deserving and demanding of utter obedience from his creatures, his disposing of all that happens in his world, his freely choosing to shower love and grace on some regardless of their lack of worth and condemnation of others, and so on. Since the medieval period and the emergence of Nominalism, such a stress in Christian theology was rendered even more potent by a voluntarist doctrine that construed God as absolute will, unconstrained even by his own nature, and hence inherently unpredictable.

In his discussion of the covenant theme in Old Testament theology, Walther Eichrodt notes how one of its key functions is to banish the spectre of arbitrariness and caprice that haunted pagan religion, thereby creating in Israel's piety an atmosphere of trust and security.[7] With the Lord she knew where she stood, both in terms of his promise and the demands it made on her. We should not overlook the fact that the political struggles of the English Civil War were largely a reaction against the longstanding model of Absolute Monarchy to which Charles I aspired, and from which the subscribers to the Solemn League and Covenant were determined to keep him. Given the persistent stress in Reformed theology on

God's absolute sovereignty and freedom, and given the insecurity and unease that reflection on the idea of divine caprice tends naturally to engender, it may well be supposed to have been unsurprising for the theologians at Westminster to turn to a metaphor that effectively transformed God from an Absolute to a Constitutional Monarch in a single stroke, at least so far as the elect were concerned. *In himself* God is and remains of course utterly free, and under no obligation to do anything for anyone. But he has, in the 'covenant of grace', placed himself under constraints and entered into a relationship within which, so long as the conditions are kept from the human side, believers may be entirely confident of his beneficence towards them.

Understood thus, the theme of covenant in a peculiar way renders God, as well as the believer, accountable for his actions, while yet managing to preserve the doctrine of his absolute freedom in the background. Hence Tyndale: 'If we meek ourselves to God, to keep all his laws, after the example of Christ, then God hath bound himself unto us, to keep and make good all the mercies promised in Christ through all the Scripture.'[8] This sort of thinking undoubtedly could and did lead some more enthusiastic articulations of the scheme into apparently un-Reformed excess. 'You may sue [God] of his own bond written and sealed,' one such informs us, 'and he cannot deny it.'[9] But we must never overlook the doctrine of Providence and secondary causality that, in the best exponents of the covenant scheme, immediately served to rob what otherwise sounded like crudely contractual language of its offence. It is finally not 'spiritual commercialism',[10] because if the elect bear the fruit of 'repentance, faith and the diligent use of the outward means whereby Christ communicates to us the benefits of his mediation', which the answer to Q.153 of the Larger Catechism refers us to as 'requirements' of the covenant, this is a matter of that disposing of their wills by grace of which the Confession speaks in its opening sections.

This leads us to a further theological circumstance that commended the covenant scheme to the Assembly's theologians; namely the need to steer a careful course between the twin errors of Arminianism and Antinomianism, both of which were in plentiful evidence in England at the time.[11] What was required, therefore, was 'explicit grounds on which to plead the necessity of "works", but to discover them without sacrificing the absolute freedom of God to choose and reject regardless of man's achievements'.[12] This covenant theology sought to do by furnishing explicit grounds both for moral obligation and individual assurance. The elect could not presume upon God's grace, because the terms of the covenant of grace could not be breached. It was not supposed that any could actually keep the moral law in this life, but that believers would strive to do so and would manifest due faith and repentance as a necessary corollary of their being in covenant with God at all.[13] On the other hand, as we have already seen, these aspects of a believer's life are the product not of his or her own effort (and hence meritorious) but of God's grace at work. God himself, in other words, supplies that which he demands and underwrites the covenant he has made.

While in precise philosophical terms this sort of compatibilist scheme appears to meet the demands of a Reformation emphasis on salvation being 'all of grace', like most versions of determinism it suffers from the singular defect that it is impossible to live as if it were true. Despite the best intentions of those who developed this theology, therefore, by driving believers to look to (God's work in) the quality of their own faith, repentance and holiness in order to confirm the truth of their participation in the 'covenant of grace', it tended in practice often to engender the twin problems of legalistic self-righteousness and guilt-ridden despair. If, as Badcock's chapter suggests, the primary warrant for the use of the covenant metaphor (in Scripture itself, or in any subsequent theological rehabilitation of it) is indeed a practical one, as an image that informs the shape of our relationship to God as Christians, then clearly the issue of the relationship between grace and law, with all its pastoral ramifications, needs to be rendered crystal clear. That covenant theology always intended to inform a life lived 'trustingly under the promises of God' is clear; but it is equally clear that some ways of unpacking the metaphor lean ironically in a semi-Pelagian direction and undermine rather than reinforce the theology of promise. Again, the question 'What sort of covenant?' is vital; and to it may be added some others: Who fulfils the covenant? and when? and how?

Christ, Covenant, and the Logic of Substitution

One of the strengths of Karl Barth's handling of the covenant metaphor (to which Badcock turns next) is to relocate it with respect to
creation and Christology. In essence, Barth orders these such that
the boundaries of the covenant are open-ended relative to those of
creation (the covenant is the internal basis for creation, and creation
the external basis for the covenant),[14] and its definitive centre is to
be located historically in the person of Christ. Badcock sees that in
effect Barth here renegotiates the logic and scope of the
soteriological concept of substitution, insisting that the covenant
between God and Israel, the church, humankind, *has been fulfilled* in
our place in the messianic, Spirit-filled humanity of God himself.
God has, as it were, taken entire responsibility for the covenant
upon himself, fulfilling its 'conditions' from both the divine and the
human side. Badcock indicates that this step effectively relativises
our significance, seemingly displacing us from places where we
ought not to be displaced. There is some truth in this, but we must
take care not to misunderstand the sense in which it is true for Barth.
Substitution that did not involve displacement would be an odd sort
of affair; but it need not erase us completely from the picture. It may
simply set us, and our actions and responses, on a different, more
secure footing.

The English theologian John Saltmarsh (d. 1647) had proposed a
Christocentric reading of the category of covenant in the seven-
teenth century, and was duly chastised for it by the Scot Samuel
Rutherford. In his treatise *Christ Dying and Drawing Sinners to
Himself* (London, 1647), Rutherford charges Saltmarsh with
Antinomianism, insisting that he confuses justification (that which
God does *for us* in Christ) with sanctification (that which God does
in us). In this context he rejects Saltmarsh's claim that Christ repents,
obeys the law or is sanctified for us, except in the uncontentious
sense that 'Christ by his grace worketh *in us* repentance, and new
obedience, and mortification, and the change of the whole man.'[15]
Rutherford's fear is that talk of Christ obeying in our stead will lead
straight to the conclusion that we need therefore not obey for
ourselves. Hence the need for sanctification in the believer is effectively displaced. In this case, he notes, 'my walking in holiness
cannot be rewarded with life eternal, nor have any influence as a

way, or means leading to the kingdom', whereas in fact, while God himself grants the power of obedience, he has ordained such obedience needful to attaining this 'reward'. Saltmarsh's claim has been that the source of assurance for the believer is to look to Christ's obedience, penitence, holiness, and so on, which God has wrought in the flesh of Jesus. This need not entail a rejection of a subsequent working of these same qualities in the believer himself. It may simply be an insistence on the complete self-substitution of the Son of God for us in our relationship with God, veiling our weakness and inadequacy at every point with his perfect new humanity. But Rutherford rejects the suggestion, insisting that the source of Christian assurance is not in Christ's obedience, because that is *in Christ* and not *in us*, and thus can furnish no evidence of *our* interest in it.[16] The gospel itself, he tells us later in the same volume, reveals only the terms on which we may be saved; the efficacy of the gospel in particular lives tells us whether or not we actually are.[17]

Antinomianism arises, it might be argued, when Christ's self-sanctification for our sakes is deemed to be entirely substitutionary. If it is not thought of in this way, however, and if there is an insistence that what God has done *for us* through the Spirit in the humanity of the Son he pledges himself and subsequently begins to do *in us* by that same Spirit, if, in other words, the intrinsic connection between substitution and participation is affirmed, then Antinomianism is rendered impossible. Neonomian legalism, on the other hand, arises when substitution and participation are separated, so that what God does *for us* by the Spirit in the humanity of the Son is understood to be logically separable from what God does *in us* by that same Spirit. No self-respecting covenant theologian would make such a claim. Nonetheless, covenant theology in its classic versions tends in this direction. Specifically, its subordination of the logic of incarnation to that of covenant results in an understanding of Christ's mediation in terms of an office through the acquittal of which he certainly *establishes* the 'covenant of grace' (purchasing benefits for the elect by both his passive and active obedience) but does not actually *fulfil* it from the human side in his own person. The covenant is *fulfilled* by each person who is drawn into it by God's irresistible call and disposal of the will through the Spirit. The covenant is certainly fulfilled by God from first to last: but his promises are, we might say, yea in

Christ, but only actually amen in us. But this, for reasons indicated, seems to be incapable in the final analysis of furnishing adequate grounds for a level and sort of assurance that, while it may well not be what Christians experience at every moment, seems to be what Luther discovered in the heart of Paul's theology, and may be deemed proper to Christian faith as such.

If, on the other hand, we think of the covenant relation between God and humans as fulfilled once and for all in the person of Jesus in a total self-substitution of his perfect new humanity for our old, and if we insist, at the same time, that our union with him can only result in a concomitant work of his Spirit in us, which, while it is not the decisive ratification or fulfilment of the covenant, is nonetheless a vital consequence of his fulfilment of it for us, then it seems that both assurance and a grounds for Christian obedience can be held meaningfully together. After this Barth was setting any discussion of Christian ethics within a framework shaped by Christological affirmation, an account of the decision made about us by God and established in the humanity of the Son by the power of the Holy Spirit. For Barth sees clearly something Reformed orthodoxy struggled to sustain: the logic of covenant is from first to last essentially a logic of promise, the promise of God that duly calls forth and generates a response of faith and trust in itself. The classic covenant formula in Scripture ('You shall be my people and I shall be your God') captures this dual aspect, standing as it does as an ethical imperative rooted in an eschatological indicative. And the logic of both is rooted and underwritten firmly in the objective actuality of what God has already done for us in Christ, in whom all God's promises are yea *and* amen. Thus, Barth insists, in Jesus we see

> the one faithful and obedient Israelite in whom Israel's justification, sanctification, and vocation are unproblematically enacted by its God ... the man in whom the whole human race is set in the light of God's grace and in relation to whom the whole human race is to be told that God's name is already hallowed in its midst, God's kingdom has already come, and God's will in and with it is already done. The history of completed fellowship between God and man, not merely commencing on one side but established on both.[18]

This is a substitution that does not in any way remove us from the picture, but it certainly relocates us from its centre to a less prominent position. For now it is the fact that God in Jesus has done all *for us* that on the one hand obliges us to respond in faith, repentance and obedience. On the other hand the same objective fact liberates us to do so unhindered by the fear and despair attendant upon that sense of personal inadequacy and failure that those who view their humanity in the light of Christ otherwise inevitably have. Indeed, now obedience will be genuine, being motivated by love for the one who gave all for us, rather than an essentially selfish concern to secure eternity by proving to ourselves that God is doing something in us.

Humility and Trust in Theological Imagination

Badcock's chapter closes with a bold appeal for a form of theological humility, remembering that even the best of what we say about God and his dealings with us falls short of who and what God actually is. Thus 'in the final analysis, we must embrace a certain agnosticism in thinking the Christian faith'. Again, though, we must ask 'what sort of agnosticism'? John of Damascus somewhere reflects on this subject, and reminds us that when we say, 'I see the sky,' we do not actually mean that we plumb the depths of the reality called 'the sky', capturing it entirely and adequately within our field of vision. We do, though, mean that we genuinely see the sky, and not something else, even though our seeing of it is partial and falls short of its full reality. What we see is not, in other words, something other than or *inappropriate* to the reality of the sky. This sort of epistemic humility seems to me to be even more vital in theology, unless we are going to fall into the trap of confusing our own human formulations and images with the reality of a God who infinitely transcends all that is proper to this world, let alone our language about it (something, incidentally, that Barth – despite Badcock's closing judgement on him – is concerned to warn us against on every page of his writings, and for the purposes of which he develops the complex doctrine of the *analogia fidei*). Every time we say the creed we should doubtless keep some such careful qualification close to hand in order to avoid the dangers of theological arrogance and idolatry.

There is, though, another form of agnosticism much more problematic in theological terms: the sort of agnosticism that eschews
altogether any attempt to speak the truth about anything, let alone
God; that casts aside what it castigates as 'metaphysics' in preference
for a purely pragmatic engagement with images and models that
seem to 'work' for us as expressions of our experience. For such an
approach, our language about God not only falls short of his reality,
but leaves it finally shrouded in complete mystery, unable to be
known or spoken of. This sort of agnosticism goes way beyond
proper humility, and is generally the flip side of a theological
constructivism that takes it upon itself to create its own images for
God, being essentially unconstrained by (having neatly liberated
itself from) any guidelines, controls or moral obligations imposed
upon it by a reality lying beyond the scope of its own imagination.
But the Christian tradition does have guidelines and controls for its
peculiar form and object of knowing. While it should never forget
that its language for God consists inevitably in the poetic stuff of
myth and metaphor (in the sense indicated at the outset of this
response), it nonetheless does not consider itself to be the *source* of
this poetry, but looks instead to a divine self-giving in which God,
through his engagement with history, furnishes the linguistic and
conceptual tools for appropriating his own self-manifestation. In
other words, all talk of humility and agnosticism needs to be worked
out in conjunction with an adequate doctrine of revelation; I would
have liked to read a little more about this in Badcock's chapter.
Heart, imagination and head (as well as will) need to be held closely
together in theology, and I have sought to make clear in this
response that genuine trust in the promises of God cannot actually
flourish for long where certain sorts or levels of agnosticism
concerning God's character or purposes towards us are entertained.

Conclusion

In what sense, then, is the God of Christians the God of the
covenant? In the sense that he has furnished us with this metaphor,
among others, in terms of which to imagine, think and speak about
him and our relationship to him. In his self-revealing, we might say,
God takes our imagination captive and reshapes it. But we should

not underestimate the epistemic significance of the metaphorical; and it matters a great deal how we then handle and develop it theologically, not least in terms of its pragmatic impact. We cannot invest trust for long in a God about whom we can say nothing with any confidence or whose 'promises' to us turn out finally to be either contingent upon or expressions of the shape and intensity of our personal piety.

Endnotes

[1] The relationship between 'analogy' and 'metaphor' is variously defined. For our purposes, I intend by 'metaphor' any language use in which one thing is spoken of in terms proper to another. I will reserve 'analogy' for the actual levels of likeness discerned between two or more objects in reality, on the basis of which metaphorical speech is deemed appropriate and illuminating. So the metaphor of God as a shepherd is warranted because there is something about God's relation to Israel that is analogous to a shepherd's relationship to his flock, and so on. The one term refers to the level of the linguistic; the other to the level of the real.

[2] Sallie McFague, *Metaphorical Theology: Models of God in Religious Language* (Augsburg Fortress, USA, 1982; London, 1983), 19.

[3] See, e.g., Jens Møller, 'The Beginnings of Puritan Covenant Theology', *Journal of Ecclesiastical History* 14.1 (1963). Møller traces the distinctives of the covenant scheme in Britain as early as the prologue to William Tyndale's 1534 edition of the New Testament.

[4] J. Lumsden, *The Covenants of Scotland* (Paisley, 1914).

[5] See on this J.B. Torrance, 'The Covenant Concept in Scottish Theology and Politics and its Legacy', *Scottish Journal of Theology* 34.3 (1981). Also, by the same author, 'Covenant or Contract? A Study of the Theological Background of Worship in Seventeenth Century Scotland', *Scottish Journal of Theology*, 23.1 (1970).

[6] The syllogism took some form such as the following:
- All who are elected to salvation manifest signs of that election in their lives.
- I exhibit the signs of election in my life.
- Therefore I am among the elect.

[7] Walther Eichrodt, *Theology of the Old Testament* (London, 1960), 1:38.

[8] Cited in Møller, 'Beginnings', 53.

[9] John Preston (1587–1628), cited in Perry Miller, *The New England Mind* (Cambridge, MA, Harvard UP, 1954), 2:389.

10   Ibid.

11   See, e.g., R.S. Paul, *The Assembly of the Lord* (Edinburgh, T. & T. Clark, 1985): 'The religious situation of the country provided a very plausible excuse for debating the Church of England's doctrinal standards, for challenging the errors that had infiltrated through the Arminian opinions of Laudian divines, and for refuting the Pelagianism that Calvinists discovered under the covers of every prayer book. On the other side there were the equally horrendous heresies among the sectarians' (82).

12   Miller, *New England Mind*, 2:368.

13   'The condition is faith, but covenant faith has in the law a way prescribed for it to walk in, and faith as the fulfilment of a covenant obliges the believer so to walk, whereas unsophisticated piety naively supposes that faith in itself is adequate for salvation regardless of how it walks' (ibid. 2:385).

14   See K. Barth, *Church Dogmatics*, 4 vols., ed. G.W. Bromiley and T.F. Torrance (Edinburgh, T. & T. Clark, 1958), 3/1, 94–329.

15   Rutherford, *Christ Dying*, 78 (my italics). T.F. Torrance appears to read this passage incorrectly when, citing what is actually a quotation from Saltmarsh, which Rutherford subsequently rejects, he presents it as Rutherford's own view. See T.F. Torrance, *Scottish Theology from John Knox to John McLeod Campbell* (Edinburgh, T. & T. Clark, 1996), 100.

16   Rutherford, *Christ Dying*, 79.

17   Ibid. 418.

18   Barth, *Church Dogmatics* 4/4, §74, published as *The Christian Life* (Grand Rapids, 1981), 11. See further on this Trevor Hart, *Regarding Karl Barth* (Carlisle, 1999), 74–99.

Health Care and Covenant: Withholding and Withdrawing Treatment

Chaplaincy Lecture 2000

Robin Gill

Is it possible to express what is distinctive about Christian ethics without denying the validity of other forms of ethics? Does Christian ethics inevitably clash with secular ethics and perhaps also with ethics drawn from other religious traditions? Or can Christian ethicists successfully work alongside other ethicists, both with those from other religious traditions and with those disavowing any religious tradition at all? As we enter the third millennium all of these questions are still unresolved among Christian ethicists: we remain polarised.

My own instincts are to be inclusive. If I can work with others without denying my own faith I always attempt to do so. More than that, in matters of social ethics in a pluralist society, I have argued that such an approach is imperative.[1] This is especially important in medical ethics. In all Western countries today Christian doctors and nurses work alongside those with other religious faiths and with none, and patients, in turn, will probably not know whether those treating them share their own faith or not. Of course there may be areas where there is a considerable conflict – as traditionalist Roman Catholics have found on reproductive issues and Jehovah's Witnesses have found on blood transfusions. Yet it is overwhelmingly in the interests of most of us that current medical practice should not conflict with our own values. Even if we cannot agree on meta-ethics – that is, on the grounds on which we justify our values – a broad set of bridging values that Christians and others can accept is highly desirable. Much of medical ethics today is committed to seeking such values and to finding ways of enshrining them in laws that are acceptable to as broad a section of society as possible. I thoroughly share this commitment. At the same time I recognise that there are other Christian and Jewish ethicists who radically disagree. For them it is more important that they challenge secular society with their own faith and with the values they believe derive directly from this faith.[2] For them conversion always takes priority over inclusion.

This chapter will illustrate this crucial difference using the vexed topic of withholding and withdrawing nutrition and hydration. This has become a contentious topic not just between Christians and secularists but also among both practising Christians and practising Jews. Those opposed to withholding and withdrawing nutrition and hydration tend to see their fellow Christians or Jews who support this as liberals simply following secular fashions. Doubtless this can happen. However, I shall argue that an understanding of covenant offers a more serious theological justification. It also allows us to see how Christian (and indeed Jewish) ethicists can properly make alliances with secular ethicists without surrendering our distinctiveness.

The Debate about Withholding/Withdrawing Nutrition/Hydration

Withholding and withdrawing nutrition and hydration has recently been considered by both the Lambeth Conference of Bishops and by the Medical Ethics Committee of the British Medical Association. In both cases I was part of the discussion that preceded their respective reports, although in neither case did I actually write the reports. Although their premises differed considerably, their main conclusions were close. They offer a useful example of parallel Christian and largely secular discussions.

The Lambeth bishops defined their subject, agreed on a set of criteria and made recommendations based carefully upon them. It is, I believe, a model report that could be used widely in church and parish discussions, but so far has been rather neglected.

The report identifies five 'bedrock principles upon which the discussion of euthanasia and related issues rest':

- Life is God-given and therefore has intrinsic sanctity, significance and worth.
- Human beings are in relationship with the created order and that relationship is characterised by such words as respect, enjoyment and responsibility.
- Human beings, while flawed by sin, nevertheless have the capacity to make free and responsible moral choices.
- Human meaning and purpose is found in our relationship with God, in the exercise of freedom, critical self-knowledge, and in our relationship with one another and the wider community.
- This life is not the sum total of human existence; we find our ultimate fulfilment in eternity with God through Christ.[3]

Having set out these principles, the bishops then reflect theologically and sensitively upon human pain and suffering and upon our responsibilities in Christ to other people. They are fully aware of strong pressures in many countries to legalise *voluntary euthanasia* (i.e. 'where a competent, informed person asks another to end his or her life and is not coerced into doing so') and even *involuntary euthanasia* (e.g. 'where a terminally ill person, who does not have the capacity for informed choice, is killed').[4] Yet they believe that a combination of the first, second and fourth principles precludes either voluntary or involuntary euthanasia. They also worry about the consequential dangers of legalising such forms of euthanasia – especially the danger of abuse, the danger of diminution of respect for human life, and the danger of damaging the doctor–patient relationship. They take a firm stand against legalising euthanasia in these forms.

Yet they are also people with wide pastoral experience. Some of the bishops responsible for this report have direct experience of being hospital and hospice chaplains. Indeed, one of the women bishops was a nurse before her ordination. As a result they are fully aware of the many ambiguous situations that modern medicine and technology can produce. For example, they believe that it is consonant with Christian faith for patients in some circumstances to refuse or terminate medical treatment. Christians do not, they argue on the basis of their fifth principle, need to cling to this life at all costs.

The bishops are also sympathetic to the House of Lords Judgement of 3 February 1993 about the tragic Anthony Bland case.[5] Bland was a victim of the Hillsborough football disaster. After being crushed by the crowd, he was left in what is sometimes termed a persistent or permanent vegetative state (PVS) for more than three years. After the judgement his nasal gastric tube was removed, he no longer received nutrition or hydration, and within two weeks he died from renal failure. The Lambeth bishops conclude that when such a person is safely diagnosed as PVS, then it can be right to withdraw life-prolonging medical treatment and medical intervention.

Representing a more pluralist constituency, a British Medical Association Medical Ethics Committee report[6] inevitably does not start from explicitly theological premises. Yet it does share the two main conclusions of the Lambeth bishops: namely, that public pressure to legalise voluntary euthanasia should be resisted, and that it can be right not to give life-prolonging treatment to patients when it simply becomes a burden to them. Essential to these conclusions is the BMA Medical Ethics Committee's initial understanding of the primary goal of medicine:

> The primary goal of medical treatment is to benefit the patient by restoring or maintaining the patient's health as far as possible, maximising benefit and minimising harm. If treatment fails, or ceases, to give a net benefit to the patient (or if the patient has completely refused the treatment) that goal cannot be realised, and the justification for providing the treatment is removed. Unless some other justification can be demonstrated, treatment that does not provide net benefit to the patient may, ethically and legally, be withheld or withdrawn, and the goal of medicine should shift to the palliation of symptoms.[7]

Several conclusions follow naturally from this understanding. The BMA authors also believe that competent patients can properly refuse treatment. In English law it has long been recognised that adults with the capacity to make decisions about their treatment do have the right to refuse life-prolonging, or even life-saving, treatment. So a competent and mature patient can properly refuse chemotherapy and opt for palliative care instead, even if this effectively shortens her or his life. In such circumstances, doctors cannot legally act against such a patient's wishes. Again, doctors cannot give a life-saving blood transfusion to adult Jehovah's Witnesses who refuse (although they can sometimes give it against their wishes to their child).

However, like the bishops, the authors of the BMA report go further than this: they believe that medical treatment can properly be withdrawn from non-competent patients if it no longer offers them actual or potential benefit. This report argues that when people like Anthony Bland can no longer interact with others, are not aware of their existence, and can never again achieve purposeful action, then life-prolonging treatment does not provide them with any real benefit. It may at that point properly be withdrawn. In the case of babies born in similar conditions, life-prolonging treatment may properly be withheld altogether.

The BMA report is written with sensitivity. It recognises that families should be approached in a considerate and pastoral manner. Doctors should consult them, and other members of medical teams, carefully. Yet it is finally doctors, and not the courts (as at present in PVS cases), who ought, the report believes, to make medical decisions about withholding and withdrawing treatment.

However, there is an important difference between the two reports. The Lambeth bishops are more cautious about describing artificial forms of feeding as 'treatment'. Instead their report talks about 'medical treatment and intervention', since they are conscious that some people regard feeding, even in artificial forms, as a part of basic care and not as treatment. The BMA report, in contrast, argues that English law already regards such feeding as treatment. For example, the 1993 House of Lords Judgement argued that the regime of nasogastric feeding and evacuation using enemas that supported Anthony Bland in his final three years does constitute 'a form of life support analogous to that provided by a ventilator which artificially breathes air in and out of the lungs of a patient incapable of breathing normally'. In the event, the bishops' distinction probably made little difference to their conclusions. On the basis of their pastoral experience they accept that most of us simply do not want doctors to prolong our lives indefinitely, and to no purpose, with artificial forms of feeding. So, leaving it to others to decide whether artificial nutrition and hydration for PVS patients constitutes 'medical treatment' or 'medical intervention', the bishops too conclude that it can, in circumstances such as those facing Anthony Bland, properly be withdrawn.

A number of more conservative religious groups remain strongly opposed to this conclusion, arguing that nutrition and hydration are a part of basic human care and should not be withdrawn from PVS patients at all. To withdraw, say, antibiotics from PVS patients may be allowable since this clearly constitutes 'treatment'. However, food and water should never be described as 'treatment' (or even 'intervention'), since if we withdraw them patients will certainly die. In contrast, if we withdraw 'treatment', patients, at most, will be allowed to die from their medical condition.

Stated in this way it might seem that this conservative group is more caring than either the BMA Medical Ethics Committee or the Lambeth bishops. They insist, after all, that it is our duty to offer patients basic care whatever their medical condition and however burdensome to society at large this might seem. True Christian or Jewish care demands nothing less. This is what *agape* requires.

Perhaps the BMA report is too blunt in insisting that artificial forms of nutrition and hydration constitute 'medical treatment'. There may even be some sleight of hand at this point. Insisting that this is now established in English law, the report then assumes that it is thereby established in ethics as well. From that point onwards it is comparatively easy to show that there are many circumstances when it is morally right to withdraw treatment. Yet this is not a wise argument since the Anthony Bland case showed that law and ethics should not always be conflated so readily. Several of the English Law Lords showed that they were remarkably ill at ease in making their historic judgement because they realised that the questions being raised went beyond their competence as lawyers and involved serious moral issues. The academic lawyer Simon Lee has exposed some of the weaknesses of their arguments at this very point, being particularly critical of the selective way Lord Hoffmann reached his ethical conclusions.[8]

Again, the Anthony Bland case revealed that the notions of withdrawing and withholding 'treatment' do not involve identical issues as is so often maintained. In this instance law and ethics pull in quite different directions. From a legal perspective it would undoubtedly have been easier if 'treatment' had been withheld from Anthony Bland in the first place rather than withdrawn three years later. Presumably this happened with other Hillsborough victims at the time, but this is seldom noticed. Yet from an ethical perspective initial 'treatment' was essential if it was to be properly established that Anthony Bland was in a persistent/permanent vegetative state. And some of us would maintain that, while it was ethically responsible to 'treat' in the first place, it was also ethically responsible (even if legally difficult) to withdraw this 'treatment' once a diagnosis of PVS had been safely established.

However, I believe that to depict the BMA report as 'uncaring' would thoroughly misrepresent it. The authors provide abundant evidence of their sensitivity and pastoral concern, as do the Lambeth bishops. Both doctors and bishops are aware that most people are anxious not to be sustained by means of medically delivered forms of nutrition and hydration indefinitely and to no purpose.

But is there really no purpose here? Religious conservatives typically use a second argument at this point, namely that withdrawing nutrition and hydration effectively involves involuntary euthanasia. For them there is little difference between ending the life of a PVS patient by means of an injection or by withdrawing nutrition and hydration. In both instances the patient dies and the doctor knows that this will happen. The only real difference is that withdrawing nutrition and hydration usually takes some two weeks to kill a patient, whereas an injection may be instantaneous. In contrast, withdrawing medical treatment, properly understood, simply allows the patient to die from her medical condition. There is, of course, an obvious weakness in the last part of this argument (to which I shall return in a moment), since withdrawing replacement forms of medical treatment from patients who cannot live without them (for example, withdrawing insulin from PVS diabetics) will just as effectively involve their death. And it could be argued that it was only artificial nutrition and hydration that prevented Anthony Bland from dying from his medical condition in the first place. These crucial points aside, there does seem to be a legitimate fear expressed by religious conservatives that a principle of not killing people is violated here.

The BMA report argues that there is a crucial difference between the two, although only

> if the purpose of doing so is to withdraw treatment which is not a
> benefit to the patient and is therefore not in the patient's best interests
> … the patient will die if treatment is not provided, but this cannot be
> the sole reason for withholding it; the overriding purpose or objective
> is to ensure that treatment which is not in the best interests of the
> patient is avoided.

The report wisely avoids a lengthy discussion of the troublesome doctrine of double-effect,[9] yet it does once again conflate two languages, namely the ethical language of 'benefits' and the legal language of 'best interests'. Here too these languages may be more distinct than is allowed in the BMA report. The very notion of 'benefit' may expose ideological and metaphysical differences that, I suspect, the authors are anxious to avoid.

The Relevance of Covenant Theology

At this point the Lambeth bishops may be better equipped to respond to those Christians and Jews who object to their conclusions. From a theological perspective, can sustaining PVS patients indefinitely constitute a benefit either to them or to society at large? Once patients can no longer interact with others, are not aware of their existence, and can never again achieve purposeful action, then surely the BMA report is correct in claiming that life-prolonging treatment does not provide them with any real benefit. I believe that a theology of covenant suggests that it does not and that once we regard people as children of God we have profound reasons why we should not burden such patients beyond endurance with our principles. In terms of a covenant theology, ethical principles are there to help and serve people; people are not there to serve principles. There are occasions when the vulnerable may need to be protected from an overzealous application of principles.

Of course this is a risky ethical stance to take. In the previous generation the Christian ethicist Joseph Fletcher thoroughly misused it, leading him to argue that all ethics is situational and that principles are at best relative guidelines. But this is surely a *reductio ad absurdum*. In contrast, covenant ethics is concerned more with the vulnerable and with victims. It is closer to the risky form of ethics practised by Jesus in the Synoptic Gospels when he claimed that the sabbath was made for people and not people for the sabbath (Mark 2:27).

Other contributors to this volume have pointed out the personal and committed character of covenants. John Goldingay sums this up well when he writes (in Ch. 2) that 'a covenant involves a relationship, but no ordinary relationship: it presupposes a level of commitment not required of most relationships, and a formalising of that commitment, which shows that we really mean it.' Gary Badcock is also helpful when he writes (in Ch. 5) that 'in the Bible, the covenant is not a doctrinal or theological construction so much as a relational or practical one, the meaning of which is possibly assumed, but the implications of which must be worked out across time in moral and religious struggle'. As it happens, I also agree with Stephen Clark that we can have this sort of relationship, or something very like it, with animals: my own relationship to my dog is indeed very personal and committed.

Interestingly, the Lambeth bishops who wrote the report on the environment also shared this perspective. They identified four major aspects to their eco-theology. The first of these is based upon covenant, in which 'God is pictured binding together all living beings, and the earth itself, into a web of inter-relatedness.'[10] The second is the sacrament of creation: that 'a deep communion exists between God and creation; indeed that creation is actually imbued with the divine presence, not in a pantheistic sense which confuses God with creation, but in a sacramental sense which maintains and affirms ontological distinctions between the natural and the divine.' The third is of people being priests for creation: that 'as the divine image-bearers, humans are uniquely called to embody and express God's will and purpose for all creation which clearly excluded its abuse and wanton destruction'. Human beings are called to be co-creators, priests and pastors of creation: 'they are to pronounce God's blessing on creation and they are also the means of expressing creation's praise and longing to God.' And they do this especially within the Eucharist. And the fourth is the notion of the sabbath feast 'enoughness':

This is achieved in two ways. Firstly, the Genesis narrative emphasises that creation reaches its crown and consummation not in the creation of humankind on the sixth day but in the peace of the Sabbath on the seventh day. Secondly, the Sabbath concept when related to the fallow season for the earth introduces a constraint on human intervention in nature and thus sets limits to the human exploitation of the natural order.[11]

Significantly, each of these four aspects is intensely personal. Indeed a number of Christian ethicists have been attracted to covenant theology precisely because it is so personal. Often they make a distinction between covenant and contract – a distinction that may be especially helpful in the contrasting roles of law and ethics in the withholding and withdrawing treatment debate.

One Christian ethicist who has done much to analyse this contrast is Joseph Allen.[12] For him a covenant model is significant for Christian ethics for three reasons. In the first place, it emphasises that human life is essentially social and that 'we are always dependent upon others and must entrust ourselves to them if we are to live at all and if we are to find what it is truly to live well.'[13] Secondly, 'a covenant model enables us to express the Christian awareness that each member of the covenant community has a value not reducible to his or her usefulness to the whole group.' And thirdly, a covenant model 'enables us to take seriously the *historical* fabric of the moral life, both of the individual and of the community, without losing our recognition of the moral unity of all people under God.'[14]

When Allen contrasts the model of covenant with that of contract in marriage its ethical importance can be seen most clearly. He argues as follows:

> As a special covenant, marriage brings together a man and a woman in the most intensive relationship possible in human life. Their mutual concerns and obligations cover the whole range of life's interests, not merely a small or specific list of subjects, as might be the case in a business transaction. Once married, the two belong essentially together ... They will be able to sustain their marriage as a growing relationship only to the extent that they commit themselves fully and steadfastly to each other and affirm each other as persons of worth, not only as

individuals having convenient or useful or praiseworthy characteristics
… A covenant model of marriage is one that expresses the essential
characteristics of covenant love in a way appropriate for this unique
kind of human relationship. In contrast to a covenant model, much
contemporary opinion views marriage as merely a limited-liability
contract for the mutual advantage of each of the two spouses.[15]

Allen at once recognises that Christian marriage services contain a
mixture of contractual and covenantal features. They rightly recognise, for example, that a valid marriage service requires the consent
of both the man and the woman and that they have identifiable
rights and corresponding obligations. Allen is not claiming that
marriage as covenant eliminates the need for marriage as contract.
Nevertheless he believes that marriage as covenant 'provides the
theological framework within which the moral obligatoriness of the
contract is to be understood, and not the reverse … particular
contractual matters within the marriage, however important, can be
seen in their proper light – as means to the full affirmation of the
other in marriage, and not as ways of pursuing private interests in
competition with the marriage.'[16]

William F. May has long argued that such a distinction between
covenant and contract is helpful for a better understanding of the
doctor–patient relationship. He argues that there are benefits in
seeing this relationship in contractual terms 'in which two parties
calculate their own best interests and agree upon some joint project
in which they both derive roughly equivalent benefits for goods
contributed by each.'[17] Such a model reduces doctor paternalism
and stresses patient consent and doctor accountability. Nevertheless, May believes that 'it would be unfortunate if professional ethics
were reduced to a commercial contract without significant
remainder … There is a donative element in the nourishing of
covenant – whether it is the covenant of marriage, friendship, or
professional relationship … in which one must serve and draw upon
the deepest reserves of another.'[18]

If contract is more to do with law, and covenant with ethics,
then perhaps the relationship between them in the withholding and
withdrawing treatment/intervention debate becomes rather
clearer. Both Allen and May – correctly in my view – believe that
covenant complements contract: contracts may be essential to

ensure basic levels of justice but without covenantal behaviour they can become arid and uncaring. So, whereas marriages lacking contracts can lead to injustice, marriages based solely upon contracts and without any covenantal love can result in joyless relationships. Writing in 1983 Allen feared that contractual understandings of marriage were too dominant. At the turn of the millennium almost the reverse now seems to be the case. An increasing number of couples throughout the Western world are choosing to live together in a covenant but without a contract. This may allow romantic love to flourish, but ironically it may also increase injustice, especially for children.

The fine line between rejecting voluntary or involuntary euthanasia and accepting, on occasions, withholding or withdrawing life-prolonging medical treatment and intervention may require a similar delicate balance between contract and covenant. If contracts in this context are rightly concerned with principles, covenants are more concerned with relationships, especially with the vulnerable. In the Torah stories of covenant, God reaches out especially to people at moments of vulnerability – to Noah after the devastating flood (Gen. 9), to Abraham and Sarah in apparently infertile old age (Gen. 15—17), and to Moses wandering in the wilderness (Exod. 34). Unlike the mutuality of a good marriage, the terminally ill are more like the vulnerable recipients of God's covenants within the Torah. The terminally ill are in particular need both of protective principles and obligations and of genuine covenant love. This, I believe, is the delicate balance required here.

Some theologians would go much further than me at this point. Both Paul Badham[19] and Hans Küng,[20] for example, have argued that voluntary euthanasia is compatible with Christian love. If someone who is terminally ill and in pain wishes to end her life, then Christian love may require that she should be helped to do so. Covenant theology, then, would be extended beyond withholding and withdrawing treatment or medical intervention. This is not the place to debate again the issue of voluntary or involuntary euthanasia. Elsewhere I have argued that, although there are grounds for being sympathetic to changing the law to allow for at least voluntary euthanasia (or 'physician assisted suicide'), I fear that such a change might have dangerous consequences.[21] A fear of procedural deterioration – whereby exceptions for difficult cases become rights for all

– has persuaded many of us that a well-meaning change in law might actually make the vulnerable more vulnerable. The situation in the Netherlands, in which doctors ending the lives of their patients still do not follow even the remarkably liberal Dutch procedures (e.g. a significant number of euthanasia cases there are not reported, as required, and some do not even involve the terminally ill), does little to reduce this fear. Most politicians outside the Netherlands have concluded that, if the vulnerable are to be properly protected, then the law does need to be clear. Legalising voluntary euthanasia, let alone legalising involuntary euthanasia, might, they believe, make serious abuse more likely than at present. Law and contract have a proper place here.

Nevertheless, there is abundant evidence from opinion polls that most people, even many churchgoers, are unhappy with the present situation.[22] Not surprisingly most of us, given the choice, simply do not wish to have our lives sustained indefinitely when we can no longer interact with others, are not aware of our existence, and can never again achieve purposeful action. In such circumstances most of us probably agree that life-prolonging treatment or medical intervention would be a burden and not a benefit at all. However much we might hesitate about withdrawing nutrition and hydration from other people, few of us doubt that we would wish them to be withdrawn from ourselves in similar circumstances. The very thought of medics indefinitely prolonging us as empty shells, imprisoned in some scientifically created limbo, is abhorrent. Just as we regard enthusiasts of cryogenics as weird, most us are appalled by the thought that others might think it their principled duty to keep us 'alive' in the manner of Anthony Bland. When other people's principles become a tyranny at our expense, then we are surely right to be worried.[23]

Inevitably the law becomes uneasy at this point. The diffidence of the English Law Lords in the Anthony Bland case is understandable. Nonetheless they were aware that it seemed inhuman to sustain him in a persistent vegetative state indefinitely. However such an awareness is to be expressed in secular language, the notion of covenant is helpful at a theological level. It insists that for Jews, Christians and Muslims – sharing a fundamental conviction about God's overwhelming concern for all people – a concern for other people, and especially for the vulnerable, should be at the very heart of ethics.[24] More than that, the new covenant is not just some external law, but is actually written in people's hearts (Jer. 31:31–4).

A similar legal ambiguity is apparent even in palliative care. Of course good palliative care has helped doctors to be more discriminate and proportionate in their use, for example, of morphine. An earlier generation of doctors was less conscious of the difference between doses of morphine that were proportionate to treating pain and those that might directly shorten the life of the patient. The successful management of pain is a real achievement of palliative medicine. Notwithstanding this, there is still some ambiguity about when a dose of morphine, even if it is proportionate to pain, might contribute to shortening the life of a patient. The doctrine of double effect has frequently been invoked to justify this, but among a number of ethicists and lawyers there are now considerable doubts about this doctrine. Properly understood, this doctrine insists that a foreseen but unintended secondary effect must not be wrong in itself – which is an obvious problem for those who believe that the medical shortening of life, whether intended or not, *is* wrong in itself. On their own premises, they should insist that an intention to relieve pain should never put at risk the principle of the sanctity of human life: pain should simply be endured if there is a risk of hastening death.[25] On strictly contractual grounds this aspect of palliative care may seem dubious. Yet on covenant grounds it does appear justifiable. Most people in severe pain do wish to receive powerful analgesics, even if they might shorten their lives. Genuine care, beyond contract, moves most doctors to respond. Indeed, a doctor who refused to give a patient morphine to ease severe pain, on the contractual ground that he risked prosecution, or even moral or theological approbation, for knowingly shortening life, would be applauded by few of us.

Good medicine does seem to require both contract and covenant. Perhaps the term 'covenant' itself is too theological for more general use within medicine. For Christians and Jews it does carry the implication that human covenants are finally to be set in the context of God's generous and abundant covenant with us. At this crucial meta-ethical level secular and religious concepts are not to be confused. However, at the level of practice I regard it as nothing but encouraging that both the Lambeth bishops and members of the BMA Medical Ethics Committee held a common pastoral compassion for the vulnerable that finally went beyond formal contracts and principles.

Endnotes

[1] See my *Moral Leadership in a Postmodern Age* (Edinburgh: T. & T. Clark, 1997).

[2] A striking example is Michael Banner's *Christian Ethics and Contemporary Moral Problems* (Cambridge: Cambridge University Press, 1999).

[3] See *The Official Report of the Lambeth Conference 1998* (Harrisburg, PA: Moorehouse, 1999).

[4] The bishops derived their definitions from *Assisted Suicide and Euthanasia: The Washington Report* (Harrisburg, PA: Moorehouse, 1997).

[5] House of Lords (Judgement: 4 February 1993): Airedale NHS Trust (Respondents) *v.* Bland (Acting by his Guardian *ad litem*) (Appellant).

[6] *Withholding and Withdrawing Life-prolonging Medical Treatment: Guidance for Decision Making* (London: BMJ, 1999).

[7] Ibid. 1.

[8] Simon Lee, 'Uneasy Cases', in Bruce Dickson and Paul Carmichael (eds.), *The House of Lords: Its Parliamentary and Judicial Roles* (Oxford: Hart, 1999), 239–52.

[9] For a critique of this see my *Euthanasia and the Churches* (London: Cassell, 1998).

[10] See *Official Report of the Lambeth Conference 1998*.

[11] Ibid.

[12] Particularly in his book *Love and Conflict: A Covenantal Model of Christian Ethics* (Nashville: Abingdon, 1984).

[13] Ibid. 46.

[14] Ibid. 47.

[15] Ibid. 226.

[16] Ibid. 227.

[17] William F. May, 'Code, Covenant, Contract or Philanthropy: A Basis for Professional Ethics', *Hastings Center Report*, December 1975, 33. See also his *The Physician's Covenant: Images of the Healer in Medical Ethics* (Philadelphia: Westminster, 1983).

[18] May, 'Code, Covenant', 33–4.

[19] See his chapter 'Should Christians Accept the Validity of Voluntary Euthanasia', in my *Euthanasia and the Churches*, 41–59.

[20] Hans Küng and Walter Jens, *A Dignified Dying* (London: SCM, 1995).

[21] See my 'Euthanasia – Response to Paul Badham', *Studies in Christian Ethics* 2.1 (Edinburgh: T. & T. Clark, 1998), 19–23.

22 For these see my *Churchgoing and Christian Ethics* (Cambridge: Cambridge University Press, 1999), 184–5.

23 See Stephen Toumlin, 'The Tyranny of Principles: Regaining the Ethics of Discretion', *Hastings Center Report*, December 1981; and Kieran Cronin, *Rights and Christian Ethics* (Cambridge: Cambridge University Press, 1992), 66–7.

24 See Garth Hallett, *Priorities and Christian Ethics* (Cambridge: Cambridge University Press, 1998).

25 See my 'Euthanasia – Response', 20.

8

Covenant and Care:
From Law to Loving-kindness

A Response to Robin Gill

Margaret Whipp

How may a distinctively theological theme contribute to the multi-faceted problems of medical ethics in a pluralistic professional environment? Robin Gill's chapter presents the concept of covenant as a useful key to unlock some of the vexed questions that surround the withholding and withdrawing of life-sustaining treatments. It may not be a key that fits every lock, yet I hope to explore some of the doors that are opened by the concept of covenant, and to pursue these openings in the further direction of a more widely accessible, while profoundly Christian, concept of care.

The Covenant Spirit

William May has promoted the image of the covenant as a fundamental key to professional identity and relationships within the situation of medical practice.[1] Setting the intensely personal quality of covenant relationships over against the more impersonal dynamics of contractual and technical relationships, he argues that some notion of covenant has been fundamental to professional medical identity since the earliest times. May's analysis of the Hippocratic oath stresses the covenantal nature of a physician's obligations. The doctor is bound by indebtedness to his teachers and colleagues to practise the healing arts within clear boundaries of propriety. Furthermore, these obligations are underpinned by an oath taken in the sight of Apollo and Asclepius, emphasising the seriously religious character of the covenant profession thus adopted.[2]

How relevant is this ontological basis of professional identity for contemporary physicians? And, indeed, how accurate is this interpretation of the Hippocratic oath in its historical setting? Randall and Downie have critically traced the various historic traditions that have contributed, in varying degree, to the core of ethical identity recognised by physicians in the contemporary pluralistic Western tradition.[3] They interpret the Hippocratic commitment against a contextual background of Greek craftsmanship. The duty to do good rather than harm to a human patient is not unlike the craftsmanlike duty of a carpenter to work on wood in a way that will not damage the essential raw material, but rather will bring out its true nature as wood. It is this proper sense of the limits of an art or craft that set the boundaries of professional interventions, according to these authors, rather than any more modern understanding of personal beneficence that is often read back into the Hippocratic corpus.

According to Randall and Downie, we must recognise a wider range of influences that have contributed to our contemporary ethical sense of medical relationships. Not least of these influences is the Gospel tradition of personal beneficence they find in the morally compelling story of the Good Samaritan, ministering with skill and sensitivity to the needs of the sick person. Other influences that spring from the Christian tradition include the commitment to noble service, epitomised by the Crusader movements and later religious orders through which people of wealth and influence devoted their resources to benevolent medical care.

More recent influences in medical ethics have been formed by Enlightenment thinking. The Kantian tradition of individual autonomy is vigorously promoted in contemporary ethical debates, often in contrast to the paternalistic stance that belonged to an older Christian impulse of *noblesse oblige*. All of these moral and philosophical ideals, and others – such as the pressing contemporary concern for justice in the allocation of scarce medical resources – have been assimilated in a complex mosaic of sources representing the pluralistic foundation on which medical ethics in a modern society must be built.

Against such a chequered background of historically shifting traditions, is it not anachronistic to appeal to the ancient concept of covenant as a credible basis for contemporary ethical reflection? Can the theological concept of covenant, which has undergone such startling evolution and development in the course of biblical and church history, offer any clear and unequivocal guidance to the intricacies of technological and biological decision-making in twenty-first century hospitals? Robin Gill's chapter makes some general ethical assertions, elevating relationships over principles,[4] always privileging the vulnerable,[5] while stressing throughout the significance of personal and moral struggle in working out the demands and dilemmas of relationships-in-covenant.[6] Yet the relevance of the covenant in his argument is focused most meaning-fully in the motivation rather than in the direction of specifically ethical behaviour.

I would argue that motivation remains the chief contribution of a religious narrative to the complexities of contemporary ethical debate. The resources of a religious vision of human relationships, identity and vocation will sustain a quality of ethical commitment that goes far beyond an elementary concern to make right decisions and avoid dangerous mistakes. The relevance of the covenant concept lies in the tremendous care that is given to such decision-making, and in the willingness to go to extraordinary lengths in the struggle to express a commitment to human relation-ships that is worthy of the divine relationships within which they find ultimate value and meaning.

Joseph Allen sums up this imperative in writing of a 'covenant standard' for relationships, which is seen in a far-reaching 'faithful-ness to one another in our various relationships, also expressible as loyalty, steadfastness and trust' as a central Christian attitude towards all moral actions.[7]

If Christian concepts of covenant function in this inspirational rather than directional way, then it is not surprising to find, as noted by Robin Gill, that the conclusions of Christian ethicists can be broadly similar to those of secular professionals in terms of the content of their practical guidance.[8] Such differences as exist lie in the vision of professional care presented as a framework for ethical activity. For the British Medical Association an emphasis on the goals of medical treatment should maximise benefit and minimise harm.[9] This concern for the proper goals of medical practice echoes the technical propriety required in the craft code of the Hippocratic formula, where physicians see themselves as accountable within properly defined boundaries. For the Lambeth bishops, in contrast, a vision of professional care was set within a larger narrative of vocational identity and purpose animated and sustained by the gift and grace of God.[10]

As a practitioner faced with frequent dilemmas in the field of withholding and withdrawing treatment, I look less to religious narratives to provide coded guidance from ancient texts for the resolution of highly complicated contemporary dilemmas, than to sustain the struggle to deal faithfully within human covenant relationships, inspired by a larger vision of personal identity and value uniquely expressed within the loving-kindness of a covenantal God.

The Struggle to Be Faithful

Consider the following scenario from palliative medicine. Jimmy is a fifty-year-old man with a large malignant tumour invading the base of his tongue. His disease is not unduly painful, yet the effects of his cancer and its treatment have been locally disfiguring, and are beginning to interfere significantly with his speech. Recently, the infiltration of tumour into Jimmy's throat has created difficulties in swallowing, such that eating and drinking are increasingly slow and distressing, punctuated by frequent coughing and choking episodes. When hospital staff noted the alarming degree of weight loss in re-cent weeks, they agreed with Jimmy to pass a small tube through the nose into the stomach to allow supplementation of food and fluid. Concerns arose when this nasogastric feeding tube inexplicably 'fell out'. While Jimmy denies any interference with the tube, it is difficult to understand why a well-positioned and carefully secured appliance should repeatedly become dislodged. For the staff, there is now the dilemma over whether to proceed to more invasive methods of nutrition, entailing the insertion of a tube directly into the stomach by percutaneous endoscopic gastrostomy (PEG). It is not easy to explore the options with Jimmy, who has become increasingly withdrawn and halting in his conversation. He has no immediate family, and his only friends are occasional drinking partners who are reluctant to discuss distressing details, and manifestly wary of involvement with official figures.

What principles are available to guide an ethical decision concerning the insertion of a PEG feeding tube? Doctors increasingly rely on the four *prima facie* principles respecting autonomy, beneficence, non-maleficence and justice.[11] Providing that none of the principles conflicts irreconcilably with another principle, a wide range of ethical problems may be addressed within this fourfold framework.

Yet Jimmy's case exemplifies the problems of principles in practice. How are we to interpret autonomy? It is exceedingly difficult to know what Jimmy himself wants from his doctors. Although he is fully conscious and able to engage in limited conversation, his behaviour communicates deep-seated depression and ambivalence whenever new initiatives and interventions are proposed. He never openly refuses treatment, yet the recurrent removal of his nasogastric tubes leads nursing staff to suppose that he is too frightened to admit that he would rather be allowed to die.

Is there a clear argument from beneficence? Who is to judge whether artificial persistence with food and fluid might be in Jimmy's best interests? The British Medical Association employs a criterion of 'futility' in advising that a treatment may be withdrawn or withheld when it is incapable of benefiting the recipient.[12] Arguably, Jimmy's quality of life is now so poor that to prolong that life with further unsought interventions is nothing more than principled cruelty. On the other hand, his evident depression might be relieved by regular medication and careful nutrition, his loneliness may be eased by the warm hospitality of hospice care, and his prognosis might extend to a further six months of comfortable and cheerful existence. There are many imponderables in the situation, which are not readily reduced to a simple calculus of risk and benefit.

Yet the risks of an invasive procedure must not be underestimated. The principle of non-maleficence warns that it is easier not to start a new treatment than to stop once a course has been embarked upon. PEG treatment is certainly not free of complications. Many malnourished patients, when fitted with a gastrostomy tube, lack the resources for tissue healing and suffer prolonged leakage and infection around the site of surgery. Sadly, the risk of such problems is increased with every delay in deciding to proceed with the PEG. Waiting a little longer to decide may mean that the decision is taken far too late.

What are the implications of justice in this contentious situation? How are the differing views and feelings of staff and carers to be weighed alongside the impenetrable fears of the patient? Typically, the nurses in this case are eager to find ways to go on nourishing their patient. They give voice to that most basic instinct which sees the provision of elemental food and fluid, not as 'treatment' but as fundamental human care. The doctors are less sentimental in their approach, quoting statistical survival figures and the impersonal language of 'futility' and 'outcomes'. Sadly however, despite all the high-minded debate that takes place in the staff office, it is painful to observe that hardly anyone gives time to involve the patient himself in discussion – because the communication has simply become too difficult.

I quote this example to illustrate some of the difficulties in practice that arise not only in respect of the substance of the ethical decision, but also, and very significantly, in the process of decision-making by which we struggle to care faithfully for those who are the vulnerable parties in the covenantal context of doctor–patient relationships.

Some of the dimensions of this struggle may be seen as issues for particular care.

1. There is a care to distinguish between reasonable and unreasonable interventions to support nutrition. Conventional ethicists, particularly in the Roman Catholic tradition, have distinguished between ordinary and extraordinary means of care, with the implication that the more 'extraordinary' and less 'natural' a treatment appears, the more justification is required for its ethical application. With the continuing advance of extraordinarily beneficial medical interventions, such a distinction is no longer considered helpful. Otherwise, such extraordinarily successful interventions as long-term

renal dialysis might be rejected as unnatural and unethical. A more recent approach seeks to distinguish between proportionate and disproportionate means, in which the value of an intervention must be weighed against some sense of the proportionate benefit the person is likely to accrue.[13]

2. There is a care to distinguish between the worth of the treatment and the worth of the patient. This point is well made in the pastorally sensitive considerations of the British Medical Association.[14] Not uncommonly, those close to a patient feel that the withdrawal of food and fluids means that staff have 'given up' on their loved one. There are deeply symbolic meanings attached to the loving administration of basic food and drink. It is no accident that in the Christian tradition the essential sacrament of the Eucharist centres on food and drink as an expression of the personal covenant love of God in Christ. For those to whom the patient is dear – and this may include staff – just as much as family and friends – feeding evokes powerful associations with the parent–child relationship and the intimacy experienced in feeding an infant. Conneley notes that 'these emotions foster feelings of love, care and compassion, helping society to accept responsibility for caring for those who are dependent.'[15] These symbolic and sentimental associations that surround feeding should not be casually dismissed, or neatly discarded in a calculated argument about 'futility'. A sensitive use of language is important in ensuring that deep feelings about the worth of a patient are not swept aside in a shallowly factual debate about the worth of a treatment.

3. For this reason, there is a care to commit serious time to sensitive communications. Being faithful in covenant relationship to a patient and her significant others is seen not so much in achieving a 'right' solution to the ethical dilemma, as in entering the personal struggle of patient, carers and staff to grapple with the painful realities that the dilemma highlights. The rich concept of covenant is a real inspiration at this point. How often the biblical writers reveal the struggle in the heart of God to fulfil his covenant commitment of faithfulness, and the anguish to communicate adequately across chasms of fear and guilt and misunderstanding. The prophets especially

portray something of the personal passion expressed in a desire to reveal the depths of covenant commitment above and beyond the mere principles of legally 'correct' behaviour. Relationships take priority over principles in a fully covenantal conception of Christian ethics.

4. Finally, there is a care to do justice to all parties in a web of interconnected covenantal relationships. Ethical dilemmas arise because of different views and feelings and priorities, dearly held by different parties. In a clinical situation it is all too easy for those with the power of status and science to dominate a debate in a way that belittles the concerns of others. Feminist ethicists have observed that an over-abstract approach to ethical debate will privilege those who are stronger in rationality than in relationships.[16] They stress the ethical importance of intimacy and emotional involvement, rather than prizing detachment and an objective analysis of rights and wrongs. Sharp gender differences between nurses and doctors are sometimes acted out in powerful conflict over the black and white distinctions that have been falsely drawn between what is termed 'basic care' and what is termed 'treatment'.[17] In a covenantal approach to ethics, it is important to honour the relational as well as the rational impulses that guide our sense of what is loyal and faithful to those in need of our care.

A Steadfast Commitment to Care

In Chapter 5 of this volume Gary Badcock shows commendable restraint in not loading the concept of covenant with more weight – historically and theologically – than it might be expected to bear. Beyond all our constructions of the religious and ethical meanings of the covenant lies the ultimate reality of a covenantal God, a God of *ḥeseḏ* or covenant faithfulness. 'The thrust of biblical language about the covenant is precisely this question of faithfulness: the point is to say that the God of the covenant is faithful.'[18]

The character of a covenantal God is imprinted on all vocational commitments undertaken in a religious spirit. This is William May's argument against merely secular contractarianism, when he asserts that a 'steadfast commitment to protect, nourish and heal the needy' will falter without the transcendent resources of a covenantal vision of faithfulness.[19] In practice, this 'covenantal image shows itself, less through a distinguishing set of duties than through a pervasive fidelity that informs the performance of all duties.'[20]

How might such a sublime vision of steadfast loving-kindness be brought to engage on the mosaic of pluralistic ethical foundations that guide contemporary medical practice? Robin Gill freely admits that the term 'covenant' itself is far too theological for direct use within daily medical practice.[21] Perhaps more accessible, while no less profound in its theological resonances, is a richly nuanced concept of 'care'. As a fruitful basis for ethical reflection, several ethicists from the feminist tradition are exploring an ethic of care as a powerful contribution to multidisciplinary education and pluralistic debate.[22]

The narrative background of covenant theology offers some rich resources for an ethic of care, suggesting those ideals of character and commitment, intimacy and intricate knowledge that are essential for effective caring. The potent ideal of 'tender loving care', which has been the hallmark of the hospice movement in this country, reflects significant aspects of the Christian story of God's covenantal devotion towards humankind. The word *ḥesed*, used to signify God's covenant affection and loyalty, is the same Hebrew word used to describe the intimate affection and passionate loyalty of kinsmen: it touches deep desires and aspirations, both ethically and emotionally.

Something of this warmth of loving-kindness is expounded in a delightful monograph *On Caring* by the philosopher Milton Mayeroff.[23] Without sinking to mere emotionalism, Mayeroff urges the fully affective element of caring alongside its more thoughtful and essentially informed rationality. He identifies eight indispensable components of caring:

1. *Knowledge.* To care I must understand the other's need. This involves explicit as well as implicit knowledge, objectively as well as intimately discerned.
2. *Alternating rhythms.* Caring alternates between closeness and distance, between interacting with others and reflecting on the consequences of that interaction.

3. *Patience.* The need to give time to relationships is paramount in caring. Not simply waiting for things to happen, but enabling others to grow in their own time and style.
4. *Honesty.* Active openness and confrontation with oneself and others.
5. *Trust.* Appreciating the independence of others and allowing them to grow in their own way.
6. *Humility.* Being willing to learn from others and being aware of one's own limitations.
7. *Hope.* The possibility of something worthy of commitment.
8. *Courage.* Makes risk-taking possible. Founded in trust of one's own and the other's ability to grow.[24]

Mayeroff's analysis touches some profoundly parallel themes to those found in the narratives of covenant. These themes of personal involvement are rarely found with such force in traditional approaches to medical ethics. Yet recent commentators are pointing out that medical ethics has stressed principles too much, to the detriment of feeling, and that 'caring', often seen as a distinctively feminine virtue, has been neglected.[25] Susan Frank Parsons has explained that an 'ethic of care' can approximate more closely to what women say about morality because it places stress in the moral life 'upon immanence rather than transcendence, upon discovering within situations and interactions what needs to be done, rather than appealing for guidance as if from outside these relationships.'[26]

All of these concerns for an ethic that is fully personal rather than merely principled approximate closely to the impassioned basis for theological ethics found in the concept of covenant. In order to care faithfully for intensely vulnerable patients approaching the end of life, I hope to have demonstrated that an element of personal commitment is at least as important as an enlightened ethical consciousness in the process of making morally 'good' decisions. This is what Downie and Macnaughton describe as a 'humane attitude' to the ethical process, which is cultivated not simply through the development of philosophical and analytical skills in ethics, but more significantly by an expansion of sympathy and imagination through rich reflection on real relationships of care.[27]

How is such an attitude to be cultivated? Downie and Macnaughton take an analogy:

Imagine a musical child who plays the Chopin D flat nocturne at a music competition. The adjudicator says to the child: 'You have played the nocturne accurately and have observed the phrasing and dynamics faithfully, but you will play it much better when you have had three love affairs and two disappointments.' The adjudicator means that, although the nocturne was played well technically, and the performance was even a musical one, it nevertheless lacked a human context, or it was played from the outside, or the inner meaning was missing. In a similar way, a doctor could treat a patient in a way that was technically excellent, and the doctor might also show compassion and respect for the patient's autonomous decision. Yet there might be something lacking ...[28]

An ethic of care, informed by the love affairs and heartaches of the ancient biblical narrative of covenant, offers something more than ethical clarity and legalistic correctness. In the exquisitely sensitive situations of end-of-life dilemmas, it looks to the fullest limits of loving-kindness.

> He has told you, O mortal, what is good;
> > and what does the Lord require of you
> but to do justice, and to love kindness,
> > and to walk humbly with your God? (Mi. 6:8)

Endnotes

[1]   W.F. May, *The Physician's Covenant: Images of the Healer in Medical Practice* (Pennsylvania: Westminster, 1983).

[2]   Ibid. 109ff.

[3]   F. Randall and R.S. Downie, *Palliative Care Ethics: A Good Companion* (Oxford: Oxford University Press, 1996), 3ff.

[4]   See Ch. 7 in this volume.

[5]   Ibid.

[6]   Ibid.

[7]   J.L. Allen, *Love and Conflict: A Covenantal Model of Christian Ethics* (Lanham, MD: University Press of America, 1995), 9.

[8]   See Ch. 7 in this volume.

[9]   British Medical Association, *Withholding and Withdrawing Life-prolonging Medical Treatment: Guidance for Decision Making* (London: BMJ, 1999), 1.

10   *The Official Report of the Lambeth Conference 1998* (Harrisburg, PA:
     Moorehouse, 1999).
11   See T.L. Beauchamp and J.F. Childress, *Principles of Biomedical Ethics*
     (Oxford: Oxford University Press, 1989).
12   British Medical Association, *Withholding and Withdrawing*, 18.
13   A discussion of the concept of proportionality can be found in the
     Sacred Congregation for the Doctrine of the Faith, *Declaration on
     Euthanasia* (Rome, 1980), 4–10.
14   British Medical Association, *Withholding and Withdrawing*, 3.
15   R. Conneley, 'The Sentiment Argument for Artificial Feeding of the
     Dying', *Omega* 20 (1989), 229–37.
16   See S.F. Parsons, *Feminism and Christian Ethics* (Cambridge:
     Cambridge University Press, 1996), 203.
17   See Randall and Downie, *Palliative Care Ethics*, 109.
18   Ch. 5 in this volume.
19   May, *Physician's Covenant*, 126.
20   Ibid. 141.
21   Ch. 7 in this volume.
22   See, e.g., N. Noddings, *Caring: A Feminine Approach to Ethics and
     Moral Education* (Los Angeles: University of California Press, 1984).
23   M. Mayeroff, *On Caring* (New York: HarperCollins, 1971).
24   Ibid. 35–6.
25   For a review of these issues, see E.D. Pellegrino and D.C. Thomasma,
     The Virtues in Medical Practice (New York: Oxford University Press,
     1994).
26   Parsons, *Feminism*, 203.
27   R.S. Downie and J. Macnaughton, *Clinical Judgement: Evidence in
     Practice* (Oxford: Oxford University Press, 2000), 86.
28   Ibid. 87.

METHODS IN MOLECULAR

Series Editor
John M. Walker
School of Life and Medical Sciences
University of Hertfordshire
Hatfield, Hertfordshire, UK

For further volumes:
http://www.springer.com/series/7651

For over 35 years, biological scientists have come to rely on the research protocols and methodologies in the critically acclaimed *Methods in Molecular Biology* series. The series was the first to introduce the step-by-step protocols approach that has become the standard in all biomedical protocol publishing. Each protocol is provided in readily-reproducible step-by-step fashion, opening with an introductory overview, a list of the materials and reagents needed to complete the experiment, and followed by a detailed procedure that is supported with a helpful notes section offering tips and tricks of the trade as well as troubleshooting advice. These hallmark features were introduced by series editor Dr. John Walker and constitute the key ingredient in each and every volume of the *Methods in Molecular Biology* series. Tested and trusted, comprehensive and reliable, all protocols from the series are indexed in PubMed.

Invariant Natural Killer T-Cells

Methods and Protocols

Edited by

Chaohong Liu

*Department of Pathogen Biology Tongji Medical College, Huazhong University of Science and Technology,
Wuhan, China*

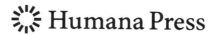 Humana Press

Editor
Chaohong Liu
Department of Pathogen Biology
Tongji Medical College
Huazhong University of Science and Technology
Wuhan, China

ISSN 1064-3745   ISSN 1940-6029   (electronic)
Methods in Molecular Biology
ISBN 978-1-0716-1777-9   ISBN 978-1-0716-1775-5   (eBook)
https://doi.org/10.1007/978-1-0716-1775-5

This Humana imprint is published by the registered company Springer Science+Business Media, LLC, part of Springer Nature.
The registered company address is: 1 New York Plaza, New York, NY 10004, U.S.A.

Preface

The invariant natural killer T-cells (iNKT cells) contribute to homeostasis and autoimmunity and also can cause various pathological responses such as allergy, infection, excessive auto-immune response, and cancer. Without antigen stimulation or requiring clonal expansion, iNKT cells directly produce a large number of cytokines when activated. They differentiate into at least three effector subsets NKT1, NKT2, and NKT17 in thymus and express an invariant T-cell receptor (TCR), α-actin, and variable (TCR) β-chain. iNKT cells are presented by MHC class I-like molecule CD1d and express TCRs with a unique Vα14-Jα18 rearrangement, which is special in recognizing glycolipid antigens including alpha-galactosylceramide (α-Galcer). When stimulated by agonistic lipid α-Galcer, the continuous expression of cytokines enables iNKT cells to engage in innate and adaptive immune response.

During the past few years, the diversity of iNKT cell functional subsets is not unveiled like other lymphocytes because of limitations in techniques. Nowadays, with the development of all kinds of high-resolution microscopy, flow cytometry, and the advance of gene analysis technology, the function of iNKT cells and the technique of analyzing have been improved gradually as well as with other lymphocytes. This volume on *Invariant Natural Killer T-Cells* focuses on various aspects of iNKT cells. Chapters 1 and 2 focus on the analysis of genes and their ligands of iNKT cells. Chapter 3 shows protocols to learn the interactions between iNKT cells and viruses. Chapters 4–7 reveal methods of iNKT cell identification and isolation in different organs of mice and humans. Chapters 8–10 outline the procedures to study iNKT cell activation and to study the activation and transformation of iNKT cells by using flow cytometry. Chapters 11–13 establish the procedures to study iNKT cell proliferation and differentiation. Chapter 14 uses intravital confocal microscopy to observe the dynamic activities of invariant natural killer T-cells in the liver of CXCR6$^{GFP/+}$ transgenic mice. Chapters 15 and 16 focus on α-GalCer transformation technology to observe in vivo cytotoxicity and the usage of α-GalCer/CD1d-scFv fusion protein technology to redirect iNKT cells for antitumor purposes. Chapter 17 characterizes the dynamic changes in metabolic profiles associated with iNKT cell development.

I have tried to give you an idea about the current advanced protocols that help with the study of iNKT cells. This volume might not provide a big picture of current research progress in iNKT cells. From my point of view, we can still make greater progress in studying iNKT cells. These years of rapid progress in this field are just the beginning. Further research on iNKT cells will help us have deeper knowledge of the human immune system. I hope the protocols published in this volume can help those immunologists who devote themselves to studying iNKT cells. I am very thankful to all contributors for their time and experience, as well as their great suggestions, in finishing this volume. The series editor John Walker has provided great help for publishing these protocols. Finally, the staff from Springer and Han Li also provided great help for editing this volume.

Wuhan, China   *Chaohong Liu*

Contents

Contributors

ORCHI ANANNYA • *Department of Microbiology and Immunology, Cornell Center for Immunology, Cornell Institute for Host Microbe and Defense, Cornell University, Ithaca, NY, USA*

KELLY J. ANDREWS • *Department of Pediatrics, University of Miami Miller School of Medicine, Miami, FL, USA; Department of Microbiology and Immunology, University of Miami Miller School of Medicine, Miami, FL, USA; Beckman Coulter, Miami, FL, USA*

AVERY AUGUST • *Department of Microbiology and Immunology, College of Veterinary Medicine, Cornell University, Ithaca, NY, USA*

LI BAI • *Hefei National Laboratory for Physical Sciences at Microscale, Laboratory of Structural Immunology, CAS Key Laboratory of Innate Immunity and Chronic Disease, Division of Life Sciences and Medicine, University of Science and Technology of China, Hefei, China*

KAMEL BENLAGHA • *INSERM, UMR-1160, Institut de Recherche St-Louis (IRSL), Universite Paris Diderot, Sorbonne, Paris, France*

NIELS OLSEN SARAIVA CAMARA • *Department of Immunology, Institute of Biomedical Sciences, University of Sao Paulo, Sao Paulo, Brazil; Nephrology Division, Department of Medicine, Federal University of Sao Paulo, Sao Paulo, Sao Paulo, Brazil*

JIAXI CHENG • *Shanghai Pudong New Area Mental Health Center, School of Medicine, Tongji University, Shanghai, China*

XUE CHENG • *Department of Immunology, School of Basic Medicine, Tongji Medical College, Huazhong University of Science and Technology, Wuhan, China*

HONGBO CHI • *Department of Immunology, St. Jude Children's Research Hospital, Memphis, TN, USA*

MARCELLA CIPELLI • *Department of Immunology, Institute of Biomedical Sciences, University of Sao Paulo, Sao Paulo, Brazil*

MENGQING CONG • *Division of Life Sciences and Medicine, Department of Medical Oncology, The First Affiliated Hospital of USTC, University of Science and Technology of China, Hefei, China; Hefei National Laboratory for Physical Sciences at Microscale, Laboratory of Structural Immunology, CAS Key Laboratory of Innate Immunity and Chronic Disease, Division of Life Sciences and Medicine, University of Science and Technology of China, Hefei, China*

CRISTHIANE FAVERO DE AGUIAR • *Department of Genetics, Evolution, Microbiology and Immunology, Institute of Biology, University of Campinas, Campinas, Brazil*

ALENA DONDA • *Translational Tumor Immunology Group, Ludwig Cancer Research, University of Lausanne, Epalinges, Switzerland; Department of Fundamental Oncology, University of Lausanne, Epalinges, Switzerland*

RUI DOU • *Department of Immunology, School of Basic Medicine, Tongji Medical College, Huazhong University of Science and Technology, Wuhan, China*

HAOPENG FANG • *Division of Life Sciences and Medicine, Department of Medical Oncology, The First Affiliated Hospital of USTC, University of Science and Technology of China, Hefei, China; Hefei National Laboratory for Physical Sciences at Microscale, Laboratory of Structural Immunology, CAS Key Laboratory of Innate Immunity and Chronic Disease,*

Division of Life Sciences and Medicine, University of Science and Technology of China, Hefei, China

WANG FEI • *School of Life Science, Anhui Medical University, Hefei, China*

YIFANG GAO • *Organ Transplantation Center, The First Affiliated Hospital, Sun Yat-sen University, Guangzhou, China; Guangdong Provincial Key Laboratory of Organ Donation and Transplant Immunology, The First Affiliated Hospital, Sun Yat-sen University, Guangzhou, P. R. China; Guangdong Provincial International Cooperation Base of Science and Technology (Organ Transplantation), The First Affiliated Hospital, Sun Yat-sen University, Guangzhou, China*

QING GE • *Department of Immunology, School of Basic Medical Sciences, Peking University, NHC Key Laboratory of Medical Immunology (Peking University), Beijing, China; Department of Integration of Chinese and Western Medicine, School of Basic Medical Sciences, Peking University, Beijing, China*

S. M. MANSOUR HAERYFAR • *Department of Microbiology and Immunology, Western University, London, ON, Canada; Department of Medicine, Division of Clinical Immunology and Allergy, Western University, London, ON, Canada; Department of Surgery, Division of General Surgery, Western University, London, ON, Canada; Centre for Human Immunology, Western University, London, ON, Canada, Lawson Health Research Institute, London, ON, Canada*

WENJING HE • *Organ Transplantation Center, The First Affiliated Hospital, Sun Yat-sen University, Guangzhou, China; Guangdong Provincial Key Laboratory of Organ Donation and Transplant Immunology, The First Affiliated Hospital, Sun Yat-sen University, Guangzhou, P. R. China; Guangdong Provincial International Cooperation Base of Science and Technology (Organ Transplantation), The First Affiliated Hospital, Sun Yat-sen University, Guangzhou, China*

ZHOU HONG • *School of Life Science, Anhui Medical University, Hefei, China*

BRIAN IMBIAKHA • *Department of Microbiology and Immunology, Cornell Center for Immunology, Cornell Institute for Host Microbe and Defense, Cornell University, Ithaca, NY, USA*

RONG JIN • *Department of Immunology, School of Basic Medical Sciences, Peking University, NHC Key Laboratory of Medical Immunology (Peking University), Beijing, China*

VIBHUTI JOSHI • *Neuro-Oncology Branch, Center for Cancer Research, National Cancer Institute, NIH, Bethesda, MD, USA*

NATASHA K. KHATWANI • *Department of Pediatrics, University of Miami Miller School of Medicine, Miami, FL, USA; Sheila and David Fuente Program in Cancer Biology, University of Miami Miller School of Medicine, Miami, FL, USA; Sylvester Comprehensive Cancer Center, University of Miami Miller School of Medicine, Miami, FL, USA*

JIHENE KLIBI • *INSERM, UMR-1160, Institut de Recherche St-Louis (IRSL), Universite Paris Diderot, Sorbonne, Paris, France*

BOFENG LI • *Division of Life Sciences and Medicine, Department of Medical Oncology, The First Affiliated Hospital of USTC, University of Science and Technology of China, Hefei, China; Hefei National Laboratory for Physical Sciences at Microscale, Laboratory of Structural Immunology, CAS Key Laboratory of Innate Immunity and Chronic Disease, Division of Life Sciences and Medicine, University of Science and Technology of China, Hefei, China*

XIANG LI • *Hefei National Laboratory for Physical Sciences at Microscale, Laboratory of Structural Immunology, CAS Key Laboratory of Innate Immunity and Chronic Disease,*

Division of Life Sciences and Medicine, University of Science and Technology of China, Hefei, China

YAN-RUIDE LI • Department of Microbiology, Immunology & Molecular Genetics, University of California, Los Angeles, Los Angeles, CA, USA

ZHIYUAN LI • Key Laboratory of Medicinal Chemistry for Natural Resource, Ministry of Education, Yunnan University, Kunming, China

CANDICE LIMPER • Department of Microbiology and Immunology, Cornell Center for Immunology, Cornell Institute for Host Microbe and Defense, Cornell University, Ithaca, NY, USA

RUI LIU • Department of Oncology, the First Affiliated Hospital of Anhui Medical University, Hefei, China; Inflammation and Immune Mediated Diseases Laboratory of Anhui Province, Hefei, China

GUANGHUI NI • Key Laboratory of Medicinal Chemistry for Natural Resource, Ministry of Education, Yunnan University, Kunming, China

TIM PIERPONT • Department of Microbiology and Immunology, Cornell Center for Immunology, Cornell Institute for Host Microbe and Defense, Cornell University, Ithaca, NY, USA

ASHA B. PILLAI • Department of Pediatrics, University of Miami Miller School of Medicine, Miami, FL, USA; Sheila and David Fuente Program in Cancer Biology, University of Miami Miller School of Medicine, Miami, FL, USA; Department of Microbiology and Immunology, University of Miami Miller School of Medicine, Miami, FL, USA; Sylvester Comprehensive Cancer Center, University of Miami Miller School of Medicine, Miami, FL, USA

THERESA RAMALHO • Department of Immunology, Institute of Biomedical Sciences, University of Sao Paulo, Sao Paulo, Brazil; Department of Medicine, University of Massachusetts Medical School, Worcester, MA, USA

JANA L. RAYNOR • Department of Immunology, St. Jude Children's Research Hospital, Memphis, TN, USA

PATRICK T. RUDAK • Department of Microbiology and Immunology, Western University, London, ON, Canada

JULIE SAHLER • Department of Microbiology and Immunology, Cornell Center for Immunology, Cornell Institute for Host Microbe and Defense, Cornell University, Ithaca, NY, USA

XIAOSHENG TAN • Department of Immunology, School of Basic Medicine, Tongji Medical College, Huazhong University of Science and Technology, Wuhan, China

MASAKI TERABE • Neuro-Oncology Branch, Center for Cancer Research, National Cancer Institute, NIH, Bethesda, MD, USA

HUA WANG • Department of Oncology, the First Affiliated Hospital of Anhui Medical University, Hefei, China; Inflammation and Immune Mediated Diseases Laboratory of Anhui Province, Hefei, China

JING WANG • Shanghai Public Health Clinical Center Affiliated to Fudan University, Shanghai, China

KE WANG • Department of Immunology, School of Basic Medical Sciences, Peking University, NHC Key Laboratory of Medical Immunology (Peking University), Beijing, China; Department of Integration of Chinese and Western Medicine, School of Basic Medical Sciences, Peking University, Beijing, China

PENG G. WANG • School of Medicine, Southern University of Science and Technology, Shenzhen, China

XIUFANG WENG • *Department of Immunology, School of Basic Medicine, Tongji Medical College, Huazhong University of Science and Technology, Wuhan, China*

XIONGWEN WU • *Department of Immunology, School of Basic Medicine, Tongji Medical College, Huazhong University of Science and Technology, Wuhan, China*

CHENGFENG XIA • *Key Laboratory of Medicinal Chemistry for Natural Resource, Ministry of Education, Yunnan University, Kunming, China*

JIANQING XU • *Shanghai Public Health Clinical Center Affiliated to Fudan University, Shanghai, China*

LILI YANG • *Department of Microbiology, Immunology & Molecular Genetics, University of California, Los Angeles, Los Angeles, CA, USA; Eli and Edythe Broad Center of Regenerative Medicine and Stem Cell Research, University of California, Los Angeles, Los Angeles, CA, USA; Jonsson Comprehensive Cancer Center, David Geffen School of Medicine, University of California, Los Angeles, Los Angeles, CA, USA; Molecular Biology Institute, University of California, Los Angeles, CA, USA*

DONGMEI YE • *Organ Transplantation Center, The First Affiliated Hospital, Sun Yat-sen University, Guangzhou, China; Guangdong Provincial Key Laboratory of Organ Donation and Transplant Immunology, The First Affiliated Hospital, Sun Yat-sen University, Guangzhou, P. R. China; Guangdong Provincial International Cooperation Base of Science and Technology (Organ Transplantation), The First Affiliated Hospital, Sun Yat-sen University, Guangzhou, China*

SAMUEL ZENG • *Department of Microbiology, Immunology & Molecular Genetics, University of California, Los Angeles, Los Angeles, CA, USA*

LIANJUN ZHANG • *Suzhou Institute of Systems Medicine, Suzhou, Jiangsu, China; Center for Systems Medicine, Institute of Basic Medical Sciences, Chinese Academy of Medical Sciences and Peking Union Medical College, Beijing, China*

WENPENG ZHANG • *School of Medicine, Southern University of Science and Technology, Shenzhen, China*

CHEN ZHAO • *Shanghai Public Health Clinical Center Affiliated to Fudan University, Shanghai, China*

XUCAI ZHENG • *Division of Life Sciences and Medicine, Department of Medical Oncology, The First Affiliated Hospital of USTC, University of Science and Technology of China, Hefei, China*

DAPENG ZHOU • *Shanghai Pudong New Area Mental Health Center, School of Medicine, Tongji University, Shanghai, China*

YANG ZHOU • *Department of Microbiology, Immunology & Molecular Genetics, University of California, Los Angeles, Los Angeles, CA, USA*

ZENG ZHUTIAN • *School of Basic Medical Sciences, University of Science and Technology of China, Hefei, China*

Chapter 1

Genetic Analysis of *i*NKT Cell Development and Function

Julie Sahler, Orchi Anannya, Candice Limper, Brian Imbiakha, Tim Pierpont, and Avery August

Abstract

Natural killer T (NKT) cells are among the immediate and early responding immune cells and are important players in autoimmune diseases and tumor immunity. This unique subset of T cells shares properties of natural killer cells and T cells. Proper identification and characterization of NKT cell subsets is essential to understand the function and involvement of these understudied immune cells in various diseases. This review aims to summarize the known methods for identifying and characterizing NKT cells. NKT cells are divided into Type I (or invariant) and Type II, with either limited or broad TCR repertoires, respectively, that generally respond to glycolipids presented on the nonclassical MHC, CD1d. Type I NKT cells or invariant NKT cells (*i*NKT) are the most well studied and can be further subdivided into NKT1, NKT2, or NKT17 populations, classified based on their functional capacity. Conversely, less is known about Type II NKT cells because they have a more diverse TCR repertoire which make them hard to identify. However, genetic analyses have shed light on the development and function of all NKT subsets, which aids in their characterization. Further exploration of the role of NKT cells in various diseases will reveal the intricacies and importance of their novel functions.

Key words α-Galactosyl ceramide, Natural killer T cells, CD1d, CD1d/α-galactosyl ceramide tetramers

1 Introduction

Natural killer T (NKT) cells are found everywhere that conventional T cells are found. In mice, NKT cells represent ~30% of the total lymphocytes in the liver (~50% of α/β T cell receptor (TCR)⁺ T cells), ~20% of the αβ T cells in the bone marrow, ~3% of the αβ T cells in the spleen, and very small percentage in the lymph node [1–3]. The most striking effector function of an activated NKT cell is

---

Julie Sahler, Orchi Anannya, Candice Limper, Brian Imbiakha, Tim Pierpont, and Avery August contributed equally to this work.
To whom corres[once should be addressed.

Chaohong Liu (ed.), *Invariant Natural Killer T-Cells: Methods and Protocols*, Methods in Molecular Biology, vol. 2388, https://doi.org/10.1007/978-1-0716-1775-5_1,
© The Author(s), under exclusive license to Springer Science+Business Media, LLC, part of Springer Nature 2021

their ability to rapidly produce large amounts of IL-2, IL-4, IFN-γ, and TNF-α. NKT cells appear to be pivotal for immediate responses to infection, prevent certain autoimmune diseases, and the immune response to cancer. NKT cells can respond to glycolipid ligands such as sulfatide, β-galactosyl ceramide, phosphatidylglycerol, phosphatidylinositol, and diphosphatidylglycerol presented by the MHC-1-like molecule CD1d. While the natural ligand presented to NKT cells by CD1d in vivo has previously been unclear, and thought to be a glycosylphosphatidylinositol, isoglobotrihexosyl-ceramide (iGb3) have been reported as an endogenous ligand for these cells [4, 5].

Since NKT cells have a variety of lineages, each with their own developmental process, markers, and functions, accurate identification and assessment of function is essential to determine the role of NKT cell in disease. The aim of this review is to provide a brief description of the main NKT cell populations, describe how they are extracted, define identification markers, and highlight important genes expressed during their development and activation. Since much of the work on NKT cells has been performed in mice, the information presented here will be referring to this model unless otherwise specified.

NKT cells are divided into two primary groups: Type I and Type II, respectively, carrying limited or diverse Vα chain variants of their TCR. Type I cells (also known as iNKT) are the most well studied and can be further subdivided into NKT1, NKT2, or NKT17 populations, each with different effector functions. Regardless of their differences, they all utilize their TCRs to respond to a limited array of lipids, including a particular synthetic glycolipid α-galactosyl ceramide (α-GalCer), which is not recognized by conventional T cells [6]. This molecule, extracted from marine sponges, has been identified as a specific ligand for both mouse and human NKT cells and has been used in complex with the CD1d as tetramers to identify iNKT cells. While Type II NKT cells can respond to a variety of ligands presented on CD1d, they express a more diverse range of TCRs and so are not identified by α-GalCer/CD1d tetramers and therefore are less well studied. Here we describe how to extract and identify these NKT subsets from mice.

1.1 General Development of NKT Cells

In addition to the invariant TCR, most NKT cells express NK1.1 (NKRP1C in human), and DX5, and mature NKT cells express Ly49 and are CD44^{Hi}/CD69^{+}/CD49b$^{-/Lo}$ and produce large amounts of IL-4 and IFN-γ upon activation [7, 8]. NKT cells, like conventional T cells, arise from thymocyte progenitor cells. Currently it is unclear how early prior to TCR expression progenitor cells become committed to the NKT lineage, since they are identified by their TCR specificity. Following TCR expression, CD1d restricted cells can be identified, based on the ability to bind α-GalCer/CD1d tetramers, even prior to the expression of

NK1.1 [9]. Based on expression of the cell surface marker DX5, developing CD1d-reactive NKT cells have been divided into four stages. The first two stages are immature, with the most immature stage lacking both DX5 and NK1.1. These cells express CD4$^+$, as do the cells in the next stage, which are DX5$^+$/NK1.1$^-$. Mature NKT cells are divided almost equally into DX5$^+$/NK1.1$^+$ and DX5$^-$/NK1.1$^+$ [7]. In contrast to conventional T cells, which can develop in the fetus and are present at birth, NKT cells are not found until approximately 5 days postpartum in mice [10].

1.2 Type I NKT Cells or iNKT Cells

Type I or *i*NKT cells express an invariant TCR α chain Vα14Jα18 and a β chain with limited variability (mostly Vβ8.2, Vβ7 or Vβ2) and recognize the prototypical antigen α-GalCer [11]. In humans, these cells express Vα24-JαQ, paired with a Vβ11 β-chain, and are also referred to as Vα14 NKT cells [2]. In the mouse where *i*NKT cell development has been the most studied, developing *i*NKT cells are positively selected from the CD4/CD8 double-positive cells by the MHC molecule CD1d, which presents glycolipid complexes [12]. A number of genes, including transcription factors, signaling molecules, and receptors, have been identified as being important for the development of *i*NKT cells. Many of these genes regulate both NK and T cell development and function, confirming the view that NKT cells branch from the developmental pathway of conventional T cells at the CD4$^+$CD8$^+$ stage following the emergence of those carrying the Vα14Jα18 TCR [13]. These genes include CD132 (the common gamma chain receptor for IL-2, IL-4, IL-7, and IL-15) mutation of which results in reduced numbers of B, T, NK, and NKT cells. Mutations in CD132 are also responsible for X-linked severe combined immunodeficiency in humans [13]. Mutations in other genes such as Rag1/2, Notch, or the NF-κB axis (RelB or NIK), as well as genes for lymphotoxin, CD122/IL-15 axis, and LFA-1, SLAMf1, and SLAMf6, also directly affect NKT cell numbers and function [13, 14]. Targeted deletion of the genes for CD1d and the cytokine GM-CSF also result in an almost complete loss of NKT cells [13]. Targeted mutations in the signaling molecules Itk, Fyn, SAP, and Vav1 affect NKT cell differentiation and function [7, 14]. Knockout of the genes for transcription factors Ets, Mef, Irf1, and Ikaros, E, and Id proteins, or the transcriptional repressor NKAP, indicates that they are important in *i*NKT subset differentiation [13, 15–17]. The ability to identify specific genes associated with NKT cell development and function allow the use of specific approaches to identify the developmental stages.

*i*NKT cells undergo positive selection by homotypic interaction of self-lipids presented by CD1d with the TCR, along with the co-stimulation of SLAM family of receptors [18, 19]. The high signaling that results from the CD1d-TCR interaction in presence of SLAM receptor ligation allows high expression of transcription factor Egr2, thereby enhancing transition into post-positive selection stage 0 iNKT cells (CD24^{Hi}, CD69^{Hi}) [20–23]. The increased expression of Egr2 subsequently allows expression of the TF PLZF, defined as the stage 1 iNKT cell (CD24^{Lo} CD44^{Lo}) [24–28]. Further rounds of cell division and expansion leads to transition into stage 2 iNKT cells (CD24^{Lo} CD44^{Hi} NK1.1$^-$) and stage 3 (CD24^{Lo} CD44^{Hi} NK1.1$^+$) [26–28]. Stage 2 and 3 of iNKT cells can be exported to the periphery where they terminally differentiate into iNKT (PLZF^{Lo}), iNKT (PLZF^{int}), and iNKT (PLZF^{Hi}) lineages, although there is plasticity within these subsets [26–28]. The stage 2 iNKT cells can differentiate into iNKT2 and iNKT17 subsets characterized by expression of the TFs GATA3 and RORγt, respectively [28–30]. The stage 3 iNKT cells differentiate into the iNKT1 subset characterized by expression of the TF Tbet, although an alternate mechanism for iNKT1 cells include direct differentiation from CD4/CD8 double negative CD25/CD44 double negative (DN4) thymocytes [28–30]. Similar to their conventional T cell counterparts, iNKT1 cells produce IFNγ, iNKT2 cells produce IL-4 and IL-13, while iNKT17 cells produce IL-17 and IL-22 [28–30]. The transcriptional regulation of these sublineages has been increasingly investigated to identify additional transcription factors that regulate their development and function. These studies have shown that Id2/3, ThPOK, Pak2 and Hdac3 are important for differentiation into iNKT1, and that the function of LEF1 and NKAP are important for the differentiation of iNKT2 and iNKT17 cells respectively [15–17, 28, 31–36]. Furthermore, an inverse relationship in expression of select transcription factors were observed in these iNKT cell subsets such that while iNKT1 cells are Id2^{Hi} Id3^{Lo} PLZF^{Lo}, iNKT2 cells are Id2^{Lo} Id3^{Hi} PLZF^{Hi}, and iNKT17 cells are intermediate for these transcription factors [15–17, 28, 31–36] (Fig. 1).

1.3 Type II NKT Cells

Like Type I iNKT cells, Type II NKT cells are CD1d restricted [37, 38]; however, unlike Type I iNKT cells, Type II NKT cells do not have a unique marker (nor do their TcRs bind to CD1d/α-GalCer tetramers that allow identification, like the Type I iNKT cells) capable of defining the cell subsets. Thus, studies of Type II NKT cells use an indirect approach to determine the presence or role of these cells in immunity. $Jα18^{-/-}$ and $CD1d^{-/-}$ mice have been used as models to study the effects of type II NKT cells on infections [39]. $Jα18^{-/-}$ mice are not able to generate a Vα14-Jα18 TCR chain, thus they lack Type I NKT cells while $CD1d^{-/-}$ mice lack both Type I and II NKT cells. Differences in the phenotypes in these mice following infections help infer the role of Type II NKT cells. As discussed previously, a unique feature that allows for the detection of Type I iNKT cells is that they bind to the α-GalCer-loaded CD1d tetramer [38]. While Type II NKT cells do not respond to α-GalCer presented on CD1d, different subsets

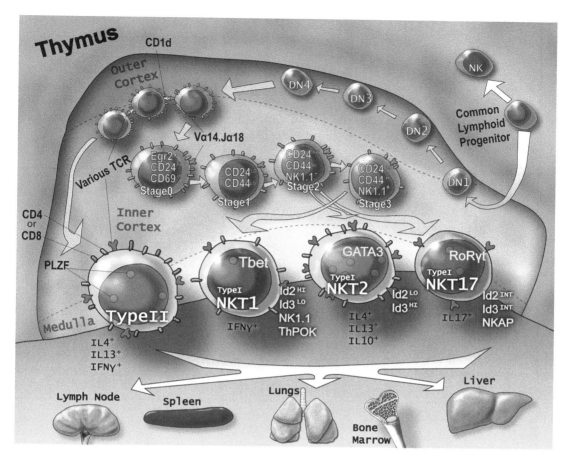

Fig. 1 NKT cells develop from common lymphoid progenitor cells that enter the thymus and undergo canonical DN1-DN4 maturation. At the $CD4^+/CD8^+$ double-positive (DP) cell stage, T cells expressing specific TCR variants undergo activation and selection by nonclassical MHC CD1d-expressing DP cells presenting endogenous glycolipids, rather than by dendritic cells as is the case for conventional T cells. DP cells expressing the invariant TCR (Mouse) [(V)Vα14-Jα18 (J)Vβ8.2, Vβ7, Vβ2] (Human) [(V)Vα24-JαQ, (J)Vβ11] become stimulated to differentiate toward **Type I NKT** cells which are defined as either **NKT1** (PLZF^{Lo}, Id2^{Hi}, Id3^{Lo}, Tbet$^+$, CD4^{Lo}, TCRB^{Lo}, IFNγ^+, NK1.1$^+$, CD122$^+$, IL-4$^+$), **NKT2** (PLZ^{Hi}, Id2^{Hi}, Id3^{Lo}, GATA3$^+$, CD4$^+$, TCRB^{Hi}, IL-4$^+$, IL-13$^+$, IL-10$^+$, PD-1$^+$), or **NKT17** (PLZF^{int}, Id2^{int}, Id3^{int}, RORγt$^+$, CD4$^-$, TCRB^{int}, IL-17$^+$, CD138$^+$, CCR6$^+$) through a common progenitor, stage 2 iNKT (CD24^{Lo}, CD44^{Hi}, NK1.1$^-$). DP cells expressing a diverse range of CD1d-restricted TCRs can be similarly stimulated to become **Type II NKT cells** (CD4$^{+/-}$, CD8$^+$, IL-4$^+$, IL-13$^+$, IFNγ^+)

react to different ligands including sulfatide, β-galactosylceramide, phosphatidylglycerol, phosphatidylinositol, and diphosphatidylglycerol presented on CD1d [40, 41]. Type II NKT cells are also characterized by the production of IL-4 and IL-13 and the expression of PLZF [42]. These IL-4$^+$, IL-13$^+$, PLZF^{int} Type II NKT cells have been suggested to differentiate from the IL-4$^+$, IL-13$^+$ PLZF$^+$ Type I NKT2 subset.

1.4 Detection of NKT Cells

There are a number of different markers used to determine the number, percent, and functional characteristics of murine NKT cells. The following protocol can be used to detect Type I and II. Regardless of the NKT cell type of interest, the majority of the procedure will remain the same. However, there will be some variation in the "cell collection" section because lymphocyte extraction varies by organ and tissue type. Carry out the following procedures on ice unless otherwise specified.

2 Materials

RPMI Media.
Heat-inactivated FBS (65 °C for 30 min).
Sodium pyruvate.
Non-essential amino acids.
0.5% HEPES.
L-glutamine.
Penicillin/streptomycin.
6 well plates.
96-well V-bottom plate.
15 mL tubes.
Bucket containing ice.
Dissection board.
Lympholyte-M.
23-gauge needle.
PBS.
Collagenase A.
Dispase II.
gentleMACS tubes.
100 µM cell strainer.
50 mL tubes.
5 mL serological pipettes.
Pipette controller.
Pins.
Tweezer.
Scissors.
70% ethanol.
Spray bottle.
70 µm cell strainer.
10 mL syringe (for the plunger).
Centrifuge (able to spin to 1000 RCF).
Flow cytometer tubes.
Flow cytometer.
Aspirator.
Antibodies (*see* Table 1).

Table 1
List of antibodies used to detect various developmental stages of *i*NKT cells and types based on identifiable surface markers, transcription factors, and cytokine profiles for respective tissues

Natural killer cell		Surface markers	Transcription factors	Cytokines	Tissues	References
Early development stage(s)	0	$CD4^+8^+$ $CD24^{Hi}$ $CD69^{Hi}$			Thymus	[20–23]
	1	$CD4^+8^+$ $TCR\beta^+$ $CD24^{Lo}$ $CD44^{Lo}$	$EGR2^+$ $PLZF^+$		Thymus	[24–28]
	2	$CD4^+8^+$ $TCR\beta^+$ $CD24^{Lo}$ $CD44^{Hi}$ $NK1.1^-$			Thymus	[26–28]
	3	$CD4^+8^+$ $TCR\beta^+$ $CD24^{Lo}$ $CD44^{Hi}$ $NK1.1^+$			Thymus	[26–28]
Type I						
NKT1		CD1d tetramer$^+$ $CD4^+$ NK1.1	$PLZF^{Lo}$ $Tbet^+$ $Id2^{Hi}$ $Id3^{Lo}$ $ThPOK^+$	$IFN\gamma^+$ $IL4^+$	Liver, spleen, thymus	[8, 9, 15–17, 28, 31–36] [28–30]
NKT2		CD1d tetramer$^+$ $CD4^+$	$PLZF^{Hi}$ $GATA3^+$ $Id2^{Lo}$ $Id3^{Hi}$	$IL4^+$ $IL13^+$ $IL10^+$	LN	[9, 28–30] [9]
NKT17		CD1d tetramer$^+$ $CD4^-8^-$ $CD138^+$ $CCR6^+$	$PLZF^{Int}$ $Id2^{Int}$ $Id3^{Int}$	$IL17^+$ $IL22^+$	Lung, LN	[9, 28–30] [15–17, 28, 31–36]
Type II		$CD4^{+/-}$ $CD8^+$	$PLZF^{Int-Hi}$	$IL4^+$ $IL13^+$ $IFN\gamma^+$	Unclear	[42]

3 Methods

3.1 Prepare Solutions

1. Make media solution to be used for resuspension of isolated single cells from specific: RPMI base, 10% heat-inactivated FBS (65 °C for 30 min), 1 mM sodium pyruvate, 1 mM non-essential amino acid, 0.5% HEPES, 1 mM L-glutamine, and 100 U/mL penicillin/streptomycin.

2. Insert one 70 μM filter per well of a 6 well plates.

3. Add 2 mL of media to each well (*see* **Note 1**).

4. Required antibodies (*see* Table 1).

3.2 Cell Collection

1. Place 6 well plate in ice bucket.

2. Euthanize the mouse according to IACUC-approved method (this usually entails the use of carbon dioxide and/or cervical dislocation).

3. Pin mouse paws to a dissection board with ventral side facing up.

4. Sterilize mouse fur using 70% ethanol with a spray bottle.

5. Lift up the mouse skin with tweezers with your nondominant hand and make an incision with your scissors and cut all the way up to the lower jaw and pin the skin down (*see* **Note 2**).

6. Isolate lymphocytes from organ(s):
   (a) Thymus.
      - The thymus is above the heart; it appears white and has two lobes. Pluck the thymus and immediately place it in a well of the 6 well plate on ice.
      - Isolate lymphocytes from the thymus by gently dissociating it through a 70 μm cell strainer using the seal portion of a 10 mL plunger.
      - Use the ice bucket to slant the plate at a 10° so the media pools preferentially at the bottom of the well.
      - With a 1000 μL pipette, pull 1000 μL of the cell suspension and wash the well to collect the majority of cells.
      - After most of the cells are pooled, filter them through the filter three times to remove large tissues.
      - Collect the samples into a 15 mL tube.
      - Bring the volume of each sample to 2 mL with complete media and count the number of cells.
   (b) Liver.
      - Obtain 10 mL syringe and 23-gauge needle and flip the liver lobes.

- Inject 10 mL of PBS in the hepatic vein; this will cause it to turn white.

- With the same needle, inject 2–5 mL 0.05% collagenase A and dispase II.

- Place the liver in gentleMACS tube with 3 mL of complete medium and dissociate tissue with gentle-MACS dissociator machine or follow procedure as aii-iv and then go to step bvi using a 100 μM filter.

- Place 100 μM filter on top of a 50 mL tube and filter homogenized tissue through the filter and rinse the filter with 5 mL of 2% FBS in PBS.

- Spin tubes at 400 RCF, for 5 min, and then aspirate supernatant.

- Resuspend the pellet in 10 mL PBS.

- Separate the cell suspension by equal parts into two 15 mL tubes.

- Slowly add 5 mL of lympholyte M to the bottom of each tube with a serological pipette and pipette controller while slowly pulling out of the liquid as it is being dispended.

- Centrifuge at 1200 RCF at room temperature for 20 min, 5 accelerate, and 0 decelerate settings.

- Extract the interface layer (around 5 mL) with a 1000 μL pipette and transfer into a 15 mL tube until the cloudy layer has been completely removed.

- Centrifuge 800 RCF for 10 min and aspirate the buffer while not disturbing the cell pellet.

- Resuspend the pellet into 1 mL of complete media and count the number of cells.

7. In a 96-well V-bottom plate and add desired cell number per well, plate extra wells for single cells controls (one well for each antibody color).

8. Make surface staining master mix: most antibodies can be stained at 1 μL:200 μL (antibody:PBS), but this may vary depending on the source of product. Make enough antibody mixture so that each sample will have 35 μL per well. The single cell controls can be stained with 100 μL of PBS with 0.5 μL antibody stock.

9. Pellet cells while in the plate in a centrifuge with 1000 RCF for 1 min.

10. Remove the media while being careful not to disrupt the cell pellet.

11. Aliquot 35 μL of the antibody master mix to each well. Resuspend the cells in the staining mixture.

12. Incubate the cells for 20–30 min at room temperature and away from light (*see* **Note 3**).

13. Resuspend cells with 200 μL of 1× PBS and centrifuge 1000 RCF for 1 min.

14. Remove the media while being careful not to disrupt the cell pellet.

15. Aspirate media off and add 250–300 μL to each well.

16. Resuspend cells in 250–300 μL of 1:1 ratio of PBS and media.

17. Transfer the cells into a flow cytometer tube and run the samples within 2 days' time (*see* **Note 4**).

4 Notes

1. The volume of media you will add will vary depending on the organ of tissue of interest.

2. The initial incision cut may vary depending on your organ or tissue of interest.

3. Make sure to stain the cells at the same time point between various experiments.

4. After cells are extracted from the mouse, the quality of the cells decrease over time, impacting the staining and subsequent analyses. It is best to run samples the same day of collection and wait no longer than the second day.

References

1. Godfrey D, Hammond K, Poulton L, Smyth M, Baxter A (2000) NKT cells: facts, functions and fallacies. Immunol Today 21:573–583

2. Berzins S, Uldrich A, Pellicci D, McNab F, Kayakawa Y, Smyth M, Godfrey D (2004) Parallels and distinctions between T and NKT cell development in the thymus. Immunol Cell Biol 82:269–275

3. Emoto M, Kaufmann S (2003) Liver NKT cells: an account of heterogeneity. Trends Immunol 24:364–369

4. Zhou D, Mattner J, Cantu C 3rd, Schrantz N, Yin N, Gao Y, Sagiv Y, Hudspeth K, Wu Y et al (2004) Lysosomal glycosphingolipid recognition by NKT cells. Science 306:1786–1789

5. Hansen D, Schofield L (2004) Regulation of immunity and pathogenesis in infectious diseases by CD1d-restricted NKT cells. Int J Parasitol 34(1):15–25

6. Crowe N, Uldrich A, Kyparissoudis K, Hammond K, Hayakawa Y, Sidobre S, Keating R, Kronenberg M, Smyth M, Godfrey D (2003) Glycolipid antigen drives rapid expansion and sustained cytokine production by NK T cells. J Immunol 171(8):4020–4027

7. Gadue P, Stein P (2002) NK T cell precursors exhibit differential cytokine regulation and require Itk for efficient maturation. J Immunol 169:2397–2406

8. Stenstrom M, Skold M, Ericsson A, Beaudoin L, Sidobre S, Kronenberg M, Leheren A, Cardell S (2004) Surface receptors identify mouse NK1.1+ T cell subsets distinguished by function and T cell receptor type. Eur J Immunol 34:56–65

9. Gumperz J, Miyake S, Yamamura T, Brenner M (2002) Functionally distinct subsets of CD1d-restricted natural killer T cells revealed by CD1d tetramer staining. J Exp Med 195:625–636

10. Pellicci D, Hammond K, Uldrich A, Baxter A, Smyth M, Godfrey D (2002) A natural killer T (NKT) cell developmental pathway iInvolving

a thymus-dependent NK1.1(−)CD4(+) CD1d-dependent precursor stage. J Exp Med 195:835–844

11. Godfrey D, Stankovic S, Baxter A (2010) Raising the NKT cell family. Nat Immunol 11:197–206

12. Cui J, Shin T, Kawano T, Sato H, Kondo E, Toura I, Kaneko Y, Koseki H, Kanno M, Taniguchi M (1997) Requirement for Valpha14 NKT cells in IL-12-mediated rejection of tumors. Science 278:1623–1626

13. Jordan M, Fletcher J, Baxter A (2004) Genetic control of NKT cell numbers. Immunol Cell Biol 82:276–284

14. Griewank K, Borowski C, Rietdijk S, Wang N, Julien A, Wei D, Mamchak A, Terhorst C, Bendelac A (2007) Homotypic interactions mediated by Slamf1 and Slamf6 receptors control NKT cell lineage development. Immunity 27:751–762

15. D'Cruz LM, Stradner MH, Yang CY, Goldrath AW (2014) E and Id proteins influence invariant NKT cell sublineage differentiation and proliferation. J Immunol 192(5):2227–2236

16. Verykokakis M, Krishnamoorthy V, Iavarone A, Lasorella A, Sigvardsson M, Kee BL (2013) Essential functions for ID proteins at multiple checkpoints in invariant NKT cell development. J Immunol 191(12):5973–5983

17. Thapa P, Das J, McWilliams D, Shapiro M, Sundsbak R, Nelson-Holte M, Tangen S, Anderson J, Desiderio S, Hiebert S, Sant'angelo DB, Shapiro VS (2013) The transcriptional repressor NKAP is required for the development of iNKT cells. Nat Commun 4:1582

18. White AJ, Lucas B, Jenkinson WE, Anderson G (2018) Invariant NKT cells and control of the thymus medulla. J Immunol 200(10):3333–3339

19. Godfrey DI, Berzins SP (2007) Control points in NKT-cell development. Nat Rev Immunol 7(7):505–518

20. Krovi SH, Gapin L (2018) Invariant natural killer T cell subsets-more than just developmental intermediates. Front Immunol 9:1393

21. Seiler MP, Mathew R, Liszewski MK, Spooner CJ, Spooner C, Barr K, Meng F, Singh H, Bendelac A (2012) Elevated and sustained expression of the transcription factors Egr1 and Egr2 controls NKT lineage differentiation in response to TCR signaling. Nat Immunol 13(3):264–271

22. Lazarevic V, Zullo AJ, Schweitzer MN, Staton TL, Gallo EM, Crabtree GR, Glimcher LH (2009) The gene encoding early growth response 2, a target of the transcription factor

NFAT, is required for the development and maturation of natural killer T cells. Nat Immunol 10(3):306–313

23. Kumar A, Suryadevara N, Hill TM, Bezbradica JS, Van Kaer L, Joyce S (2017) Natural killer T cells: an ecological evolutionary developmental biology perspective. Front Immunol 8:1858

24. Kovalovsky D, Uche OU, Eladad S, Hobbs RM, Yi W, Alonzo E, Chua K, Eidson M, Kim HJ, Im JS, Pandolfi PP, Sant'Angelo DB (2008) The BTB-zinc finger transcriptional regulator PLZF controls the development of invariant natural killer T cell effector functions. Nat Immunol 9(9):1055–1064

25. Savage AK, Constantinides MG, Han J, Picard D, Martin E, Li B, Lantz O, Bendelac A (2008) The transcription factor PLZF directs the effector program of the NKT cell lineage. Immunity 29(3):391–403

26. Kwon DI, Lee YJ (2017) Lineage differentiation program of invariant natural killer T cells. Immune Network 17(6):365–377

27. Constantinides MG, Bendelac A (2013) Transcriptional regulation of the NKT cell lineage. Curr Opin Immunol 25(2):161–167

28. Shissler SC, Webb TJ (2019) The ins and outs of type I iNKT cell development. Mol Immunol 105:116–130

29. Watarai H, Sekine-Kondo E, Shigeura T, Motomura Y, Yasuda T, Satoh R, Yoshida H, Kubo M, Kawamoto H, Koseki H, Taniguchi M (2012) Development and function of invariant natural killer T cells producing T(h)2- and T(h)17-cytokines. PLoS Biol 10(2):e1001255

30. Wang H, Hogquist KA (2018) How lipid-specific T cells become effectors: the differentiation of iNKT subsets. Front Immunol 9:1450

31. Li J, Wu D, Jiang N, Zhuang Y (2013) Combined deletion of Id2 and Id3 genes reveals multiple roles for E proteins in invariant NKT cell development and expansion. J Immunol 191(10):5052–5064

32. Wang L, Carr T, Xiong Y, Wildt KF, Zhu J, Feigenbaum L, Bendelac A, Bosselut R (2010) The sequential activity of Gata3 and Thpok is required for the differentiation of CD1d-restricted CD4+ NKT cells. Eur J Immunol 40(9):2385–2390

33. Thapa P, Romero Arocha S, Chung JY, Sant'Angelo DB, Shapiro VS (2017) Histone deacetylase 3 is required for iNKT cell development. Sci Rep 7(1):5784

34. O'Hagan KL, Zhao J, Pryshchep O, Wang CR, Phee H (2015) Pak2 controls acquisition of NKT cell fate by regulating expression of the transcription factors PLZF and Egr2. J Immunol 195(11):5272–5284

35. Carr T, Krishnamoorthy V, Yu S, Xue HH, Kee BL, Verykokakis M (2015) The transcription factor lymphoid enhancer factor 1 controls invariant natural killer T cell expansion and Th2-type effector differentiation. J Exp Med 212(5):793–807

36. Gapin L (2016) Development of invariant natural killer T cells. Curr Opin Immunol 39:68–74

37. Cardell S, Tangri S, Chan S, Kronenberg M, Benoist C, Mathis D (1995) CD1-restricted CD4+ T cells in major histocompatibility complex class II-deficient mice. J Exp Med 182(4):993–1004

38. Park SH, Weiss A, Benlagha K, Kyin T, Teyton L, Bendelac A (2001) The mouse CD1d-restricted repertoire is dominated by a few autoreactive T cell receptor families. J Exp Med 193(8):893–904

39. Genardi S, Visvabharathy L, Cao L, Morgun E, Cui Y, Qi C, Chen YH, Gapin L, Berdyshev E, Wang CR (2020) Type II natural killer T cells contribute to protection against systemic methicillin-resistant Staphylococcus aureus infection. Front Immunol 11:610010

40. Rhost S, Löfbom L, Rynmark BM, Pei B, Månsson JE, Teneberg S, Blomqvist M, Cardell SL (2012) Identification of novel glycolipid ligands activating a sulfatide-reactive, CD1d-restricted, type II natural killer T lymphocyte. Eur J Immunol 42(11):2851–2860

41. Tatituri RV, Watts GF, Bhowruth V, Barton N, Rothchild A, Hsu FF, Almeida CF, Cox LR, Eggeling L, Cardell S, Rossjohn J, Godfrey DI, Behar SM, Besra GS, Brenner MB, Brigl M (2013) Recognition of microbial and mammalian phospholipid antigens by NKT cells with diverse TCRs. Proc Natl Acad Sci U S A 110(5):1827–1832

42. Zhao J, Weng X, Bagchi S, Wang CR (2014) Polyclonal type II natural killer T cells require PLZF and SAP for their development and contribute to CpG-mediated antitumor response. Proc Natl Acad Sci U S A 111(7):2674–2679

Chapter 2

Genetic Studies of Natural Glycosphingolipid Ligands for NKT Cells

Dapeng Zhou, Chengfeng Xia, Peng G. Wang, Zhiyuan Li, Wenpeng Zhang, Guanghui Ni, and Jiaxi Cheng

Abstract

Glycosphingolipids (GSL) are natural ligands of NKT cells. Several laboratories have reported the in vitro activity of isoglobotriosylceramide (iGb3) in stimulating NKT cells. However, the knockout mice of iGb3 synthase showed no deficiency in development and function of NKT cells. There is a lack of knowledge on the genetics of redundant natural glycosphingolipid ligands. We have identified additional glycosphingolipid with stimulatory activity to NKT cells, including fucosyl lactosylceramide (H antigen). Here we describe the procedures to generate mice with deficiencies in Fut1, Fut2, and Sec1 genes to deplete H antigen through BAC engineering for the generation of ES cell-targeting construct, as well as the mice with deficiency of both blood group H-GSL ligand and isoglobotriosylceramide.

Key words Blood group H, α-2-Fucosyltransferease, Isoglobotriosylceramide, Natural killer T cells

Abbreviations

Blood group A	GalNAc α3 Fuc α2 Gal β
Blood group B	Gal α3 Fuc α2 Gal β
Blood group H	Fuc α2 Gal β
CFG	Consortium of functional glycomics
Fut1	α-2 fucosyltransferase I
Fut2	α-2 fucosyltransferase II
NKT	natural killer T cells
Sec1	α-2 fucosyltransferase III

Supplementary Information The online version of this chapter (https://doi.org/10.1007/978-1-0716-1775-5_2) contains supplementary material, which is available to authorized users.

Chaohong Liu (ed.), *Invariant Natural Killer T-Cells: Methods and Protocols*, Methods in Molecular Biology, vol. 2388,
https://doi.org/10.1007/978-1-0716-1775-5_2,

1   Introduction

Invariant natural killer T (iNKT) cells restrictedly recognize glyco-lipid antigens presented by the major histocompatibility complex class I-like protein CD1d [1–4]. The iNKT cells express natural killer receptors and a conserved, semi-invariant T-cell antigen receptor (TCR) composed of an invariant variable (Vα14)-joining (Jα18) chain (Vα24-Jα18 in human) combined with a limited but not invariant TCRβ repertoire dominated by Vβ8.2, Vβ7, or Vβ2 (Vβ11 in human) [5]. The distinguishing feature of iNKT cells is their capacity to rapidly secrete copious cytokines within minutes to hours of antigenic stimulation. Because of this characteristic release of both T helper 1 (Th1) and Th2 cytokines, including interferon-γ (IFN-γ), interleukin-4 (IL-4), IL-10, IL-12, and IL-13, iNKT cells play a unique role in protection against infection, suppression of autoimmunity, and increase of antitumor immunity and a signifi-cant role in allergic airway inflammation and some other immune system-related diseases and symptoms [6, 7].

The glycosphingolipid α-galactosylceramide (α-GalCer, Fig. 1) was originally discovered in an extract from a marine sponge [8, 9] and was found to strongly activate iNKT cells at very low concen-trations. The salient structural feature that distinguishes α-GalCer from mammalian glycoceramides is the α-linkage between the

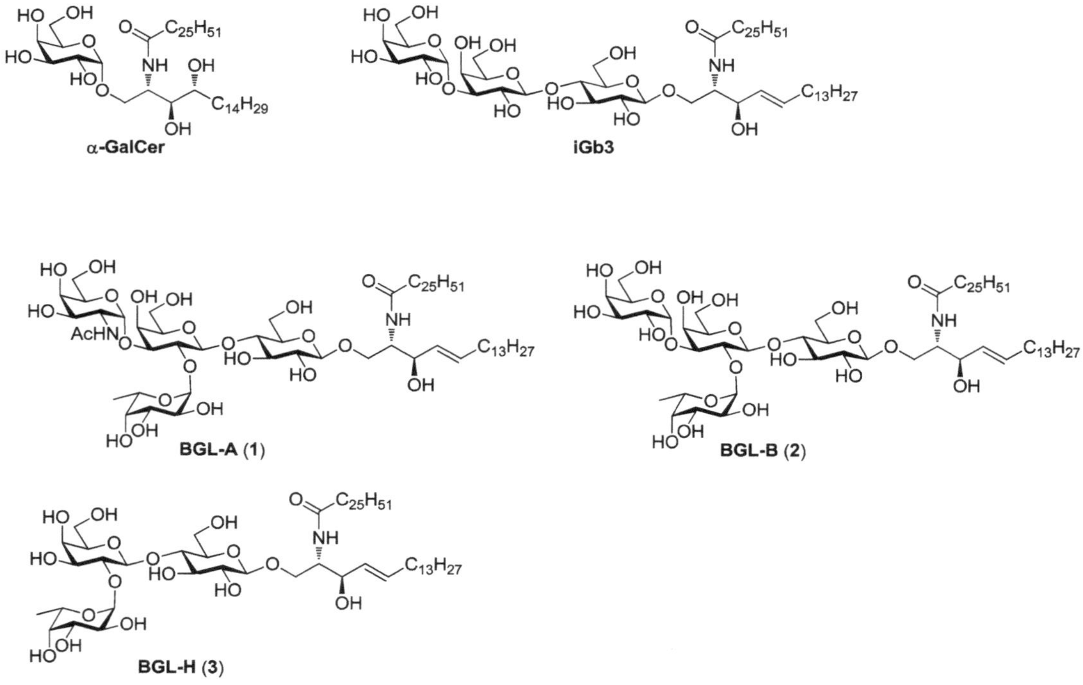

Fig. 1 Structures of α-GalCer, iGb3, and blood group glycosphingolipids

saccharide and ceramide moieties. When this molecule is presented to iNKT cells by antigen-presenting cells, it triggers a rapid, transient, and massive response of iNKT cells, causing accumulation of Th1 and Th2 cytokines and initiation of downstream immunological cascades, including responses to pathogens, tumors, tissue grafts, allergens, and other non-self-agents.

Efficient development of iNKT cells from the T-cell precursor pool in the thymus requires presentation of an endogenous antigen by CD1d to the randomly generated TCR. Although α-GalCer and its analogs from bacterial origin [10–12] exhibits strong iNKT cell stimulation leading to secretion of various cytokines, this glycolipid is not a natural product of mammalian cells. The structures of the mammalian glycolipids that serve as endogenous antigens in the thymus for iNKT cells are still unknown. Identification of these endogenous antigens is essential for understanding the process of iNKT cell maturation in the thymus and the mechanism of its activation. It will also help in exploration of endogenous ligands with different iNKT cell stimulation profiles.

Isoglobotrihexosylceramide (iGb3; Fig. 1) was the first endogenous lysosomal glycolipid reported by several groups to activate iNKT cells from mice and humans, albeit weakly [13]. However, it has been suggested that iGb3 is not a principal endogenous iNKT cell antigen [14, 15]. Gröne et al. generated mice that cannot produce iGb3 because they are deficient in iGb3 synthase (*iGb3S*, also known as α1,3-galactosyltransferase 2 [A3galt2]) [14]. The *iGb3S*$^{-/-}$ mice showed normal numbers of iNKT cells in the thymus, spleen, and liver with selected TCR Vβ chains identical to controls. Upon administration of α-GalCer, activation of iNKT cells and dendritic cells was similar in *iGb3S*$^{-/-}$ and *iGb3S*$^{+/-}$ mice. These results strongly suggest that iGb3 is not required for selection of iNKT cells in the thymus. The presence of iGb3 in mouse and human thymuses remains a controversy, mainly because of conflicting results due to different analytical methods [16–18]. Speak et al. could not detect iGb3 in mouse and human thymuses by high-performance liquid chromatography [16]. Li et al. used ion-trap mass spectrometry to analyze thymic lipids and detected both iGb3 and iGb4 [17, 18].

Thus, even though it is not disputed that iGb3 is a mammalian agonist ligand for iNKT cells, other redundant endogenous antigens that control iNKT cell development must exist. A β-glucosylceramide synthase-deficient cell line, GM95, was shown to be defective in iNKT cell stimulation [19]. β-glucosylceramide was reported as a ligand that activates peripheral NKT cells when co-stimulatory signals to NKT cells are present [20], although there is no evidence that it selects NKT cells during the positive selection stage. β-glucosylceramide does not stimulate autoreactive NKT clones, unlike ligands that mediate positive selection of NKT cells [21]. In thymic organ culture experiments, inhibition of β-glucosylceramide synthesis abolished development of NKT cells but not conventional CD4[+] and CD8[+] T cells, suggesting the role of β-glucosylceramide-derived glycosphingolipids in mediating positive selection of NKT cells [16]. β-glucosylceramide is catalyzed by lactosylceramide synthase to give β-lactosylceramide [22], which is then further extended to different series of glycosylceramides such as the lacto and neolacto series, ganglio series, isoglobo series, and globo series.

During the search for NKT ligands, several groups including ours reported an iGb3-related structure, fucosylated iGb3 (Gal α3 [Fuc α2] Gal β4 Glc β1 Cer), in pig cells [23, 24]. Its precursor Fuc α2 Gal β4 Glc β1 Cer was also identified [24, 25]. This series of findings beg the question whether this iGb3-related structure, which is a type of B blood group glycosphingolipid antigen in human ABO blood group system, is an agonist ligand for NKT cells.

The human ABO blood group system, which is based on the presence or absence of blood group antigens A and B, comprises four major blood groups. Individuals of all four blood groups synthesize blood group glycolipid H (BGL-H), which is the precursor of BGL-A and BGL-B. Individuals of blood group AB catalyze the biosynthesis of both BGL-A and BGL-B, while blood group A individuals and blood group B individuals catalyze only the synthesis of BGL-A or BGL-B, respectively. Blood group O individuals catalyze the synthesis of neither BGL-A nor BGL-B, only BGL-H (Fig. 2). The blood group carbohydrate structures A, B,

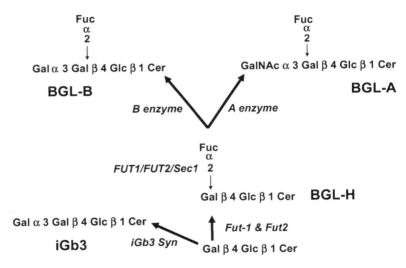

Fig. 2 Genetics of iGb3-related blood group glycosphingolipids. Fut1, α 1,2 fucosyltransferase 1 (EC 2.4.1.69); Fut2, α 1,2 fucosyltransferase 2 (EC 2.4.1.69); iGb3 Syn, α 1,3 galactosyltransferase 2 (EC 2.4.1.87); A enzyme, α 1,3 N-acetylgalactosaminyltransferase (EC 2.4.1.41); B enzyme, beta-D-galactosyl-1,4-N-acetyl-D-glucosaminide α 1,3 galactosyltransferase (EC 2.4.1.87)

and H are found at the termini of oligosaccharide chains of glycolipids and glycoproteins on the surface of erythrocytes and of
endothelial and most epithelial cells [26, 27]. Pigs have a blood
group AO system comparable to the ABO system in humans [28],
and two of the prospective antigens, BGL-A and BGL-H, have
been characterized in pigs by the Breimer group [25]. Mice, in
contrast to pig and human, have only a cisAB blood group, which is
encoded by a cisAB enzyme that has both α3-galactosyltransferase
and α3-acetylgalactosaminyltransferase enzyme activities [29]. We
have conducted in vitro experiments aimed at revealing the activities of these blood group lipids as stimulatory ligands for NKT
cells.

The biosynthesis of blood group ABO structures is initiated by
α-2-fucosyltransfearse (EC: 2.4.1.3441). Three members have
been cloned for mouse α-2-fucosyltransfearse gene family. Enzyme
activities were reported for mouse Fut1 and Fut2, while no enzyme
activity has been reported for Sec1 [30, 31].

The Fut1 and Fut2 gene are located in the same chromosome
with a 30 kb distance (Fig. 3a). This short genetic distance prevents
the homologous recombination process required for generating
double knockout mice. In this study, we sequentially depleted
Fut1 gene and Fut2/Sec1 gene in ES cells and generated triple
knockout mice with total deficiency of α1,2-fucosyltransferase
enzyme. We also generated mice deficiency of all blood group H
ligands and iGb3, which serve as a tool for further in vivo assays of
endogenous ligands for NKT cells.

2   Materials

2.1   Mice and Embryonic Stem (ES) Cells

1. Fut1 KO mice, B6.129-Fut1^{tm1Sdo}/J, Jackson Laboratory.
2. Fut2 KO mice, B6.129X1-*Fut2*^{tm1Sdo}/J, Jackson Laboratory.
3. ES cell clone iTL BA1 (C57BL/6 x 129/SvEv), Ingenious Targeting Laboratory, Ronkonkoma, NY.

2.2   GSLs (Chemically Synthesized, Note 1)

1. Isoglobotriosylceramide (iGb3).
2. Blood group H GSL, Fuc α2 Gal β4 Glc β1 Cer.
3. Blood group A, GalNAc α3 Fuc α2 Gal β4 Glc β1 Cer.
4. Blood group B, Gal α3 Fuc α2 Gal β4 Glc β1 Cer.

2.3   NKT Cell Hybridoma Cells (Note 2)

The DN32.D3 [21], representing iNKT cells, were from Dr. Albert
Bendelac (University of Chicago). These hybridomas were maintained in RPMI1640 medium containing 10% fetal calf serum
(FCS), 2 mM sodium pyruvate, 2 mM L-glutamine, and 50 μM
2-mercaptoethanol.

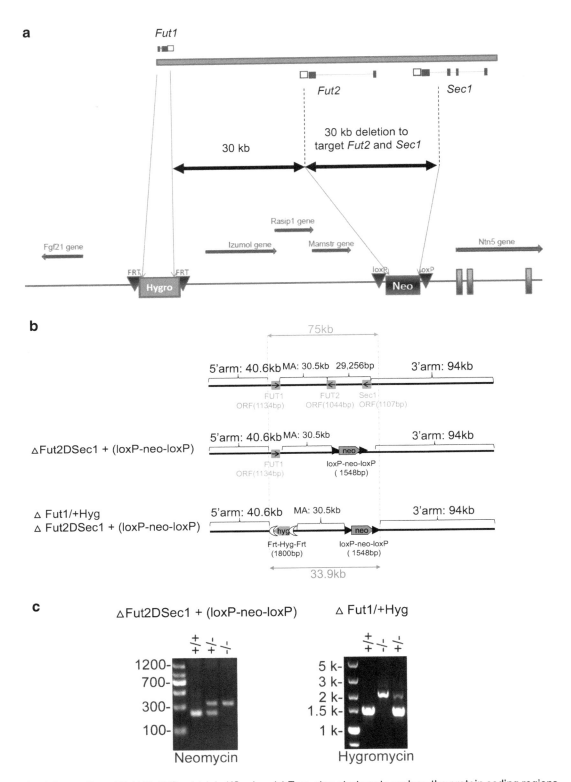

Fig. 3 Generation of Fut1/Fut2/Sec1 triple KO mice. (**a**) Two-step strategy to replace the protein coding regions (marked as empty boxes) of Fut1, Fut2, and Sec1 by targeting constructs containing neomycin and hygromycin selection markers; (**b**) scheme of genetic locus for wild-type ES cell line, △Fut2DSec1 + (loxP-neo-loxP) ES cell line, and △ Fut1/+Hyg △ Fut2DSec1 + (loxP-neo-loxP) ES cell line; (**c**) PCR results of the product lengths of wild-type allele, △ Fut1/+Hyg allele, and △Fut2DSec1 + (loxP-neo-loxP) allele

2.4   Antibodies and Glycolipid Tetramers

The PBS57-loaded mouse CD1d tetramer was from NIAID tetramer facility [32].

The anti-mouse CD3 antibody was from BioLegend.

3   Methods

3.1   Generation of Mice Deficient of FUT1, FUT2, and Sec1 (Note 3)

1. Engineering of Bacmid

   The Fut1, Fut2, and Sec1 loci are located in chromosome 7 in a 77 kb region (Table 1). A two-step knockout strategy was used to generate the mice with protein-coding regions of all three genes mutated. Firstly, a LoxP-neomycin-LoxP cassette was used to replace a 30 kb region which contains protein coding regions of both Fut2 and Sec1. Secondly, a FRT-hygromycin-FRT cassette was used to replace the protein coding region of Fut1. BAC clone RP23-223G1 was purchased from Children's Hospital Oakland Research Institute BACPAC Resources Center, and mutated constructs were made by Red/ET recombination technology [33] (Fig. 3b).

2. Generation of Fut1/Fut2/Sec1 Triple KO Mice

   Mutated constructs were electroporated into iTL BA1 (C57BL/6 × 129/SvEv) by Ingenious Targeting Laboratory, NY. Hybrid embryonic stem cells and ES clones bearing mutated loci were selected by neomycin and hygromycin resistance sequentially. Targeted iTL BA1 (C57BL/6 × 129/SvEv) hybrid embryonic stem cells were microinjected into C57BL/6 blastocysts. Resulting chimeras with a high percentage agouti coat color were mated to wild-type C57BL/6 N mice to generate F1 heterozygous offspring. Tail DNA was analyzed as described below from pups with agouti or black coat color. Primers F1385hygS and R1385hygS (Table 2, Data S1) were used to determine the mutation of Fut1 locus (replaced by FRT-hygromycin-FRT cassette). Primers Wt1, R1385neoS, and N2 were used to determine the mutation of Fut2 and Sec1 locus (replaced by LoxP-neomycin-LoxP cassette). Triple knockout mice with deletion of Fut1, Fut2, and Sec1 were genotyped by PCR (Fig. 3c, Table 2).

Table 1
Location of Fut1, Fut2, and Sec1 in mouse genome

Gene	Chromosome	Location	Centimorgan	Strand
Fut1	7	45617289-45621059	29.39	+
Fut2	7	45648591-45666394	29.41	−
Sec1	7	45677686-45694402	29.43	−

Table 2
Primers used for genotyping for Fut1/Fut2/Sec1 KO mice

Loci	Primer	Sequence	PCR product length
Hygromycin	F1385hygS	5'- CTG TGA GGT TCC CAG AAG GC -3'	1.47 kb for WT
	R1385hygS	5'- GCT TAC AGT GCT GAC TTG GG -3'	1.47 kb and 2.14 kb for heterozygous
			2.14 kb for homozygous
Neomycin	wt1	5'- AGA GGT AGA AGG TGG AGA GG -3'	231 bp for WT
	N2	5'- TTC CTC GTG CTT TAC GGT ATC G -3'	333 bp and 231 bp for heterozygous
	R1385neoS	5'- AGT AAG ACC CAT CAC GTT G -3'	333 bp for homozygous

3. PCR Reaction to Amplify the Hygromycin Cassette

   Tail DNA was extracted by TransDirect mouse genotyping kit (Transgen, Beijing, China). To amplify the hygromycin cassette, tail DNA samples from correctly targeted mice were amplified with primers F1385hygS and R1385hygS. F1385hygS is located upstream of the Hygro cassette, and R1385hygS is located downstream of the Hygro cassette. F1385hygS/R1385hygS amplifies a wild-type fragment of 1.47 kb in length. Hygro cassette presence is indicated by a band 2.14 kb long. PCR for Hygro cassette was performed by Expand High Fidelity PCR System (Roche catalog # 04738276001), in a 25 μL mixture containing the following: 1.5 μL DNA (100 ng).

   200 μM dNTP.

   4% DMSO.

   1 μM Primers F1385hygS/R1385hygS.

   2.5 μL PCR buffer with 15 mM MgCl2.

   Add ddH$_2$O to final volume 25 μL.

   After a 10 min hot start at 99 °C, 0.125 μL of Taq polymerase was added to each PCR sample followed by a layer of two drops of mineral oil. Then the reaction was at 94 °C for 5 min, 95 °C × 30 s followed by 58 °C × 1 min (annealing step), and 72 °C for 2 min and 10 s (elongation step), for 35 cycles. The PCR product was run on a 0.8% gel with a 1 KB ladder as reference.

4. PCR Reaction to Amplify the Neomycin Cassette

   Tail DNA samples from correctly targeted mice were amplified with primers wt1, R1385neoS, and N2. N2 is located inside the Neo cassette, R1385neoS is located downstream of the Neo cassette, and wt1 is located on the targeted wild-type sequence replaced with the Neo cassette. Primer set wt1/R1385neoS amplifies a wild-type band 231 bp in length, and N2/R1385neoS amplifies a fragment of 333 bp in length indicating Neo presence. PCR for neomycin cassette was performed by the Exo-PCR System (Roche catalog# 04738420001) in a 25 μL mixture containing the following: 1.5 μL DNA.

200 μM dNTP.

20% GC rich solution.

1 μM Primers wt1, R1385neoS, and N2.

2.5 μL PCR buffer with 15 mM MgCl2.

Add ddH$_2$O to final volume 25 μL.

After a 5 min hot start at 99 °C, 0.125 μL of Taq polymerase was added to each PCR sample followed by a layer of two drops of mineral oil. Then the reaction was at 94 °C for 5 min, 94 °C × 30 s followed by 60 °C × 1 min (annealing step), and 72 °C for 1 min (elongation step), for 30 cycles. The PCR product was run on a 2% gel with a 100 bp ladder as reference.

3.2 Generation of Mice Deficient of iGb3 Synthase (A3galt2)

A3galt2 knockout mice were generated by CRISPR/Cas9-based approach.

1. Two sgRNAs (ACTGAGCTGGACAACCCTTGGGG GTGT GGGAACCCCAATACCT AGG) were designed by CRISPR design tool (http://crispr.mit.edu) to target either a region upstream of the exon 5 or 3′UTR (Fig. 4) and then were screened for on-target activity using a Universal CRISPR Activity Assay (UCATM, Biocytogen Inc., Beijing, China) [34].

2. T7 promoter sequence was added to the Cas9 or sgRNA templates by PCR. Cas9 mRNA and sgRNAs were prepared and co-injected into the cytoplasm of fertilized oocytes (one cell stage, C57BL/6 strain).

3. The injected zygotes were transferred into oviducts of pseudo-pregnant females (Kunming strain, Biocytogen Inc., Beijing, China) to generate F0 mice. F0 mice with expected genotype were confirmed by PCR analysis of tail genomic DNA. Two

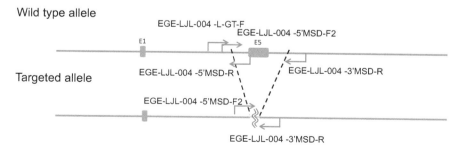

Fig. 4 Generation of A3galt2 KO mice

Table 3
Primers used for genotyping of A3galT2 KO mice

Primer	Sequence (5′-3′)	PCR product (bp)
EGE-LJL-004-5′MSD-F	CAAGGGTGGACAGACCCTTG TAGG	552 for mutant allele, 1822 for wild type allele
EGE-LJL-004-5′MSD-R	GTGTTCCAGGTACTTCTCCAGG TAC	
EGE-LJL-004-3′MSD-F	GCCAACATCTTTGGCACTACC TTAAG	598 for wild type allele
EGE-LJL-004-3′MSD-R	GTAACA TGAAGGAAGAGCCAGCATAGC	

pairs of primers were designed to amplify the exon 5-deleted mutant allele and the wild-type allele, respectively (Fig. 4, Table 3). F0 mice were mated with C57BL/6 mice to establish germline-transmitted F1 heterozygous mice.

4. PCR reaction to amplify the wild-type allele: Tail DNA samples from correctly targeted mice were amplified with primers EGE-LJL-004-L-GT-F and EGE-LJL-004-5′MSD-R, which generate a 598 bp product in wild-type allele but no signal in mutant allele. PCR for wild-type allele was performed in 10 μL volume of mixture containing the following:
1 μL tail DNA (100 ng).

1 μM Primers EGE-LJL-004-L-GT-F and EGE-LJL-004-5′MSD-R.

5 μL Easy Mix (from Transgen, Beijing, China).

Add ddH$_2$O to 10 μL.

The PCR reaction was at 94 °C for 5 min, 94 °C × 30 s followed by 62 °C × 30 s (annealing step), and 72 °C for 45 s (elongation step), for 35 cycles. The PCR product was run on a 2% gel with a 100 bp ladder as reference.

5. PCR reaction to amplify the A3galt2 mutant allele: Tail DNA samples from correctly targeted mice were amplified with primers EGE-LJL-004-5′MSD-F2 and EGE-LJL-004-3′MSD-R, which generate a 552 bp product in mutant allele and 1822 bp for the wild-type allele. PCR for mutant allele was performed in 10 μL volume of mixture containing the following:
1 μL tail DNA (100 ng).

1 μM Primers EGE-LJL-004-5′MSD-F2 and EGE-LJL-004-3′MSD-R.

5 μL Easy Mix (from Transgen, Beijing, China).

Add ddH2O to 10 μL.

The PCR reaction was at 94 °C for 5 min, 94 °C × 30 s followed by 62 °C × 30 s (annealing step), and 72 °C for 45 s (elongation step), for 35 cycles. The PCR product was run on a 2% gel with a 100 bp ladder as reference.

3.3 Generation of Mice Deficient of FUT1/FUT2/Sec1/A3galt2

1. FUT1/FUT2/Sec1/A3galt2$^{-/-}$ mice were generated by breeding FUT1/FUT2/Sec1$^{-/-}$ mice and A3galt2$^{-/-}$ mice.

2. The development of NKT cells in FUT1/FUT2/Sec1/A3galt2$^{-/-}$ mice was measured by PBS57/CD1d tetramer staining (*see* **Note 4**).

4 Notes

1. Chemical synthesis of blood-group-related GSL ligands. The GSLs were synthesized as described in Data S4 and S5.

2. Stimulation of NKT cell hybridoma by GSL ligands. The NKT cell hybridomas were stimulated by mouse bone marrow-derived dendritic cells as described in Data S2.

3. This strain has been deposited in Jackson laboratory as B6.Cg-*Fut1*^{tm1Dzhou} Del(7Fut2-Sec1)1Dzhou/J).

4. The development of NKT cells in mice deficient of Fut1/Fut2/Sec1 and A3galt2 (iGb3 synthase) was measured by PBS57/CD1d tetramer staining as described in Data S3.

Acknowledgments

This work was supported by US NIH grant AI079232 (DZ), National Key Research and Development Plan grant 2021YFE0200500 and 2017YFA0505901 (DZ), Fundamental Research Funds for the Central Universities 22120210292 (DZ), National Natural Science Foundation of China grant 81570007 and 31870972 (DZ), Shanghai Science and Technology Committee grant 20410713500, and the Outstanding Clinical Discipline Project of Shanghai Pudong Grant Number: PWYgy2018–10 (DZ). All these sponsors have no roles in the study design or the collection, analysis, and interpretation of data.

References

1. Kronenberg M (2005) Toward an understanding of NKT cell biology: progress and paradoxes. Annu Rev Immunol 23:877–900

2. De Libero G, Mori L (2005) Recognition of lipid antigens by T cells. Nat Rev Immunol 5:485–496

3. Van Kaer L (2005) α-Galactosylceramide therapy for autoimmune diseases: prospects and obstacles. Nat Rev Immunol 5:31–42

4. Porcelli SA, Modlin RL (1999) The CD1 system: antigen-presenting molecules for T cell

recognition of lipids and glycolipids. Annu Rev Immunol 17:297–329

5. Godfrey DI, MacDonald HR, Kronenberg M, Smyth MJ, Van Kaer L (2004) NKT cells: what's in a name? Nat Rev Immunol 4:231–237

6. Taniguchi M, Harada M, Kojo S, Nakayama T, Wakao H (2003) The regulatory role of Va14 NKT cells in innate and acquired immune response. Annu Rev Immunol 21:483–513

7. Major AS, Van Kaer L (2005) The role of natural killer T cells in atherosclerosis. Curr Immunol Rev 1:261–274

8. Natori T, Koezuka Y, Higa T (1993) Agelasphins, novel a-galactosylceramides from the marine sponge *Agelas mauritianus*. Tetrahedron Lett 34:5591–5592

9. Kawano T, Cui J, Koezuka Y, Toura I, Kaneko Y, Motoki K, Ueno H, Nakagawa R, Sato H, Kondo E, Koseki H, Taniguchi M (1997) CD1d-restricted and TCR-mediated activation of Vα14 NKT cells by glycosylceramides. Science 278:1626–1629

10. Mattner J, Debord KL, Ismail N, Goff RD, Cantu C 3rd, Zhou D, Saint-Mezard P, Wang V, Gao Y, Yin N, Hoebe K, Schneewind O, Walker D, Beutler B, Teyton L, Savage PB, Bendelac A (2005) Exogenous and endogenous glycolipid antigens activate NKT cells during microbial infections. Nature 434(7032):525–529

11. Kinjo Y, Wu D, Kim G, Xing GW, Poles MA, Ho DD, Tsuji M, Kawahara K, Wong CH, Kronenberg M (2005) Recognition of bacterial glycosphingolipids by natural killer T cells. Nature 434(7032):520–525

12. Sriram V, Du W, Gervay-Hague J, Brutkiewicz RR (2005) Cell wall glycosphingolipids of Sphingomonas paucimobilis are CD1d-specific ligands for NKT cells. Eur J Immunol 35(6):1692–1701

13. Zhou D et al (2004) Lysosomal glycosphingolipid recognition by NKT cells. Science 306:1786–1789

14. Porubsky S et al (2007) Normal development and function of invariant natural killer T cells in mice with isoglobotrihexosylceramide (iGb3) deficiency. Proc Natl Acad Sci U S A 104:5977–5982

15. Speak AO et al (2007) Implications for invariant natural killer T cell ligands due to the restricted presence of isoglobotrihexosylceramide in mammals. Proc Natl Acad Sci U S A 104:5971–5976

16. Li Y et al (2009) Immunologic glycosphingolipidomics and NKT cell development in mouse thymus. J Proteome Res 8:2740–2751

17. Li Y et al (2008) Sensitive detection of isoglobo and globo series tetraglycosylceramides in human thymus by ion trap mass spectrometry. Glycobiology 18:158–165; Erratum in: Glycobiology 18, 568 (2008)

18. Zhou D (2006) The immunological function of iGb3. Curr Protein Pept Sci 7:325–333

19. Stanic AK et al (2003) Defective presentation of the CD1d1-restricted natural Va14Ja18 NKT lymphocyte antigen caused by beta-D-glucosylceramide synthase deficiency. Proc Natl Acad Sci U S A 100:1849–1854

20. Brennan PJ et al (2011) Invariant natural killer T cells recognize lipid self antigen induced by microbial danger signals. Nat Immunol 12:1202–1211

21. Bendelac A (1995) Positive selection of mouse NK1+ T cells by CD1-expressing cortical thymocytes. J Exp Med 182:2091–2096

22. Chatterjee S, Kolmakova A, Rajesh M (2008) Regulation of lactosylceramide synthase (glucosylceramide beta 1->4 galactosyltransferase); implication as a drug target. Curr Drug Targets 9:272–281

23. Diswall M, Angström J, Schuurman HJ, Dor FJ, Rydberg L, Breimer ME (2007) Studies on glycolipid antigens in small intestine and pancreas from alpha1,3-galactosyltransferase knockout miniature swine. Transplantation 84(10):1348–1356

24. Puga Yung GL, Li Y, Borsig L, Millard AL, Karpova MB, Zhou D, Seebach JD (2012) Complete absence of the αGal xenoantigen and isoglobotrihexosylceramide in α1,3galactosyltransferase knock-out pigs. Xenotransplantation 19(3):196–206

25. Holgersson J, Jovall PA, Samuelsson BE, Breimer ME (1990) Structural characterization of non-acid glycosphingolipids in kidneys of single blood group O and A pigs. J Biochem 108(5):766–777

26. Watkins W (1980) Biochemistry and genetics of the ABO, Lewis, and P blood group systems. Adv Hum Genet 10:1

27. Clausen H, Hakomori S (1989) ABH and related histo-blood group antigens; immunochemical differences in carrier isotypes and their distribution. Vox Sang 56:1–20

28. Bell K (1983) Red blood cells of domestic mammals. Elsevier Science Publishers, Amsterdam, pp 133–164

29. Yamamoto M et al (2001) Murine equivalent of the human histo-blood group ABO gene is a cis-AB gene and encodes a glycosyltransferase with both A and B transferase activity. J Biol Chem 276:13701–13708

30. Domino SE, Zhang L, Lowe JB (2001) Molecular cloning, genomic mapping, and expression of two secretor blood group alpha (1,2)fucosyltransferase genes differentially regulated in mouse uterine epithelium and gastrointestinal tract. J Biol Chem 276(26):23748–23756

31. Lin B, Saito M, Sakakibara Y, Hayashi Y, Yanagisawa M, Iwamori M (2001) Characterization of three members of murine alpha1,2-fucosyltransferases: change in the expression of the Se gene in the intestine of mice after administration of microbes. Arch Biochem Biophys 388(2):207–215

32. Liu Y, Goff RD, Zhou D, Mattner J, Sullivan BA, Khurana A, Cantu C 3rd, Ravkov EV, Ibegbu CC, Altman JD, Teyton L, Bendelac A, Savage PB (2006) A modified alpha-galactosyl ceramide for staining and stimulating natural killer T cells. J Immunol Methods 312(1–2):34–39

33. Bird AW, Erler A, Fu J, Hériché JK, Maresca M, Zhang Y, Hyman AA, Stewart AF (2011) High-efficiency counter selection recombineering for site-directed mutagenesis in bacterial artificial chromosomes. Nat Methods 9 (1):103–109

34. Lin Z, Li S, Feng C, Yang S, Wang H, Ma D, Zhang J, Gou M, Bu D, Zhang T, Kong X, Wang X, Sarig O, Ren Y, Dai L, Liu H, Zhang J, Li F, Hu Y, Padalon-Brauch G, Vodo D, Zhou F, Chen T, Deng H, Sprecher E, Yang Y, Tan X (2016) Stabilizing mutations of KLHL24 ubiquitin ligase cause loss of keratin 14 and human skin fragility. Nat Genet 48(12):1508–1516

Chapter 3

Retroviral Transduction of NKT Hybridoma Cells

Ke Wang, Rong Jin, and Qing Ge

Abstract

Natural killer T (NKT) cells have been shown to bridge innate and adaptive immunity. However, the rare population and hard-to-transfect of primary NKT cells slow down our understanding of cellular and molecular mechanisms of NKT development and function. To overcome these drawbacks, NKT hybridomas, especially DN32.D3 cells, are applied to study NKT cells in vitro and becoming a valuable tool. Here, we describe the method in the genetic manipulation of DN32.D3 cells by retrovirus, including the generation and concentration of retrovirus, retroviral transduction of DN32.D3 cells, and evaluation of transduction efficiency.

Key words iNKT, NKT hybridomas, DN32.D3, Retroviral transduction, Vector

1 Introduction

Natural killer T (NKT) cells are a type of innate-like unconventional αβ T lymphocytes that recognize self and exogenous glycolipid antigens and hydrophobic peptides presented by β2 microglobulin (β2m)-associated non-polymorphic MHC class I-like molecule CD1d [1, 2]. NKT cells share many features of both T cells and NK cells, thus orchestrating or even participating in innate and adaptive immune responses to protect against a variety of tumors and pathogens and contribute to tissue homeostasis and in some cases tissue damage [3–6]. There are two types of NKT cells according to their differences in TCR usage. Type I or invariant NKT (iNKT) cells express an invariant germline TCR α-chain (Vα14-Jα18 (TRAV11-TRAJ18) in mice, Vα24-Jα18 (TRAV10-TRAJ18) in humans) paired with a limited array of non-germline TCR β-chain (Vβ8.2/7/2 in mice and Vβ11 in humans) [7–9]. iNKT cells in mice represent 1–3% of T cells in most tissues and up to 50% of T cells in the liver and adipose tissue [10, 11]. In human, however, iNKT cells account for less than 1% of T cells in the blood and liver while up to 50% in adipose tissue [7, 11–13]. Type II NKT cells express polyclonal TCRαβ and are more

Chaohong Liu (ed.), *Invariant Natural Killer T-Cells: Methods and Protocols*, Methods in Molecular Biology, vol. 2388,
https://doi.org/10.1007/978-1-0716-1775-5_3,

abundant in humans while much less in mice [14]. Compared with iNKT cells, type II NKT cells are much less studied largely due to technical limitations to specifically identify them [15].

DN32.D3 cells are derived from a murine CD4⁻CD8⁻ (DN) iNKT hybridoma expressing TCR-Vα14/Vβ8.2 [16]. Like primary iNKT cells, DN32.D3 cells produce IL-2 upon stimulation [17, 18]. This characteristic has been used to identify iNKT-specific ligands [17, 19]. In addition, DN32.D3 cells are used for testing the capacity of lipid presentation of CD1d-expressing cells based on their IL-2 production [20–22]. DN32.D3 cells also express IFN-γ, IL-4, IL-10, and several genes critical for iNKT cell development and function, such as *Egr2* and *Zbtb16* (encoding PLZF) [23, 24]. Therefore, a number of groups used DN32.D3 cells as iNKT cells in their studies [25–27]. Furthermore, DN32.D3 cells can be used to investigate the molecular mechanisms of iNKT cells as genetic modifications can be easily performed in these cells [25, 28, 29].

Retroviral transduction is a fast and efficient method to introduce genetic materials into the murine primary T cells [30], hematopoietic stem cells [31], and any actively dividing cells [32]. Retroviral vectors provide a stable genetic modification in the infected cells because they integrate into the genome of the target cells. The gene(s)-of-interest harboring retroviral backbone needs Gag, Pol, and Env proteins for packaging [33]. Gag proteins form viral core structural proteins; Pol proteins are enzymes involved in viral replication; and Env proteins function as viral envelope glycoproteins [34]. These three elements are cotransfected with retroviral backbone in an independent vector (e.g., pCL-Eco helper vector [33]) or provided in a retroviral packaging cell line (e.g., Platinum-E cell line [35]). The Env proteins determine the host range of a retrovirus [36]. The retrovirus produced by cotransfection with pCL-Eco helper vector that we used in this protocol can infect murine and rat cells but not human cells and therefore can be safely used.

2   Materials

1. DN32.D3 cells, a kind gift from Dr. Li Bai at the University of Science and Technology of China, are used for retroviral transduction. HEK 293T cells are used for retroviral package.

2. DN32.D3 growth medium: RPMI 1640, 10% fetal bovine serum, 1% penicillin/streptomycin, 2 mM L-glutamine, and 0.1 mM β-mercaptoethanol. HEK 293T growth medium: DMEM, 10% fetal bovine serum, 1% penicillin/streptomycin, 2 mM L-glutamine, and 0.1 mM β-mercaptoethanol.

3. Plasmids: retroviral backbone pMSCV-ubc-EGFP and helper vector pCL-Eco are kind gifts from Dr. Zhongjun Dong at Tsinghua University.

4. Lipofectamine 2000 transfection reagent is used for HEK 293T transfection with retroviral package plasmids.

5. Opti-MEM I is used for diluting Lipofectamine 2000 and plasmids.

6. PBS: 8.0 g NaCl, 0.20 g KCl, 3.63 g $Na_2HPO_4 \cdot 12H_2O$, and 0.24 g KH_2PO_4 are dissolved in 1000 ml of H_2O, and the pH is adjusted to 7.20 using HCl. PBS is filtered through 0.22 μm pore size syringe filter.

7. 4 mg polybrene is dissolved in 1 ml of sterile PBS. 4 μg/ml of polybrene is used during retroviral transduction.

8. 0.45 μm pore size syringe filter is used for filtering medium containing retrovirus.

3 Methods

3.1 Retroviral Package in HEK 293T

1. One day before transfection, seed HEK 293T cells (*see* **Note 1**) in 10 cm dish with 15 ml of DMEM growth medium to make sure cells will be 70–90% confluent at the time of retroviral plasmids transfection.

2. At the day of seeding HEK 293T cells, thaw a vial of frozen DN32.D3 cells used for step "Transduction of DN32.D3 by retrovirus," culture them in RPMI 1640 growth medium, and passage them every day at split ratio of 1:2 (*see* **Note 2**).

3. At the day of transfection, dilute 10 μg of pMSCV-ubc-EGFP and 20 μg of pCL-Eco with Opti-MEM I to a volume of 1.5 ml and mix them gently. Dilute 60 μl of Lipofectamine 2000 with Opti-MEM I to a volume of 1.5 ml and mix them gently. Incubate them for 5 min at room temperature (*see* **Note 3**).

4. After the incubation, mix the diluted plasmids with the diluted Lipofectamine 2000 gently and incubate for 20 min at room temperature.

5. Add the 3 ml of complexes to different sites of 10 cm dish containing HEK 293T cells. Shake the dish gently.

6. Incubate the cells at 37 °C in 5% CO_2 incubator. Change the medium with 15 ml of pre-warmed fresh DMEM growth medium very gently (*see* **Note 4**) after 8 h of transfection.

7. After 24 h of transfection, collect the supernatant containing retrovirus. Add 15 ml of pre-warmed fresh DMEM growth medium into 10 cm dish very gently (*see* **Note 4**). Filter the collected supernatant through a 0.45 μm pore size syringe filter and store at 4 °C.

8. After 48 h of transfection, collect the supernatant containing retrovirus. Filter the collected supernatant through a 0.45 μm pore size syringe filter and store at 4 °C. Dispose of 10 cm dish containing HEK 293T cells properly.

3.2 Concentration of Retrovirus by Centrifugation (See Note 5)

1. Combine the retrovirus-containing supernatant collected from above steps. Aliquot them to 1 ml into 1.5 ml tube. Centrifuge (*see* **Note 6**) for 2 h at $17,700 \times g$ (*see* **Note 7**) at 4 °C.

2. After centrifugation, the white retrovirus pellet appears at the bottom of 1.5 ml tube. Transfer 900 μl of supernatant very gently and discard. Save the rest of 100 μl of supernatant containing retrovirus pellet (*see* **Note 8**). Vertex for 10 s to resuspend the pellet and combine the aliquots into two tubes. Store at 4 °C.

3.3 Transduction of DN32.D3 by Retrovirus (See Note 9)

1. Use one tube of concentrated retrovirus-containing supernatant immediately after the harvest to prepare the mixture for the transduction. Add 5% of fetal bovine serum (*see* **Note 10**) and 4 μg/ml of polybrene (*see* **Note 11**) into concentrated retrovirus-containing supernatant. Mix them gently.

2. Collect and count DN32.D3 cells. Seed 1.8×10^5 cells per well of 48-well plate with 500 μl of transduction mixture. Centrifuge the 48-well plate for 2 h at $1500 \times g$ at 32 °C (*see* **Note 12**).

3. After centrifugation, incubate the cells at 37 °C in 5% CO_2 incubator. Change the medium with 500 μl of pre-warmed fresh RPMI 1640 growth medium after 1 h of incubation.

4. After 24 h of transduction, proceed to the second round of transduction. Repeat **step 1–3** by using another tube of concentrated retrovirus-containing supernatant.

5. After 24 h of the second transduction, passage the infected cells at split ratio of 1:2.

6. After 48 h of the second transduction, proceed to downstream of experiments depending on the following applications. The infected DN32.D3 cells can be used for flow cytometry and western blot.

3.4 Determination of Transduction Efficiency by Flow Cytometry (See Note 13)

1. The transduction efficiency of infected DN32.D3 cells can be determined after 48 h of the second transduction. Collect the cells and wash with 1 ml of PBS containing 1% FBS once. Centrifuge for 5 min at $450 \times g$ at 4 °C.

2. Resuspend the cell pellet with 300 μl of PBS containing 1% FBS and transfer into 5 ml flow cytometry tube.

3. Run sample on flow cytometer. As shown in Fig. 1, the percentage of positive infected cells of one experiment is 94.5% (*see* **Note 14**).

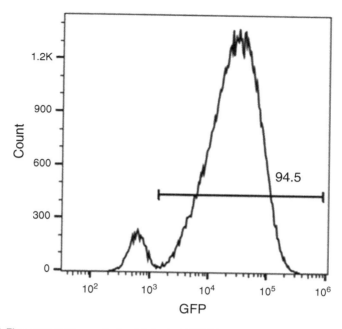

Fig. 1 Flow cytometry analysis of infected DN32.D3 cells

4   Notes

1. Use less than ten generations of HEK 293T cells after thawing to acquire high transfection efficiency.

2. Thawing DN32.D3 cells at this time point can make them ready for retroviral transduction immediately after harvesting concentrated retrovirus-containing supernatant.

3. Proceed to next step within 25 min.

4. Changing the medium for HEK 293T cells should be very gentle. Add pre-warmed fresh DMEM growth medium from side of 10 cm dish slowly and avoid disturbing the cells.

5. This concentration step improves the transduction efficiency of DN32.D3 cells.

6. Mark the position of 1.5 ml tube, and the pellet can be easily found at the bottom of the side away from the center of centrifuge.

7. 17,700 × g is the maximum speed of Kitman-T24 micro centrifuge (TOMY); this speed may be adjusted depending on different centrifuge. Our protocol for retrovirus concentration can be done without having ultracentrifuge.

8. The retrovirus pellet is tiny and incompact. Save 100 μl of supernatant at the bottom of the tube instead of discarding all of supernatant to decrease the loss of retrovirus.

9. Always use freshly made retrovirus to achieve high transduction efficiency.

10. The transduction is performed in the presence of additional FBS to improve the viability of cells.

11. The addition of polybrene, a cationic polymer, can enhance the efficiency of retroviral transduction.

12. Pre-warm the centrifuge to 32 °C before using.

13. The retroviral backbone pMSCV-ubc-EGFP contains a fluorophore gene. The infected cells express EGFP as an indicator of transduction efficiency, which can be detected by flow cytometry.

14. We usually achieve 94.0–99.8% of transduction efficiency with this protocol.

Acknowledgments

The authors thank Dr. Li Bai at the University of Science and Technology of China for the DN32.D3 hybridomas and Dr. Zhongjun Dong at Tsinghua University for the pCL-Eco and pMSCV-ubc-EGFP vectors. This work was supported by grants from the National Key Research and Development Program of China (2017YFA0104500), the National Natural Science Foundation of China (32070897, 31671244, 31872734), the Foundation for Innovative Research Groups of the National Natural Science Foundation of China (81621001), Beijing Natural Science Foundation (7202079), and the Non-Profit Central Research Institute Fund of Chinese Academy of Medical Sciences, 2019PT320006.

References

1. Kronenberg M (2005) Toward an understanding of NKT cell biology: progress and paradoxes. Annu Rev Immunol 23:877–900. https://doi.org/10.1146/annurev.immunol.23.021704.115742

2. Nishioka Y, Masuda S, Tomaru U et al (2018) CD1d-restricted type II NKT cells reactive with endogenous hydrophobic peptides. Front Immunol 9:548. https://doi.org/10.3389/fimmu.2018.00548

3. Crosby CM, Kronenberg M (2018) Tissue-specific functions of invariant natural killer T cells. Nat Rev Immunol 18(9):559–574. https://doi.org/10.1038/s41577-018-0034-2

4. Bassiri H, Das R, Nichols KE (2013) Invariant NKT cells: killers and conspirators against cancer. Onco Targets Ther 2(12):e27440. https://doi.org/10.4161/onci.27440

5. Kakimi K, Guidotti LG, Koezuka Y et al (2000) Natural killer T cell activation inhibits hepatitis B virus replication in vivo. J Exp Med 192(7):921–930. https://doi.org/10.1084/jem.192.7.921

6. Geissmann F, Cameron TO, Sidobre S et al (2005) Intravascular immune surveillance by CXCR6+ NKT cells patrolling liver sinusoids. PLoS Biol 3(4):e113. https://doi.org/10.1371/journal.pbio.0030113

7. Kawano T, Cui J, Koezuka Y et al (1997) CD1d-restricted and TCR-mediated activation of valpha14 NKT cells by glycosylceramides. Science 278(5343):1626–1629. https://doi.org/10.1126/science.278.5343.1626

8. Shimamura M, Ohteki T, Beutner U et al (1997) Lack of directed V alpha 14-J alpha 281 rearrangements in NK1+ T cells. Eur J

Immunol 27(6):1576–1579. https://doi.org/10.1002/eji.1830270638

9. Kronenberg M (2014) When less is more: T lymphocyte populations with restricted antigen receptor diversity. J Immunol 193 (3):975–976. https://doi.org/10.4049/jimmunol.1401491

10. Das R, Sant'Angelo DB, Nichols KE (2010) Transcriptional control of invariant NKT cell development. Immunol Rev 238(1):195–215. https://doi.org/10.1111/j.1600-065X.2010.00962.x

11. Lynch L, Nowak M, Varghese B et al (2012) Adipose tissue invariant NKT cells protect against diet-induced obesity and metabolic disorder through regulatory cytokine production. Immunity 37(3):574–587. https://doi.org/10.1016/j.immuni.2012.06.016

12. Santodomingo-Garzon T, Swain MG (2011) Role of NKT cells in autoimmune liver disease. Autoimmun Rev 10(12):793–800. https://doi.org/10.1016/j.autrev.2011.06.003

13. Lynch L, O'Shea D, Winter DC et al (2009) Invariant NKT cells and CD1d(+) cells amass in human omentum and are depleted in patients with cancer and obesity. Eur J Immunol 39 (7):1893–1901. https://doi.org/10.1002/eji.200939349

14. Sebode M, Wigger J, Filpe P et al (2019) Inflammatory phenotype of intrahepatic Sulfatide-reactive type II NKT cells in humans with autoimmune hepatitis. Front Immunol 10:1065. https://doi.org/10.3389/fimmu.2019.01065

15. Singh AK, Tripathi P, Cardell SL (2018) Type II NKT cells: an elusive population with immunoregulatory properties. Front Immunol 9:1969. https://doi.org/10.3389/fimmu.2018.01969

16. Lantz O, Bendelac A (1994) An invariant T cell receptor alpha chain is used by a unique subset of major histocompatibility complex class I-specific CD4+ and CD4-8- T cells in mice and humans. J Exp Med 180(3):1097–1106. https://doi.org/10.1084/jem.180.3.1097

17. Bendelac A, Lantz O, Quimby ME et al (1995) CD1 recognition by mouse NK1+ T lymphocytes. Science 268(5212):863–865. https://doi.org/10.1126/science.7538697

18. Brutkiewicz RR, Bennink JR, Yewdell JW et al (1995) TAP-independent, beta 2-microglobulin-dependent surface expression of functional mouse CD1.1. J Exp Med 182(6):1913–1919. https://doi.org/10.1084/jem.182.6.1913

19. Kain L, Webb B, Anderson BL et al (2014) The identification of the endogenous ligands of natural killer T cells reveals the presence of mammalian alpha-linked glycosylceramides. Immunity 41(4):543–554. https://doi.org/10.1016/j.immuni.2014.08.017

20. Zhou D, Cantu C 3rd, Sagiv Y et al (2004) Editing of CD1d-bound lipid antigens by endosomal lipid transfer proteins. Science 303 (5657):523–527. https://doi.org/10.1126/science.1092009

21. Freigang S, Zadorozhny V, McKinney MK et al (2010) Fatty acid amide hydrolase shapes NKT cell responses by influencing the serum transport of lipid antigen in mice. J Clin Invest 120 (6):1873–1884. https://doi.org/10.1172/JCI40451

22. Albu DI, VanValkenburgh J, Morin N et al (2011) Transcription factor Bcl11b controls selection of invariant natural killer T-cells by regulating glycolipid presentation in double-positive thymocytes. Proc Natl Acad Sci U S A 108(15):6211–6216. https://doi.org/10.1073/pnas.1014304108

23. Jordan-Williams KL, Poston S, Taparowsky EJ (2013) BATF regulates the development and function of IL-17 producing iNKT cells. BMC Immunol 14:16. https://doi.org/10.1186/1471-2172-14-16

24. Yang SH, Kim SJ, Kim N et al (2008) NKT cells inhibit the development of experimental crescentic glomerulonephritis. J Am Soc Nephrol 19(9):1663–1671. https://doi.org/10.1681/ASN.2007101117

25. Wang Y, Yun C, Gao B et al (2017) The lysine acetyltransferase GCN5 is required for iNKT cell development through EGR2 acetylation. Cell Rep 20(3):600–612. https://doi.org/10.1016/j.celrep.2017.06.065

26. van Eijkeren RJ, Morris I, Borgman A et al (2020) Cytokine output of adipocyte-iNKT cell interplay is skewed by a lipid-rich microenvironment. Front Endocrinol (Lausanne) 11:479. https://doi.org/10.3389/fendo.2020.00479

27. Huh JY, Kim JI, Park YJ et al (2013) A novel function of adipocytes in lipid antigen presentation to iNKT cells. Mol Cell Biol 33 (2):328–339. https://doi.org/10.1128/MCB.00552-12

28. Wang K, Zhang X, Wang Y et al (2019) PDCD5 regulates iNKT cell terminal maturation and iNKT1 fate decision. Cell Mol Immunol 16(9):746–756. https://doi.org/10.1038/s41423-018-0059-2

29. Kim HS, Kim HS, Lee CW et al (2010) T cell Ig domain and mucin domain 1 engagement on invariant NKT cells in the presence of TCR stimulation enhances IL-4 production but inhibits IFN-gamma production. J Immunol

184(8):4095–4106. https://doi.org/10.4049/jimmunol.0901991

30. Yu B, Zhang K, Milner JJ et al (2017) Epigenetic landscapes reveal transcription factors that regulate CD8(+) T cell differentiation. Nat Immunol 18(5):573–582. https://doi.org/10.1038/ni.3706

31. Yang M, Li D, Chang Z et al (2015) PDK1 orchestrates early NK cell development through induction of E4BP4 expression and maintenance of IL-15 responsiveness. J Exp Med 212(2):253–265. https://doi.org/10.1084/jem.20141703

32. Shang Y, Coppo M, He T et al (2016) The transcriptional repressor Hes1 attenuates inflammation by regulating transcription elongation. Nat Immunol 17(8):930–937. https://doi.org/10.1038/ni.3486

33. Naviaux RK, Costanzi E, Haas M et al (1996) The pCL vector system: rapid production of helper-free, high-titer, recombinant retroviruses. J Virol 70(8):5701–5705. https://doi.org/10.1128/JVI.70.8.5701-5705.1996

34. Ciuculescu MF, Brendel C, Harris CE et al (2014) Retroviral transduction of murine and human hematopoietic progenitors and stem cells. Methods Mol Biol 1185:287–309. https://doi.org/10.1007/978-1-4939-1133-2_20

35. Morita S, Kojima T, Kitamura T (2000) Plat-E: an efficient and stable system for transient packaging of retroviruses. Gene Ther 7(12):1063–1066. https://doi.org/10.1038/sj.gt.3301206

36. Lounkova A, Kosla J, Prikryl D et al (2017) Retroviral host range extension is coupled with Env-activating mutations resulting in receptor-independent entry. Proc Natl Acad Sci U S A 114(26):E5148–E5E57. https://doi.org/10.1073/pnas.1704750114

Chapter 4

Methods for Studying Mouse and Human Invariant Natural Killer T Cells

Yang Zhou, Yan-Ruide Li, Samuel Zeng, and Lili Yang

Abstract

Invariant natural killer T (iNKT) cells are a unique subset of T lymphocytes that recognize lipid antigens presented by nonpolymorphic major histocompatibility complex (MHC) I-like molecule CD1d. iNKT cells play essential roles in regulating immune responses against cancer, viral infection, autoimmune disease, and allergy. However, the study and application of iNKT cells have been hampered by their very small numbers (0.01–1% in mouse and human blood). Here, we describe protocols to (1) generate mouse iNKT cells from mouse mononuclear cells or from mouse hematopoietic stem cells engineered with iNKT T cell receptor (TCR) gene (denoted as mMNC-iNKT cells or mHSC-iNKT cells, respectively), (2) generate human iNKT cells from human peripheral blood mononuclear cells or from human HSC cells engineered with iNKT TCR gene (denoted as hPBMC-iNKT cells or hHSC-iNKT cells, respectively), and (3) characterize mouse and human iNKT cells in vitro and in vivo.

Key words Invariant natural killer T (iNKT) cell, CD1d, T cell receptor (TCR), Alpha-galactosylceramide (α-GalCer), Glycolipid, Gene engineering, Hematopoietic stem cell (HSC), Cancer immunotherapy

1 Introduction

Invariant natural killer T (iNKT) cells are a unique subpopulation of innate T lymphocytes that express both natural killer (NK) cell markers and a restricted αβ T cell receptor (TCR). The restricted TCR is comprised of a canonical invariant TCRα chain (Vα14-Jα18 in mice; Vα24-Jα18 in human) paired with a semi-variant TCRβ chain (mostly Vβ8.2 in mice; mostly Vβ11 in human) [1, 2]. The early developmental stages of iNKT cells are similar to classical MHC-restricted CD4$^+$ and CD8$^+$ conventional T (Tc) cells [2, 3]. Lymphoid precursor cells arising from hematopoietic stem

Yang Zhou and Yan-Ruide Li contributed equally to this work.

Chaohong Liu (ed.), *Invariant Natural Killer T-Cells: Methods and Protocols*, Methods in Molecular Biology, vol. 2388,
https://doi.org/10.1007/978-1-0716-1775-5_4,

cells (HSCs) migrate to the thymus, undergo rearrangement of the TCRβ chain, and develop into CD4 and CD8 double-positive (DP) thymocytes. DP thymocytes then randomly rearrange their TCRα loci to generate intact TCR complexes expressed on the cell surface. However, unlike Tc cells that are selected by peptides presented on MHC-I or MHC-II of thymic epithelial cells, iNKT DP precursors are positively selected by glycolipids presented on CD1d expressed by DP thymocytes themselves [4]. The iNKT TCR-glycolipid-CD1d interaction, along with signals through the signaling lymphocytic activated molecules (SLAM) receptor family, provides co-stimulation for the further development of iNKT cells [3]. Owing to their unique developmental path, iNKT cells exit the thymus expressing a memory T cell phenotype. They further mature in the periphery through upregulating their expression of NK cell markers [5].

Functionally mature iNKT cells are powerful modulators of the immune response [4, 6–8]. Their most notable function is secreting copious amounts of cytokines upon stimulation, including T helper (Th)1-like (IFN-γ), Th2-like (IL-4, IL-13), Th17-like (IL-17, IL-22), and regulatory (IL-10) cytokines [4]. What cytokines are produced depends on the mechanism of cell activation, the location, and the iNKT cell subsets. iNKT cells also produce cytolytic proteins such as perforin and granzyme B and surface molecules involved in cytotoxicity such as Fas Ligand (FasL) and tumor necrosis factor α (TNF-α)-related apoptosis-inducing ligand (TRAIL) [9, 10]. Collectively, iNKT cells can profoundly influence many other immune cells, including dendritic cells, macrophages, neutrophils, NK cells, T cells, and B cells, thereby orchestrating the immune responses during infection, autoimmune disease [11], allergy [12], and cancer [9, 13, 14].

However, the extremely low number of iNKT cells, particularly in human peripheral blood (0.01–1% in healthy humans; 0.001–0.1% in cancer patients), is a significant obstacle for studying iNKT cell biology and developing iNKT cell-based therapies [5]. In our lab, we have developed methods to effectively generate large numbers of mouse and human iNKT cells through genetic engineering of HSCs (denoted as mHSC-iNKT cells and hHSC-iNKT cells, respectively [15–17]); we also routinely expand mouse iNKT cells from mouse mononuclear cells (denoted as mMNC-iNKT cells) and expand human iNKT cells from human peripheral blood mononuclear cells (denoted as hPBMC-iNKT cells) following established protocols with certain modifications [15, 17]. Here, we share our lab protocols on (1) generating mMNC-iNKT and mHSC-iNKT cells; (2) generating hPBMC-iNKT and hHSC-iNKT cells; (3) characterizing mouse and human iNKT cells with in vitro and in vivo assays.

2   Materials

Prepare all media in sterile hood (unless otherwise indicated).

2.1   Generation of Mouse iNKT Cells

2.1.1   Isolate and Expand mMNC-iNKT Cells

1. Mice: C57BL/6J (B6-WT) mouse.
2. Fetal bovine serum (FBS).
3. Phosphate-buffered saline (PBS).
4. 33% Percoll: 33% (vol/vol) of 100% Percoll, 67% (vol/vol) of 1× PBS solution.
5. 40% Percoll: 40% (vol/vol) of 100% Percoll, 60% (vol/vol) of 1× PBS solution.
6. 60% Percoll: 60% (vol/vol) of 100% Percoll, 40% (vol/vol) of 1× PBS solution.
7. Anti-mouse CD16/32 Fc block.
8. Anti-mouse CD19 microbeads.
9. Anti-mouse CD1d-Tetramer-PE.
10. Anti-PE microbeads.
11. 70 μm cell strainer.
12. Mouse iNKT culture medium: C10 medium supplemented with recombinant mouse IL-2 (final concentration 10 ng/ml) and IL-12 (final concentration 1 ng/ml).
13. Equipment: Magnetic beads separator (MACS), MACS Columns (LS column, LD column), water bath, sonicator, irradiator, pH meter.

2.1.2   Generate mHSC-iNKT Cells

1. Mice: C57BL/6J (B6-WT) mice.
2. Mouse iNKT TCR sequence [15].
3. 5-Fluorouracil (*see* **Note 1**).
4. Mouse iNKT retrovirus (*see* **Note 2**).
5. Human embryonic kidney cell line HEK293.T.
6. Polybrene.
7. Recombinant mouse IL-3.
8. Recombinant mouse IL-6.
9. Murine stem cell factor (SCF).
10. Antibiotics: sulfamethoxazole and trimethoprim.
11. Other reagents, material, and equipment were described in Subheading 2.1.

2.2 Generation of Human iNKT Cells

2.2.1 Isolate and Expand hPBMC-iNKT Cells

1. Human blood from healthy donors.
2. Ficoll-Paque Plus.
3. Anti-human iNKT MicroBeads.
4. Recombinant human IL-7.
5. Recombinant human IL-15.
6. Tris-buffered ammonium chloride buffer (TAC buffer or red blood cell lysis buffer): 0.16 M NH_4CL, 0.17 M Tris, ddH_2O.
7. MACS sorting buffer: phosphate-buffered saline (PBS), 0.5% bovine serum albumin (BSA), and 2 mM EDTA.
8. C10 medium: RPMI1640 supplemented with 10% (vol/vol) FBS, 1% (vol/vol) penicillin/streptomycin/glutamine, 1% (vol/vol) MEM NEAA, 10 mM HEPES, 1 mM sodium pyruvate, and 50 μM β-ME.
9. Human iNKT culture medium: C10 medium supplemented with recombinant human IL-7 (final 10 ng/ml) and human IL-15 (final concentration 10 ng/ml).
10. α-GalCer medium: C10 medium supplemented with α-galactosylceramide (final concentration 5 μg/ml).

2.2.2 Generate hHSC-iNKT Cells

1. Mice: NOD.Cg-Prkdc^{SCID}Il2rg^{tm1Wjl}/SzJ (NOD/SCID/IL-2Rγ$^{-/-}$, NSG) mice.
2. Human CD34$^+$ hematopoietic stem cells (CD34$^+$ HSCs) (see **Note 3**).
3. Human fetal thymus tissues.
4. Human iNKT TCR sequences [17].
5. RetroNectin.
6. 2% BSA.
7. X-VIVO-15 serum-free medium.
8. Carprofen.
9. Recombinant human IL-3.
10. Human Flt3-Ligand (Flt3-L).
11. Human stem cell factor (hSCF).
12. Human thrombopoietin (TPO).
13. 6-well non-tissue culture treated plates.
14. Other reagents, materials, and equipment were described in Subheading 2.1.

2.3   Characterization of Mouse or Human iNKT Cells

2.3.1   Phenotype Analysis of Mouse or Human iNKT Cells

1. Antibodies (*see* Table 1).
2. Phorbol-12-myristate-13-acetate (PMA): 1 mg PMA dissolved in 400 μl DMSO.
3. Ionomycin: 1 mg ionomycin dissolved in 400 μl DMSO.
4. GolgiStop.
5. BD fixation/permeabilization solution kit.
6. Recombinant mouse and human IFN-γ (ELISA, standard).
7. Recombinant mouse and human IL-4 (ELISA, standard).
8. Anti-mouse and human IFN-γ (ELISA, capture).
9. Anti-mouse and human IFN-γ (ELISA, detection).
10. Anti-mouse and human IL-4 (ELISA, capture).
11. Anti-mouse and human IL-4 (ELISA, capture).
12. Nunc-Immuno ELISA plate.
13. ELISA coating buffer: 325 ml of 0.1 M $NaHCO_3$, 50 ml of 0.1 M Na_2CO_3, PH = 9.4, store at room temperature (RT).
14. ELISA borate buffered saline (BBS) dilution buffer: 6.07 g H_3BO_3 (0.1 M), 7.32 g NaCl (0.012 M), 20 g 2% BSA, 1 L ddH_2O, PH = 8, store at 4 °C.
15. ELISA wash buffer (20×): 1 M Tris (PH = 8.0), 163.5 g NaCl, 10 ml Tween-20.
16. Tetramethylbenzidine (TMB).
17. Streptavidin-HRP conjugate.
18. TMB reaction stop solution (1 M H_3PO_4): 68.2 ml 85% phosphoric acid, 1 L ddH_2O, store at RT.

2.3.2   Function Analysis of Mouse or Human iNKT Cells

1. Human CD14 microbeads.
2. NK isolation kit.
3. Mouse melanoma cell line B16.F10.
4. Human multiple myeloma cell line MM.1S.
5. Human multiple myeloma cell line MM.1S-FG and MM.1S-hCD1d-FG (*see* **Note 4**).
6. Human chronic myelogenous leukemia cancer cell line K562.
7. Human chronic myelogenous leukemia cancer cell line K562-FG (*see* **Note 5**).
8. Human melanoma cell line A375.
9. Human melanoma cell line A375-A2-Eso-FG (*see* **Note 6**).
10. D-luciferin.
11. Isoflurane.
12. Zeiss Stemi 2000-CS microscope (Carl Zeiss AG).
13. IVIS 100 imaging system (Xenogen/PerkinElmer).

Table 1
List of antibodies

Antibodies		
Anti-human CD45 (Clone H130)	BioLegend	CAT#304026, RFID: AB_893337
Anti-human TCRαβ (Clone I26)	BioLegend	CAT#306716, RRID: AB_1953257
Anti-human CD4 (Clone OKT4)	BioLegend	CAT#317414, RRID: AB_571959
Anti-human CD8 (Clone SK1)	BioLegend	CAT#344714, RRID: AB_2044006
Anti-human CD45RO (Clone UCHL1)	BioLegend	CAT#304216, RRID: AB_493659
Anti-human CD161 (Clone HP-3G10)	BioLegend	CAT#339928, RRID: AB_2563967
Anti-human CD69 (Clone FN50)	BioLegend	CAT#310914, RRID: AB_314849
Anti-human CD56 (Clone HCD56)	BioLegend	CAT#318304, RRID: AB_604100
Anti-human CD62L (Clone DREG-56)	BioLegend	CAT#304822, RRID: AB_830801
Anti-human CD14 (Clone HCD14)	BioLegend	CAT#325608, RRID: AB_830681
Anti-human CD1d (Clone 51.1)	BioLegend	CAT#350308, RRID: AB_10642829
Anti-mouse TCRβ (Clone 1B3.3)	BioLegend	CAT#156305, RRID: AB_2800701
Anti-mouse NK1.1 (Clone PK136)	BioLegend	CAT#108710, RRID: AB_313397
Anti-mouse CD62L (Clone MEL-14)	BioLegend	CAT#104411, RRID: AB_30566881
Anti-mouse CD44 (Clone IM7)	BioLegend	CAT#103012, RRID: AB_312963
Anti-mouse CD4 (Clone GK1.5)	BioLegend	CAT#100412, RRID: AB_312697
Anti-mouse CD8 (Clone 53-6.7)	BioLegend	CAT#100712, RRID: AB_312751
Anti-mouse CD3 (Clone 17A2)	BioLegend	CAT#100236, RRID: AB_2561456
Anti-mouse IFN-γ (Clone XMG1.2)	BioLegend	CAT#505809, RRID: AB_315403
Anti-mouse IL-4 (Clone 11B11)	BioLegend	CAT#504103, RRID: AB_315317
Anti-mouse CD1d (Clone K253)	BioLegend	CAT#140805, RRID: AB_10643277
Anti-human CD34 (Clone 581)	BD Biosciences	CAT#555822, RRID: AB_396151
Anti-human TCR Vα24-Jβ18 (Clone 6B11)	BD Biosciences	CAT#552825, RRID: AB_394478
Anti-human Vβ11	Beckman-Coulter	CAT#A66905
Human Fc Receptor Blocking Solution (TrueStain FcX)	BioLegend	CAT#422302
Mouse Fc Block (anti-mouse CD16/32)	BD Biosciences	CAT#553142, RRID: AB_394657
LEAF purified anti-human CD1d antibody (Clone 51.1)	BioLegend	CAT#350304
LEAF purified Mouse IgG2b, k isotype ctrl (Clone MG2b-57)	BioLegend	CAT#401212
Mouse Fluorochrome-conjugated mCD1d/PSC-57 tetramer	NIH Tetramer Core Facility	

3   Methods

3.1   Generation of mMNC-iNKT Cells

3.1.1   Prepare MNCs from Mouse Spleen and Liver (Fig. 1a)

1. Euthanize mice by CO_2.

2. Clean the skin by spraying with 70% ethanol. Dissect the mouse and collect the spleen, located on the left flank. The liver is preferably flushed of circulating blood prior to collection. To do so, shift the intestines away from the body to uncover the inferior vena cava, and use a 5 ml syringe to push approximately 5 ml of PBS through it. The liver should turn yellow/white as a result.

3. Harvested spleen and liver should be collected in separate tubes containing 3–5 ml sterile C10 medium (*see* **Note 7**).

4. In a sterile hood, disperse the liver and spleen into single cell suspensions by placing each tissue in a 70 μm cell strainer and mashing with a plunger from a 3 ml syringe. Rinse the plunger and cell strainer with C10 medium and transfer the cell suspension into a new 15 ml conical tube.

5. Liver and spleen samples are processed differently. **Steps 6–11** refer to processing the liver, while **steps 12** and **13** refer to processing the spleen.

6. Add 3 ml of 60% Percoll into a new 15 ml tube.

7. Spin down ($600 \times g$) the liver cells and resuspend the cell pellet in 3 ml of 40% Percoll in PBS (*see* **Note 8**).

8. Gently layer the 40% Percoll cell suspension on top of the 60% Percoll. To do this, tilt the conical tube until it is almost horizontal and add the 40% suspension drop by drop. If performed correctly, one should see a sharp demarcation between the 40% and 60%.

9. Spin at $800 \times g$ for 30 min with no brakes at RT (*see* **Note 9**).

10. Aspirate the floating debris. There should be a thin layer of cells around the 3 ml line. Collect those cells while avoiding the red blood cells found at the bottom of the tube.

11. Add 5 ml C10 medium to the collection and mix well. Spin down for 5 min at 4 °C. Aspirate the supernatant and resuspend in 5 ml C10 medium.

12. Spin down ($600 \times g$) the spleen cells and resuspend in 5 ml TAC buffer at room temperature for 10–20 min to lyse the red blood cells.

13. Add an additional 5 ml C10 medium to neutralize the buffer, spin down ($600 \times g$). Aspirate the supernatant and resuspend the pellet with 5 ml C10 medium. Cells clumps may be observed. Filter through a 70 μm cell strainer to remove dead cell clumps.

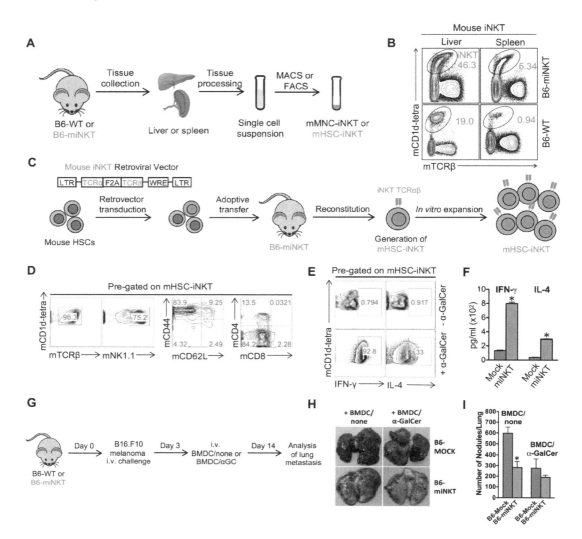

Fig. 1 Generation and characterization of mouse iNKT cells. (**a**) Diagram depicting the isolation of mMNC-iNKT cells and mHSC-iNKT cells. (**b**) FACS detection of mouse iNKT cells in liver and spleen of B6-miNKT mice or B6-WT mice. (**c**) Experimental design for generating mHSC-iNKT cells in a B6-miNKT mouse model. (**d**) FACS detection of the surface markers of mHSC-iNKT cells. These iNKT cells were detected in the liver of B6-miNKT mice for up to 6 months after HSCs adoptive transfer. (**e, f**) Functionality of mHSC-iNKT cells tested in vitro. Spleen cells collected from B6-miNKT mice were cultured in vitro in the presence of α-GalCer (100 ng/ml) (**e**) FACS detection of intracellular cytokine production in mHSC-iNKT cells 3 days post α-GalCer stimulation. (**f**) ELISA analysis of cytokine production of mHSC-iNKT cells in the cell culture medium 3 days post α-GalCer stimulation. (**g–i**) Study in vivo antitumor efficacy of mHSC-iNKT cells using an B16.F10 melanoma lung metastasis mouse model. (**g**) Experimental design. (**h**) Photos of lung tumor nodules. Representative of two experiments. (**i**) Enumeration of lung tumor nodules. Data were presented as the mean ± SEM. *$P < 0.01$, by Student's *t* test. (Note that **d–i** were reproduced from Ref. 15 with permission from NAS, copyright (2015) National Academy of Sciences)

14. Count live cell numbers. Cell resuspension can be kept at 4 °C, ready for sorting or FACS staining (*see* **Note 10**).

3.1.2 Magnetic
Separation
of mMNC-iNKT Cells

1. Resuspend MNCs from Subheading 3.1.1 in 2% FBS/PBS buffer.

2. Centrifuge the cell mixture, aspirate the supernatant, and resuspend in 100 μl of 2% FBS/PBS.

3. Add 10 μl of anti-mouse CD16/CD32 mAb to block nonspecific binding to Fcγ receptors and incubate for 5 min at 4 °C.

4. Add 20 μl of anti-mouse CD19 microbeads and incubate for 15 min at 4 °C.

5. Meanwhile, prepare a LD column and equilibrate with 2 ml of 2% FBS/PBS buffer.

6. Wash the cells with 2% FBS/PBS buffer and centrifugation at $600 \times g$ for 5 min at 4 °C.

7. Resuspend cells in 500 μl of buffer and add to the LD column.

8. Collect the CD19$^-$ fraction into a clean 15 ml conical tube. Wash the column twice with 1 ml of 2% FBS/PBS each time and keep collecting the flow through.

9. Spin down the CD19$^-$ fraction and stain with 20 μl of anti-mouse CD1d-Tetramer-PE in 30 μl of 2% FBS/PBS for 20 min on ice.

10. Wash the cells with 2% FBS/PBS buffer and centrifugation at $600 \times g$ for 5 min at 4 °C.

11. Stain with 20 μl of anti-PE microbeads in 100 μl of 2% FBS/PBS for 15 min on ice.

12. Meanwhile, prepare another LD column and equilibrate with 2 ml of 2% FBS/PBS.

13. Wash the cells with 2% FBS/PBS buffer and centrifuge at $600 \times g$ for 5 min at 4 °C. Resuspend cells in 500 μl of buffer.

14. Load cell suspension into LD column. Mouse iNKT cells will bind to the column by positive selection. Wash the column twice with 1 ml of 2% FBS/PBS each time. The flow through can be discarded but can also be kept for troubleshooting.

15. Remove the LD column from the magnetic field and elute the cells from column.

16. The purity of the iNKT cells can be checked by FACS staining and can be further improved via FACS sorting (Fig. 1b).

3.1.3 In Vitro Expansion
of mMNC-iNKT Cells

1. Count the number of mMNC-iNKT cells from Subheading 3.1.2.

2. Seed cell at 2×10^6 cells per well in the C10 medium, with or without the addition of α-GalCer (final concentration 100 ng/ml) for 5 days (*see* **Note 11**).

3. On day 3 and day 5, collect cells and run assays for mMNC-iNKT cell expansion using flow cytometry.

3.2 Generation of Mouse HSC-iNKT Cells (mHSC-iNKTs)

3.2.1 Generate HSC-iNKT Mouse (See Note 12) (Fig. 1c)

1. Day 0, treat B6 mice with 5-fluorouracial (250 μg per gram body weight).

2. Day 5, harvest bone marrow (BM) cells from mouse and culture the cells for 4 days in BM cell culture medium containing recombinant mouse IL-3 (20 ng/ml), IL-6 (50 ng/ml), and SCF (50 ng/ml).

3. Day 7 and 8, BM cells were spin-infected with retroviruses (see Note 13) supplemented with 8 μg/ml of polybrene, at $770 \times g$, 30 °C for 90 min.

4. Day 9, BM cells were collected and intravenously injected into B6 recipients that had received 1200 rads of total body irradiation ($\sim$1–2 $\times$ 10^6 transduced BM cells per recipient) (see Note 14).

5. The BM recipient mice were maintained on the combined antibiotics sulfamethoxazole and trimethoprim oral suspension in a sterile environment for 6–8 weeks until analysis or use for subsequent experiments.

3.2.2 Isolate and Expand mHSC-iNKT Cells (Refer Subheading 3.1)

1. Purify mHSC-iNKT cells following the steps of magnetic separation of mMNC-iNKT cells (refer Subheading 3.1.2).

2. Count the number of mHSC-iNKT cells, seed cells at 2 $\times$ 10^6 cells per well in the C10 medium, with or without the addition of α-GalCer (final concentration 100 ng/ml) for 5 days.

3. On day 3 and day 5, collect cells and run assays for mHSC-iNKT cell expansion using flow cytometry.

3.3 Generation of hPBMC-iNKT Cells

3.3.1 Isolate PBMCs from Human Peripheral Blood (Fig. 2a)

1. Obtain peripheral blood from healthy donors in blood collection tubes with heparin 1000 U/ml.

2. Centrifuge at 400 $\times$ g for 15 min with no brakes at RT.

3. Aspirate the supernatant and resuspend the cell pellet with PBS (10–12 ml/tube).

4. Transfer the mixture to a 50 ml conical tube. Wash once more using RT PBS (10–12 ml/tube).

5. Aspirate the supernatant and resuspend with 14 ml PBS.

6. Gently layer 14 ml of room temperature Ficoll on top of the mixture, using a 25 ml pipette (see Note 15).

7. Centrifuge at 970 $\times$ g for 20 min with no brakes at RT.

8. Aspirate the upper PBS layer.

9. Using a 5 ml pipette, carefully collect the PBMCs at the interface.

10. Wash with 10–20 ml PBS and centrifuge at 400 $\times$ g for 7 min at RT.

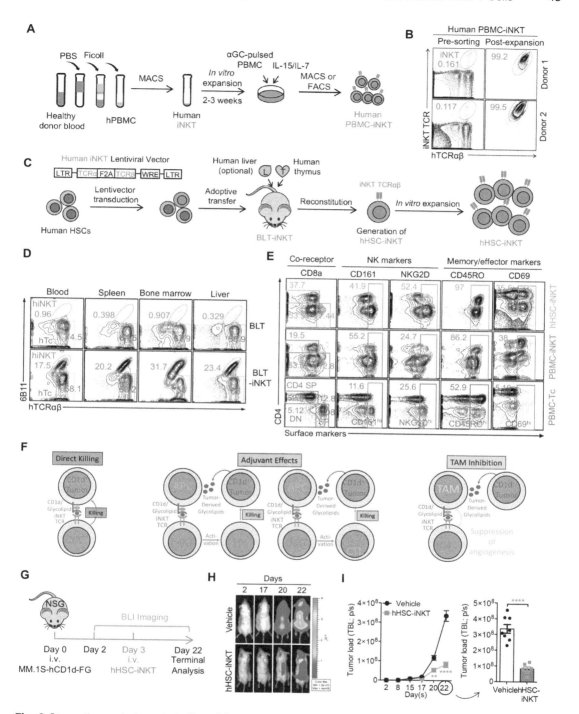

Fig. 2 Generation and characterization of human iNKT cells. (**a**) Diagram depicting the isolation and in vitro expansion of hPBMC-iNKT cells. (αGC: α-GalCer.). (**b**) FACS detection of hPBMC-iNKT cells before or after MACS sorting using anti-human iNKT microbeads. (**c**) Experimental design to generate hHSC-iNKT cells in a bone marrow-liver-thymus (BLT) humanized mouse model. (**d**) FACS detection of hHSC-iNKT cells in control BLT and BLT-iNKT mice tissues, at week 20 post-HSC transfer. Control BLT mice were generated by

11. Aspirate the supernatant and resuspend the PBMC pellet in 10 ml TAC buffer for 10–20 min at RT.

12. Centrifuge at $600 \times g$ for 5 min and remove the supernatant.

13. Wash PBMCs with C10 medium once and resuspend cells in 10 ml of C10 medium.

14. Count live cell numbers.

3.3.2 Magnetic Separation of hPBMC-iNKT Cells

1. Count the number of cells in PBMC sample (*see* **Note 16**).

2. Centrifuge cell suspension at $300 \times g$ for 10 min.

3. Aspirate supernatant completely and resuspend cell pellet in 400 μl of MACS sorting buffer per 1×10^8 total cells.

4. Add 100 μl of anti-human iNKT microbeads per 1×10^8 total cells. Mix well and incubate for 15 min in the refrigerator (2–8 °C).

5. Wash cells by adding 1–2 ml of buffer per 1×10^8 cells and centrifuge at $300 \times g$ for 10 min. Aspirate supernatant completely and resuspend up to 1×10^8 cells in 500 μl of buffer.

6. Place column in the magnetic field of a suitable MACS separator.

7. Equilibrate column by rinsing with the appropriate amount of buffer (LS: 3 ml).

8. Apply cell suspension into the column. Collect flow-through containing unlabeled cells (*see* **Note 17**).

9. Wash column with the appropriate amount of buffer. Collect unlabeled cells that pass through and combine with the effluent (LS: 3×3 ml).

10. Remove column from the separator and place it on a clean 15 ml conical tube.

11. Pipette 3 ml of buffer onto the column. Immediately flush out the magnetically labeled cells by firmly pushing the plunger into the column (*see* **Note 18**).

12. Check the purity of human iNKT cells with FACS staining.

Fig. 2 (continued) adoptively transferring mock-transduced human HSCs into NSG mice engrafted with human thymus. (**e**) FACS detection of the surface markers of hHSC-iNKT cells isolated from the spleen of BLT-iNKT mice. Human PBMC-iNKT cells and human PBMC-derived conventional αβ T (PBMC-Tc) cells were included as controls. (**f**) Diagram showing the possible mechanisms used by human iNKT cells to attack tumor cells. APC, antigen presenting cell; NK, natural killer cell; DC, dendritic cell; CTL, cytotoxic T lymphocyte; TAM, tumor-associated macrophage. (**g–i**) Study in vivo antitumor efficacy of hHSC-iNKT cells using an MM.1S-hCD1d-FG human MM xenograft NSG mouse model. (**g**) Experimental design. (**h**) BLI images showing tumor burden in experimental mice over time. Representative of three experiments. (**i**) Quantification of (**h**) ($n = 6$–8). Data were presented as the mean ± SEM. ****$P < 0.0001$, by Student's t test. (Note that **d–i** were reproduced from Ref. 17 with permission from Elsevier, copyright (2019) Elsevier)

3.3.3 In Vitro Expansion of hPBMC-iNKT Cells

1. Count the number of PBMC-iNKT cells from magnetic separation. (Usually around 5×10^8 PBMC will yield 0.5–2×10^6 iNKT cells.)

2. Load a portion of the negative fraction (1–2×10^8 per 5 ml) with α-GalCer (5 μg/ml) (*see* **Note 19**) and irradiate (~70% yield, 6000 rads); freeze down the remaining negative portion.

3. Seed cells at 1×10^6 iNKT: 2×10^6 α-GalCer-pulsed PBMC per 3 ml C10 medium per well of a 6-well plate. Add IL-7 and IL-15 at 10 ng/ml to the culture.

4. Monitor cell growth daily. As cells reach saturation, add C10 medium containing human IL-7 and IL-15 at 10 ng/ml and split cultures.

5. Cells can expand five- to tenfold and reach ~80% iNKT cell confluency during the first week. At day 7, cells can be restimulated (repeat **steps 2** and **3**). Cells can expand around tenfold per stimulation.

6. Take a small aliquot of iNKT culture for FACS staining (Fig. 2b).

7. The culture reaches >95% iNKT cell during the second week. iNKT cells can be frozen down and kept in liquid nitrogen for long-term storage (*see* **Note 20**).

3.4 Generation of Human HSC-iNKT Cells

*3.4.1 Generate HSC-iNKT Humanized Mouse (Fig. 2c) (See **Note 21**)*

1. Day 1, thaw and prestimulate CD34+ PBSCs.
   (a) Coat 6-well non-tissue culture treated plates with Retro-Nectin (RN, 20 μg per vial in PBS) at RT for 2 h.
   (b) Aspirate and replace with 1 ml of 2% BSA for 30 min at RT.
   (c) Aspirate and replace with 2 ml PBS (*see* **Note 22**).
   (d) Thaw CD34+ PBSC using X-VIVO-15 medium, spin at $300 \times g$ for 7 min.
   (e) Aspirate supernatant and resuspend in 5 ml of X-VIVO-15 medium and count cell number.
   (f) Spin down at $300 \times g$ for 7 min and aspirate supernatant.
   (g) Prepare 10 ml of X-VIVO-15 medium supplemented with hSCF (50 ng/ml), hFLT3L (50 ng/ml), hTPO (50 ng/ml), and hIL-3 (10 ng/ml).
   (h) Resuspend CD34+ cells in X-VIVO-15/hSCF/hFLT3L/hTPO/hIL-3 medium (1×10^6 cells/ml).
   (i) Aspirate PBS in RN-coated well and seed the cells (1×10^6 per well).
   (j) Incubate at 37 °C, 5% CO_2.

2. Day 2, transduce CD34+ PBSCs with lentivirus (*see* **Note 23**).

(a) Thaw concentrated virus supernatant on ice.

(b) Pipet thawed supernatant and add directly to well (*see* **Note 24**). Rock plate gently to mix.

(c) Incubate cells at 37 °C, 5% CO_2 for 24 h.

3. Day 3, prepare thymus pieces and intravenously inject transduced PBSCs to NSG mice.

(a) Prepare fetal thymus fragments and irradiate with 500 rads (*see* **Note 25**).

(b) Incubate irradiated thymus in C10 medium with antibiotics until surgery. Make sure to wash thymus thoroughly and keep on ice until surgery.

(c) Irradiate NSG mice with 270 rads.

(d) Harvest and count transduced human CD34$^+$ cells 24 h post transduction, and then resuspend in X-VIVO-15 medium (*see* **Note 26**).

(e) Implant thymus pieces under the kidney capsule of pre-irradiated NSG mouse. Additionally, give retro-orbital injections of transduced PBSCs to each mouse.

(f) Suture and staple the incision.

(g) Subcutaneously inject 300 µl of 1:100 carprofen diluted in PBS (*see* **Note 27**).

4. Day 4, 5, daily injection with 300 µl of 1:100 carprofen diluted in PBS.

5. Day 7, remove the staples and monitor the conditions of BLT-iNKT mice.

6. Starting from week 6 post injection, bleed mice monthly and check human cell reconstitution by FACS staining (*see* **Note 28**).

3.4.2 hHSC-iNKT Cells from Humanized Mouse (Fig. 2d)

1. Euthanize mice by CO_2.

2. Place mouse in dorsal recumbency and clean the skin by spraying with 70% ethanol.

3. Cut the skin and expose both the abdomen and chest.

4. Puncture the heart with 26-gauge on 1 ml syringe to collect blood in a heparin-coated collection tube.

5. Collect the lung, liver, spleen, and bone marrow from humanized mouse and store the tissues on ice.

6. Disperse tissues into mononuclear cell suspension:

(a) For blood, incubate in 5 ml TAC buffer for 20 min at RT; spin down to remove supernatant and resuspend in 1 ml C10 medium. Store at 4 °C. Sample is ready for staining (refer Subheading 3.5.1).

(b) For spleen, lung, and liver, mash tissues in C10 medium through a 70 μm cell strainer using plungers from 5 ml syringes. Collect the single cell suspension in a 15 ml conical tubes, spin down to remove supernatant, and resuspend in 14 ml 33% Percoll in PBS (spleen samples can skip Percoll separation and directly proceed to TAC lysis). Spin at 800 × g for 30 min with no brakes at RT. Aspirate the supernatant and resuspend the pellet in 5 ml TAC buffer. Incubate for 10 min at RT, and then add additional C10 medium and filter through cells strainer. Spin down and resuspend in fresh C10 medium. Store samples at 4 °C. Samples are ready for staining or cryopreservation (refer to Subheading 3.5.1).

(c) For bone marrow, use forceps to hold leg bones over a 15 ml conical tube and flush with C10 medium using 25-gauge needle fitted onto a 10 ml syringe. Spin down to remove the supernatant and resuspend in 10 ml TAC buffer. Incubate for 10 min at RT, and then filter through a 70 μm cell strainer. Spin down, aspirate the supernatant, and wash with 2 ml C10 medium. Resuspend the sample in C10 medium, and store at 4 °C. Sample is ready for staining or cryopreservation (refer Subheading 3.5.1).

3.4.3 In Vitro Expansion of hHSC-iNKT Cells

1. Healthy donor PBMCs were loaded with α-GalCer (by culturing 1×10^8 PBMCs in 5 ml C10 medium containing 5 μg/ml α-GalCer for 1 h in 6-well TC plate), irradiated at 6000 rads, and then used to stimulate iNKT cells.

2. To expand iNKT cells, pooled hHSC-iNKT humanized mouse tissue cells were mixed with α-GalCer-pulsed PBMCs (ratio 1:1 or 1:1.5; e.g. 1×10^6 iNKT tissue cells were mixed with 1.5×10^6 irradiated α-GalCer-pulsed PBMCs) and cultured in C10 medium for 7 days. Cells were plated in 6-well plate (2.5×10^6/ml, 3 ml/well). Recombinant human IL-7 (10 ng/ml) and IL-15 (10 ng/ml) were added to cell cultures starting from day 2. Cells were split 1:2 once confluent (about every 2–3 days).

3. On day 7, cell cultures were collected and iNKT cells were sorted out using flow cytometry (identified as hCD45$^+$hTCRαβ$^+$6B11$^+$ cells).

4. The sorted iNKT cells (>99% purify based on flow cytometry analysis) were expanded further with α-GalCer-pulsed PBMCs and human IL-7/IL-15 for another 7 to 14 days (*see* **Note 29**).

5. Expanded iNKT cells were aliquoted and frozen in LN storage tanks (e.g., 1×10^7 cells per vial for in vitro assay and 1×10^8 cells per vial for in vivo assay).

3.5 Characterization of Mouse or Human iNKT Cells

3.5.1 iNKT Cell Phenotype Analysis

1. Surface and intracellular marker staining (Figs. 1d, e, and 2e):

    (a) Aliquot cells into labeled FACS tubes.

    (b) Wash cells with 1 ml C10 media, spin down, and aspirate the supernatant.

    (c) Wash cells with 1 ml PBS, spin down, and aspirate the supernatant.

    (d) Resuspend cells in 50 μl PBS with human FcR Block and Fixable Viability Dye e506 (*see* **Note 30**).

    (e) Incubate cells at 4 °C for 15 min shielded from light.

    (f) Wash cells with 1 ml PBS, spin down, and aspirate the supernatant.

    (g) Resuspend cells in 50 μl PBS with antibody cocktails.

    (h) Incubate cells at 4 °C for 15 min shielded from light.

    (i) Wash cells with 1 ml PBS, spin down, and aspirate the supernatant.

    (j) For surface staining, resuspend the cell pellet in 100–200 μl PBS for flow cytometry.

    (k) For intracellular staining, add 250 μl of BD fixation/permeabilization buffer to the cell pellet.

    (l) Incubate cells at 4 °C for 20–30 min, shielded from light.

    (m) Spin at 600 g for 5 min, and aspirate the supernatant.

    (n) Wash twice with BD washing buffer.

    (o) Spin and resuspend the cell pellet in 50 μl intracellular antibodies cocktail.

    (p) Incubate cells at 4 °C for 30 min shielded from light.

    (q) Wash cells twice with 1 ml wash buffer.

    (r) Resuspend cells in 100–200 μl PBS for flow cytometry.

2. Stimulate cytokine production (PMA/Ionomycin stimulation):

    (a) Resuspend cells at 1×10^6/ml in C10 medium containing PMA (final concentration 50 ng/ml) and ionomycin (final concentration 500 ng/ml).

    (b) Transfer 1 ml of cells into capped FACS tubes.

    (c) Add GolgiStop to cells (4 μl GolgiStop per 6 ml of C10 medium) and tightly close caps on FACS tubes.

    (d) Incubate at 37 °C, 5% CO_2 for 4–6 h.

    (e) Samples are ready for FACS staining (refer Subheading 3.5.1, **step 1**).

3. ELISA (following standard protocol from BD bioscience) (Fig. 1f).

(a) Coat Nunc Immunoplates with purified capturing anti-body diluted in ELISA coating buffer. Add 50 μl/well and incubate for 2 h at 37 °C or overnight at 4 °C.

(b) Wash plate four times with ELISA wash buffer.

(c) Block plate with 100 μl/ well of ELISA BBS buffer. Incubate for 30 min at 37 °C or overnight at 4 °C.

(d) Wash plate four times with ELISA wash buffer.

(e) Add samples at 25 μl or 50 μl per well. Incubate for 3 h at 37 °C or 4 °C overnight.

(f) Wash plate four times with ELISA wash buffer.

(g) Add 50 μl of the biotinylated detection antibody diluted in BBS solution buffer. Incubate for 45 min at RT.

(h) Wash plate four times with ELISA wash buffer.

(i) Add 50 μl/ well of the streptavidin-HRP, diluted 1:1000 in BBS dilution buffer. Incubate for 30 min at RT, shielded from light.

(j) Wash plate eight times with ELISA wash buffer.

(k) Mix the TMB developing solution and add 50 μl/ well. Incubate at RT.

(l) Monitor the blue color change and stop reaction by adding 50 μl/well of TMB reaction stop solution.

(m) Read absorbance at 450 nm within 30 min.

3.5.2 iNKT Cell Function Analysis

1. mHSC-iNKT cell in vivo antitumor efficacy study—mouse B16 melanoma lung metastasis mouse model [15] (Fig. 1g–i):

(a) C57BL/6 J (B6) mice received intravenous (i.v.) injection of $0.5-1 \times 10^6$ B16.F10 melanoma cells to model lung metastasis over the course of 2 weeks.

(b) On day 3 post tumor challenge, the experimental mice received i.v. injection of 1×10^6 bone marrow-derived dendritic cells (BMDCs) that were either unloaded or loaded with α-GalCer.

(c) On day 14, mice were humanely euthanized, and their lungs were collected and analyzed for melanoma metastasis by counting tumor nodules.

2. hHSC-iNKT cell tumor-attacking mechanism study [17] (Fig. 2f):

(a) In vitro direct tumor cell killing assay. Human multiple myeloma cell line MM.1S was used. MM.1S-FG or MM.1S-hCD1d-FG tumor cells ($5-10 \times 10^3$ cells per well) were co-cultured with hHSC-iNKT cells (ratio 1:1, 1:2, 1:5, and 1:10) in Corning 96-well clear bottom black plates for 24–48 h, in X-VIVO™ 15 medium with or without the addition of α-GalCer (100 ng/ml). At the end of culture, live tumor cells were quantified by adding 150 mg/ml of D-luciferin to cell cultures and reading out luciferase activities. In order to verify CD1d-dependent tumor killing mechanism, we blocked CD1d by adding 10 mg/ml LEAF™ purified anti-human CD1d antibody or LEAF™ purified mouse IgG2b κ isotype control antibody to tumor cell cultures at least 1 h prior to adding hHSC-iNKT cells. At the end of culture, live tumor cells were quantified by adding D-Luciferin to cell cultures and reading out luciferase activities.

(b) In vitro NK adjuvant effect assay. Primary human NK cells were isolated from healthy donor PBMCs through an NK Cell Isolation Kit according to the manufacturer's instructions. K562-FG cells (5×10^4 cells per well) were co-cultured with NK cells and hHSC-iNKT cells (at ratio of 1: 2: 2) in Corning 96-well clear bottom black plates for 24 h, in C10 medium with or without α-GalCer-pulsed irradiated PBMCs as antigen-presenting cells (APCs). Live tumor cells were quantified by adding D-luciferin (150 mg/ml) to the cell cultures and reading out luciferase activities.

(c) In vitro dendritic cells (DC)/cytotoxic T lymphocyte (CTL) adjuvant effect assay. CD1d⁺/HLA-A2⁺ human monocyte-derived dendritic cells (MoDCs) were generated by isolating CD14⁺ monocytes from HLA-A2⁺ healthy donor PBMCs using anti-human CD14 beads, followed by a 4-day culture in R10 medium supplemented with recombinant human GM-CSF (100 ng/ml) and IL-4 (20 ng/ml). The NY-ESO-1 specific CD8⁺ human CTLs were co-cultured with CD1d⁺/HLA-A2⁺ MoDCs in C10 medium for 3 days, with or without hHSC-iNKT cells (cell ratio 1:1:1) and α-GalCer (100 ng/ml). Tumor-killing potential of ESO-T cells was measured by adding A375-A2-ESO-FG tumor cells (1:1 ratio to input ESO-T cells) to the ESO-T/MoDC co-culture 24 h post co-culture setup and quantifying live tumor cells by luciferase activity reading in another 24 h (*see* **Note 31**).

(d) In vitro macrophage inhibition assay. CD14⁺ monocytes were isolated from healthy donor PBMCs, followed by co-culturing with hHSC-iNKT cells (ratio 1:1) for 24–48 h in C10 medium with or without the addition of α-GalCer (100 ng/ml). At the end of culture, cells were collected for flow cytometry analysis.

3. hHSC-iNKT cell in vivo antitumor efficacy study—MM.1S human multiple myeloma xenograft NSG mouse model [17] (Fig. 2g–i):

(a) NSG mice were pre-conditioned with 175 rads of total body irradiation and inoculated with $0.5–1 \times 10^6$ MM.1S-hCD1d-FG or MM.1S-FG cells intravenously (day 0) to develop multiple myeloma over the course of about 3 weeks.

(b) Three days post-tumor inoculation (day 3), mice received i.v. injection of vehicle (PBS) or 1×10^7 hHSC-iNKT cells. Recombinant human IL-15 was intraperitoneally injected to experimental animals to support the peripheral maintenance of hHSC-iNKT cells twice per week starting from day 3 (500 ng per animal per injection).

(c) The tumor burden was monitored twice per week by bioluminescence (BLI) measurement.

(d) At around week 3, mice were humanely euthanized (refer to Subheading 3.4.2), and tissues (peripheral blood, spleen, liver, and bone marrow) were collected for flow cytometry analysis.

4   Notes

1. 5-Fluorouracil (5-FU) is a chemotherapy drug used to treat cancer. 5-FU can inhibit thymidylate synthetase function during pyrimidine synthesis. The carcinogenicity and acute toxicity of 5-FU require proper handling from lab personnel.

2. The generation of mouse iNKT TCR gene delivery retroviral vector was described in our previous publication [15].

3. Human CD34$^+$ HSCs are commercially available from Hema-Care Corporation (Northridge, California, USA).

4. Human multiple myeloma (MM) cell line MM.1S, human chronic myelogenous leukemia cancer cell line K562, and human melanoma cell line A375 were all purchased from the American Type Culture Collection (ATCC) (Manassas, Virginia, USA) and cultured in ATCC recommended media. The stable MM.1S-FG and MM.1S-hCD1d-FG tumor cell lines were engineered by transducing the parental MM.1S cell line with the lentiviral vectors encoding the intended gene(s) to overexpress human CD1d and/or firefly luciferase and enhanced green fluorescence protein (GFP) dual-reporters (FG). CD1d$^+$ and/or GFP$^+$ cells were sorted by flow cytometry 72 h post viral transduction to generate stable cell lines.

5. The stable K562-FG tumor cell line was engineered by transducing the parental K562 cell line with lentiviral vectors

encoding FG. GFP⁺ cells were sorted by flow cytometry post 72 h of virus transduction to generate stable cell line.

6. The stable A375-A2-Eso-FG tumor cell line was engineered by transducing the parental A375 cell line with lentiviral vectors encoding human HLA-A2.1, human NY-ESO-1, and FG.

7. Keeping tissues on ice during processing improves the viability of cells.

8. 33%, 40%, and 60% Percoll can be prepared beforehand and stored long term at 4 °C. However, Percoll must be warmed back to RT before usage.

9. Centrifuge must be equilibrated to RT before starting and the centrifuge brakes must be turned off. Excessive deceleration can remix the separating layers.

10. Cells from spleen and liver can be combined for in vitro expansion if needed. Cells from multiple mice can be combined if needed.

11. mMNC-iNKT cells may be expanded and cultured in vitro for up to 3 weeks using repetitive stimulations with anti-CD3ε and anti-CD28 every 7–8 days [18]. α-GalCer stimulation leads to apoptosis and is not suitable for long-term expansion of mouse iNKT cells [18].

12. We have established a B6-miNKT mouse model through genetic engineering of hematopoietic stem cells [15] to produce large numbers of iNKT cells. Compared to B6-WT mice, B6-miNKT mice provide a significantly higher yield of iNKT cells.

13. Spin infections on two sequential days increase retrovirus transduction rate. Preferably, the second infection should be performed within 12–15 h after the first one to infect cells at different stages of the cell cycle.

14. For a secondary BM transfer, fresh whole BM cells harvested from the primary BM recipients are intravenously injected into secondary B6 recipient mice that had received 1200 rads of total body irradiation (~1 × 10^7 total BM cells per recipient). Details were described in previous publications [15, 16].

15. Tilt the tube and bring the pipette close to surface of the blood/PBS mixture. Slowly pipette out 1–2 ml. Then detach the pipette to allow gravity to dispense the remainder of the Ficoll. When the flow stops, reattach the pipette to push out any remaining Ficoll before removing the pipette from the conical tube. Be extremely careful at this step to make sure that the interface is not disturbed.

16. Choose the right column to use based on the sample cell number. For example, if there are ~2 × 10^8 total PBMCs, use one LS column.

17. Do not let the column dry out and avoid adding bubbles into the column. Bubbles inside the column can interfere with the sample and decrease selection efficacy.

18. To increase the purity, the eluted fraction can be enriched over a second column. Repeat the magnetic separation procedure as described if needed.

19. α-GalCer glycolipid and DMSO are immiscible at RT. To prepare the stock α-GalCer (1 µg/µl), add the proper volume of DMSO into the α-GalCer powder and heat it at 80 °C in a water bath for 10 min, followed by 10 min of sonication at 50 °C. Then, vortex the vial for full 2 min until the solution turns clear. Aliquot it into glass vials and store them in a −20 °C freezer. To prepare the α-GalCer working solution (5 µg/ml), heat the aliquot at 80 °C for 5 min followed by 5 min of sonicating at 50 °C. Then vortex the aliquot for a full 60 s and add 200 µl of pre-warmed C10 medium. Sonicate for another 5 min and vortex for 60 s. Add the rest of the pre-warmed C10 medium to make the final concentration 5 µg/ml. α-GalCer aliquots from −20 °C are single-used. Do not refreeze after diluting with media.

20. Cell expansion fold is donor-dependent. iNKT cells from different donors can be in vitro expanded for up to 3 weeks.

21. Standard BLT (human bone marrow-liver-thymus engrafted NOD/SCID/γc$^{-/-}$) humanized mouse is established by co-implanting human fetal liver and thymus pieces under the renal capsule of NSG mouse together with intravenous injection of human CD34$^+$ HSCs. In our modified approach, only thymus pieces are placed under the renal capsule together with intravenous injection of engineered CD34$^+$ HSC.

22. RN-coated plate with PBS can be left for several hours in the hood.

23. Pre-stimulate CD34$^+$ cells for 12–18 h before transduction. One option is to coat the plate in the late afternoon and seed cells at around 6 pm. The next morning, add the virus for transduction.

24. The generation of human iNKT lentivirus is described in our prior publication [15]. Do not vortex, just very gently mix the concentrated virus. If necessary, adding poloxamer and PEG-2 can improve virus transduction rate [19].

25. Both fresh and frozen fetal thymus can be used for implantation. Fetal thymus should be pre-cut into 1 mm^3 cube size. Each mouse can be implanted with one to two pieces of thymus fragments.

26. Keep small portions of un-transduced and transduced CD34$^+$ cells in X-VIVO-15 media supplemented with cytokines post

virus transduction for a 72-h culture. Collect cells and perform intracellular staining of Vβ11 to detect the virus transduction efficacy.

27. Carprofen works as painkiller to relieve the pain from surgery. It can be substitute with other analgesics based on institution recommendation.

28. The viral transduction rate, the quality of human fetal thymus, and the quality of surgery will all contribute to the quality of HSC reconstitutions. BLT-iNKT mice can live around 6 months to 1 year.

29. Sorted iNKT cells are expected to expand tenfold in the first week and another tenfold in the second week.

30. Optimize antibody dilution beforehand.

31. NY-ESO-1 specific CD8$^+$ human cytotoxic T lymphocytes (CTLs, or ESO-T cells) were generated through engineering human CD34$^+$ HSCs with a TCR gene encoding a 1G4 TCR (HLA-A2- restricted, NY-ESO-1 tumor antigen-specific) and differentiating the TCR gene-engineered HSCs into CD8+ CTLs in an artificial thymic organoid (ATO) culture [17].

Acknowledgments

We thank the University of California, Los Angeles (UCLA) animal facility for providing animal support and the UCLA Virology Core for providing human blood from healthy donors. This work was supported by a Director's New Innovator Award from the NIH (DP2 CA196335, to L.Y.), a Partnering Opportunity for Translational Research Projects Award from the California Institute for Regenerative Medicine (CIRM TRAN1-08533, to L.Y.), a Stem Cell Research Award from the Concern Foundation (to L.Y.), a Research Career Development Award from the STOP CANCER Foundation (to L.Y.), and a BSCRC-RHF Research Award from the Rose Hills Research Foundation (to L.Y.). Y.-R.L. is a predoctoral fellow supported by the UCLA Whitcome Predoctoral Fellowship in Molecular Biology. We acknowledge Tasha Tsao and Emily Peng for proofreading the content.

References

1. Bendelac A, Savage PB, Teyton L (2007) The biology of NKT cells. Annu Rev Immunol 25:297–336. https://doi.org/10.1146/annurev.immunol.25.022106.141711

2. Bennstein SB (2017) Unraveling natural killer T-cells development. Front Immunol 8:1950. https://doi.org/10.3389/fimmu.2017.01950

3. Mori L, Lepore M, De Libero G (2016) The immunology of CD1- and MR1-restricted T cells. Annu Rev Immunol 34:479–510. https://doi.org/10.1146/annurev-immunol-032414-112008

4. Godfrey DI, Stankovic S, Baxter AG (2010) Raising the NKT cell family. Nat Immunol 11

(3):197–206. https://doi.org/10.1038/ni.1841

5. Godfrey DI, Berzins SP (2007) Control points in NKT-cell development. Nat Rev Immunol 7 (7):505–518. https://doi.org/10.1038/nri2116

6. Fujii SI, Shimizu K (2019) Immune networks and therapeutic targeting of iNKT cells in cancer. Trends Immunol 40(11):984–997. https://doi.org/10.1016/j.it.2019.09.008

7. Nagato K, Motohashi S, Ishibashi F, Okita K, Yamasaki K, Moriya Y, Hoshino H, Yoshida S, Hanaoka H, Fujii S, Taniguchi M, Yoshino I, Nakayama T (2012) Accumulation of activated invariant natural killer T cells in the tumor microenvironment after alpha-galactosylceramide-pulsed antigen presenting cells. J Clin Immunol 32(5):1071–1081. https://doi.org/10.1007/s10875-012-9697-9

8. Exley MA, Friedlander P, Alatrakchi N, Vriend L, Yue S, Sasada T, Zeng W, Mizukami Y, Clark J, Nemer D, LeClair K, Canning C, Daley H, Dranoff G, Giobbie-Hurder A, Hodi FS, Ritz J, Balk SP (2017) Adoptive transfer of invariant NKT cells as immunotherapy for advanced melanoma: a phase I clinical trial. Clin Cancer Res 23 (14):3510–3519. https://doi.org/10.1158/1078-0432.CCR-16-0600

9. Takami M, Ihara F, Motohashi S (2018) Clinical application of iNKT cell-mediated antitumor activity against lung cancer and head and neck cancer. Front Immunol 9:2021. https://doi.org/10.3389/fimmu.2018.02021

10. Bedard M, Salio M, Cerundolo V (2017) Harnessing the power of invariant natural killer T cells in cancer immunotherapy. Front Immunol 8:1829. https://doi.org/10.3389/fimmu.2017.01829

11. Torina A, Guggino G, La Manna MP, Sireci G (2018) The Janus face of NKT cell function in autoimmunity and infectious diseases. Int J Mol Sci 19(2):440. https://doi.org/10.3390/ijms19020440

12. Lundblad LKA, Gulec N, Poynter ME, DeVault VL, Dienz O, Boyson JE, Daphtary N, Aliyeva M, Ather JL, Scheuplein F, Schaub R (2017) The role of iNKT cells on the phenotypes of allergic airways in a mouse model. Pulm Pharmacol Ther 45:80–89. https://doi.org/10.1016/j.pupt.2017.05.003

13. Nair S, Dhodapkar MV (2017) Natural killer T cells in cancer immunotherapy. Front Immunol

8:1178. https://doi.org/10.3389/fimmu.2017.01178

14. de Lalla C, Rinaldi A, Montagna D, Azzimonti L, Bernardo ME, Sangalli LM, Paganoni AM, Maccario R, Di Cesare-Merlone A, Zecca M, Locatelli F, Dellabona P, Casorati G (2011) Invariant NKT cell reconstitution in pediatric leukemia patients given HLA-haploidentical stem cell transplantation defines distinct CD4+ and CD4- subset dynamics and correlates with remission state. J Immunol 186 (7):4490–4499. https://doi.org/10.4049/jimmunol.1003748

15. Smith DJ, Liu S, Ji S, Li B, McLaughlin J, Cheng D, Witte ON, Yang L (2015) Genetic engineering of hematopoietic stem cells to generate invariant natural killer T cells. Proc Natl Acad Sci U S A 112(5):1523–1528. https://doi.org/10.1073/pnas.1424877112

16. Smith DJ, Lin LJ, Moon H, Pham AT, Wang X, Liu S, Ji S, Rezek V, Shimizu S, Ruiz M, Lam J, Janzen DM, Memarzadeh S, Kohn DB, Zack JA, Kitchen SG, An DS, Yang L (2016) Propagating humanized BLT mice for the study of human immunology and immunotherapy. Stem Cells Dev 25(24):1863–1873. https://doi.org/10.1089/scd.2016.0193

17. Zhu Y, Smith DJ, Zhou Y, Li YR, Yu J, Lee D, Wang YC, Di Biase S, Wang X, Hardoy C, Ku J, Tsao T, Lin LJ, Pham AT, Moon H, McLaughlin J, Cheng D, Hollis RP, Campo-Fernandez B, Urbinati F, Wei L, Pang L, Rezek V, Berent-Maoz B, Macabali MH, Gjertson D, Wang X, Galic Z, Kitchen SG, An DS, Hu-Lieskovan S, Kaplan-Lefko PJ, De Oliveira SN, Seet CS, Larson SM, Forman SJ, Heath JR, Zack JA, Crooks GM, Radu CG, Ribas A, Kohn DB, Witte ON, Yang L (2019) Development of hematopoietic stem cell-engineered invariant natural killer T cell therapy for cancer. Cell Stem Cell 25(4):542–557. e549. https://doi.org/10.1016/j.stem.2019.08.004

18. Watarai H, Nakagawa R, Omori-Miyake M, Dashtsoodol N, Taniguchi M (2008) Methods for detection, isolation and culture of mouse and human invariant NKT cells. Nat Protoc 3 (1):70–78. https://doi.org/10.1038/nprot.2007.515

19. Masiuk KE, Zhang R, Osborne K, Hollis RP, Campo-Fernandez B, Kohn DB (2019) PGE2 and Poloxamer Synperonic F108 enhance transduction of human HSPCs with a beta-globin lentiviral vector. Mol Ther Methods Clin Dev 13:390–398. https://doi.org/10.1016/j.omtm.2019.03.005

Chapter 5

Isolation and Detection of Murine iNKT Cells in Different Organs

Mengqing Cong, Xiang Li, Haopeng Fang, Li Bai, Xucai Zheng, and Bofeng Li

Abstract

The invariant NKT (iNKT) cells are innate-like lymphocytes that share phenotypic and functional characteristics with NK cells and T cells, playing an important role in both human and mouse physiology and disease and bridging the gap between the innate and adaptive immune responses. The frequency and subtypes of iNKT cells in major immune organs are different, which also determines the regional immune characteristics of iNKT cells. Here, we report a protocol about the isolation of iNKT cells in the thymus, spleen, and liver of C57BL/6, CD1d$^{-/-}$, and Jα18$^{-/-}$ mice.

Key words iNKT cells, Spleen, Thymus, Liver

1 Introduction

1.1 The Characteristics of iNKT Cells

The invariant NKT (iNKT) cells are innate-like lymphocytes that are conserved in mice and humans and share phenotypic and functional characteristics with NK cells and T cells, connecting the innate and adaptive immune responses [1, 2]. iNKT cells have relatively constant TCR chains (Vα24-Jα18/Vβ11 in humans, Vα14-Jα18/Vβ8.2, Vβ7, Vβ2 in mice), which recognize glycolipid antigens and can be efficiently activated through recognition of α-galactosylceramide (α-GalCer) in the context of CD1d, a monomorphic MHC class I-like molecule [3–5]. After the activation, NKT cells produce large amount of Th1 and Th2 cytokines (IL-2, IL-4, IL-6, IL-10, IL-17, IFN-γ, and TNF-α), enabling them to act as powerful regulators of the immune system [1, 6], including modulating Th1/Th2 immune balance, and affecting the function of other immune cells such as T cells, B cells, DCs, and

---

Mengqing Cong and Xiang Li contributed equally to this work.

Chaohong Liu (ed.), *Invariant Natural Killer T-Cells: Methods and Protocols*, Methods in Molecular Biology, vol. 2388, https://doi.org/10.1007/978-1-0716-1775-5_5,

macrophages [7]. iNKT cells also express typical markers of NK cells, including inhibitory and activated killer receptors, such as NK1.1, CD16, and CD122, exerting cytotoxic effects in certain condition [8].

1.2 The Function of iNKT

iNKT cells play a crucial role in a number of immune-related diseases. They not only help the antitumor immunity and anti-infection effect but also induce immunosuppression in a series of autoimmune diseases and organ transplantation rejection, such as type 1 diabetes mellitus, autoimmune encephalomyelitis (EAE), multiple sclerosis (MS), systemic lupus erythematosus (SLE), and rheumatoid arthritis (RA) [8–11]. In addition, iNKT cells play an indispensable role in immune and metabolic-related diseases, including obesity, type 2 diabetes, and cardiovascular diseases (CVD) [12].

1.3 iNKT Cells Development

iNKT precursor cells are derived from thymus $CD4^+CD8^+$ double-positive cells and escaped the traditional T cell development pathway [13]. However, they still need to go through positive selection and negative selection to obtain appropriate, semi-invariant and CD1d-dependent TCR and self-tolerance [14, 15]. In addition to positive selection and negative selection, iNKT cells then mature through the following four stages based on the different expression of cell surface proteins CD24, CD44, and NK1.1, including stage 0 ($CD24^+CD44^{lo}NK1.1^{lo}$), stage 1 ($CD24^-CD44^{lo}NK1.1^{lo}$), stage 2 ($CD24^-CD44^{hi}NK1.1^{lo}$), and stage 3 ($CD24^-CD44^{hi}NK1.1^+$) [16, 17]. During the process of maturation, some iNKT cells begin to leave thymus and migrate into peripheral organs for further maturation at stage 2 [18, 19].

1.4 The Subtypes of iNKT Cells

According to the different transcription factors and cell functions, iNKT cells are distributed in the peripheral tissues in the form of at least three major subpopulations (NKT1, NKT2, and NKT17 cells) and play various roles by releasing different cytokines (inflammatory and anti-inflammatory) [20–24]. The frequency and subtypes of iNKT cells in different tissues and organs of mice are variable greatly, which also determines the regional immune characteristics of iNKT cells. Different organs have different isolation methods. Here, we describe a modified version of this protocol about isolating iNKT cells from the spleen, liver, and thymus, based on previous report [25, 26]. We compared the percentage and number of total iNKT cells in the thymus, spleen, and liver of C57BL/6, $CD1d^{-/-}$, and $J\alpha18^{-/-}$ mice by using CD1d tetramers and TCRβ to gate iNKT cells.

2   Materials

2.1   Mice

1. Wild-type C57BL/6J mice: Purchase from Charles River Laboratories.

2. CD1d$^{-/-}$ mice: On the C57BL/6 background were provided by Prof. Albert Bendelac.

3. Jα18$^{-/-}$ mice: On the C57BL/6 background were provided by Prof. Albert Bendelac.

2.2   Materials and Solutions

1. 75% alcohol.

2. 10× PBS: 80 g NaCl, 2 g KCl, 29 g Na$_2$HPO$_4$·12H$_2$O and 2 g KH$_2$PO$_4$ in 1 L ddH$_2$O.

3. 1× PBS: Diluted from 10× PBS by ddH$_2$O.

4. Hemolysis buffer: Beyotime, Cat #: C3702-120 Ml.

5. The stock solution of Percoll: GE Healthcare, Lot: 10276722. 100% Percoll: Use Percoll stock solution with 10*PBS in accordance with volume ratio 9:1.

   40% Percoll: Diluted from 100% Percoll by 1× PBS.

   70% Percoll: Diluted from 100% Percoll by 1× PBS.

6. Antibodies:
   Purified anti-mouse CD16/CD32 antibody: BioLegend, Cat#: 101302, clone: 93, working dilution 1/200.

   PerCP/Cyanine5.5 anti-mouse CD45: BioLegend, Cat #: 103132, clone: 30-F11, working dilution 1/100.

   FITC anti-mouse TCR β chain antibody: BioLegend, Cat #: 109206, clone: H57-597, working dilution 1/100.

   PE anti-mouse CD24: BioLegend, Cat #: 138504, clone: 30-F1, working dilution 1/100.

   PerCP/Cyanine5.5 anti-mouse/human CD44 Antibody: BioLegend, Cat #: 103032, clone: IM7, working dilution 1/100.

   CD1d-tetramers: Provide by NIH, working dilution 1/200.

   PE/Cyanine7 anti-mouse NK-1.1 Antibody: BioLegend, Cat #: 108714, clone: PK136, working dilution 1/300.

7. DAPI: Sigma-Aldrich, Cat #: D9542, working concentration: 2 μg/mL.

8. 200 mesh iron gauze net (70 μm strainer): Purchase from Consumables Company in China.

9. 200 mesh nylon mesh (70 μm strainer): Purchase from Consumables Company in China.

10. Scissors and tweezers: Purchase from Consumables Company in China.

11. 1 mL syringe plunger: Purchase from Consumables Company in China.

12. 1.5 mL Eppendorf tube: Purchase from Consumables Company in China.

13. 15 mL and 50 mL centrifuge tube: NEST company.

14. Hemocytometer chamber: Purchase from Consumables Company in China.

15. FACS tubes: BD, cat#: 352008-Falcon.

2.3 Equipment

1. Cryogenic Centrifuge: Xiangyi, L535R.

2. Vortexer: DLVB.

3. FACS DIVA: BD FACSVerse.

2.4 Software

1. FlowJo™ 10 software.

2. GraphPad Prism 7.04.

3 Methods

3.1 Preparation of Tissue Samples from C57BL/6, CD1d$^{-/-}$, and Jα18$^{-/-}$ Mice

1. 8 to 12 weeks male C57BL/6, CD1d$^{-/-}$, or Jα18$^{-/-}$ mice are used as experimental mice (5 mice in each group).

2. Mice are euthanized via cervical dislocation, and the abdominal fur of mice is disinfected with 75% alcohol, the liver and spleen in abdominal cavity and thymus in the chest are carefully harvested by dissection tools, and put them in 1 x PBS on ice for later use.

3.2 Isolation of Splenocytes

1. Put 200 mesh iron gauze net (70 μm strainer) on the 50 mL centrifugal tube, cut the spleen separated in Subheading 3.1 step into several small segments with scissors and apply the spleen on it, rinse the strainer with 1× PBS, splenocytes are collected in PBS and gently homogenize through a 70 μm cell strainer using the hard end of a syringe plunger, and keep rinsing the strainer with PBS while homogenizing the spleen until all the residual tissues are white connective tissue (*see* **Note 1**). Centrifuge at 650 × *g* for 10 min at 4 °C.

2. After centrifugation, remove the supernatant, and add 1 mL hemolysis buffer; incubate 5 min at room temperature to lyse redundant erythrocytes (*see* **Note 2**).

3. After RBCs fully lysis, 10 mL 1× PBS is added to terminate the lysis and then passed through a 70 μm cell strainer to obtain a single cell suspension. Centrifuge at 650 × *g* for 10 min at 4 °C,

and collect cell pellet at the bottom of the tube, washing cells with 1× PBS again.

4. The cells at the bottom of the tube are splenocytes. Resuspend cells with an appropriate volume of 1× PBS, cells are counted using a hemocytometer chamber, and stored at 4 °C for subsequent FACS analysis.

3.3 Isolation of Thymocytes

1. Put 200 mesh iron gauze net (70 μm strainer) on the top of the 50 mL centrifuge tube, cut the thymus separated in Subheading 3.1 step into several small segments with scissors, rinse the gauze with 1× PBS, thymocytes are collected in PBS and gently homogenized through a 70 μm cell strainer using the hard end of the syringe plunger, and keep rinsing the strainer with PBS while homogenizing the thymus until all the residual tissues are white connective tissue (*see* **Note 1**). Centrifuge at 650 × g for 10 min at 4 °C.

2. Cells pellet at the bottom of the tube are thymocytes. Resuspend cells with an appropriate volume of 1× PBS. Cells are counted using a hemocytometer chamber and stored at 4 °C for subsequent FACS analysis.

3.4 Harvest Lymphocytes from the Liver

1. Experimental preparation: the stock solution of Percoll is mixed with 10× PBS at 9:1 ratio to acquire 100% Percoll, which is further diluted to 40% Percoll with 1× PBS (*see* Subheading 2.2, **item 5**).

2. Put 200 mesh iron gauze net (70 μm strainer) on the top of the 50 mL centrifuge tube, cut the liver separated in Subheading 3.1 into several small segments with scissors, rinse the gauze with 1× PBS, liver single cells are collected in PBS and gently homogenize through a 70 μm cell strainer using the hard end of the syringe plunger, and keep rinsing the strainer with PBS while homogenizing the liver until all the residual tissues are connective tissue (*see* **Note 1**).

3. Add 1× PBS up to 50 mL, centrifuge at 50 × g for 2 min at 4 °C, and only keep the cell supernatant.

4. Repeat **step 3** for 2–3 times to remove hepatocytes to the most extent, and only keep the cell supernatant, then centrifuge at 650 × g for 10 min at 4 °C, and collect cells at the bottom of the tube.

5. Cells are resuspended with 3–4 mL 40% Percoll solution and then added on 3 mL 70% Percoll along the wall of centrifugal tube carefully; keep the interface between 40% and 70% Percoll clear and no shaking as far as possible (*see* **Notes 3** and **4**). Centrifuge at 1260 × g for 30 min at room temperature, with the speed increased by 6 and decreased by 2.

6. After centrifugation, cells at the interface between 40% and 70% Percoll layer are retained and resuspended with 1× PBS, centrifuge at 650 × g for 10 min at 4 °C (*see* **Note 5**). Cells at the bottom of the tube were collected and washed again with 1× PBS.

7. Cells pellet at the bottom of the centrifuge tube are liver lymphocytes, which are resuspended with 1× PBS, counted using a hemocytometer chamber and stored at 4 °C for subsequent FACS analysis.

3.5 Detection iNKT Cells by Flow Cytometry

1. Take the spleen, thymus, and liver lymphocytes prepared in Subheadings 3.2, 3.3, and 3.4, respectively. Adjust the number of cells per test ranging from 2×10^5 to 1×10^6 cells in 100 μL PBS each tube.

2. Purified anti-mouse CD16/CD32 antibody was added to each sample in **step 1** (dosage see antibodies in Subheading 2.2, **item 6**), which blocks antibodies unspecific binding sites on cells, and incubated at 4 °C for 15 min.

3. The combined flow cytometric antibodies (dosage see antibodies in Subheading 2.2, **item 6**) were added into each tube. The antibodies used in the study are listed here: PerCP/Cyanine5.5 anti-mouse CD45, FITC anti-mouse TCR β chain antibody, PE anti-mouse CD24, PerCP/Cyanine5.5 anti-mouse/human CD44 Antibody, CD1d-tetramers, and PE/Cyanine7 anti-mouse NK1.1 Antibody. Antibodies are added into each sample in **step 2** and incubated in dark at 4 °C for 45 min (*see* **Note 6**).

4. Wash with 1 mL 1× PBS, and then centrifuge at 650 × g for 10 min at 4 °C. Collect cells at the bottom of the tube, and resuspend with 200 μL 1× PBS. Cells are filtered into the flow tube through 200 mesh nylon mesh and placed on the ice for recording by flow cytometry.

5. 5 min before flow cytometry record, DAPI (used to distinguish dead and living cells) is added and mixed well. Then record cells by FACS DIVA.

6. All flow cytometry data are analyzed with FlowJo™ 10 software and GraphPad Prism 7.04 software.

3.6 Representative Results

We detected the percentage and number of total iNKT cells in the thymus, spleen, and liver of C57BL/6, CD1d$^{-/-}$, and Jα18$^{-/-}$ mice by using CD1d-tetramers and TCR β to label iNKT cells. The scheme of the iNKT gating in the liver, spleen, and thymus of C57BL/6, CD1d$^{-/-}$, and Jα18$^{-/-}$ mice is shown in Fig. 1, CD1d-tetramer$^+$ TCRβ$^+$ cells are considered as iNKT cells. The detailed proportions and numbers of total iNKT cells in the liver,

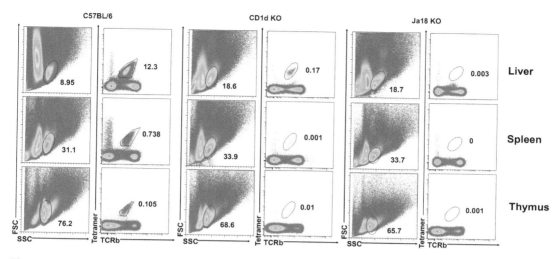

Fig. 1 Scheme of the iNKT gate in the liver, spleen, and thymus of C57BL/6, CD1d$^{-/-}$, and Jα18$^{-/-}$ mice. Five male C57BL/6, CD1d$^{-/-}$, or Jα18$^{-/-}$ mice aged from 8 to 12 weeks were sacrificed, removing the liver, spleen, and thymus to harvest the single cell suspension. iNKT cells were gated on CD1d-tetramer$^+$ TCRβ$^+$ by FACS

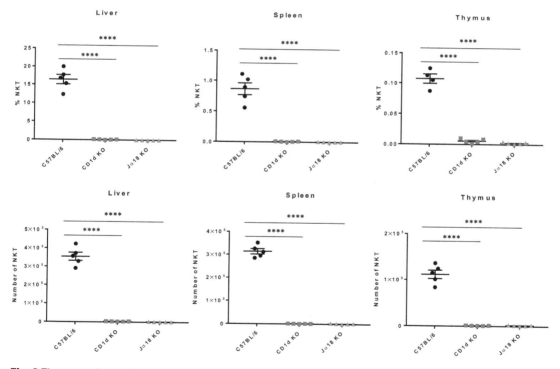

Fig. 2 The proportion and number of total iNKT cells in the liver, spleen, and thymus of C57BL/6, CD1d$^{-/-}$, and Jα18$^{-/-}$ mice. The liver, spleen, and thymus were harvested, and cells were stained directly ex vivo by CD1d tetramers and TCRβ, showing the proportion and number of iNKT cells in CD45$^+$ cells. Symbols represent individual animals. Data are shown by mean plus SEM. Significant was determined by unpaired t-test ($n = 5$ mice per group). * $p < 0.05$,*** $p < 0.001$, *** $p < 0.001$,**** $p < 0.0001$

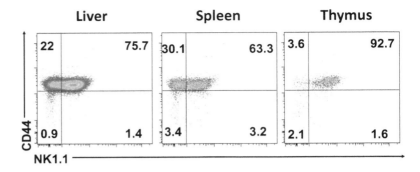

Fig. 3 The stage of iNKT cell development in the liver, spleen, and thymus of C57BL/6 mice. C57BL/6 mice aged from 8 to 12 weeks were sacrificed, removing the liver, spleen, and thymus to harvest the single cell suspension and detecting the developmental stage of iNKT cells by FACS according to using anti-mouse CD24, CD44, and NK1.1 antibody. NKT stage 0 and 1, $CD44^{lo}$ $NK1.1^{lo}$; NKT stage 2, $CD44^{hi}$ $NK1.1^{lo}$; NKT stage 3, $CD44^{hi}NK1.1^{+}$

spleen, and thymus of C57BL/6, $CD1d^{-/-}$, and $J\alpha18^{-/-}$ mice are shown in Fig. 2. Moreover, we also detected the stage of iNKT cell development in the liver, spleen, and thymus of C57BL/6 mice which divided into four stages according to the different expression of cell surface proteins CD24, CD44, and NK1.1: stage 0 ($CD24^{+}CD44^{lo}NK1.1^{lo}$), stage 1 ($CD24^{-}CD44^{lo}NK1.1^{lo}$), stage 2 ($CD24^{-}CD44^{hi}NK1.1^{lo}$), and stage 3 ($CD24^{-}CD44^{hi}NK1.1^{+}$). Due to very few iNKT cells in these organs, we did not detect the iNKT cells development in $CD1d^{-/-}$ and $J\alpha18^{-/-}$ mice (Fig. 3).

3.7 Discussion

The invariant NKT (iNKT) cells bridge the gap between the innate and adaptive immune responses and played an important role in both human and mouse physiology and disease. iNKT was distributed variously in different tissues, which also determines the regional immune characteristics of iNKT cells. Here, we detect the proportions, numbers, and developmental stage of iNKT cells in the thymus, spleen, and liver of C57BL/6, $CD1d^{-/-}$, and $J\alpha18^{-/-}$ mice. Our results showed that the proportions and numbers of iNKT were abundant in the liver of C57BL/6 mice, occupying around 20% of total immune cells, while that in spleen and thymus is only about 1% (Figs. 1 and 2). Moreover, in the liver and spleen of C57BL/6 mice, iNKT is mainly at stage 2 and stage 3, indicating most iNKT cells are mature in these organs. In the thymus, almost all iNKT cells in the thymus are at stage 3, rather than other immature stages (Fig. 3). During the development of iNKT, TCR rearrangement and positive and negative selection are required, which $J\alpha18$ and CD1d play an indispensable role [27]. Once lost the gene of $J\alpha18$ or CD1d, iNKT cells fail to reach maturity and go through death. Our results also confirm this result, because in CD1d$^{-/-}$ or Jα18$^{-/-}$ mice, it is hard to detect iNKT cells in the liver, spleen, and thymus (Fig. 3).

Notably, considering the inconvenient of liver perfusion and there was no significant difference between the effect of traditional grinding liver and liver perfusion on iNKT separation, we prefer to use the traditional liver grinding method to isolate liver iNKT cells.

In summary, we provide a modified protocol and basic data about NKT cells distribution in different organs for further NKT research.

4   Notes

1. During homogenizing the spleen, thymus, and liver through a 70 μm cell strainer using the hard end of a syringe plunger, pay attention to vertical grinding up and down, rather than grinding left and right, and wash the isolated single cells into the centrifuge tube in time to prevent the secondary damage to the cells by grinding (*see* Subheading 3.2, **step 1**, Subheading 3.3, **step 1**, and Subheading 3.4, **step 2**).

2. When lysis RBCs, keep in mind of homogenizing the cells by vortex immediately to ensure sufficient lysis of red blood cells, where the cell suspension change from turbid to clear (*see* Subheading 3.2, **step 2**).

3. In order to have an effective separation of lymphocytes, Percoll should be kept at room temperature; otherwise, low temperature will affect the density of Percoll (*see* Subheading 3.4, **step 5**).

4. In order to keep the interface between 40% and 70% Percoll clear and no shaking, the centrifuge tube should be tilted, and 40% Percoll should be added on 70% Percoll at a constant speed, which is beneficial to the effective separation of lymphocytes (*see* Subheading 3.4, **step 5**).

5. Collecte the cells at the edge of the interface of 40% and 70% percoll layer, and dilute the collected cell suspension with 1 x PBS as much as possible and mixing it well, which can prevent the loss of target cells as much as possible (*see* Subheading 3.4, **step 6**).

6. In order to reduce the operation error between samples, mix the antibodies as much as possible, and then add it to each sample evenly (*see* Subheading 3.5, **step 3**).

References

1. Bendelac A, Savage PB, Teyton L (2007) The biology of NKT cells. Annu Rev Immunol 25:297–336

2. Gumperz JE (2006) The ins and outs of CD1 molecules: bringing lipids under immunological surveillance. Traffic 7(1):2–13

3. Exley M, Garcia J, Balk SP, Porcelli S (1997) Requirements for CD1d recognition by human invariant Valpha24+ CD4-CD8- T cells. J Exp Med 186(1):109–120

4. Gumperz JE, Miyake S, Yamamura T, Brenner MB (2002) Functionally distinct subsets of CD1d-restricted natural killer T cells revealed by CD1d tetramer staining. J Exp Med 195 (5):625–636

5. Kawano T, Cui J, Koezuka Y, Toura I, Kaneko Y, Motoki K, Ueno H, Nakagawa R, Sato H, Kondo E, Koseki H, Taniguchi M (1997) CD1d-restricted and TCR-mediated activation of valpha14 NKT cells by glycosylceramides. Science 278(5343):1626–1629

6. Ververs FA, Kalkhoven E, Van't Land B, Boes M, Schipper HS (2018) Immunometabolic activation of invariant natural koiller T Cells. Front Immunol 9:1192. https://doi.org/10.3389/fimmu.2018.01192

7. Brigl M, Brenner MB (2004) CD1: antigen presentation and T cell function. Annu Rev Immunol 22:817–890

8. Kohlgruber AC, Donado CA, LaMarche NM, Brenner MB, Brennan PJ (2016) Activation strategies for invariant natural killer T cells. Immunogenetics 68(8):649–663. https://doi.org/10.1007/s00251-016-0944-8

9. Brennan PJ, Brigl M, Brenner MB (2013) Invariant natural killer T cells: an innate activation scheme linked to diverse effector functions. Nat Rev Immunol 13(2):101–117. https://doi.org/10.1038/nri3369

10. Cohen NR, Garg S, Brenner MB (2009) Antigen presentation by CD1 lipids, T cells, and NKT cells in microbial Immunity. Adv Immunol 102:1–94. https://doi.org/10.1016/S0065-2776(09)01201-2

11. Kim EY, Lynch L, Brennan PJ, Cohen NR, Brenner MB (2015) The transcriptional programs of iNKT cells. Semin Immunol 27 (1):26–32. https://doi.org/10.1016/j.smim.2015.02.005

12. van Eijkeren RJ, Krabbe O, Boes M, Schipper HS, Kalkhoven E (2018) Endogenous lipid antigens for invariant natural killer T cells hold the reins in adipose tissue homeostasis. Immunology 153(2):179–189. https://doi.org/10.1111/imm.12839

13. Egawa T, Eberl G, Taniuchi I, Benlagha K, Geissmann F, Hennighausen L, Bendelac A, Littman DR (2005) Genetic evidence supporting selection of the Valpha14i NKT cell lineage from double-positive thymocyte precursors. Immunity 22(6):705–716

14. Bendelac A (1995) Mouse NK1+ T cells. Curr Opin Immunol 7(3):367–374

15. Godfrey DI, Berzins SP (2007) Control points in NKT-cell development.Nature reviews. Immunology 7(7):505–518

16. Tuttle KD, Gapin L (2018) Characterization of Thymic development of natural killer T cell subsets by multiparameter flow cytometry. Methods Mol Biol 1799:121–133. https://doi.org/10.1007/978-1-4939-7896-0_11

17. Benlagha K, Wei DG, Veiga J, Teyton L, Bendelac A (2005) Characterization of the early stages of thymic NKT cell development. J Exp Med 202(4):485–492

18. Benlagha K, Kyin T, Beavis A, Teyton L, Bendelac A (2002) A thymic precursor to the NK T cell lineage. Science 296(5567):553–555

19. Pellicci DG, KJL H, Uldrich AP, Baxter AG, Smyth MJ, Godfrey DI (2002) A natural killer T (NKT) cell developmental pathway iInvolving a thymus-dependent NK1.1(−)CD4(+) CD1d-dependent precursor stage. J Exp Med 195(7):835–844

20. Wei DG, Lee H, Park S, Beaudoin L, Teyton L, Lehuen A, Bendelac A (2005) Expansion and long-range differentiation of the NKT cell lineage in mice expressing CD1d exclusively on cortical thymocytes. J Exp Med 202 (2):239–248

21. Savage AK, Constantinides MG, Han J, Picard D, Martin E, Li B, Lantz O, Bendelac A (2008) The transcription factor PLZF directs the effector program of the NKT cell lineage. Immunity 29(3):391–403. https://doi.org/10.1016/j.immuni.2008.07.011

22. Kovalovsky D, Uche OU, Eladad S, Hobbs RM, Yi W, Alonzo E, Chua K, Eidson M, Kim H, Im JS, Pandolfi PP, Sant'Angelo DB (2008) The BTB-zinc finger transcriptional regulator PLZF controls the development of invariant natural killer T cell effector functions. Nat Immunol 9(9):1055–1064. https://doi.org/10.1038/ni.1641

23. Lee YJ, Holzapfel KL, Zhu J, Jameson SC, Hogquist KA (2013) Steady-state production of IL-4 modulates immunity in mouse strains and is determined by lineage diversity of iNKT cells. Nat Immunol 14(11):1146–1154. https://doi.org/10.1038/ni.2731

24. Kwon D, Lee YJ (2017) Lineage differentiation program of invariant natural killer T cells. Immune Netw 17(6):365–377. https://doi.org/10.4110/in.2017.17.6.365

25. Watarai H, Nakagawa R, Omori-Miyake M, Dashtsoodol N, Taniguchi M (2008) Methods for detection, isolation and culture of mouse and human invariant NKT cells. Nat Protoc 3(1):70–78. https://doi.org/10.1038/nprot.2007.515

26. Fang X, Du P, Liu Y, Tang J (2010) Efficient isolation of mouse liver NKT cells by perfusion. PLoS One 5(4):e10288. https://doi.org/10.1371/journal.pone.0010288

27. Zhang J, Bedel R, Krovi SH, Tuttle KD, Zhang B, Gross J, Gapin L, Matsuda JL (2016) Mutation of the Traj18 gene segment using TALENs to generate natural killer T cell deficient mice. Sci Rep 6(1). https://doi.org/10.1038/srep27375

Chapter 6

Identifying, Isolation, and Functional Use of Human Liver iNKT Cells

Wenjing He, Dongmei Ye, and Yifang Gao

Abstract

It is widely accepted that iNKT cells are abundant in the liver and play a role in various liver disorders. In here, we describe an optimized protocol in identifying and isolating invariant natural killer T (iNKT) cells by magnetic beads to further use in functional assays.

Key words iNKT, Proliferation, Flow cytometry

1 Introduction

In recent years, innate T cells have been increasingly recognized as an important cell group in regulating immune responses. Three major populations within the innate T cell group are known, namely, invariant NKT cells (iNKT cells), mucosal associated invariant T cells (MAIT cells), and gamma delta T cells ($\gamma\delta$ T cells) [1]. Unlike their conventional counterparts, these cells rapidly recognize foreign pathogen signals and manifest immediate effector functions post-activation. This allows innate T cells to perform effector immune responses much earlier than conventional T cells.

Variations in the frequency of these cells have been found in numerous disease compared to healthy controls. For example, iNKT cells are one of the most well-studied innate T cell populations; their frequencies are significantly reduced in multiple sclerosis, systemic lupus erythematosus, rheumatoid arthritis, and cancer, compared with healthy controls [2]. Studies also found a lower percentage of gamma delta T cells in various cancer states [3]. As the newest member in this family, MAIT cells were found to be decreased in varies infectious disease including HIV and HCV [4, 5].

Chaohong Liu (ed.), *Invariant Natural Killer T-Cells: Methods and Protocols*, Methods in Molecular Biology, vol. 2388,
https://doi.org/10.1007/978-1-0716-1775-5_6,
© The Author(s), under exclusive license to Springer Science+Business Media, LLC, part of Springer Nature 2021

It is widely accepted that iNKT cells are abundant in liver and highly conserved in mammals. The percentage of these innate T cells could direct or indirectly influence the outcome of immunotherapy for cancer and/or autoimmunity. [6–8] The number of certain innate T cells, i.e., iNKT cells, has become an entry criteria for certain trials [9–11]. Hence, an efficient and reliable analysis of percentage of these innate T cells is important. So that it can be used for monitoring the number of these cells in patient using limited amount of sample.

Multi-parameter flow cytometry base assay has been the main tool to study the innate T cells. Analysis of these cells is particularly challenging since their frequency among peripheral blood T cells is relatively low, i.e., the mean percentage of iNKT cells is around 0.1% (ranging from less than 0.01% to 1%). In current practice, iNKT cells are identified with either TCR markers Vα24/Vβ11 or CD1d tetramer, whereas MAIT cells are identified with Vα7.2/CD161, Vα7.2/IL-18R, or MR1 tetramer [12]. In here, we described an optimized protocol in isolating invariant natural killer T(iNKT) cells by magnetic beads to further use in functional assays.

2   Materials

1. Human iNKT cell isolation kit (6B11; Miltenyi Biotec).
2. Human recombinant protein IL-2 (PeproTech).
3. MACS isolation buffer (Miltenyi Biotec).
4. KRN7000(Avanti).
5. PMA (Sigma)/ionomycin (Sigma).
6. Brefeldin A (Invitrogen).
7. Ficoll-Paque (GE Healthcare).
8. Phosphate-buffered solution(Sigma, 0.01 M phosphate buffer + 0.0027 M potassium chloride + 0.137 M sodium chloride, pH 7.2–7.6).
9. Collagenase from *Clostridium histolyticum* (Sigma).
10. CellBanker 2 (Zenoaq).
11. FACS lysing solution (BD).
12. Antibodies: 20 μl Vα24 FITC (C15) (Beckman Coulter, USA); 20 μl Vβ11 PE (C21) (Beckman Coulter, USA); 20 μl CD161 APC (DX21) (BD, USA); 20 μl Vα7.2 PE (3C10) (BioLegend, USA); 5 μl of TCRγδ Pacific Blue (B1) (BD, USA); 20 μl of CD3 PerCP (SK7) (BD, USA); 5 μl CD8β APC (2ST8.5H7) (BD, USA); 5 μl CD8α AmCyan (SK1) (BD, USA);5 μl CD4 PE-Cy7 (RPA-T4) (BD, USA); Purified anti-human CD3(BD, USA); Purified anti-human CD28(BD, USA).

13. 70 μm nylon mesh, sterile (Sorfa).

14. FACSCanto with FACS Diva software (BD).

15. BD Multicolor CompBeads for compensation (BD).

3   Methods

3.1   Sample Collection and Preparation

Obtain human liver specimens from surgical specimens. Liver specimens should be stored at room temperature for a maximum of 4 h before performing the assay. For analysis of the stability of the marker, blood samples can be stored at CellBanker 2 solution at 4 °C and process as soon as possible.

3.2   Liver Cells Preparation

Process liver specimens as described previously [3].

1. Perfuse tissues with 1 mg/ml collagenase at 37 °C for 20 min to dissociate collagen fibrils in connective tissues (Fig. 1).

2. Mechanically dissociate undigested tissues by passing through a 70 μm mesh.

3.3   Isolation of Mononuclear Cells from Liver Sample

The mononuclear cells from liver specimens can be isolated by density gradient as follows:

1. Add Ficoll-Paque (15 ml) to a 50 ml centrifuge tube.

2. Warm up RPMI1640 medium at 37 °C.

3. Mix the meshed liver cells with 30 ml RPMI1640, and carefully layer the diluted sample (30 ml) on Ficoll-Paque (*see* **Note 3**).

4. Centrifuge at $400 \times g$ for 25–30 min at 18–20 °C.

5. Carefully remove the sample from centrifuge without disturbing the layers and collect the interphase from each sample (cloudy layer with clear layer below and straw layer above) into 50 ml (Falcon) tubes.

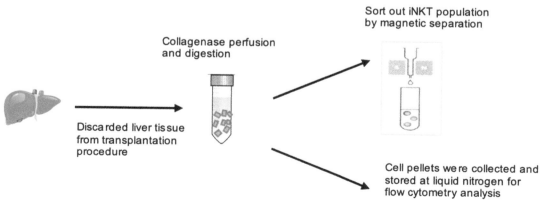

Fig. 1 Schematic diagram of liver iNKT separation

6. Add PBS (phosphate buffered solution) to make up to 50 ml. Spin at 300 × *g* for 5 min, discard the supernatant.

7. Resuspend the cells by adding pre-warmed RPMI1640.

8. Isolate iNKT cells.
   (a) Suspend the cells in 1 ml cold MACS isolation buffer, and isolate the iNKT cells using the human iNKT cell isolation kit, according to the manufacturer's protocols (*see* **Note 2**).
   (b) Centrifuge the purified iNKT cells for 5 min at 400 × *g* and resuspend in 2 ml RPMI1640 medium; count the cells and use for functional assay.

3.4 One Tube Innate T Cells for Identifying iNKT Cells and MAIT Cells

1. Add a minimum of 10^5 cells into 5 ml polystyrene FACS Tubes.

2. Stain samples with the anti-human antibodies for 15 min at room temperature per recommended by the manufacturer:
   20 μl Vα24 FITC (C15) (Beckman Coulter, USA); 20 μl Vβ11 PE (C21) (Beckman Coulter, USA); 20 μl CD161 APC (DX21) (BD, USA), 20 μl Vα7.2 PE (3C10) (BioLegend, USA); 5 μl of TCRγδ Pacific Blue (B1) (BD, USA); 20 μl of CD3 PerCP (SK7) (BD, USA); 5 μl CD8β APC (2ST8.5H7) (BD, USA); 5 μl CD8α AmCyan (SK1) (BD, USA); and 5 μl CD4 PE-Cy7 (RPA-T4) (BD, USA). As a parallel comparison, tubes containing only iNKT cells (CD3/Vα24/Vβ11/CD161/CD4/CD8) and MAIT cells (CD3/Vα7.2/CD161/CD4/CD8) identification can also be labeled.

3. Add 3 ml of FACS lysing solution (BD) for an additional 15 min at 4 °C.

4. Wash samples twice with FACS buffer and analyze straight away.

3.5 Gating Strategy and Sample Analysis

1. Run samples on a FACSCanto with FACS Diva software.

2. For quality control, set up compensation using BD Comp-Beads for each experiment.

3. Identify lymphocyte population with FSC and SSC.

4. Gate to acquire 100,00 CD3 positive T cells, and then calculate the number of iNKT cells by gating on CD3+TCRγδ-Vα24+-Vβ11+, and it is recorded as percentage of alpha beta T cells.

5. Create a "NOT GATE" to further identify the MAIT cells.
   The number of MAIT cells can be calculated on the population of non-iNKT αβ T cells by gating on CD3+TCRγδ-Vα7.2+CD161+ T cells.

6. Analyze the further phenotype of all innate T cells (iNKT cells and MAIT cells) with CD4 and CD8 markers.

3.6 Cytokine Production by Innate T Cells

1. Incubate whole blood cultures with anti-CD3 (1 µg/ml)/CD28(1 µg/ml) or PMA (100 ng/ml)/ionomycin (100 ng/ml) for 6 h at 37 °C with 5% CO_2.

2. Add Brefeldin A (BFA, 5 µg/ml) after an hour initial activation.

3. Wash the cells with FACS washing buffer and label with monoclonal antibodies to surface molecules: CD3 PerCP; Vα7.2PE; Vβ11PE; CD161APC; IFNγ PE-Cy7; TCRγδ Pacific Blue; and CD8 AmCyan for 10 min at room temperature.

4. Lyse erythrocytes and fix leukocytes using FACS lysing solution at 4 °C for 10 min simultaneously.

5. Then wash cells with FACS wash buffer and permeabilize with permeabilization solution 2 to 10 min at room temperature.

6. Wash cells again with FACS wash buffer and stain for intracellular cytokine IFN-γ and iNKT TCR Vα24-FITC for 10 min at room temperature in the dark.

7. Wash cells two times with FACS wash buffer and proceed for acquisition.

3.7 Functional Assay of iNKT Cells

1. Suspend 5×10^5 LMC in 1 ml of complete RPMI1640 culture medium with 100 IU/ml of recombinant human IL-2 and 100 ng/ml of the KRN7000 (*see* **Note 1**).

2. Incubate cells at 37 °C with 5% CO_2 for 7 days.

3. Assess proliferation of iNKT cells at day 7 using the FACS panel. Proliferation index can be calculated by comparing the total number of iNKT cells pre-proliferation to the total number of iNKT cells post-proliferation.

4 Notes

1. The high concentration of IL-2 and KRN7000 are critical for the expansion of iNKT cells. Otherwise, more exhausted iNKT cells will be found in the system.

2. The number of iNKT cells in the liver specimen varied from case to case. In a typical liver tissue, it can make up around 10–20% of the liver mononuclear cells. However, the number will be much lower in certain liver disorders. It should pay attention that the purity of iNKT cells will be much lower in the tissues with low numbers of iNKT cells. In this case, FACS sorting can further increase the purity of the sorting.

3. If performing cell to cell co-culture in liver system, Percoll methods is preferred compared to Ficoll. Percoll gradient will allow isolate hepatic non-parenchymal cells. Cells could perform in various densities.

Acknowledgments

YG is supported by the Natural Science Foundation of Guangdong Province (Grant number: 2018A030313019), National Natural Science Foundation of China (Grant number:31800758), Guangdong Provincial Key Laboratory of Organ Donation and Transplant Immunology, The First Affiliated Hospital, Sun Yat-sen University, Guangzhou, China (2017B030314018, 2020B1212060026), and Guangdong Provincial International Cooperation Base of Science and Technology (Organ Transplantation), The First Affiliated Hospital, Sun Yat-sen University, Guangzhou, China (2015B050501002).

References

1. Gao Y, Williams AP (2015) Role of innate T cells in anti-bacterial immunity. Front Immunol 6:302. https://doi.org/10.3389/fimmu.2015.00302
2. Godfrey DI, Uldrich AP, McCluskey J, Rossjohn J, Moody DB (2015) The burgeoning family of unconventional T cells. Nat Immunol 16(11):1114–1123. https://doi.org/10.1038/ni.3298
3. Paul S, Lal G (2016) Regulatory and effector functions of gamma-delta (gammadelta) T cells and their therapeutic potential in adoptive cellular therapy for cancer. Int J Cancer 139(5):976–985. https://doi.org/10.1002/ijc.30109
4. Barathan M, Mohamed R, Vadivelu J, Chang LY, Saeidi A, Yong YK, Ravishankar Ram M, Gopal K, Velu V, Larsson M, Shankar EM (2016) Peripheral loss of CD8(+) CD161(++) TCRValpha7.2(+) mucosal-associated invariant T cells in chronic hepatitis C virus-infected patients. Eur J Clin Investig 46(2):170–180. https://doi.org/10.1111/eci.12581
5. Cosgrove C, Ussher JE, Rauch A, Gartner K, Kurioka A, Huhn MH, Adelmann K, Kang YH, Fergusson JR, Simmonds P, Goulder P, Hansen TH, Fox J, Gunthard HF, Khanna N, Powrie F, Steel A, Gazzard B, Phillips RE, Frater J, Uhlig H, Klenerman P (2013) Early and nonreversible decrease of CD161++ / MAIT cells in HIV infection. Blood 121(6):951–961. https://doi.org/10.1182/blood-2012-06-436436
6. Faveeuw C, Trottein F (2014) Optimization of natural killer T cell-mediated immunotherapy in cancer using cell-based and nanovector vaccines. Cancer Res 74(6):1632–1638. https://doi.org/10.1158/0008-5472.CAN-13-3504
7. Gomes AQ, Martins DS, Silva-Santos B (2010) Targeting gammadelta T lymphocytes for cancer immunotherapy: from novel mechanistic insight to clinical application. Cancer Res 70(24):10024–10027. https://doi.org/10.1158/0008-5472.CAN-10-3236
8. Guo T, Chamoto K, Hirano N (2015) Adoptive T cell therapy targeting CD1 and MR1. Front Immunol 6:247. https://doi.org/10.3389/fimmu.2015.00247
9. Ishikawa A, Motohashi S, Ishikawa E, Fuchida H, Higashino K, Otsuji M, Iizasa T, Nakayama T, Taniguchi M, Fujisawa T (2005) A phase I study of alpha-galactosylceramide (KRN7000)-pulsed dendritic cells in patients with advanced and recurrent non-small cell lung cancer. Clin Cancer Res 11(5):1910–1917. https://doi.org/10.1158/1078-0432.CCR-04-1453
10. Motohashi S, Nagato K, Kunii N, Yamamoto H, Yamasaki K, Okita K, Hanaoka H, Shimizu N, Suzuki M, Yoshino I, Taniguchi M, Fujisawa T, Nakayama T (2009) A phase I-II study of alpha-galactosylceramide-pulsed IL-2/GM-CSF-cultured peripheral blood mononuclear cells in patients with advanced and recurrent non-small cell lung cancer. J Immunol 182(4):2492–2501. https://doi.org/10.4049/jimmunol.0800126
11. Motohashi S, Ishikawa A, Ishikawa E, Otsuji M, Iizasa T, Hanaoka H, Shimizu N, Horiguchi S, Okamoto Y, Fujii S,

Taniguchi M, Fujisawa T, Nakayama T (2006) A phase I study of in vitro expanded natural killer T cells in patients with advanced and recurrent non-small cell lung cancer. Clin Cancer Res 12(20 Pt 1):6079–6086. https://doi.org/10.1158/1078-0432.CCR-06-0114

12. Salio M, Silk JD, Jones EY, Cerundolo V (2014) Biology of CD1- and MR1-restricted T cells. Annu Rev Immunol 32:323–366. https://doi.org/10.1146/annurev-immunol-032713-120243

Chapter 7

Isolation and Characterization Methods of Human Invariant NKT Cells

Liu Rui and Wang Hua

Abstract

Natural killer T cells (NKT) are abundant in the hepatic sinuses and account for about 20–50% of rat liver lymphocytes. Type I or invariant NKT cells (iNKT) exert a powerful pro-inflammatory effect when activated, while type II NKT cells are more heterogeneous and mainly play an immunomodulatory role. Here we mainly introduced the isolation and characterization methods of human invariant NKT cells. Through immunomagnetic beads and flow cytometry, iNKT cells can be isolated specifically, and that explains functional analysis can be further established.

Key words Invariant NKT cells (iNKT), Isolation, Characterization, Immunomagnetic beads, Flow cytometry

1 Introduction

Conventional CD4$^+$ and CD8$^+$ T cells are the most studied T cell subgroups, but the nonconventional T cells have become a hot topic in recent years, and their number and influence are more abundant than previously thought [1, 2]. The main subpopulations of unconventional T cells include natural killer T (NKT) cells, mucosal-associated invariant T (MAIT) cells and invariant T cells; in general, these T cells account for about 10% of circulating T cells, usually they are the majority of T cells in tissues such as liver and intestinal mucosa [3]. Natural killer T cells (NKT) are abundant in the hepatic sinuses and account for about 20–50% of rat liver lymphocytes [4].

In recent research, iNKT cells have been shown to play an important role in inflammation, fibrosis, tissue repair, viral infection, and tumor immunology. For example, iNKT cells can directly kill tumor cells through antigen recognition or enhance the anti-tumor response by depleting tumor-associated macrophages (TAM) and promoting the cytotoxic T lymphocytes (CTLs) and

Chaohong Liu (ed.), *Invariant Natural Killer T-Cells: Methods and Protocols*, Methods in Molecular Biology, vol. 2388,
https://doi.org/10.1007/978-1-0716-1775-5_7,

natural killer (NK) cells activation [5]. iNKT are mostly CD4$^+$ or CD4$^-$ CD8$^-$ ("double negative"), although a few CD8$^+$ iNKT can be found in some humans, and they are innate-like CD1d-restricted T cells that express the invariant T cell receptor (TCR) composed of Vα24 and VB11 in humans [6]. In this article, we detail the isolation, in vitro expansion, and functional characterization methods of human iNKT cells.

2   Materials

Use ultrapure water (prepared by purified deionized water, with a sensitivity of 18 MΩ-cm at room temperature) and analytical grade reagents to prepare all solutions. Prepare and store all reagents (unless otherwise noted) at 4 °C. When disposing of waste, all waste disposal regulations must be carefully observed. Sodium azide is not added to the reagents.

2.1 Isolation of Invariant NKT Cells by Immunomagnetic Beads

1. Human blood (heparinized blood).
2. Ficoll-Hypaque solution.
3. Phosphate-buffered saline (PBS).
4. PBS/EDTA: PBS with 2 mM EDTA.
5. FcR-blocking reagent (Human IgG).
6. Binding buffer: PBS (APPENDIX 2A) with 2 mM EDTA and 2% (v/v) human serum.
7. α-GalCer [7].
8. DMSO freezing mixture: 90% FBS/10% DMSO.
9. T cell medium (see **Note 1**): RPMI-1640 supplemented with 10% fetal bovine serum (FBS), 15 mM HEPES, 1× non-essential amino acids, 1× essential amino acids, 4 mM glutamine final (including additional 2 mM from standard medium), 5.5 × 10^{-5} M 2-mercaptoethanol, 10μg/ml gentamicin, 100 IU/ml human IL-2, 4 °C once IL-2 has been added.
10. Unconjugated or PE-conjugated anti-Vα24 mAb (Coulter).
11. Unconjugated or PE-conjugated 6B11 anti-invariant TCRα mAb.
12. Goat anti-mouse IgG or anti-PE microbeads (Miltenyi Biotec).
13. MS columns (for up to 10^8 starting cells; Miltenyi Biotec).
14. LS columns (for up to 10^8 starting cells; Miltenyi Biotec).
15. Magnetic separation device (Miltenyi Biotec).
    The above reagent can be replaced by direct 6B11-conjugated microbeads/iNKT kit (Miltenyi Biotec). Alternatives to α-GalCer are PHA-P (Difco) or mitogenic CD3 mAb.

2.2 Isolation of Invariant NKT Cells by Flow Cytometry

See Subheading 2.1 (**steps 1–9**); for additional materials, see below:

1. Conjugated anti-Vα24 mAb (clone C15B2, PE, or FITC conjugate).

2. Conjugated 6B11 anti-invariant TCR mAb or α-GalCer (or its stable analog such as PBS-57)-loaded CD1d tetramer.

3. Conjugated anti-Vβ11 mAb (clone C21D2, Coulter FITC, or PE conjugates).

4. Conjugated isotype matched control mAbs (Coulter, PharMingen).

5. IgG1 isotype control for 6B11 or unloaded CD1d tetramer control conjugate.

6. FACS buffer: PBS with 1% human serum and 1% FBS.

7. Fluorescence-activated cell sorting (FACS) instrument.

2.3 Recognition and Quantitation of Invariant NKT Cells

See Subheading 2.2; for additional materials, see below:

1. Flow cytometry buffer (FC buffer): PBS (APPENDIX 2A) with 1% human serum, 1% FBS, 0.1% sodium azide.

2. PBS with 4% (w/v) paraformaldehyde.

3   Methods

3.1 Isolation of Invariant NKT Cells by Immunomagnetic Beads

Immunomagnetic beads can be used to isolate Vα24$^+$ or 6B11$^+$ T Cells [8, 9] from small amount of peripheral blood. Although this method is suitable for small samples, it is more efficient when the sample size is larger. The method described below can upregulate or downregulate the sample size based on samples of 10^8 PBMC cells.

1. Put fresh heparinized blood into a 15/50 ml conical centrifuge tube, add an equal volume of room temperature PBS, and mix well.

2. Centrifuge at $200 \times g$ for 15 min at room temperature, and then remove the supernatant suspension containing platelets and cell debris. (When isolating cells from a leukapheresis donor, dilute blood with PBS (1:4 blood/PBS).)

3. Add an equal volume of PBS at room temperature.

4. Insert the tip of the pipet containing Ficoll-Hypaque deep into the bottom of the sample tube, and slowly inject the Ficoll-Hypaque solution at the bottom of the cell mixture (*see* **Note 2**).

5. Centrifuge at 2000 rpm ($900 \times g$) for 20 to 30 min at room temperature with a deceleration rate of 0.

6. Remove the upper layer containing the plasma and most of the remaining cell platelets. Transfer the mononuclear lymphocyte cell layer (white turbid band between the plasma and Ficoll-Hypaque layer) to another centrifuge tube.

7. Wash the PBMCs twice, each time in 15 ml PBS/EDTA (*see* **Note 3**), 1000 × *g* centrifugation for 6–10 min, room temperature or chilled, resuspend in binding buffer at 10^8 cells/ml, and place on ice for 15 min.

8. Add Vα24 or 6B11 monoclonal antibody (*see* **Note 4**) to the remaining cells at a concentration of approximately 10μg/ml, and incubate on ice for 20 to 30 min.

9. Wash the cells twice with 1.5 ml PBS/EDTA, 1000 × *g* each time, centrifuge at room temperature or chilled for 6–10 min, and resuspend 10^8 cells in 0.8 ml binding buffer. Add 0.2 ml goat anti-mouse IgG beads, incubate for 20–30 min, and shake on ice.

10. Pre-wash the Miltenyi column with 3 ml binding buffer and then assemble on magnet. Wash the cells twice with PBS/EDTA, resuspend in 1 ml binding buffer, and spread the cells on the column. Wash the column three times, using 3 ml PBS/EDTA each time, and collect the eluate (containing unbound cells). Equal portions of unbound PBMCs (10^7) are set aside for irradiation and use as feeder cells (**step 7**).

11. Remove the column from the magnet and elute bound cells with 3 ml PBS/EDTA. Wash the cells in 1.5 ml T cell culture medium, centrifuge at 1000 × *g* room temperature or chilled for 6–10 min, and resuspend in 0.1 ml T cell culture medium. Count viable cells in iNKT-enriched cell preparation. The recovered cells can be examined directly by flow cytometry to determine the success of the separation (*see* **Note 5**).

12. Add the same amount of irradiated autologous PBMCs (set aside in **step 5** as feeder cells) and purified iNKT-containing cell preparations to the wells of the 96-well plate (*see* **Note 6**). Add 20 ng α-GalCer and use T cell culture medium (final 100 ng/ml α-GalCer) to bring the final volume to 200μl/well. Autotrophic cells are preferred because they should not stimulate allogenic responses.

13. Without changing the medium, culture in a CO_2 incubator containing T cell culture medium for about 2 weeks. Then gently remove about 150μl and replace with fresh T cell culture medium. This step should be updated every 2 to 3 days until most of the hole is occupied. Cells could then be divided into 96-well plates in a ratio of 1:2, or if the growth rate is very wide, cells from the 96-well plate can be transferred to one of the 24-well plate.

14. Cultured by the above method, the cells will continue to proliferate for several weeks. When cell proliferation slows down or stops, cells can be restimulated selectively or with polyclonal mitogens. Or, if stationary cells need to be produced for functional assays, they can be switched to a low-IL-2 (10 U/ml) T-cell medium. In this case, IL-2 concentration should be gradually moved from 100 to 50 to 20 and gradually moved to 10 U/ml after the last week or so to avoid cell death.

3.2 Isolation of Invariant NKT Cells by Flow Cytometry

Flow cytometry sorting is an alternative method to immunomagnetic beads. FACS can also set multiple parameters, while magnetic beads usually can only use a single sort or sequence of negative and positive selection. This section introduces the application of FACS system to isolate iNKT cells. Reliable detection of very small Numbers of cells using flow cytometry requires the use of at least two antibodies and attention to blocking the nonspecific background.

1. Separate PBMCs from 50–100 ml of blood (see above) by Ficoll-Hypaque to obtain at least 10^8 cells. Set aside half for irradiation and use as feeder cells.

2. Centrifuge the remaining cells at $1000 \times g$ in 15 ml PBS/EDTA for 6–10 min at room temperature or chilled, resuspend at 10^7 to 10^8 cells/ml in FACS buffer, and place them on ice for 15 min (see **Note 4**).

3. Take out a part of the cells (10^6 cells in 0.1 ml), and then add 1μg of control FITC-bound mAb. Add FITC-Vα24 mAb to the remaining cells at a concentration of 10μg/ml and incubated on ice for 30 min.

4. Identify the Vα24$^+$ population and gate on these cells for sorting. In order to maximize cell viability, cells are sorted directly into a tube containing TCM.

5. Wash the sorted cells twice in T cell medium and culture with feeder cells set previously and α-GalCer as described above for the beads purification.

3.3 Recognition and Quantitation of Invariant NKT Cells

The content of iNKT cells in human peripheral blood is relatively low. Flow cytometry is usually used for identification and quantitative analysis of iNKT in human peripheral blood. CD3 mAb can most directly differentiate T cell populations and is included in the laser channel of multicolor FACS. 6B11mAb can detect Vα24-Jα18 CDR3 independently of TCRβ, so it is more selective than Vα24 or Vβ11. However, 6B11 may also have weak nonspecific binding to other monocytes that are mainly FcR$^+$. In this case, two specific labeled antibodies are of great significance for explicit recognition. Another staining scheme that can accurately identify iNKT is the double staining of Vα24 and Vβ11 mAB [10]. Vα24mAb can specifically recognize iNKT, as well as all Vα24$^+$ T cells, and the combination with Vβ11 greatly improves the specificity. The experimental methods of the two staining schemes are basically the same, except that different binding antibodies are replaced. The following takes the 6B11mAb staining scheme to describe the specific steps.

1. Separate PBMCs from 50 to 100 ml of blood (see above) by Ficoll-Hypaque to obtain at least 10^8 cells. Set aside half for irradiation and use as feeder cells.

2. Centrifuge at $1000 \times g$, room temperature or chilled for 6–10 min, wash a total of 1×10^6 PBMCs twice with PBS, and then resuspend in the FC buffer for 1×10^7 cells/ml. Incubate on ice for at least 15 min.

3. Divide 100µl of cell suspension in a special tube for flow cytometry.

4. Add PE-conjugated Vα24 and FITC-conjugated 6B11 and compatibly conjugated CD3 (see **Note 4**) and/or other mAbs to a 0.1 ml total volume. (The control should include a single isotype-matched non-specific monoclonal antibody and a monoclonal antibody that binds to each specific monoclonal antibody.)

5. Wash once with FC buffer and resuspend in 0.5 ml FC buffer for flow cytometry.

6. Analyze with flow cytometry within a few hours or fix the cells with 4% paraformaldehyde in PBS to preserve the sample.

In addition, there are still CD4, CD8, CD56, CD161, and NKG2D [11–13] which are often used to further define the markers of iNKT cells. These protocols are similar to the flow cytometric identification of iNKT cells mentioned above, and different combinations of markers can be used for personalized analysis.

4   Notes

1. TCM can be stored at 4 °C for a month and for a longer time without glutamine, 2-mercaptoethanol, or IL-2.

2. Use 3 ml Ficoll-Hypaque per 10 ml blood/PBS mixture. Use up to 10 ml Ficoll-Hypaque per 40 ml white blood cell/RBC/PBS mixture.

3. The second washing with FcR blocking agent may reduce background, especially when washing PBMC.

4. The concentration of antibody is determined according to the relevant instructions of the purchased manufacturer and product. Antibodies at the appropriate dilution should be filter sterilized through a 0.22µm filter just prior to use.

5. After cell isolation, flow cytometry should be performed to determine cell purity, proportion, and viability, especially when the expected iNKT cell line cannot be produced in subsequent culture.

6. Up to 10^4 per well in a round-bottomed 96-well plate, up to 10^5 per well in a flat bottom plate. In the absence or presence of autogenous APC, allogeneic cells can be used as a source of $CD1d^+$ APC due to the considerable specificity provided by α-GalCer.

References

1. Georgiev H, Peng C, Huggins MA, Jameson SC, Hogquist KA (2021) Classical MHC expression by DP thymocytes impairs the selection of non-classical MHC restricted innate-like T cells. Nat Commun 12(1):2308

2. Weng X, Kumar A, Cao L, He Y, Morgun E, Visvabharathy L et al (2021) Mitochondrial metabolism is essential for invariant natural killer T cell development and function. Proc Natl Acad Sci U S A 118(13)

3. Pellicci DG, Koay HF, Berzins SP (2020) Thymic development of unconventional T cells: how NKT cells, MAIT cells and gammadelta T cells emerge. Nat Rev Immunol 20 (12):756–770

4. Bovens AA, Wesselink TH, Behr FM, Kragten NAM, van Lier RAW, van Gisbergen K et al (2020) Murine iNKT cells are depleted by liver damage via activation of P2RX7. Eur J Immunol 50(10):1515–1524

5. Fu S, He K, Tian C, Sun H, Zhu C, Bai S et al (2020) Impaired lipid biosynthesis hinders anti-tumor efficacy of intratumoral iNKT cells. Nat Commun 11(1):438

6. Aoki T, Takami M, Takatani T, Motoyoshi K, Ishii A, Hara A et al (2020) Activated invariant natural killer T cells directly recognize leukemia cells in a CD1d-independent manner. Cancer Sci 111(7):2223–2233

7. Ma J, He P, Zhao C, Ren Q, Dong Z, Qiu J et al (2020) A designed alpha-GalCer analog promotes considerable Th1 cytokine response by activating the CD1d-iNKT Axis and CD11b-positive monocytes/macrophages. Adv Sci 7(14):2000609

8. Xu X, Huang W, Heczey A, Liu D, Guo L, Wood M et al (2019) NKT cells Coexpressing a GD2-specific chimeric antigen receptor and IL15 show enhanced in vivo persistence and antitumor activity against neuroblastoma. Clin Cancer Res 25(23):7126–7138

9. Exley MA, Friedlander P, Alatrakchi N, Vriend L, Yue S, Sasada T et al (2017) Adoptive transfer of invariant NKT cells as immunotherapy for advanced melanoma: a phase I clinical trial. Clin Cancer Res 23(14):3510–3519

10. Nicol AJ, Tazbirkova A, Nieda M (2011) Comparison of clinical and immunological effects of intravenous and intradermal administration of alpha-galactosylceramide (KRN7000)-pulsed dendritic cells. Clin Cancer Res 17 (15):5140–5151

11. Pauken KE, Shahid O, Lagattuta KA, Mahuron KM, Luber JM, Lowe MM et al (2021) Single-cell analyses identify circulating anti-tumor CD8 T cells and markers for their enrichment. J Exp Med 218(4)

12. Yang R, Peng Y, Pi J, Liu Y, Yang E, Shen X et al (2021) A CD4+CD161+ T-cell subset present in unexposed humans, not Tb patients, are fast acting cells that inhibit the growth of intracellular mycobacteria involving CD161 pathway, perforin, and IFN-gamma/autophagy. Front Immunol 12:599641

13. Dubois SP, Miljkovic MD, Fleisher TA, Pittaluga S, Hsu-Albert J, Bryant BR et al (2021) Short-course IL-15 given as a continuous infusion led to a massive expansion of effective NK cells: implications for combination therapy with antitumor antibodies. J Immunother Cancer 9(4)

Chapter 8

Detection of Mouse Type I NKT (iNKT) Cells by Flow Cytometry

Vibhuti Joshi and Masaki Terabe

Abstract

Flow cytometry is an effective tool in immunology that uses laser as a light source to yield scattered and fluorescent light signals read by photomultiplier tubes or photodiodes for detection. Flow cytometry allows immunophenotyping using fluorescently conjugated antibodies for the identification of subgroups of immune cells at a single-cell level. Natural killer T (NKT) cells are CD1d-restricted T cells, which recognize lipid antigens, unlike conventional T lymphocytes that recognize peptide antigens presented by class I or class II MHC. The unique T cell receptor (TCR) of type I NKT or invariant natural killer T (iNKT) cells are comprised of an invariant α-chain that pairs with a limited repertoire of β-chains. Type I NKT cells play an essential role in the orchestration of the innate and adaptive immune responses against various diseases. Here, we will review the process of identifying mouse type I NKT cells by flow cytometry, which serves as a foundational technique for studying these cells.

Key words Spleen, Thymus, Lymph node, NKT cells, Flow cytometry, CD1d tetramers, Antibody

1 Introduction

Natural killer T (NKT) cells are unconventional T cells that recognize lipid antigens presented by a monomorphic nonclassical class I like MHC molecule, CD1d [1]. There are two main groups of NKT cells currently known: designated as type I or invariant (iNKT) and type II NKT cells. Type I NKT cells are characterized by a semi-invariant T cell receptor (TCR) α chain that is comprised of Vα14Jα18 gene segments in the majority of cells paired with Vβ8, 7, or 2 in mice and Vα24Jα18 with Vβ11 in humans. In type II NKT cells, both the α chain and β chain of the TCR are variant/diverse [2]. In mice, type I NKT cells have a frequency of approximately 0.5% of the T cell population in the blood and peripheral lymph nodes, 0.5% of T cells in the thymus, and 2.5% of T cells in the spleen, mesenteric, and pancreatic lymph nodes, and up to 30% of T cells in the liver [3]. Although NKT cells make up a small

Chaohong Liu (ed.), *Invariant Natural Killer T-Cells: Methods and Protocols*, Methods in Molecular Biology, vol. 2388,
https://doi.org/10.1007/978-1-0716-1775-5_8,
© The Author(s), under exclusive license to Springer Science+Business Media, LLC, part of Springer Nature 2021

fraction of T cells, they play an important role in immune regulation of metabolic disorders, inflammation, infections, and cancer in part to their ability to quickly produce a wide range of cytokines upon activation leading to the regulation of innate and adaptive immune cell functions [4–7]. In this chapter, we will be focusing on the detection of the type I NKT cells.

Type I NKT cells can be classified based on surface marker expressions, cytokine productions, and transcription factor expressions. In mice, type I NKT cells mostly consist of $CD4^+$ single-positive and $CD4^-CD8^-$ double-negative (DN) cells [6]. Mouse studies have defined functional subsets based on the expression of the transcription factors PLZF, T-bet, and RORγ-t, produced from common progenitor cells which express transcription factor PLZF [8, 9]. Functional subsets of NKT cells, NKT1 (T-bet$^+$), NKT2 (PLZF^{hi}), and NKT17 (RORγ-t$^+$) cells, generally correspond to Th1, Th2, and Th17 of $CD4^+$ helper T cell subsets, respectively [9]. Additionally, IL-10 producing E4BP4$^+$NKT10 [10, 11], IL-21 producing Bcl-6$^+$NKT$_{FH}$ [12, 13], and Foxp3$^+$NKT$_{reg}$ cells have also been reported [14]. More recently, a high-dimensional single-cell analysis of thymic type I NKT cells has shown developmental type I NKT trajectories. They showed various type I NKT cell subsets with unique biology (designated iNKT0, iNKT17, iNKT2a, iNKT2b, iNKT1a, iNKT1b, iNKTb, and iNKTc) and, notably, did not identify NKT10 and NKT$_{FH}$ subsets that have been previously identified in peripheral organs [7].

Detection of type I NKT cells by flow cytometry is an essential requirement for studying these cells. Although various methods have been used to identify type I NKT cells, the development of CD1d tetramers loaded with α-GalCer or its analogs has significantly enhanced the specificity of type I NKT cell detection through flow cytometry [15, 16]. Here, we will describe a method for identifying type I NKT cells from the mouse tissues by using flow cytometry. It is difficult to detect NKT10, NKT$_{reg}$, and NKT$_{FH}$ subsets without specific stimulation, so in this chapter, we are only focusing on the detection of NKT1, NKT2, and NKT17 subsets of type I NKT cells.

2   Materials

2.1   Mouse Tissue Experiment Materials

2.1.1   Mice

C57BL/6 mice and BALB/c mice (7–8 weeks old) were used to perform all the protocols. Mouse lymphoid organs (spleen, thymus, and lymph nodes) were used to detect type I NKT cells in this chapter.

2.1.2   Media and Buffers

1. RPMI-1640. Store at 4 °C.
2. RPMI-1640 with 10% FBS. Store at 4 °C.

3. Phosphate-buffered saline (1x PBS). Store at room temperature.

4. Ammonium-chloride-potassium (ACK) lysis buffer. Store at room temperature.

5. Flow cytometry (FACS) buffer: Hank's buffered salt solution (HBSS) with 0.05% bovine serum albumin (BSA), 0.05% sodium azide (NaN_3). Store at 4 °C.

6. True-Nuclear™ Transcription Factor Buffer Set (BioLegend). Store at 4 °C.

2.1.3 Instruments and Plasticwares

1. Hemocytometer or cell counter.

2. Flow cytometer (we used MACS Quanta Analyzer 16 (Miltenyi Biotec) to obtain the data presented in this chapter).

3. High-speed table-top centrifuge.

4. 15 mL tubes.

5. 50 mL tubes.

6. Transfer pipette.

7. FACS tubes.

8. Cell strainer or nylon membrane (40µm pore size).

9. Petri dish (60 × 15 mm).

2.1.4 Antibodies, Staining Kit, and Other Fluorochrome-Labeled Reagents

1. LIVE/DEAD™ Fixable Aqua Dead Cell Stain Kit (Thermo Fisher Scientific). Store at −20 °C.
   Note: Reagents used for the staining should be titrated prior to the experiment.

2. Antibodies and other fluorochrome reagents used are summarized in Table 1.

3. Staining panels used in this experiment are shown in Table 2.
   Note: Fluorescence Minus One (FMO) control, which is the same as the full staining panel except there is one reagent removed, is frequently used to identify cells expressing a desired marker. Having this type of control is extremely important in studying a low frequency cell population like iNKT cells. However, since antibodies for intracellular or intranuclear staining frequently create a significant amount of signals in cells that do not express the marker, we did not use FMO in this experiment. Instead, we used Panel A which does not include reagents to stain intranuclear proteins to check the background signal level of gated type I NKT cells. Another useful approach to reduce a noise or background signal level is to use a cocktail of antibodies with the same fluorochrome against cell surface molecules that are known not to be expressed on iNKT cells such as anti-CD19, anti-CD11c, and CD11b.

Table 1
Antibodies and other fluorochrome-labeled reagents required for the detection of mouse type I NKT cells by flow cytometry

	Antibody	Fluorochrome	Clone	Company
1	Anti-CD3	FITC	17A2	BioLegend
2	Anti-CD4	Alexa Fluor 700	GK1.5	BioLegend
3	Anti-CD8α	PerCP-Cy5.5	53.6.7	BioLegend
4	Anti-T-bet	BV421	4B10	BioLegend
5	Anti-RORγ-t	PE	AFKJS-9	eBioscience
6	Anti-PLZF	PE-Cy7	9E12	BioLegend
7	PBS57/CD1d-tetramer	APC		NIH-tetramer Core Facility
8	TruStain FcX (anti-CD16/32)	–	93	BioLegend

Table 2
Staining panels for mouse type I NKT cell detection by flow cytometry

Panel A		
	Reagent	Fluorochrome
1	anti-CD3	FITC
2	anti-CD8α	PerCP-Cy5.5
3	PBS57/CD1d-Tetramer	APC
4	anti-CD4	Alexa Fluor 700
5	LIVE/DEAD	Aqua
Panel B (full staining panel)		
	Reagent	Fluorochrome
1	anti-CD3	FITC
2	anti-CD8α	PerCP-Cy5.5
3	PBS57/CD1d-tetramer	APC
4	anti-CD4	Alexa Fluor 700
5	LIVE/DEAD	Aqua
6	anti-RORγ-t	PE
7	anti-PLZF	PE-Cy7
8	anti-T-bet	Brilliant Violet 421

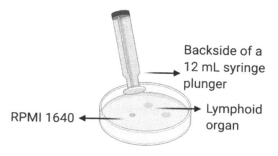

Fig. 1 Illustration of tissue mashing method. The figure depicts the method to mash lymphoid organs by using the backside of the plunger for preparing a single-cell suspension

3   Methods

3.1   Detection of Type I NKT Cells from Mouse Tissue by Flow Cytometry

3.1.1   Preparation of Single-Cell Suspension from a Mouse Spleen

1. Euthanize the mouse.

2. Harvest the spleen into the 60×15 mm petri dish filled with RPMI 1640 (2 mL) and mash it with the backside of the 12 mL syringe plunger (Fig. 1).

3. Loosen the cell aggregates by pipetting the cell suspension. After passing the cell suspension through a cell strainer using a transfer pipette, transfer the suspension into a fresh 15 mL tube.

4. Centrifuge at $300 \times g$, for 5 min at room temperature.

5. Discard supernatant and loosen the cell pellet.

6. Add 1–3 mL ACK lysis buffer by using a 5 mL pipette and mix gently 8–10 times; quickly add the fresh RPMI 1640 to make the total volume 15 mL.

7. Centrifuge at $300 \times g$, for 5 min at room temperature.

8. Discard supernatant, loosen the cell pellet well, and resuspend the cells in 10 mL of RPMI 1640.

9. Pass through a cell strainer.

10. Centrifuge at $300 \times g$, for 5 min at room temperature.

11. Discard supernatant, loosen the cell pellet well, and resuspend the cells in 10 mL of RPMI 1640.

12. Centrifuge at $300 \times g$, for 5 min at room temperature.

13. Repeat **steps 11** and **12**.

14. After discarding supernatant and loosening the cell pellet, resuspend the cells in an appropriate volume of RPMI 1640 with 10% FBS.

15. Count the cells.

*3.1.2 Preparation
of Single-Cell Suspension
from the Thymus
and Lymph Nodes*

1. Euthanize the mouse and harvest the thymus and lymph nodes (subiliac and axillary) into two separate 60×15 mm petri dishes with approximately 2 mL of RPMI 1640 each. Mash the tissue with the backside of the 12 mL syringe plunger.

   Note: Approximately 1×10^6 cells will be obtained from one lymph node. Combining multiple lymph nodes is recommended to obtain an adequate number of cells if necessary.

   We used accessory axillary lymph nodes and subiliac lymph nodes [17] in the present analysis.

2. Loosen the cell aggregates by pipetting the cell suspension. After passing the cell suspension through a cell strainer using a transfer pipette, transfer the suspension into a fresh 15 mL tube.

   Note: Collect thymus cells in a 50 mL tube to minimize the damage of cells during centrifuge.

3. Centrifuge at $300 \times g$, for 5 min at room temperature.

4. Discard supernatant, loosen the cell pellet well, and resuspend the thymocytes and lymph node cells in RPMI 1640 with 10% FBS.

5. Count the cells.

3.1.3 Staining Dead Cells

The staining procedure is the same for all cell types. In the present protocol, we used LIVE/DEAD™ Fixable Aqua Dead Cell Stain Kit (Thermo Fisher Scientific); other similar types of dyes can be used to stain dead cells.

Thaw DMSO of the kit (Component B) while preparing cells.

1. Aliquot $1-3 \times 10^6$ cells into FACS tubes.

2. Add 1–2 mL of FACS buffer to each tube. Centrifuge at $300 \times g$, for 5 min at 4 °C, and discard supernatant.

3. Loosen the pellet and resuspend the cells in 1–2 mL PBS.

4. Centrifuge at $300 \times g$, for 5 min at 4 °C. Discard supernatant and loosen the pellet well.

5. Add 50μL of DMSO (Component B of the kit) to a vial of LIVE/DEAD dye powder (Component A) as recommended in the manufacturer's protocol. Mix well.

   It is recommended to use as soon as possible.

6. Add LIVE/DEAD dye to the cells and mix well. Incubate for 30 min at room temperature in the dark.

7. Add 1–2 mL FACS buffer and centrifuge at $300 \times g$, for 5 min at 4 °C.

8. Discard supernatant and loosen the pellet well.

3.1.4   Cell Surface Protein Staining

1. Add 1μg of TruStain FcX™ (anti-mouse CD16/32) antibody in each sample tube to block a Fcγ receptor that prevents nonspecific binding of IgG to cells.

2. Incubate for at least 10 min at 4 °C in the dark.

3. Without washing, add CD1d tetramers and incubate for 30 min at 4 °C in the dark.

4. Add antibodies to stain cell surface markers (anti-CD3, anti-CD4, anti-CD8α) and incubate again for 30 min at 4 °C in the dark.

5. After incubation, add 1–2 mL FACS buffer and centrifuge at $300 \times g$, for 5 min at 4 °C. Discard supernatant and loosen the pellet well.

6. Repeat **step 5** two more times.

3.1.5   Intranuclear Transcription Factor Staining

Different subsets of type I NKT cells in mice are detected by using various transcription factors. Staining of these transcription factors require special processing of samples with the True-Nuclear Transcription Factor buffer set from BioLegend.

It is critical to have well loosened the cell pellet before adding True-Nuclear™ 1× Fix buffer.

1. Add 1 mL of True-Nuclear™ 1× Fix buffer to each tube, vortex gently, and incubate for 60 min at room temperature in the dark. Follow manufacture's protocol to prepare True-Nuclear™ 1× Fix buffer.

   Note: We can suspend the protocol at this step by using Cyto-Last™ Buffer (BioLegend) and storing at 4 °C in the dark up to 12–18 h. After completion of **step 1**, centrifuge at $300 \times g$, for 10 min at room temperature. Loosen the pellet and resuspend the cells with 0.5 mL/tube Cyto-Last™ buffer. Store tubes at 4 °C in the dark up to 12–18 h. To resume the staining, centrifuge at $300 \times g$, for 10 min at room temperature and discard Cyto-Last™ buffer before proceeding to **step 2**.

2. Add 2 mL of the True-Nuclear™ 1× Perm Buffer to each tube. Follow manufacture's protocol to prepare True-Nuclear™ 1× Perm buffer.

3. Centrifuge at $300 \times g$, for 10 min at room temperature. Discard supernatant and loosen the pellet well.

4. Add 2 mL of the True-Nuclear™ 1× Perm Buffer to each tube. Centrifuge at $300 \times g$ for 10 min at room temperature and discard supernatant.

5. Resuspend the cell pellet in 100μL of True-Nuclear™ 1× Perm buffer.

6. Add antibodies against transcription factors diluted in True-Nuclear™ 1× Perm buffer (anti-T-bet, anti-PLZF and anti-RORγ-t).

7. Incubate the tubes for 30 min at room temperature in the dark.

8. Add 2 mL of the True-Nuclear™ 1× Perm Buffer, and centrifuge tubes at 300 × g, for 10 min at room temperature.

9. Discard the supernatant and add 2 mL of FACS buffer.

10. Centrifuge the sample tubes at 300 × g, for 10 min at room temperature, and discard the supernatant.

11. Loosen the cell pellet and resuspend in 400μL of FACS buffer to acquire the data on a flow cytometer.

   Note: Always vortex the tube before acquiring a data on flow cytometer.

3.1.6 Data Acquisition

Data acquisition procedures vary among flow cytometers used to acquire data from the samples. We used MACS Quanta Analyzer 16 (Miltenyi Biotec), after performing the recommended calibration to check laser settings and cleaning procedure.

3.1.7 Data Analysis

The data was analyzed by the FlowJo software (Becton Dickinson and Company).

Type I NKT Cell Identification Gating Strategy

For type I NKT cell identification, first, gate on live cells by using the signals from LIVE/DEAD aqua and forward scatter area (FSC-A) channels. Then, select singlets among live cells by using forward scatter height (FSC-H) and FSC-A channels, and select lymphocytes among live singlets by using side scatter area (SSC-A) and FSC-A channels. Next, gate on type I NKT cells (iNKT) as PBS57-loaded CD1d tetramer positive and CD3 intermediate cells (Fig. 2).

The frequency of type I NKT cells in each lymphoid organ is different. It is also known that the frequencies are different among inbred strains of mice [8]. Here, we show a representative data from BALB/c and C57BL/6 mice organs (Fig. 3).

Identification of Type I NKT Cell Subsets

CD4 expression is one way to identify subsets of type I NKT cells. In contrast to conventional T cells, which can be identified as either CD4$^+$CD8$^-$ or CD4$^-$CD8$^+$, most mouse NKT cells are either CD4$^-$CD8$^-$ double-negative (DN) or CD4$^+$ (Figs. 2 and 3).

The three major functional subsets of type I NKT cells are NKT1, NKT2, and NKT17.

They can be identified by using combinations of three transcription factors PLZF, T-bet, and RORγ-t. NKT1, NKT2, and NKT17 cells are identified as T-bet$^+$RORγ-t$^-$ PLZF^{low}, PLZF^{hi}RORγ-t$^-$T-bet$^-$, and PLZF^{int} RORγ-t^{hi} T-bet$^-$, respectively (Figs. 2 and 4). The levels of PLZF expression are frequently

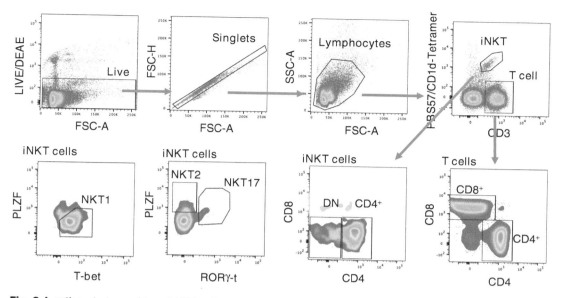

Fig. 2 A gating strategy of type I NKT cells and their functional subsets

observed as overlapping. Thus, it is not recommended to define the subsets simply based on PLZF expression levels. Here, we defined NKT2 and NKT17 by using PLZF and RORγ-t as PLZF$^+$RORγ-t$^-$ and PLZF^{int}RORγ-t$^+$ cells, respectively. NKT1 is better defined by using a two-dimensional plot with PLZF and T-bet as PLZF^{lo}T-bet$^+$ cells (Figs. 2 and 4).

Similar to the frequencies of type I NKT cells, the frequencies of NKT1, NKT2, and NKT17 are also different among lymphoid organs and among strains of mice (Fig. 4) [8, 9].

4   Notes

1. Titrating reagents for staining is highly recommend in order to use the optimal concentration of each reagent. Fluorochrome-labeled reagents used in this protocol have been optimized before the experiment.

2. PBS57 loaded on CD1d tetramers is an analog of α-GalCer which has been shown to have similar activity with α-GalCer (KRN7000) [18].

3. Prepare appropriate single strain control by cells or by beads to compensate fluorescence signals.

4. Loosening the cell pellet well after centrifuging is critical for all reagents to work optimally.

5. It is highly recommended to use 50 mL tubes for thymus cells centrifugation in order to reduce damage to cells.

A

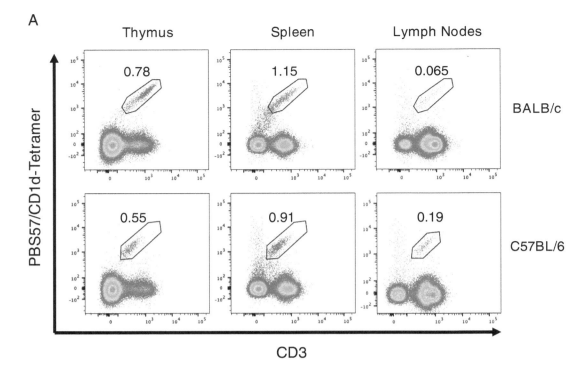

B

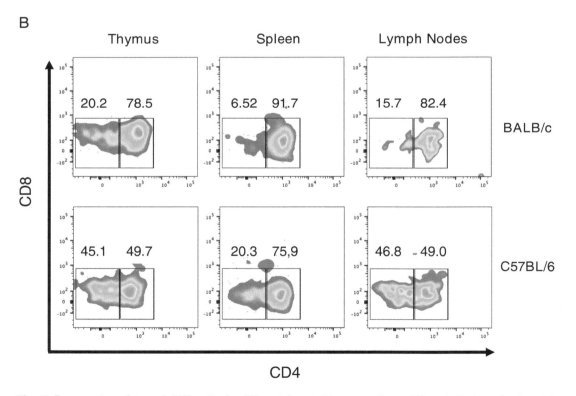

Fig. 3 Frequencies of type I NKT cells in different lymphoid organs from different strains of mice. (a) Frequencies of type I NKT cells in the thymus, spleen, and lymph nodes from BALB/c and C57BL/6 mice. (b) Frequencies of CD4⁺CD8⁻ and CD4⁻CD8⁻ DN subsets of type I NKT cells in thymus, spleen, and lymph nodes of BALB/c and C57BL/6 mice

A

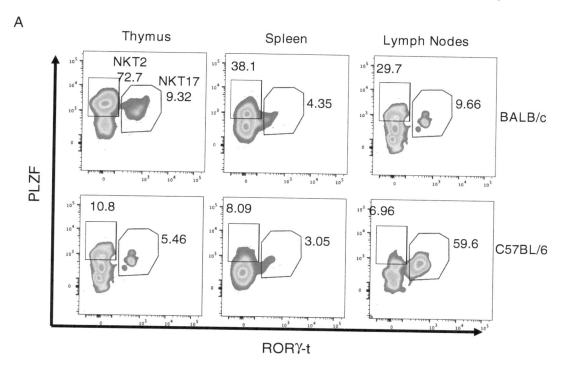

B

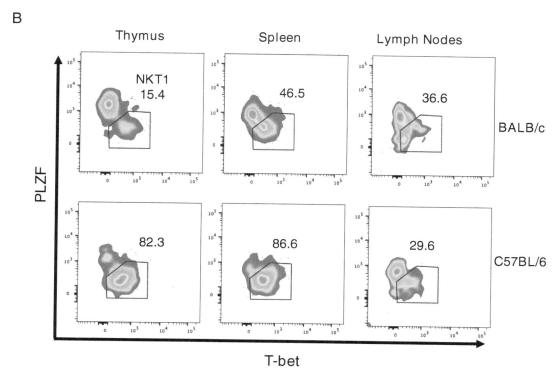

Fig. 4 Frequencies of type I NKT functional subsets in different lymphoid organs from different strains of mice.
(**a**) Frequencies of NKT2 and NKT17 in the thymus, spleen, and lymph nodes from BALB/c and C57BL/6 mice.
(**b**) Frequencies of NKT1 in the thymus, spleen, and lymph nodes from BALB/c and C57BL/6 mice

6. Combining 2 to 5 lymph node is necessary for detection of NKT cells as single lymph node do not provide enough number of cells for analysis.

7. Prepare buffers by following manufacturer's instructions.

8. It is optimal to acquire data as soon as samples are prepared.

Acknowledgments

This work was supported by Intramural Research Program of the NIH, NCI.

References

1. Godfrey DI, MacDonald HR, Kronenberg M, Smyth MJ, Van Kaer L (2004) NKT cells: what's in a name? Nat Rev Immunol 4 (3):231–237

2. Cameron G, Pellicci DG, Uldrich AP, Besra GS, Illarionov P, Williams SJ, La Gruta NL, Rossjohn J, Godfrey DI (2015) Antigen specificity of type I NKT cells is governed by TCR beta-chain diversity. J Immunol 195 (10):4604–4614. https://doi.org/10.4049/jimmunol.1501222

3. Bendelac A, Savage PB, Teyton L (2007) The biology of NKT cells. Annu Rev Immunol 25:297–336. https://doi.org/10.1146/annurev.immunol.25.022106.141711

4. Tiwary S, Berzofsky JA, Terabe M (2019) Altered lipid tumor environment and its potential effects on NKT cell function in tumor immunity. Front Immunol 10:2187. https://doi.org/10.3389/fimmu.2019.02187

5. Terabe M, Berzofsky JA (2018) Tissue-specific roles of NKT cells in tumor immunity. Front Immunol 9:1838. https://doi.org/10.3389/fimmu.2018.01838

6. Godfrey DI, Stankovic S, Baxter AG (2010) Raising the NKT cell family. Nat Immunol 11 (3):197–206. https://doi.org/10.1038/ni.1841

7. Baranek T, Lebrigand K, de Amat HC, Gonzalez L, Bogard G, Dietrich C, Magnone V, Boisseau C, Jouan Y, Trottein F, Si-Tahar M, Leite-de-Moraes M, Mallevaey T, Paget C (2020) High dimensional single-cell analysis reveals iNKT cell developmental trajectories and effector fate decision. Cell Rep 32 (10):108116. https://doi.org/10.1016/j.celrep.2020.108116

8. Lee YJ, Wang H, Starrett GJ, Phuong V, Jameson SC, Hogquist KA (2015) Tissue-specific distribution of iNKT cells impacts their cytokine response. Immunity 43(3):566–578. https://doi.org/10.1016/j.immuni.2015.06.025

9. Lee YJ, Holzapfel KL, Zhu J, Jameson SC, Hogquist KA (2013) Steady-state production of IL-4 modulates immunity in mouse strains and is determined by lineage diversity of iNKT cells. Nat Immunol 14(11):1146–1154. https://doi.org/10.1038/ni.2731

10. Sag D, Krause P, Hedrick CC, Kronenberg M, Wingender G (2014) IL-10-producing NKT10 cells are a distinct regulatory invariant NKT cell subset. J Clin Invest 124 (9):3725–3740. https://doi.org/10.1172/JCI72308

11. Lynch L, Michelet X, Zhang S, Brennan PJ, Moseman A, Lester C, Besra G, Vomhof-Dekrey EE, Tighe M, Koay HF, Godfrey DI, Leadbetter EA, Sant'Angelo DB, von Andrian U, Brenner MB (2015) Regulatory iNKT cells lack expression of the transcription factor PLZF and control the homeostasis of T (reg) cells and macrophages in adipose tissue. Nat Immunol 16(1):85–95. https://doi.org/10.1038/ni.3047

12. King IL, Fortier A, Tighe M, Dibble J, Watts GF, Veerapen N, Haberman AM, Besra GS, Mohrs M, Brenner MB, Leadbetter EA (2011) Invariant natural killer T cells direct B cell responses to cognate lipid antigen in an IL-21-dependent manner. Nat Immunol 13 (1):44–50. https://doi.org/10.1038/ni.2172

13. Chang PP, Barral P, Fitch J, Pratama A, Ma CS, Kallies A, Hogan JJ, Cerundolo V, Tangye SG, Bittman R, Nutt SL, Brink R, Godfrey DI, Batista FD, Vinuesa CG (2011) Identification of Bcl-6-dependent follicular helper NKT cells that provide cognate help for B cell responses. Nat Immunol 13(1):35–43. https://doi.org/10.1038/ni.2166

14. Moreira-Teixeira L, Resende M, Devergne O, Herbeuval JP, Hermine O, Schneider E, Dy M, Cordeiro-da-Silva A, Leite-de-Moraes MC (2012) Rapamycin combined with TGF-beta converts human invariant NKT cells into suppressive Foxp3+ regulatory cells. J Immunol 188(2):624–631. https://doi.org/10.4049/jimmunol.1102281

15. Matsuda JL, Naidenko OV, Gapin L, Nakayama T, Taniguchi M, Wang CR, Koezuka Y, Kronenberg M (2000) Tracking the response of natural killer T cells to a glycolipid antigen using CD1d tetramers. J Exp Med 192(5):741–754

16. Benlagha K, Weiss A, Beavis A, Teyton L, Bendelac A (2000) In vivo identification of glycolipid antigen-specific T cells using fluorescent CD1d tetramers. J Exp Med 191 (11):1895–1903

17. Van den Broeck W, Derore A, Simoens P (2006) Anatomy and nomenclature of murine lymph nodes: descriptive study and nomenclatory standardization in BALB/cAnNCrl mice. J Immunol Methods 312(1–2):12–19. https://doi.org/10.1016/j.jim.2006.01.022

18. Liu Y, Goff RD, Zhou D, Mattner J, Sullivan BA, Khurana A, Cantu C 3rd, Ravkov EV, Ibegbu CC, Altman JD, Teyton L, Bendelac A, Savage PB (2006) A modified alpha-galactosyl ceramide for staining and stimulating natural killer T cells. J Immunol Methods 312(1–2):34–39. https://doi.org/10.1016/j.jim.2006.02.009

Chapter 9

Identification of Rare Thymic NKT Cell Precursors by Multiparameter Flow Cytometry

Jihene Klibi and Kamel Benlagha

Abstract

Mouse invariant natural killer T (NKT) cells are a subset of T lymphocytes which have been shown to play a significant role in innate and adaptive immune responses. Features of innate responses are attributed to these cells because they can be stimulated simultaneously with the same ligand to produce quickly and in large amount cytokines without prior immunization. Because these characteristics could be exploited for clinical applications, NKT cells have attracted considerable interest. Many studies have investigated the molecular mechanisms through which they are selected and differentiate. These studies are based on developmental models that serve as a scaffold to understand the specific roles played by various factors and to identify checkpoints during cellular development. Analysis of NKT cell precursors at the HSA^{high} stage, stage 0, can reveal potential selection defects, whereas analysis of NKT cells at the HSA^{low} stage can shed light on defects in the maturation/differentiation of the different NKT cell subsets (NKT1, 2, and 17). Unlike HSA^{low} NKT cell subsets, HSA^{high} NKT cell precursors are not accurately identified by flow cytometry because of their extreme rarity. Here, we describe an NKT cell enrichment strategy to identify unambiguously NKT cell precursors at the HSA^{high} stage that can be used to assess their distribution and characteristics by multicolor flow cytometry.

Key words NKT cells, Flow cytometry, Early precursors, Thymocyte development

1 Introduction

Flow cytometry is a powerful technique to count and measure cell properties [1]. This technique makes it possible to measure and analyze, simultaneously, and on a large number of cells, several constituents of the same element defined by several parameters: size (FSC, forward scatter), graininess or texture (SSC, side scatter), and fluorescence (FL). The technology involves cells carried in a liquid vein passing in front of a laser beam. The cells are thus aligned, one behind the other, and can be analyzed by combining an optical system with electronics (photomultipliers), to record their light scattering and fluorescent parameters. In addition to

Chaohong Liu (ed.), *Invariant Natural Killer T-Cells: Methods and Protocols*, Methods in Molecular Biology, vol. 2388,
https://doi.org/10.1007/978-1-0716-1775-5_9,
© The Author(s), under exclusive license to Springer Science+Business Media, LLC, part of Springer Nature 2021

being a multiparametric technology, flow cytometry can be used to analyze cell subpopulations, even when represented in small proportions, within a mixture of several cell types on the condition that they differ by at least one parameter. Subpopulation identification and counting can be useful to help us understand disease pathogenesis.

The immune cell types represented at low levels in lymphoid organs include invariant natural killer T (NKT) cells. Conventional mature HSA^{high} T cells express either CD4 or CD8, whereas mature HSA^{high} NKT cells in mice express only CD4 or neither of these receptors (DN). These cells represent around 0.5% of the cells in the thymus; conventional CD4 and CD8 T cells represent around 15% of thymic cells [2]. NKT cells express a restricted TCR repertoire which contrasts with the polyclonal repertoire of alpha beta (αβ) TCRs expressed on conventional T cells. The NKT receptor is composed of an invariant Vα14 alpha chain paired with Jα18, Vα14-Jα18, and a variable beta chain essentially consisting of Vβ8, Vβ7, or Vβ2 [3]. Functionally, there are also differences between NKT and conventional T cells; the latter recognize peptides presented by MHCI and MHCII molecules, whereas NKT cells recognize glycolipids presented by the nonclassical MHCI molecule CD1d [2]. The study of NKT cells benefited greatly from the generation of CD1d tetramers and the identification of the NKT cell ligand α-galactosylceramide [4]. For example, CD1d tetramers loaded with α-galactosylceramide can be used to track mature HSA^{low} NKT cells based on their TCR specificity rather than their expression of NK or activation markers, such as NK1.1 and CD44 (*see* **Note 1**) [5]. Ontogeny studies using CD1d tetramers revealed that before reaching the final NK1.1^{+}CD44^{+} stage, or stage 3 (whereafter they are termed NKT1 cells), NKT cells passed through a transitional stage, stage 2, when they express CD44 but not NK1.1. These CD44-positive stage 2 NKT cells derive from stage 1 NKT cells, which express neither NK1.1 nor CD44. Based on these observations, a linear developmental model was proposed for mature HSA^{low} NKT cells, which was subsequently used in most studies investigating the specific role of the factors controlling NKT cell development (Fig. 1a) [5].

In terms of cytokines, NKT1 cells produce mainly IFN-γ, but NKT cells producing IL-17 (called NKT17) and IL-4/IL-13 (called NKT2) have also been described [6–8]. These subpopulations mirror the Th cell subgroups described for mainstream T cells, in that they produce Th1, Th17, and Th2 cytokines, respectively. Analysis of the intracellular expression patterns for the transcription factors controlling cytokine production, such as T-bet, RORγt, GATA3, and PLZF—the master gene necessary for the development of all subsets—was used to distinguish these NKT cell subsets. Thus, three groups were defined: NKT1, NKT17, and NKT2 [9]. Based on these data, an alternative NKT lineage

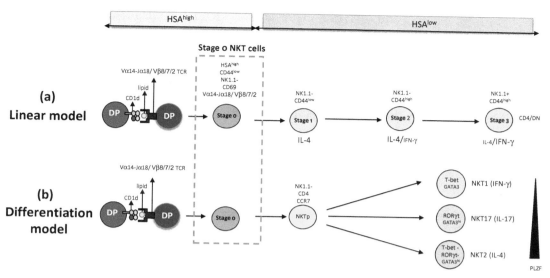

Fig. 1 Linear and differentiation models of NKT cell development. (**a**) The linear development model describes three steps through which NKT cell progress during their development, based on the differentiation markers CD44 and NK1.1. Stage 1 and 2 cells undergo massive expansion before acquiring the phenotypic and functional markers related to the NK lineage characterizing developmental stage 3 cells. (**b**) The differentiation model relies on intracellular staining patterns for lineage-specific transcription factors such as T-bet, GATA3, PLZF, and RORγt. Three functional iNKT subsets are distinguished in the thymus, designated as iNKT1, iNKT2, and iNKT17. The NKTp population represents precursors of NKT cell subsets and is defined by its CCR7 expression pattern. The HSA^{high} CD44^{low} stage 0 NKT cells highlighted by the dashed red box are common to both models and represent the earliest NKT cell precursors detected, the closest to thymic positive selection. These cells are quiescent and show a bias in Vβ8 usage like that described for their later HSA^{low} derivatives. This population expresses the early activation marker CD69, reflecting a strong TCR signal transmitted during their agonist selection. DP: double positive; NKTp: natural killer T cell precursors; HSA: heat-stable antigen

differentiation model was proposed for HSA^{low} NKT cells, in which terminally differentiated cells produce several cytokines derived from common precursors (Fig. 1b) [9].

The earliest precursors of NKT cells were detected at the HSA^{high} stage [10]. This stage is called stage 0 and is common to both the linear and the differentiation models (Fig. 1a and b). These cells represent the NKT cell developmental stage that is closest to positive selection, and the original study describing them proposed that HSA^{high} stage 0 cells could represent a branch point between NKT and conventional T lineages [10]. These cells are rare and difficult to unambiguously detect because they are not cycling like the cells at developmental stages 1 and 2. Several studies have investigated the proportion and absolute numbers of stage 0 NKT cells in the thymus. However, many of these studies do not use appropriate strategies and controls to determine whether the stage 0 cells identified are bona fide NKT cells [11]. Stage 0 cells can only be unambiguously identified without recourse to intracellular staining by using a minimum of six parameters: expression of TCRβ, HSA, and Vβ8; non-expression of NK1.1 and CD44; and binding CD1d tetramers [10]. A bias in their beta chain usage, skewed toward Vβ8 expression, demonstrates that the cells analyzed are bona fide NKT cells (*see* **Note 2**). However, because stage 0 cells are rare, enrichment strategies are necessary before these cells can be characterized by flow cytometry. This enrichment step is important and necessary because HSA^{high} cells analyzed without appropriate enrichment will include contaminant cells and thus provide skewed results [11]. In this chapter, we provide a protocol to enrich NKT cells before polychromatic flow cytometry to identify these cells at the earliest HSA^{high} stage 0 of their development (Fig. 2).

2   Materials

1. FACS solution (for cell harvesting and staining): 1× PBS, 5% fetal calf serum (FCS), 1% sodium azide, 25 mM HEPES.
2. 1.5-mL Eppendorf tubes for tissue collection.
3. Plunger from a 1 mL syringe for tissue dissociation.
4. 40-μm-pore cell strainer.
5. 50-mL Falcon tube for recovery of cell suspension from dissociated tissue.
6. MACS buffer: 1× PBS, 0.5% bovine serum albumin, 25 mM HEPES.
7. NIH-prepared CD1d tetramers loaded with PBS57 (CD1d-PBS57).
8. Anti-fluorochrome (APC) microbeads (Miltenyi Biotec).
9. 15 mL Falcon tubes and 5 mL FACS tubes for cell labeling.
10. Fluorochrome-conjugated antibodies specific for the appropriate surface markers (Table 1).
11. Viability dye.

2.1   Equipment

1. AutoMACS Pro separation system (Miltenyi Biotec).
2. Flow cytometer for data collection.

3   Methods

3.1   Staining Design

To design appropriate multicolor panels for cell staining, it is necessary to have information on the cytometer and fluorochromes that will be used. It is important to know how the flow cytometer works, and how fluorescence is generated, and detected as this information is critical to design an appropriate polychromatic panel (*see* **Note 3**) [12]. The antibodies used in the panel should be titrated using equivalent numbers of cells to the number that will be used in the experimental samples.

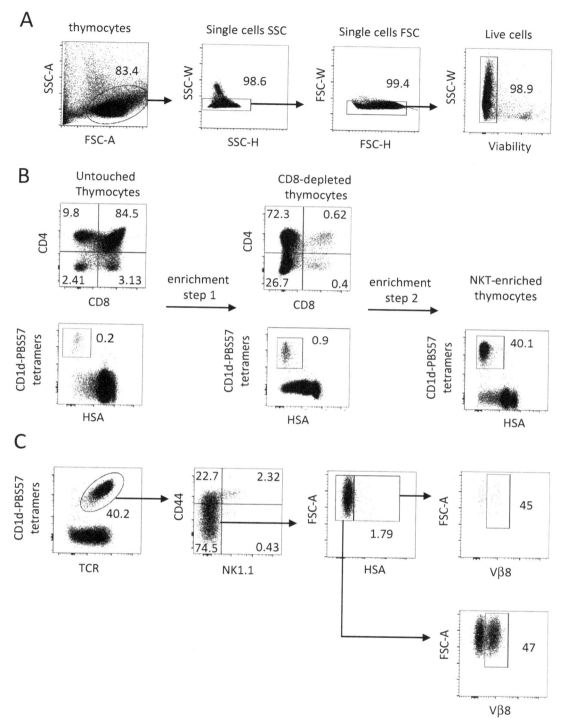

Fig. 2 NKT enrichment steps and identification of stage 0 NKT cells. CD1d-PBS57 tetramer-positive thymocytes from 2-week-old C57BL/6 x BALB/c F1 mice (*see* **Note 1**) were enriched prior to analysis. Expression of the markers outlined in Table 1 was analyzed. (**A**) Dot plots indicate the gating strategy used to identify live single cells. (**B**) NKT cell enrichment by depletion of CD8-positive cells (step 1) then by positive selection of NKT cells from CD8-depleted thymocytes using CD1d-PBS57 tetramers (step 2). The efficiency of

3.2 Isolation of Thymic NKT Cells

Due to their rarity, identification of stage 0 NKT cells requires an enrichment step. The standard method used to reveal populations present at such low levels is to enrich for thymic NKT cells. The enrichment protocol outlined below uses a two-step magnetic bead-based enrichment procedure: the first step is to deplete CD8-positive cells, and the second pulls down NKT cells from the CD8-depleted thymocytes using CD1d-PBS57 tetramers, a variant of α-galactosylceramide [13] (*see* **Note 4**). The protocol was optimized for the Miltenyi AutoMACS Pro Separator using the recommended programs that come as standard on that system.

3.2.1 Preparing the Thymocyte Suspension and Enriching for NKT Cells by Depleting CD8-Positive Cells

1. To preserve cell viability, pre-cool all buffers. In addition, throughout the procedure, cells should be kept cold on ice or in the fridge at 4 °C, unless otherwise specified.

2. Place a 40-μm-pore cell strainer on the top of a 50 mL Falcon tube.

Table 1
Sample staining panel to characterize stage 0 NKT cells

Laser	LP	BP	Fluorophore	Antigen	Clone
Red (640 nm)	750	780/60	APC-Cy7	Viability dye	
	None	670/14	APC	TCRβ	H57-597
Violet (405 nm)	505	525/50	BV510	CD24 (HSA)	M1/60
	690	710/50	BV711	CD4	GK1.5
	600	610/20	BV605	CD8	H1.2F3
	None	450/50	BV421	NK1.1	PK136
UV (355 nm)	690	740/35	BUV737	CD44	IM7
Blue (488 nm)	505	530/30	FITC	Vβ8.1/.2	KJ16-133
Yellow-green (561 nm)	570	586/15	PE	CD1d-PBS57 tetramers	NIH[a]
FC block			Purified	CD16/32	2.4G2

Flow cytometry panel to characterize stage 0 thymic NKT cells post-selection, designed for analysis on a BD LSRFortessa X-20 equipped with five lasers. Numbers in the first column indicate the wavelength emitted by the lasers. The wavelengths of light detected are also indicated, for long-pass (LP) and bandpass (BP) filters, for each channel used
[a]Provided by the NIH tetramer facility

Fig. 2 (continued) CD8 depletion and NKT cell enrichment is assessed based on CD4/CD8 and HSA/CD1d-PBS57 tetramer expression. (**C**) Identification of stage 0 NKT cells. Positively selected NKT cells from enrichment step 2, defined as expressing TCR and binding PBS57-CD1d tetramers, comprise stage 0 NKT cells defined as HSA-expressing CD44[low]NK1.1[−] cells. These cells show a bias in Vβ8 expression akin to that of their HSA[low] derivatives, which indicates that they represent bona fide NKT cells

3. Recover the thymus into a 1.5 mL Eppendorf tube containing 1 mL FACS buffer.

4. Pour the contents of the Eppendorf tube (thymus + buffer) onto the 40-μm-pore cell strainer and gently dissociate tissue by teasing the thymus apart by applying rotary movements with a 1 mL Syringe plunger. Rinse the strainer with two 10 mL volumes of FACS buffer. Remove the strainer and make up the volume of the suspension to 40 mL with FACS buffer (*see* **Note 5**).

5. Centrifuge the cell suspension at $300 \times g$-force for 10 min. All centrifugation steps should be performed at 4 °C to preserve cell viability.

6. Resuspend the cell pellet in 10 mL of MACS buffer and count cells.

7. Remove an aliquot of 3×10^6 cells to assess CD4/CD8, and NKT/HSA expression within the whole thymus. This aliquot may be reserved on ice for later staining, in parallel to the NKT-enriched fractions.

8. Centrifuge cell suspension at $300 \times g$-force for 10 min and resuspend cells at 5×10^7/mL.

9. Transfer cells to a 15-mL Falcon tube.

10. Add Fc-receptor block (1/500), and incubate for 10 min, followed by APC-conjugated anti-CD8 antibodies (1/200) to label cells for 20 min. Incubation should be performed on ice and in the dark.

11. Wash cells by adding 10 mL of FACS buffer and centrifuge at $300 \times g$-force for 10 min.

12. Resuspend cells in 10 mL MACS buffer.

13. Centrifuge cell suspension at $300 \times g$-force for 10 min.

14. Resuspend cell pellet in 80μL of MACS buffer per 10^7 total thymocytes.

15. Add 10μL of anti-APC microbeads per 10^7 total thymocytes (*see* **Note 6**), and incubate for 20 min at 4 °C (*see* **Note 7**).

16. Wash cells by adding 10 mL of MACS buffer to cells and centrifuging at $300 \times g$-force for 10 min (wash step may be repeated, if desired).

17. Prepare thymocytes for separation by resuspending them in MACS buffer at a concentration of 10^8 cells per 500μL. Using the AutoMACS Pro Separator and the DEPLETES program (appropriate for normal or strong antigen expression, which is the case for CD8 expression on thymocytes), separate the CD8-positive cells from the negative fraction. The separator will deposit each fraction in separate collection tubes.

18. Count cells in the CD8-depleted fraction (negative fraction or flow through).

19. Centrifuge at $300 \times g$-force for 10 min.

20. Resuspend the cell pellet at 5×10^6 cells per 100μL.

3.2.2 Enriching NKT Cells from CD8-Depleted Thymocytes by Positive Selection

1. Label the CD8-depleted thymocytes with PE-conjugated CD1d tetramers loaded with PBS57 (PE CD1d-PBS57). Incubate for 20 min at 37 °C or 45 min at 4 °C (*see* **Note 8**).

2. Wash cells by adding 10 mL of MACS buffer to cells, and remove an aliquot of 1×10^6 cells to allow assessment of CD4/CD8 and NKT/HSA cell expression (*see* **Note 9**). This aliquot may be reserved on ice with the whole-thymus aliquot and stained later alongside the NKT-enriched fraction.

3. Centrifuge the remaining cells at $300 \times g$-force for 10 min.

4. Resuspend the cell pellet in 80μL of MACS buffer per 10^7 total thymocytes.

5. Add 10μL of anti-PE microbeads per 10^7 total thymocytes and incubate for 20 min at 4 °C (*see* **Note 10**).

6. Wash cells by adding 10 mL of MACS buffer and centrifuging at $300 \times g$-force for 10 min (wash step may be repeated, if desired).

7. Prepare thymocytes for separation by resuspending them at 10^8 cells per 500μL in MACS buffer. Using the AutoMACS Pro Separator and the POSSELD program (appropriate for normal or strong antigen expression and for a frequency of selected cells <5–10%, which is the case for NKT cells in the CD8-depleted thymus fraction), separate the tetramer-positive cells from the negative fraction. The separator will deposit each fraction in separate collection tubes.

8. Count cells in the positive fraction and pellet them by centrifugation. Resuspend them in FACS buffer at 0.5×10^6 cells per 100μL. Transfer the cell suspension to a 5-mL FACS tube for subsequent staining steps.

3.2.3 Surface Staining

All steps should be performed at 4 °C unless otherwise specified. Samples should be protected from light to prevent photobleaching and to maintain the integrity of the fluorophores.

1. Antibodies for surface staining should be prepared as a 10× master mix. Prepare enough mix to stain each sample with 10μL of the 10× stock mixture, including one extra stain volume (10μL) to allow for pipetting loss. Antibodies should be diluted in FACS buffer to the appropriate concentration, as determined previously by titration. Remember to prepare a 10× single stain solution, containing only one of each

antibody, for every fluorochrome in the panel. These single stains should be applied to samples of thymocytes with no prior staining.

2. Add 10μL 10× master mix to the 100μL samples and incubate for 20–25 min at 4 °C.

3. Wash cells by adding 2 mL FACS buffer and centrifuging at 300 × g-force for 5 min (wash step may be repeated, if desired).

4. Resuspend cell pellets in 100μL FACS buffer and add 1μL of fixable viability dye Zombie NIR. Incubate for 10 min at room temperature in the dark (*see* **Note 11**).

5. Wash cells by adding 2 mL FACS buffer cells and centrifuging at 300 × g-force for 5 min (wash step may be repeated, if desired).

6. Resuspend cell pellets in 200μL of FACS buffer and analyze by flow cytometry (*see* **Note 12**).

4   Notes

1. Mature NKT cells express phenotypic and functional features of NK cells, e.g., they express NK1.1 and produce IFN-γ [2]. However, not all mouse strains express the NK1.1 marker (e.g., BALB/c mice). In these cases, other differentiation markers such as CD69 and CD122 could be used instead. NK markers such as NKG2D, expressed only by a fraction of NK1.1-positive cells, could also be used.

2. Mainstream T cells express a variable repertoire of 21 functional TCR β chain [14]. In the case of NKT cells, the Vβ repertoire is composed mainly of Vβ8, Vβ7, or Vβ2 chains as a result of bias [2]. As a consequence, the frequency of Vβ8-, Vβ7-, or Vβ2-expressing cells is higher in NKT cells compared to mainstream T cells. Thus, around 15% of mainstream T cells express Vβ8, compared to around 50% for NKT cells (using anti-Vβ8.1.2 mAbs) [11]. Thus, the Vβ8 expression pattern can be efficiently used to identify true NKT cells when analyzing rare stage 0 NKT cells or unidentified cells.

3. Multiple parameters can be analyzed on each cell thanks to the possibility to measure a large number of colored dyes simultaneously. As a general rule, the type of lasers and detectors available in the cytometer used will determine the fluorochromes that can be deployed. It is important to mention that the brightness of a fluorochrome will differ depending on the instrument used. The intensity and relative brightness of a fluorochrome used should also be considered. The brightest fluorochromes should be reserved for dim antigens or markers of rare populations. In our panel, PE (coupled to

CD1d-PBS57 tetramers) and APC (coupled to TCRβ), considered among the brightest fluorochromes, are used to label NKT cells. The colors selected for our panel use dyes excited by five different lasers. The excitation and emission spectra for these dyes, and the filters used to detect the fluorescence emitted by these dyes are shown in Table 1. Because of the spectral overlap, each fluorochrome will contribute signal to several detectors, therefore the contribution in detectors not assigned to that fluorochrome must be subtracted from the total signal through a process termed compensation.

4. Stage 0 NKT cells are exceedingly rare, and their proportions have been reported to represent between 0.2% and 0.5% of NKT cells in 2–5-week-old C57BL/6 mice [10]. The quiescent state of HSA^{high} stage 0 NKT explains their low frequency compared to their expanding HSA^{low} NKT cell progeny at subsequent developmental stages, stages 1 and 2 [10]. The rationale behind depleting CD8 thymocytes to enrich NKT cells is related to the fact that mature HSA^{low} NKT cells are reported not to express CD8, rather they are CD4$^+$ or CD4$^-$CD8$^-$ (DN). Hence, the HSA^{high} cells that we detect using the proposed protocol will not be CD4$^+$CD8$^+$ cells. It is worth mentioning that strategies detecting stage 0 NKT cells by direct pull-down without prior CD8 depletion result in the detection of 50% CD4$^+$CD8$^+$ NKT cells; these cells are false positives [15, 16].

5. The thymus should be teased apart gently until the capsule becomes clear in the wet filter (the filter will be wetted by the MACS buffer poured with the thymus from the tissue collection tube). To avoid clogging of the filter and cell loss upon centrifugation due to high cell density, do not use more than one thymus per filter. This is particularly important when working with young thymuses which contain up to 250×10^6 thymocytes. To increase cell viability during this relatively lengthy protocol, we included HEPES buffer in the MACS and FACS buffers to stabilize the pH throughout the prolonged processing.

6. Miltenyi recommends using 20μL of MACS beads per 10^7 cells. We performed titrations with these beads and found that 10μL was sufficient for this first step of NKT cell enrichment using anti-CD8 mAbs and separation equipment.

7. The CD8 depletion step could also be performed using Mouse Depletion Dynabeads from Invitrogen, that are superparamagnetic polystyrene beads (4.5μm diameter) coated with a polyclonal sheep anti-rat IgG antibody, in conjunction with rat monoclonal antibodies binding to mouse CD8, and Invitrogen DynaMag magnets. These magnets instantly pull the

Dynabeads-bound target to the tube wall allowing recovery of the untouched cell suspension containing enriched NKT cells. We have tested this technique and found it to give equivalent results to those obtained with anti-fluorochrome (APC) microbeads and the AutoMACS Pro Separator system (Miltenyi Biotec).

8. Preparation of tetramers may vary depending on the source. NIH-prepared CD1d tetramers loaded with PBS57 (CD1d-PBS57) come at a concentration of approximately 1 to 1.5 mg/mL. They should be titrated before use (http://tetramer.yerkes.emory.edu).

9. When staining total thymocytes, we stain 3×10^6 cells per sample to compensate for the low frequency of NKT cells, which is more accentuated in 2–3-week-old mice as NKT cells accumulate with age [6]. As the CD8-depleted fraction is enriched in NKT cells, we stain only 1×10^6 of these cells. Titrations to select optimal working dilutions of antibodies should be performed on the number of cells that will be stained during the experiment.

10. Miltenyi recommends using 20μL of MACS beads per 10^7 cells. We performed titrations with these beads and found that 10μL was sufficient for this second step in the enrichment of NKT cells using CD1d-PBS57 tetramers and separation equipment.

11. Like fluorescence-labelled antibodies, viability dye should be titrated using the number of cells that will be stained in the experiment. This is doubly important in the case Zombie NIR, as this dye will react with and binds to some proportion of proteins present in FACS buffer (serum proteins in our case), and thus a higher amount may be required.

12. Cells could be fixed and stored in FACS buffer for analysis the next day or up to 5 days after fixation. Remember to also fix single-stained cell suspensions for compensation adjustment, and store them in parallel.

References

1. Bendall SC, Nolan GP, Roederer M, Chattopadhyay PK (2012) A deep profiler's guide to cytometry. Trends Immunol 33:323–332

2. Bendelac A, Rivera MN, Park SH, Roark JH (1997) Mouse CD1-specific NK1 T cells: development, specificity, and function. Annu Rev Immunol 15:535–562

3. Lantz O, Bendelac A (1994) An invariant T cell receptor alpha chain is used by a unique subset of major histocompatibility complex class I-specific CD4+ and CD4-8- T cells in mice and humans. J Exp Med 180:1097–1106

4. Benlagha K, Weiss A, Beavis A, Teyton L, Bendelac A (2000) In vivo identification of glycolipid antigen-specific T cells using fluorescent CD1d tetramers. J Exp Med 191:1895–1903

5. Benlagha K, Kyin T, Beavis A, Teyton L, Bendelac A (2002) A thymic precursor to the NK T cell lineage. Science 296:553–555

6. Doisne JM, Becourt C, Amniai L, Duarte N, Le Luduec JB, Eberl G, Benlagha K (2009) Skin and peripheral lymph node invariant NKT cells are mainly retinoic acid receptor-

related orphan receptor (gamma)t+ and respond preferentially under inflammatory conditions. J Immunol 183:2142–2149

7. Michel ML, Keller AC, Paget C, Fujio M, Trottein F, Savage PB, Wong CH, Schneider E, Dy M, Leite-de-Moraes MC (2007) Identification of an IL-17-producing NK1.1(neg) iNKT cell population involved in airway neutrophilia. J Exp Med 204:995–1001

8. Terashima A, Watarai H, Inoue S, Sekine E, Nakagawa R, Hase K, Iwamura C, Nakajima H, Nakayama T, Taniguchi M (2008) A novel subset of mouse NKT cells bearing the IL-17 receptor B responds to IL-25 and contributes to airway hyperreactivity. J Exp Med 205:2727–2733

9. Lee YJ, Holzapfel KL, Zhu J, Jameson SC, Hogquist KA (2013) Steady-state production of IL-4 modulates immunity in mouse strains and is determined by lineage diversity of iNKT cells. Nat Immunol 14:1146–1154

10. Benlagha K, Wei DG, Veiga J, Teyton L, Bendelac A (2005) Characterization of the early stages of thymic NKT cell development. J Exp Med 202:485–492

11. Klibi J, Amable L, Benlagha K (2020) A focus on NKT cell subset characterization and developmental stages. Immunol Cell Biol 98:607

12. Baumgarth N, Roederer M (2000) A practical approach to multicolor flow cytometry for immunophenotyping. J Immunol Methods 243:77–97

13. Liu Y, Goff RD, Zhou D, Mattner J, Sullivan BA, Khurana A, Cantu C 3rd, Ravkov EV, Ibegbu CC, Altman JD, Teyton L, Bendelac A, Savage PB (2006) A modified alpha-galactosyl ceramide for staining and stimulating natural killer T cells. J Immunol Methods 312:34–39

14. Su C, Nei M (2001) Evolutionary dynamics of the T-cell receptor VB gene family as inferred from the human and mouse genomic sequences. Mol Biol Evol 18:503–513

15. Tuttle KD, Gapin L (2018) Characterization of Thymic development of natural killer T cell subsets by multiparameter flow cytometry. Methods Mol Biol 1799:121–133

16. Tuttle KD, Krovi SH, Zhang J, Bedel R, Harmacek L, Peterson LK, Dragone LL, Lefferts A, Halluszczak C, Riemondy K, Hesselberth JR, Rao A, O'Connor BP, Marrack P, Scott-Browne J, Gapin L (2018) TCR signal strength controls thymic differentiation of iNKT cell subsets. Nat Commun 9:2650

Chapter 10

iNKT Cel Transfer: The Use of Cell Sorting Combined with Flow Cytometry Validation Approach

Marcella Cipelli, Theresa Ramalho, Cristhiane Favero de Aguiar, and Niels Olsen Saraiva Camara

Abstract

Natural killer T (NKT) cells are an innate-like T cell subset that recognize lipid antigens presented by CD1d-expressing antigen presenting cells (APCs), such as dendritic cells, macrophages, and B cells. They can be subdivided into two different subsets according to the variation in $\alpha\beta$ TCR chains: type I and type II NKT cells. Type I, also called invariant NKT cells (iNKT), express restricted TCRs with an invariant α-chain ($V\alpha24$-$J\alpha18$ in humans and $V\alpha14$-$J\alpha18$ in mice) and limited β-chains. Here we have established a protocol in which iNKT cells are isolated from a donor wild-type mouse and transferred into iNKT KO ($J\alpha18^{-/-}$) mouse. Below we will explore the methods for cell sorting of splenic iNKTs, iNKT cells transfer, and detection of transferred cells into the liver using flow cytometry technique.

Key words iNKT cell, Cell sorting, Cell transfer, Flow cytometry, $J\alpha18^{-/-}$ mice, Retro-orbital injection, Isolation of splenocytes, Liver lymphocytes isolation

1 Introduction

Natural killer T (NKT) cells are an innate-like T cell subset that has lipid antigens as ligands. CD1d-expressing antigen presenting cells (APCs), such as dendritic cells, macrophages, and B cells, present lipid antigens to NKT cells through the CD1 molecule [1]. CD1 is a major histocompatibility complex (MHC) class I-like molecule adapted for self- and non-self-glycolipid antigens [1]. The CD1d lipid-enriched antigens that NKT T cell receptor (TCR) recognizes include isoglobotrihexosylceramide, a mammalian glycosphingolipid, as well as microbial α-glycuronyl ceramides found in the cell wall of Gram-negative lipopolysaccharide-negative bacteria [2]. -α-Galactosylceramide (α-GalCer), a bioactive compound with anti-

Marcella Cipelli and Theresa Ramalho contributed equally to this work.

Chaohong Liu (ed.), *Invariant Natural Killer T-Cells: Methods and Protocols*, Methods in Molecular Biology, vol. 2388, https://doi.org/10.1007/978-1-0716-1775-5_10,
© The Author(s), under exclusive license to Springer Science+Business Media, LLC, part of Springer Nature 2021

tumoral activity found in marine sponges, is the most potent KNT TCR ligand yet described [2]. α-GalCer potentially activates both human and mouse NKT cells. Also, due to a high degree of conservation, α-GalCer presented by a human CD1d is able to activate murine NKT cells and vice versa [3].

NKT cells can be subdivided into two different subsets according to the variation in αβ TCR chains: type I and type II NKT cells. Type I, also called invariant NKT cells (iNKT), expresses a restricted TCRs with an invariant α-chain (Vα24-Jα18 in humans and Vα14-Jα18 in mice) and limited β-chains [4]. Type I iNKT cells include two subpopulations: a CD4+ and a CD4−CD8− double-negative (DN) population. Yet, type II, also referred as noninvariant NKT (niNKT), expresses Vα3.2-Jα9/Vβ8, Vα8/Vβ8, and other TCRs. The TCR repertoire of type II niNKTs varies considerably between human and mice [5].

It is known if distinct subsets of NKT cells mediate different responses specifically. However, it is clear that such subsets exerts regulatory and/or protective immune functions through tissue-specific stimuli [4]. In the context of antitumoral response, studies have suggested that type I iNKTs subset mediate antitumoral responses in mice [6], yet type II niNKT cells downregulate such antitumoral immunosurveillance [7]. In addition, it has been reported autoreactive responses of the type II subset to endogenous myelin-derived glycolipid sulfatide in mice [8]. Studies in human has proposed that DN NKT cells mediate tumor rejection since they predominantly secrete Th1 cytokines. In contrast, CD4 NKT cells produce Th2 cytokines mostly. In this sense, it has been suggested that distinct NKT populations may regulate themselves, similarly to the regulatory interplay of Th1/Th2 cells [4].

In addition to Th1 and Th2 cytokines, NKT cells also produce IL-17, contributing to Th17 responses [9]. This subtype, called NKT17, rapidly produces IL-17 dependently of IL-7 in response to IL-23 RORγT activation [10]. Contrastingly, it has been reported that strong activation of iNKTs with α-GalCer induces a regulatory state, far from deactivated or anergic, which secretes IL-10 and expresses PD-1 [11]. This subtype is called NKT10 [11]. Moreover, depending on the context, iNKT cells also secrete granulocyte-macrophage colony-stimulating factor (GM-CSF) and chemokines, such as RANTES and MIPs [12–14]. In addition, iNKT cells exert cytotoxic function due to their capability to express and secrete cytolytic proteins, such as granzyme and perforin, and membrane ligands, such as FasL [12, 15].

Since NKTs have crucial importance in regulatory, protective, and harmful immune responses, there is a need to explore deeply the role of these cells using different tools. Murine models of iNKT cell deficiency have unravel the importance of NKT cells in host survival in the context of infections, antitumoral response, transplant tolerance, and autoimmunity [4]. iNKT cell-deficient mouse models include CD1d$^{-/-}$ and Jα281KO (Jα18$^{-/-}$ or Traj18$^{-/-}$) mice. The CD1d$^{-/-}$ mouse strain is not able to efficiently induce the positive selection of iNKT cells during thymus differentiation. Yet Jα18$^{-/-}$ mice that lack the *Trajl8* gene segment does not develop the invariant TCRα chain which is essential for iNKT development [16].

Here we have stablished a protocol in which iNKT cells are isolated from a donor wild-type mouse. Once isolated, the cells are prepared to be transferred into iNKT KO (Jα18$^{-/-}$) mice. Below we will explore the methods for cell sorting of splenic iNKTs, iNKT cells transfer, and detection of transferred cells into selected tissues using flow cytometry. Such protocol was stablished by our group for a study in which we investigated how iNKT cells regulate intestinal homeostasis and gut microbiota [17]. Also, our protocol can be used in donor mouse models with fluorescent NKTs cells [18] whose fluorescence can be detected in a recipient mouse.

2   Materials

2.1   Mouse Strains

Use mouse strains C57BL/6 and Jα18$^{-/-}$ (iNKT KO) male mice, aged 8–12 weeks. Jα18$^{-/-}$ mice have a specific deletion of the Jα281 gene segment, which codes for the iNKT-specific joining region of the TCR; thus, the invariant Vα14-Jα18 TCR is not expressed in these mice and consequently iNKT cells do not develop. Animal experiments must always be performed following guidelines of the corresponding Ethics Committee for Animal Experimentation.

2.2   General Reagents

1. Isoflurane.

2. Sterile phosphate-buffered saline 1× (PBS 1×): 137 mM NaCl, 10 mM Phosphate, 2.7 mM KCl, pH 7.4.

3. PBS 1× + 2% fetal bovine serum (FBS).

4. Sorting medium: RPMI 1640 medium + 3% FBS.

5. RPMI 1640 medium + 10% FBS.

6. ACK Lysis Buffer: 0.15 M NH$_4$Cl, 10 mM KHCO$_3$, 0.1 mM Na$_2$EDT, adjust PH to 7.2–7.4) (*see* **Note 1**).

7. APC-conjugated anti-mouse TCRβ antibody (BioLegend, clone H57-597).

8. PE-labeled mouse CD1d-PBS57 tetramer (kindly provided by NIH tetramer core facility).

9. PerCP-conjugated anti-mouse CD45 antibody (BioLegend, clone 30-F11).

10. Digestion solution: collagenase VIII (Sigma) 0.5 mg/mL and 10 U/mL DNase I, grade II (Roche) diluted in PBS 1× + 2% FBS.

11. Percoll solution: make a 1.5 M solution of NaCl, and then to 9 parts of Percoll (Sigma) add 1 part of 1.5 M NaCl. For example, for a 100 mL final solution, mix 10 mL of 1.5 M NaCl solution in 90 mL of Percoll. This solution is equivalent to Stock Isotonic Percoll (SIP) or 100% Isotonic Percoll.

12. 40% and 70% Isotonic Percoll solutions: to make 40% and 70% Isotonic Percoll solutions, add 4 mL of Isotonic Percoll in 6 mL of PBS 1× and 7 mL of Isotonic Percoll in 3 mL of PBS 1×, respectively.

2.3 Equipment

1. Scissors.
2. Forceps.
3. Cell strainer 70 μm and 100 μm.
4. Disposable syringe 1 mL plunger.
5. Syringe needles gauge 26G.
6. 15 and 50 mL conical centrifuge tubes.
7. 5 mL round-bottom polystyrene tubes.
8. Professional adjustable-volume micropipette (1000, 200, 20 μL).
9. Micropipette tips (1000, 200, 20 μL).
10. Heating pad or other warming device.
11. Precision laboratory balance.
12. Thermal incubator with rotation unit.
13. Cell culture centrifuge.
14. BD FACS Aria III.
15. BD FACS Canto II.
16. Software package for analyzing flow cytometry data (FlowJo v10).

3 Methods

3.1 Isolation of Splenocytes from WT Mice (Donor) and iNKT Cells Staining

1. Euthanize WT mice using isoflurane and cervical dislocation as a secondary means to assure death. After euthanasia, open the peritoneal cavity using scissors and forceps and remove the spleen.

2. Place the organs on a Petri dish and mash through it using a syringe plunger and PBS 1× solution. Filter cell suspension in a 70 μm cell strainer over a 50 mL conical centrifuge tube and then centrifuge (400 × g, 5 min, 4 °C), discarding the supernatant after that (Fig. 1).

3. Add 1 mL per spleen of ACK lysing buffer to cells and homogenize. Incubate for 5 min at room temperature, add three times

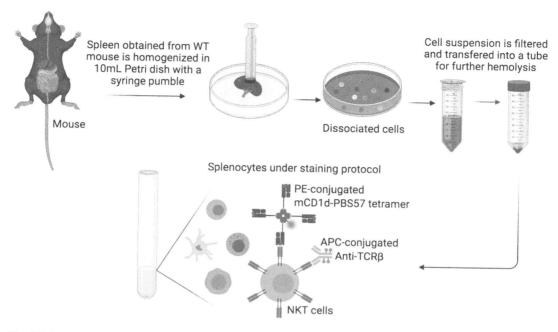

Fig. 1 Schemes of isolation of splenocytes from wild-type mice (donor) followed by staining. In this stage, the cell suspension is obtained from the whole organ and proceeded into iNKT molecules staining using antibodies conjugated to fluorochromes

the initial volume of PBS 1× to stop the reaction, and centrifuge (400 × g, 5 min, 4 °C).

4. Resuspend the pellet with PBS 1× + 2% FBS and transfer all the volume into a 15 mL conical centrifuge tube.

5. Add 100 μL PBS 1× + 2% FBS containing APC-conjugated anti-mouse TCRβ antibody and PE-labeled mouse CD1d-PBS57 to stain cells for 30 min at 4 °C, protected from light (Fig. 1).

6. After that time, add excess PBS 1× + 2% FBS to wash unbound antibody and centrifuge the cells.

7. Discard the supernatant and resuspend the pellet in RPMI medium + 3% FBS to proceed to cell sorting (Fig. 1).

3.2 WT iNKT Cell Sorting and Cell Transfer into Jα18⁻/⁻ Mice (Recipient)

1. Run the cell suspension obtained in the previous step in a BD FACS Aria III cell sorter, selecting iNKT cells as TCRβ^{int}/mCD1dPBS57$^+$ population (*see* **Note 2**).

2. Collect sorted cells in a 15 mL conical centrifuge tube containing sterile RPMI + 10% FBS and count cells (*see* **Note 3**).

3. Centrifuge (400 × g, 10 min, 4 °C) and resuspend in sterile PBS 1× for injection of around 2–3 × 10^5 iNKT cells in a final volume of 150 μL per mouse.

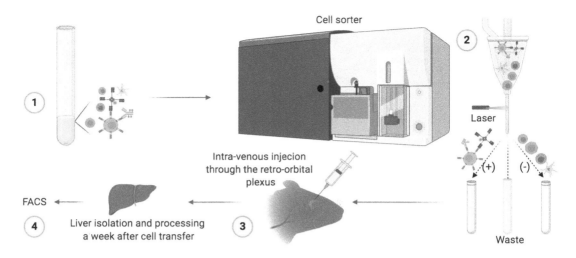

Fig. 2 Cell sorting and iNKT transfer scheme. After staining with antibodies (1), the cells are sorted under aseptic conditions by BD FACS Aria III, selecting TCRβ^{int}/mCD1dPBS57$^+$ population (2). Then, a cell suspension containing 2–3 × 10^5 iNKT cells in a final volume of 150 μL PBS 1× are prepared and injected intravenously through the retro-orbital sinus of Jα18$^{-/-}$ mouse (3). One week after injection, the mouse is euthanized and liver is harvested. Afterward, liver cells are isolated and proceeded with staining of iNKT cells, followed by flow cytometry detection (4)

4. Inject intravenously (*see* **Note 4**) the cell suspension through the retro-orbital sinus using a 1 mL disposable syringe with needle gauge 26G into isoflurane-anesthetized Jα18$^{-/-}$ mouse placed on a heating pad covered with a protective layer of paper toweling or gauze to prevent any thermal injury (Fig. 2).

3.3 iNKTs Detection by Flow Cytometry in Liver of Jα18$^{-/-}$ Mice After WT Cells Transference

1. One week after iNKT cell transfer, euthanize Jα18$^{-/-}$ mice, open the peritoneal cavity using scissors and forceps, and remove the liver.

2. For liver digestion: Place and chop (using scissors) the organs in a 15 mL conical centrifuge tube containing 3 mL per liver of digestion solution and incubate at 37 °C with agitation (200 rpm) for 20 min. After that time, filter the digested organ suspension through a 100 μm cell strainer, mashing the remaining pieces with a syringe plunger and wash with excess PBS 1× to stop the reaction (Fig. 3).

3. Centrifuge the liver cells suspension (400 × *g*, 5 min, 4 °C) and discard the supernatant.

4. Put 3 mL 70% Isotonic Percoll solution in the 15 mL centrifuge conical tube.

5. Resuspend cells in 5 mL of 40% Isotonic Percoll solution and overlay on the 70% Isotonic Percoll solution previously placed in the tube.

6. Centrifuge the tube at 500 × *g* for 25 min at room temperature, without break.

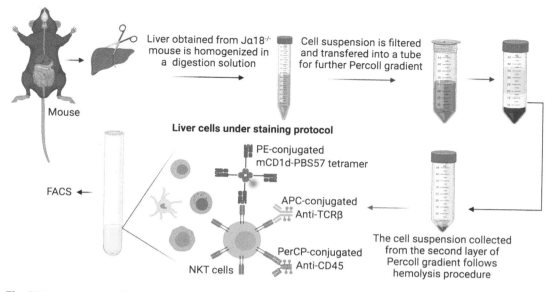

Fig. 3 Liver processing for further detection of transferred iNKT cells in $J\alpha18^{-/-}$ mouse liver. Liver is collected and processed in a digestion solution. After hemolysis, cell suspension follows a staining protocol with PE-conjugated mCD1d-PBS57 tetramer, APC-conjugated Anti-TCRβ, and PerCP-conjugated anti-CD45 antibodies. The fluorescence of the antibodies is later detected by BD FACSCanto II representing the detection of iNKT cells

7. Collect the cells that remained at the interface between the two solutions, transfer to a new tube, centrifuge ($400 \times g$, 5 min, 4 °C) and then discard the supernatant (Fig. 3).

8. After isolation of lymphocytes from liver, add 1 mL of ACK lysis buffer in the pellet, homogenize, and incubate for 3 min at room temperature. Add 3 volumes of PBS 1× to stop the reaction and centrifuge (Fig. 3).

9. Resuspend the pellet in 100 μL PBS 1× + 2% FBS containing the staining antibodies and tetramer: anti-CD45 (PerCP), anti-TCRβ (APC), and mCD1dPBS57 tetramer (PE). After 30 min of incubation at 4 °C protected from light, wash the cells by adding excess PBS 1× + 2% FBS and centrifuge (Fig. 3).

10. Resuspend the pellet in 200 μL PBS 1× each and run the cells in BD FACSCanto II flow cytometer. Analyze data using FlowJo v10 to create the dot plots (Fig. 4). Perform debris and doublets from your data selecting exactly the population of FSC-H x FSC-A gate. Select the iNKT cell population (TCRβ⁺ mCD1d-PBS57⁺) from CD45⁺ cells gate.

4   Notes

1. Used for the lysis of red blood cells in samples containing white blood cells.

2. To avoid contamination is necessary to perform an aseptic sort.

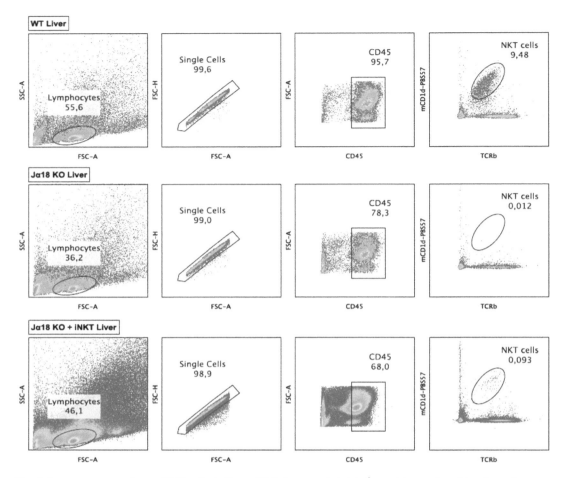

Fig. 4 Gate strategy to detect iNKT cells in liver of WT donor and Jα18$^{-/-}$ recipient mice. After liver digestion and lymphocytes isolation by Percoll gradient technique, the cell suspension is stained with the antibodies, and frequency of iNKT cells can be observed in WT, Jα18$^{-/-}$ and Jα18$^{-/-}$ + iNKT mice 1 week after iNKT cell transfer by flow cytometry

3. In all the steps of iNKT cells injections, preparation is necessary for the use of sterile reagents and perform all the procedures in a laminar flow hood previously cleaned with 70% alcohol and 15 min of UV sterilization.

4. Carefully put the anesthetize mouse laterally lying with its head facing to the right side. Protrude the mouse's eyeball applying a very delicate pressure to the skin in the dorsal and ventral directions to the eye. Do not apply excessive pressure, because this could obstruct the blood flow and hamper the injection. It is also very important not to apply exacerbated pressure to the trachea, because this could hinder mouse's breathing. Carefully introduce the needle at an angle of approximately 30°, into the

medial eye angle, following the edge of the eyeball down until the needle tip is at the base of the eye. Then, slowly injects the cell suspension and do not aspirate before injection. After that, withdraw the needle carefully and slowly. The injection procedure takes only a short time, then the mouse can be gentle placed in the cage without the heating pad, and within 45 s to 1 min after the injection, it will be moving normally.

Acknowledgments

We thank Fernando Pretel from the flow cytometry at CEFAP USP for his technical assistance. We also thank the NIH Tetramer Core Facility for providing PE-labeled mCD1d tetramer. Marcella Cipelli and Theresa Ramalho contributed equally to this work.

References

1. Barral DC, Brenner MB (2007) CD1 antigen presentation: how it works. Nat Rev Immunol 7:929–941

2. Bendelac A, Savage PB, Teyton L (2007) The biology of NKT cells. Annu Rev Immunol 25:297–336

3. Brossay L, Chioda M, Burdin N, Koezuka Y, Casorati G, Dellabona P, Kronenberg M (1998) CD1d-mediated recognition of an alpha-galactosylceramide by natural killer T cells is highly conserved through mammalian evolution. J Exp Med 188:1521–1528

4. Seino K, Taniguchi M (2005) Functionally distinct NKT cell subsets and subtypes. J Exp Med 202:1623–1626

5. Pellicci DG, Uldrich AP (2018) Unappreciated diversity within the pool of CD1d-restricted T cells. Semin Cell Dev Biol 84:42–47

6. Crowe NY, Coquet JM, Berzins SP, Kyparissoudis K, Keating R, Pellicci DG, Hayakawa Y, Godfrey DI, Smyth MJ (2005) Differential antitumor immunity mediated by NKT cell subsets in vivo. J Exp Med 202:1279–1288

7. Terabe M, Swann J, Ambrosino E, Sinha P, Takaku S, Hayakawa Y, Godfrey DI, Ostrand-Rosenberg S, Smyth MJ, Berzofsky JA (2005) A nonclassical non-Valpha14Jalpha18 CD1d-restricted (type II) NKT cell is sufficient for down-regulation of tumor immunosurveillance. J Exp Med 202:1627–1633

8. Jahng A, Maricic I, Aguilera C, Cardell S, Halder RC, Kumar V (2004) Prevention of autoimmunity by targeting a distinct, noninvariant CD1d-reactive T cell population reactive to sulfatide. J Exp Med 199:947–957

9. Michel ML, Keller AC, Paget C, Fujio M, Trottein F, Savage PB, Wong CH, Schneider E, Dy M, Leite-de-Moraes MC (2007) Identification of an IL-17-producing NK1.1(neg) iNKT cell population involved in airway neutrophilia. J Exp Med 204:995–1001

10. Webster KE, Kim HO, Kyparissoudis K, Corpuz TM, Pinget GV, Uldrich AP, Brink R, Belz GT, Cho JH, Godfrey DI, Sprent J (2014) IL-17-producing NKT cells depend exclusively on IL-7 for homeostasis and survival. Mucosal Immunol 7:1058–1067

11. Sag D, Krause P, Hedrick CC, Kronenberg M, Wingender G (2014) IL-10-producing NKT10 cells are a distinct regulatory invariant NKT cell subset. J Clin Invest 124:3725–3740

12. Eberl G, MacDonald HR (2000) Selective induction of NK cell proliferation and cytotoxicity by activated NKT cells. Eur J Immunol 30:985–992

13. Rothchild AC, Jayaraman P, Nunes-Alves C, Behar SM (2014) iNKT cell production of GM-CSF controls *Mycobacterium tuberculosis*. PLoS Pathog 10:e1003805

14. Coquet JM, Chakravarti S, Kyparissoudis K, McNab FW, Pitt LA, McKenzie BS, Berzins SP, Smyth MJ, Godfrey DI (2008) Diverse cytokine production by NKT cell subsets and identification of an IL-17-producing CD4-NK1.1- NKT cell population. Proc Natl Acad Sci U S A 105:11287–11292

15. Gansert JL, Kiessler V, Engele M, Wittke F, Röllinghoff M, Krensky AM, Porcelli SA,

Modlin RL, Stenger S (2003) Human NKT cells express granulysin and exhibit antimycobacterial activity. J Immunol 170:3154–3161

16. Crosby CM, Kronenberg M (2016) Invariant natural killer T cells: front line fighters in the war against pathogenic microbes. Immunogenetics 68:639–648

17. de Aguiar CF, Castoldi A, Amano MT, Ignacio A, Terra FF, Cruz M, Felizardo RJF, Braga TT, Davanzo GG, Gambarini V, Antonio T, Antiorio ATFB, Hiyane MI, Morais da Fonseca D, Andrade-Oliveira V, Câmara NOS (2020) Fecal IgA levels and gut microbiota composition are regulated by invariant natural killer T cells. Inflamm Bowel Dis 26:697–708

18. Humeniuk P, Geiselhart S, Battin C, Webb T, Steinberger P, Paster W, Hoffmann-Sommergruber K (2019) Generation of a Jurkat-based fluorescent reporter cell line to evaluate lipid antigen interaction with the human iNKT cell receptor. Sci Rep 9:7426

Chapter 11

Expansion of Human iNKT Cells Ex Vivo

Jing Wang, Chen Zhao, and Jianqing Xu

Abstract

Invariant natural killer T (iNKT) cells are credited with antitumor activity by preclinical studies and clinical trials. Efficient expansion of iNKT cells ex vivo is essential for their translational usage. The culturing procedure described here provides an optimized method for ex vivo expansion of iNKT cells using recombinant human IL-15 (rhIL-15) and recombinant human IL-12 (rhIL-12), which results in cell products with enhanced cytokine secretion and cytotoxicity while maintaining the purity and viability of iNKT cells.

Key words rhIL-15, rhIL-12, Antigen-presenting cells, α-GalCer, Cytokine secretion, Cytotoxicity

1 Introduction

iNKT cells are characterized by their exclusive usage of invariant Vα14Jα18 antigen receptor, which mostly paired with Vβ8.2 in mice and Vβ11 pair in human to recognize lipid antigens presented by CD1d molecule [1, 2]. The importance of iNKT cells in mediating protection against tumors is highlighted by several findings [3–5]. Efficient expansion of iNKT cells ex vivo is essential for their translational usage. A synthetic glycolipid, α-galactosylceramide (-α-GalCer), was identified as the prototypic ligand for iNKT cells [6]. Upon ligand ligation, iNKT cells are activated and elicited effector cell functions by releasing cytokines, functioning as a bridge between innate and adaptive immune responses [7]. The activities of iNKT cells are regulated by cytokines produced by the immune cells they interact with. One of the best-known cytokine regulators of iNKTs is IL-12, which is produced by mature dendritic cells (DCs) that have been activated through Toll-like receptors [8]. The IL-12-triggerd iNKT cells mainly release IFN-γ, which provides an adjuvant effect by inducing activation and expansion of NK cells and other immune cells, including neutrophils, DCs, or macrophages in the innate immune system and CD4+ Th1

Chaohong Liu (ed.), *Invariant Natural Killer T-Cells: Methods and Protocols*, Methods in Molecular Biology, vol. 2388,
https://doi.org/10.1007/978-1-0716-1775-5_11,

or CD8+ T cells in the adaptive immune system. In contrast, when iNKT cells are engaged with marginal zone B cells or regulatory DCs, which produce IL-10 instead of IL-12, they no longer produce IFN-γ, but rather produce IL-10 to mediate regulatory responses [9, 10].

With an improved knowledge of iNKT cells, it has been widely accepted that both ligand recognition and cytokine-mediated stimulation are required for ex vivo expansion of iNKT cells. Along this line, a classic culturing method of iNKT cells first described by Masaru Taniguchi et al. [11] employed α-GalCer presented by autologous DCs in combination with the cytokine rhIL-2. Here we presented an effective iNKT cell culturing method modified from the original α-GalCer-rhIL-2 approach, which is optimized to enhance the functionality of the cell products. It should be noted that this method is primarily used for culturing human iNKT cells ex vivo from human PBMCs without enrichment.

2   Materials

2.1   Preparation of Human PBMCs from Human Peripheral Blood

Ficoll-Paque plus.

Sterile phosphate buffer saline (PBS).

Serum-free cell medium suitable for culturing cells. RPMI 1640 medium with 10% FBS (V/V) can be used for research purpose.

2.2   Expansion of iNKT Cells

α-GalCer, rhIL-2, rhIL-7, rhIL-15, and rh IL-12. Prepare the solution following the manufacturer instruction, divided into small aliquots prior to storage at -20 °C to avoid repeated freezing and thawing.

Serum-free cell medium is suitable for culturing cells. RPMI 1640 medium with 10% FBS (V/V) can be used for research purpose.

2.3   Expansion of DCs

rhIL-4 and GM-CSF. Prepare the solution following the manufacturer instruction, divided into small aliquots prior to storage at -20 °C to avoid repeated freezing and thawing.

Serum-free cell medium suitable for culturing cells. RPMI 1640 medium with 10% FBS (V/V) can be used for research purpose.

2.4   Assessment of the Purity of iNKT Cells in the Cell Products

Staining buffer (PBS, 2% FBS, V/V).

Antibodies: PE-conjugated anti-human Vα24 TCR and fluorescence-conjugated anti-human Vβ11 TCR.

2.5   Measurement of Cytokine Secreted by iNKT Cells

Detection kit of enzyme-linked immunosorbent assay (ELISA) or cytometric bead array (CBA) for human IFN-γ and human IL-4.

3   Methods

3.1   Preparation of Human PBMCs from Human Peripheral Blood

1. Transfer 10 mL of anti-coagulated human peripheral blood into a plastic tube (*see* **Note 1**).

2. Dilute the whole blood with two volumes of PBS.

3. Place 15 mL of Ficoll-Paque plus in a 50 mL tube. Carefully lay up 30 mL of the diluted blood sample without disturbing the interface.

4. Centrifuge at $600 \times g$ for 30 min at room temperature (RT) with acceleration at level 3 and deceleration at level 2.

5. Human PBMCs should be visible at the PBS/Ficoll-Paque plus interface. Carefully remove the upper PBS layer and harvest PBMCs at the interface by a pipette.

6. Wash twice with 30 mL of PBS. Between wash, pellet the PBMC by centrifugation at $800 \times g$ for 5 min at RT without limitation on acceleration or deceleration.

7. Resuspend PBMCs with 20 mL of serum-free culture medium and count live cell by Trypan blue staining.

8. Keep a fraction of PBMCs in liquid nitrogen as antigen-presenting cells (APCs) for restimulation of human iNKT cells during the culture period.

3.2   Culture of Human iNKT Cells

1. Wash 1×10^7 isolated PBMCs twice with serum-free cell medium by centrifugation at $800 \times g$ for 5 min at RT. Resuspend the cell pellet in serum-free medium to a final density of 2×10^6 cells/mL.

2. Plate the cells in T25 flask, add α-GalCer to make a final concentration of 100 ng/mL, and culture in the 5% CO_2 incubator for 7 days. Refeed the cells with serum-free medium supplemented with 100 ng/mL α-GalCer on day 3.

3. Add recombinant human IL-2 (rhIL2) and recombinant human IL-7 (rhIL-7) into the culture medium at the concentration of 100 IU/mL and 10 ng/mL, respectively, on day 7.

4. Add a-GalCer-pulsed autologous DCs on day 7 to restimulate iNKT cells.

   For preparation of APCs containing DCs from peripheral blood, quickly thaw autologous PBMCs stored in liquid nitrogen, plate in flask, and keep in the cell incubator for 1 h (*see* **Note 2**). Loosen non-adherent cells by swirling the plate and aspirate the medium. Add serum-free medium containing 50 ng/mL of recombinant human granulocyte-macrophage colony-stimulating factor (rhGM-CSF) and 100 ng/mL of recombinant human IL-4 (rhIL-4) to the flask. Keep in the cell incubator for 7 days. Pulse the cell culture with 200 ng/mL of a-GalCer for 24 h. Collect the cells by centrifugation, wash twice with serum-free medium, resuspend in serum-free medium supplemented with α-GalCer, rhIL-2, and rhIL-7, and then add into the iNKT culture.

5. Replenish the iNKT culturing with α-GalCer-pulsed autologous DCs in the presence of a final concentration of 10 ng/mL of rhIL-15 on day 14.

6. Add rhIL-12 to the iNKT culturing flask to a final concentration of 10 ng/mL on day 20.

7. Refeed the cells every 3–4 days (*see* **Note 3**). Put off the addition of rhIL-12 if the cell counting on day 20 is low. IL-12 could be added into the culturing medium 24–48 h before harvest (*see* **Note 4**).

Anticipated Results.

Human iNKT cells can be expanded by culturing human PBMCs over a period of 3–4 weeks (*see* **Note 5**). The approximate yield of iNKT cells is 10^8 per 10^7 human PBMCs without enrichment.

3.3 Assessment of iNKT Cell Population by FACS

For FACS-based assessment, iNKT cells can be stained with α-GalCer/human CD1d dimer, anti-human αβ TCR, or a combination of anti-human Vα24 TCR anti-human Vβ11 TCR [11]. The procedure described below uses PE-conjugated anti-human Vα24 TCR and FITC-conjugated anti-human Vβ11 TCR as an example (*see* **Note 6**).

1. Resuspend 1×10^6 cells in 50μL staining buffer containing 1μg human IgG; incubate for 10 min at 4 °C to block nonspecific binding to Fcg receptors (FcγRs).

2. Wash the cells twice with 50μL staining buffer. Between the washes, the cells are pelleted by centrifugation at $800 \times g$ for 5 min at 4 °C.

3. Resuspend the cells in 50μL staining buffer containing PE-conjugated anti-human Vα24 TCR and FITC-conjugated anti-human Vβ11 TCR mAbs; incubate for 30 min at 4 °C in the dark. For the negative control, cells are stained with isotype-matched control antibody.

4. Wash the cells with staining buffer by centrifugation at $800 \times g$ for 5 min at 4 °C and resuspend in FACS buffer. Keep the cells on ice in the dark before being analyzed on flow cytometer.

5. iNKT population is identified as double Va24- and Vb11-positive cells (Fig. 1a).

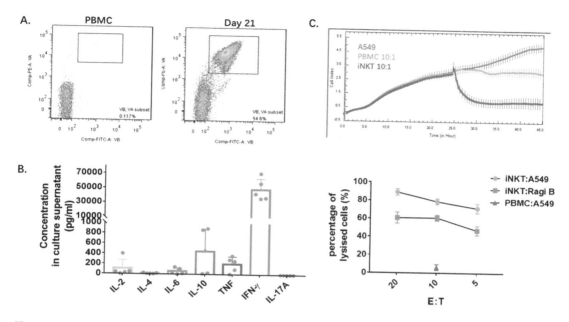

Fig. 1 Characterization of iNKT cell product. The ex vivo-expanded iNKT cells from five health volunteers were evaluated for the abundance of iNKT cells and their functionality. (**a**) Example of FACS-mediated assessment of iNKT subpopulation, identified as TCR Vα24 + Vβ11+ cells, in PBMC and the derived 21-day culture. (**b**) Quantification of the cytokines in the medium of 21-day culture using cytometric bead array. (**c**) Cytotoxicity of iNKT cells against the model cell lines of A549 and Raji B assessed by real-time cell analysis system. Upper panel: raw picture. Lower panel: analyzed data

Anticipated Results.

Generally, iNKT cells are less than 0.5% of human PBMCs. There are significant variations among individuals in the percentages of iNKT cells in human PBMCs. As shown in Fig. 1a, our method has the capacity to expand the concentration of iNKT cell population by hundred-to-thousand-fold.

3.4 Assessment of the Antitumor Functionality of iNKT Cells

1. Measurement of cytokines secreted by iNKT cells.

   The ratio of IFN-γ/IL-4 has been regarded as an effective indicator to the antitumor activity of iNKT cells [12]. Cytokines can be quantitatively detected by either enzyme-linked immunosorbent assay (ELISA) or cytometric bead array (CBA) following manufacturer protocol (Fig. 1b).

2. Cytotoxicity of iNKT cells.

   The antitumor cytotoxicity of iNKT cells can be evaluated by measuring the ratio of cytolyzed tumor cells after co-incubation with the iNKT cells being assayed. This measurement would be facilitated by machine that can perform real-time cell analysis, allowing a convenient monitoring of killing dynamics (Fig. 1c).

4   Notes

1. Although PBMCs used here were buffy coat which are separated from whole blood, it is feasible to use leukapheresis from the donor.

2. Monocytes are separated here by using their differentiated capacity of attachment to the bottom of the flask. It is also feasible to use CD16+ monocyte isolation kit to separate monocyte from other cell populations.

3. Cell density is a key impactor to the purity of iNKT cells in the final cell product. Seed 2×10^6 cells/mL PBMCs to the flask at the very beginning of cell culture, and keep the density at 1×10^6 cells/mL when refeed the culture system with fresh medium.

4. The culture procedure could be separated into three periods with different cytokines added. In the first 7 days, iNKT cells are enriched with sole α-GalCer added into the medium. Viability and cell count decreases, while debris increases in the system. The proliferation curve begins to go up after the addition of IL-2, and IL-7 are added on day 7. Cells proliferate quickly, especially iNKT cells, which were activated with α-GalCer before. In the last 7 days, IL-15 and IL-12 are added to enhance the secretion of IFN-γ and cytotoxicity of iNKT cells.

5. Cytokines are added according to the anticipant concentration based on the volume of medium refeeded into the system, other than the total volume of the culture.

6. TCR-Vα24+TCR-Vβ11+ cells are regarded as iNKT cells by using flow cytometry here. CD1d-dimer can replace anti-TCR-Vα24 antibody to detect iNKT cells with anti-TCR-Vβ11 antibody.

Acknowledgments

This work was supported by National Key R&D Program of China 2016YFC1303402 (2016YFC1303402) and National Major Projects of China (2017ZX10202102). The functional enhancement of ex vivo expanded iNKT cells by rhIL-15 and rhIL-12 has been included in a Chinese patent: ZL201611031666.9. The method for culturing iNKT cells ex vivo has been applied to an investigator-initiated clinical trial (NCT03093688).

References

1. Lantz O, Bendelac A (1994) An invariant T cell receptor alpha chain is used by a unique subset of major histocompatibility complex class I-specific CD4+ and CD4-8- T cells in mice and humans. J Exp Med 180(3):1097–1106

2. Taniguchi M, Harada M, Kojo S, Nakayama T, Wakao H (2003) The regulatory role of Valpha14 NKT cells in innate and acquired immune response. Annu Rev Immunol 21:483–513

3. Molling JW, Kolgen W, van der Vliet HJ et al (2005) Peripheral blood IFN-gamma-secreting Valpha24+Vbeta11+ NKT cell numbers are decreased in cancer patients independent of tumor type or tumor load. Int J Cancer 116(1):87–93

4. Yanagisawa K, Seino K, Ishikawa Y, Nozue M, Todoroki T, Fukao K (2002) Impaired proliferative response of V alpha 24 NKT cells from cancer patients against alpha-galactosylceramide. J Immunol 168 (12):6494–6499

5. Schneiders FL, de Bruin RC, van den Eertwegh AJ et al (2012) Circulating invariant natural killer T-cell numbers predict outcome in head and neck squamous cell carcinoma: updated analysis with 10-year follow-up. J Clin Oncol 30(5):567–570

6. Kawano T, Cui J, Koezuka Y et al (1997) CD1d-restricted and TCR-mediated activation of valpha14 NKT cells by glycosylceramides. Science 278(5343):1626–1629

7. Matsuda JL, Mallevaey T, Scott-Browne J, Gapin L (2008) CD1d-restricted iNKT cells, the 'Swiss-Army knife' of the immune system. Curr Opin Immunol 20(3):358–368

8. Takeda K, Seki S, Ogasawara K et al (1996) Liver NK1.1+ CD4+ alpha beta T cells activated by IL-12 as a major effector in inhibition of experimental tumor metastasis. J Immunol 156(9):3366–3373

9. Kojo S, Seino K, Harada M et al (2005) Induction of regulatory properties in dendritic cells by Valpha14 NKT cells. J Immunol 175 (6):3648–3655

10. Venken K, Decruy T, Aspeslagh S, Van Calenbergh S, Lambrecht BN, Elewaut D (2013) Bacterial CD1d-restricted glycolipids induce IL-10 production by human regulatory T cells upon cross-talk with invariant NKT cells. J Immunol 191(5):2174–2183

11. Watarai H, Nakagawa R, Omori-Miyake M, Dashtsoodol N, Taniguchi M (2008) Methods for detection, isolation and culture of mouse and human invariant NKT cells. Nat Protoc 3 (1):70–78

12. Altman JB, Benavides AD, Das R, Bassiri H (2015) Antitumor responses of invariant natural killer T cells. J Immunol Res 2015:652875

Chapter 12

The Expansion and Cytotoxicity Detection of Human iNKT Cells

Xue Cheng, Xiaosheng Tan, Rui Dou, Xiongwen Wu, and Xiufang Weng

Abstract

Invariant natural killer T (iNKT) cell is a type of innate-like T cell subsets with both T and NK cell phenotype and functions. They recognize lipid antigens presented by CD1d molecules and can be specifically activated by alpha-galactosylceramide (α-GalCer) in vitro. After activation, iNKT cells expand efficiently and exert direct killing effects. Based on it, we mainly introduce the protocols of detection of human iNKT cell functions in vitro, including in vitro expansion and their cytotoxicity to tumor cells.

Key words iNKT cells, Expansion, Cytotoxicity

1 Introduction

Compared with conventional T cells, iNKT cells are more limited in the diversity of T cell receptors, which usually use Vα24-Jα18 paired Vβ11 in humans and Vα124-Jα18 paired Vβ8.2, 7 or 2 in mouse [1]. iNKT cells are abundant in the liver and also found in peripheral blood, lung, intestine, thymus, bone narrow, spleen, and adipose tissue [2]. iNKT cell recognize lipid antigens presented by CD1d, a non-polymorphic major histocompatibility complex class I-like antigen-presenting molecule [3, 4]. The alpha-galactosylceramide (α-GalCer), a synthetic lipid of a chemical purified from the deep sea sponge *Agelas mauritianus* [5], can activate iNKT cells specifically in vitro. Upon activation, iNKT cells can release a large number of cytokines instantly, expand efficiently [6], directly kill tumor cells, and cross-talk with other immune cells to activate both innate and adaptive immune responses [3, 4, 7]. Although they are relatively low frequent in humans, the unique characteristics make them essential for the immune responses in pathological conditions including autoimmunity, infection diseases, and cancers [2, 3,

Chaohong Liu (ed.), *Invariant Natural Killer T-Cells: Methods and Protocols*, Methods in Molecular Biology, vol. 2388,
https://doi.org/10.1007/978-1-0716-1775-5_12,
© The Author(s), under exclusive license to Springer Science+Business Media, LLC, part of Springer Nature 2021

8]. Here, we mainly introduce methods of detection of human iNKT cell functions in vitro, including α-GalCer-induced iNKT cell expansion and their direct cytotoxicity to tumor cells.

2   Materials

2.1 Expansion of Human iNKT Cells In Vitro

1. Plastic tubes: 1.5 ml tube, 15 ml tube, 50 ml tube.
2. Flat-bottom 96-well culture plates.
3. Hemocytometer.
4. Ultrasonic cleaner.
5. Phosphate-buffered saline (PBS) without calcium and magnesium.
6. RPMI medium 1640 basic ($1\times$).
7. Complete RPMI1640 culture medium: RPMI1640 medium supplemented with 10% heat-inactivated fetal bovine serum (FBS), 100 U/ml penicillin, 100 mg/ml streptomycin, 10 mM HEPES buffer solution, 0.1 mM MEM nonessential amino acids, 1 mM sodium pyruvate, and 5.5 mM 2-mercaptoethanol (2-ME).
8. Ficoll-Paque Plus.
9. α-GalCer.
10. Human recombinant interleukin-2 (IL-2).
11. Trypan blue staining solution, 0.4% (wt/vol).
12. Allegra X-15R centrifuge.
13. Flow cytometer.

2.2 Isolation of Human iNKT Cells

1. Phosphate-buffered saline (PBS) without calcium and magnesium.
2. Bovine serum albumin (BSA) albumin fraction V.
3. Separation buffer: PBS, PH7.2, 0.5% BSA, and 2 mM EDTA.
4. APC-labeled PBS57/CD1d-tetramer: provided by the Tetramer Core Facility of the National Institutes of Health, USA (http://research.yerkes.emory.edu/tetramer   core/MR1-Tetramers.html).
5. Anti-APC MicroBeads.
6. MS Column.
7. OctoMACS Separator.
8. Hemocytometer.
9. Allegra X-15R centrifuge.
10. Flow cytometer.

2.3 Cytotoxicity Assay of Human iNKT Cells

1. CD1d transfectant of HepG2 cell line (HepG2-tmCD1d) with highly surface CD1d expression.

2. Phosphate-buffered saline (PBS) without calcium and magnesium.

3. Fetal bovine serum (FBS).

4. Tag-it Violet™ Proliferation and Cell Tracking Dye.

5. FITC Annexin V Apoptosis Detection Kit I.

6. Hemocytometer.

7. Incubator.

8. Allegra X-15R centrifuge.

9. Flow cytometer.

3 Methods

3.1 Human iNKT Cells Expansion from Human Peripheral Blood Mononuclear Cells (PBMCs)

3.1.1 Preparation of Human Peripheral Blood Mononuclear Cells (PBMCs)

1. Dilute the peripheral blood with equal volume of $1 \times$ PBS.

2. Add 5 ml Ficoll-Paque Plus to the 15 ml centrifuge tube, and add the diluted blood onto the Ficoll-Paque Plus along the wall of the centrifuge tube carefully to prevent break of the separation interface.

3. Centrifuge at $900 \times g$ for 25 min at room temperature, where the accelerating and decelerating rates are both 4 (*see* **Note 1**).

4. After centrifugation, the liquid is divided into four layers from top to bottom, including the plasma layer, the ring-shaped milky white cell layer, the transparent separation liquid layer, and the red blood cell layer, respectively.

5. Carefully draw the cell layer into another 15 ml centrifuge tube, add at least twice the volume of $1 \times$ PBS, mix well, and centrifuge at $500 \times g$ for 10 min.

6. Discard the supernatant, add 5 ml $1 \times$ PBS to resuspend the cell pellet, and centrifuge at $500 \times g$ for 10 min.

7. Discard the supernatant and resuspend the cell pellet in complete RPMI 1640 culture medium.

8. Check cell viability by Trypan blue staining, and count the amounts of live cells on a hemocytometer under an optical microscope.

3.1.2 Human iNKT Cells Expansion in Response to α-GalCer/IL-2 In Vitro

1. Adjust the cell density of PBMCs to 5×10^6/ml.

2. Seed the cells into 96-well culture plate (100 μl/well).

3. Add 100 μl complete RPMI 1640 culture medium containing 400 ng/ml α-GalCer with or without 100 U/ml IL-2. α-GalCer should be dissolved by ultrasonic for 30 min at room temperature.

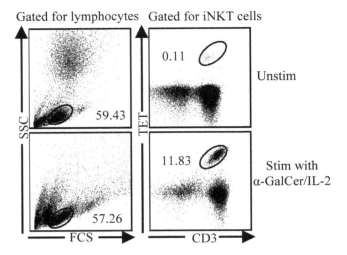

Gated for lymphocytes   Gated for iNKT cells

Fig. 1 Human iNKT cells expand from PBMCs upon α-GalCer/IL-2 stimulation PBMCs from heathy donor were stimulated with α-GalCer and IL-2 for 7 days, followed by flow cytometry detection with anti-CD3 antibody and PBS57/CD1d tetramer. Representative plots are shown

4. Mix well and incubate at 37 °C in the incubator with 5% CO_2.

5. Collect 100 μl supernatant, and then supply 100 μl complete RPMI 1640 culture medium containing 50 U/ml IL-2 on the third day of cell culture.

6. Collect the cells and detect the expansion ratio of CD3+PBS57-CD1d-TET+iNKT cells by flow cytometry on the seventh day.

7. The result shows iNKT cells are efficiently expanded with higher ratio (Fig. 1).

3.2 Cytotoxicity Assay of Human iNKT Cells

3.2.1 Enrichment of Human iNKT Cells

1. Collect the expanded cells and centrifuge at $500 \times g$ for 6 min.

2. Aspirate supernatant completely, resuspend cell pellet ($<5 \times 10^7$) in 200 μl complete RPMI 1640 culture medium with 1 μl APC-labeled PBS57/CD1d-tetremer, mix well, and incubate for 30 min at 4 °C in the dark.

3. Wash the cells with 5 ml separation buffer by centrifuging at $500 \times g$ for 6 min.

4. Aspirate supernatant completely, resuspend cell pellet in 90 μl complete RPMI 1640 culture medium and 10 μl anti-APC microbeads, mix well, and incubate for 30 min at 4 °C in the dark (*see* **Note 2**).

5. Wash the cells with 5 ml separation buffer by centrifuging at $500 \times g$ for 6 min.

6. Resuspend the cells with 2 ml separation buffer.

7. Insert MS Columns to OctoMACS™ (*see* **Note 3**).

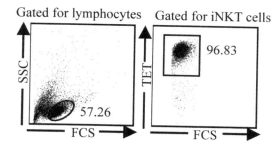

Fig. 2 Purity of enriched iNKT cells. The purity of enriched iNKT cells was detected by flow cytometry with PBS57/CD1d tetramer. Representative plots are shown

8. Prepare MS Columns by rinsing with separation buffer.

9. Apply cell suspension onto the prepared column twice and wash for three times with 1 ml separation buffer.

10. Remove the column from the magnet and place it on a suitable collection tube.

11. Pipette 2 ml separation buffer onto the MS column. Immediately flush out the retained cells within the column with the magnetically labeled cells by firmly pushing the plunger into the column.

12. Collect the cells by centrifuging at $500 \times g$ for 6 min and resuspend with 1 ml complete RPMI 1640 culture medium.

13. Check the cells viability by Trypan blue staining, count live cell amounts on a hemocytometer under an optical microscope, and check the purity of isolated cells by flow cytometry.

14. The purity of enriched iNKT cells is shown in Fig. 2.

3.2.2 Prepare of Targets

1. Collect HepG2-tmCD1d cells and wash three times with PBS by centrifuging at $400 \times g$ for 5 min.

2. Prepare a 5 μM working solution by diluting 1 ul of 5 mM Tag-it Violet™ stock solution in 1 ml RPMI 1640 (*see* **Note 4**).

3. Resuspend the cells at 1×10^7 to 1×10^8/ml in 5 μM Tag-it Violet™ working solution, mix well, and incubate for 20 min at 37 °C in the dark.

4. Quench the staining by adding half of the original staining volume of FBS, and incubate at 37 °C for 5 min in the dark.

5. Wash three times with PBS by centrifuging at $400 \times g$ for 5 min.

6. Resuspend the cells with 1 ml complete RPMI 1640 culture medium.

7. Check the cells viability by Trypan blue staining, and count live cell amounts on a hemocytometer under an optical microscope.

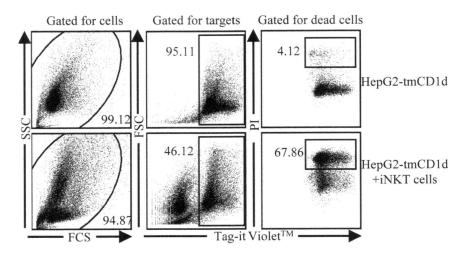

Fig. 3 Killing activity of iNKT cells against HepG2-tmCD1d. The enriched iNKT cells were co-cultured with Tag-it Violet™-labeled HepG2-tmCD1d for 24 h, followed by PI staining. Representative plots for PI positively stained targets are shown

3.2.3   Cytotoxicity Assay

1. Adjust the cell concentration of targets to 5×10^5/ml, and then seed the cells to 96-well culture plates (100 μl/well).

2. Adjust the cell concentration of effectors to 1×10^6/ml, and then seed the cells to 96-well culture plates (100 μl/well).

3. Mix well and incubate at 37 °C for 24 h in an incubator with 5% CO_2.

4. Detect the PI-positive stained targets using FITC Annexin V Apoptosis Detection Kit I by flow cytometry.

5. Figure 3 shows the ratios of PI positively stained dead cells (PI+ %) in indicated groups. Killing activity (% lysis) was calculated by subtracting PI+% in control group (HepG2-tmCD1d) from that in experiment group (HepG2-tmCD1d+iNKT cells).

4   Notes

1. The centrifugal force and time can be adjusted appropriately according to the blood sample volume to achieve the best separation effect.

2. The antibody and microbeads dosage need to be adjusted appropriately according to the numbers of total cells.

3. It is necessary for choosing an appropriate MACS column and MACS Separator depending on the number of total cells and magnetically labeled cells.

4. Adjust the appropriate dosage of Tag-it Violet™ according to the number of total cells.

References

1. Lantz O, Bendelac A (1994) An invariant T cell receptor alpha chain is used by a unique subset of major histocompatibility complex class I-specific CD4+ and CD4-8- T cells in mice and humans. J Exp Med 180:1097–1106

2. Terabe M, Berzofsky JA (2018) Tissue-specific roles of NKT cells in tumor immunity. Front Immunol 9:1838

3. Crosby CM, Kronenberg M (2018) Tissue-specific functions of invariant natural killer T cells. Nat Rev Immunol 18:559–574

4. Brennan PJ, Brigl M, Brenner MB (2013) Invariant natural killer T cells: an innate activation scheme linked to diverse effector functions. Nat Rev Immunol 13:101–117

5. Kawano T, Cui J, Koezuka Y, Toura I, Kaneko Y, Motoki K, Ueno H et al (1997) CD1d-restricted and TCR-mediated activation of valpha14 NKT cells by glycosylceramides. Science 278:1626–1629

6. Stetson DB, Mohrs M, Reinhardt RL, Baron JL, Wang ZE, Gapin L, Kronenberg M et al (2003) Constitutive cytokine mRNAs mark natural killer (NK) and NK T cells poised for rapid effector function. J Exp Med 198:1069–1076

7. Berzins SP, Smyth MJ, Baxter AG (2011) Presumed guilty: natural killer T cell defects and human disease. Nat Rev Immunol 11:131–142

8. Van Kaer L, Parekh VV, Wu L (2013) Invariant natural killer T cells as sensors and managers of inflammation. Trends Immunol 34:50–58

Ex Vivo Expansion of Th2-Polarizing Immunotherapeutic iNKT Cells from Human Peripheral Blood

Natasha K. Khatwani, Kelly J. Andrews, and Asha B. Pillai

Abstract

iNKT cells, classified as innate lymphocytes with invariant TCRs, have been highlighted as a putative, "off-the-shelf" cellular immunotherapeutic strategy for the treatment of malignant and nonmalignant diseases. However, their paucity in human blood limits their immunotherapeutic applications. Herein we describe a rigorously optimized 21-day ex vivo expansion method to achieve log-fold increases in immunotherapeutic human iNKT cells.

Key words iNKT cells, NKT cells, Immunotherapy, Cancer immunotherapy, Adoptive cellular therapy, Hematopoietic stem cell transplantation, Bone marrow transplantation, Transplantation, Cytotoxicity, Leukemia

1 Introduction

Human invariant natural killer T (iNKT) cells are a specialized subset of $\alpha\beta$ T lymphocytes that express an invariant TCR α-chain (Vα24Jα18), paired with the TCR β-chain, Vβ11 [1–3]. Unlike conventional $\alpha\beta$ T lymphocytes, iNKT cells neither recognize peptide antigens nor are restricted by conventional polymorphic MHC/HLA molecules; instead, they recognize glycolipid antigens, such as the synthetic glycolipid, α-galactosylceramide (-α-GalCer), presented on the non-polymorphic glycoprotein molecule CD1d [4–7]. Once stimulated by CD1d-presented glycolipids, iNKT cells can rapidly secrete both Th1 and Th2 cytokines. iNKT cells have been extensively studied for their potent role in immunoregulation, given their ability to promote direct and indirect tolerogenic effects [7–11]. After allogeneic transplantation, for example, iNKT cells have been found to regu-

---

Natasha K. Khatwani, Kelly J. Andrews contributed equally to this work.

Chaohong Liu (ed.), *Invariant Natural Killer T-Cells: Methods and Protocols*, Methods in Molecular Biology, vol. 2388, https://doi.org/10.1007/978-1-0716-1775-5_13,

late graft-versus-host disease (GvHD), while simultaneously maintaining potent graft-versus-tumor (GVT) effects. This separation of undesirable GvHD from the salutary GVT driven by allogeneic T cells is considered the "holy grail" of hematopoietic stem cell transplantation (HSCT) [12–15]. However, the advancement of iNKT cellular immunotherapies is significantly hindered by their low frequency in peripheral blood (< 0.01%).

To address this need, we have developed a highly reproducible and robust 21-day method for the ex vivo expansion of human peripheral blood iNKT cells. Our protocol incorporates concepts from conventional three-step signaling mechanisms in T cell activation [16] tailored specifically for optimal iNKT cell expansion, namely, the use of α-GalCer (**signal 1:** antigen-iTCR engagement) presented on PBMC-derived APCs (**signal 2:** co-stimulation) and supplemented with recombinant human (rh)IL-2 and (rh)IL-7 (**signal 3:** cytokines/growth factors) to achieve a striking 320-fold (median) increase of iNKT cells from day 0 to day 21 [17]. Additionally, we show via the ^{51}Cr release assay, that a single-step signal 1/signal 2 activation of expanded and sorted iNKT cells can significantly enhance their cytotoxicity against the CD1d-expressing Jurkat (T-ALL) cell line as compared to expansion alone.

2 Materials

2.1 iNKT Cell Expansion and Culture

1. Human PBMCs: may be purchased or isolated from single-donor blood products by Ficoll-Paque Plus® density gradient (*see* **Note 1**).

2. iNKT Media: RPMI 1640® w/ L-glutamine, 10 mM HEPES, 0.02 mg/mL gentamicin, 10% human AB serum (*see* **Note 2**). Store at 4 °C and warm to 37 °C prior to use in culture.

3. Sterile 0.45 μm CA membrane vacuum filtration unit (*see* **Note 3**).

4. Cytokines and growth factors: 100 U/mL rhIL-2, 0.4 ng/mL or 4 ng/mL rhIL-7, and 100 ng/mL α-galactosylceramide (α-GalCer) (*see* **Note 4**).

5. Stimulating antibody: 1 μg/mL anti-CD3 monoclonal antibody (MoAb).

6. Irradiator (*see* **Note 5**).

7. 0.1% Trypan blue.

8. Hemocytometer or automated cell counter.

9. T-75 sterile cell culture flasks (*see* **Note 6**).

Table 1
Recommended human iNKT sort panel

Sort Panel		
Antibody target	**Fluorophore**	**Clone**
CD3	APC	HIT3a
Vα24	PE-Cy7	6B11
Live/dead	PI or DAPI	–

Table 2
Recommended human iNKT flow cytometry panel

Flow cytometry panel		
Antibody target	**Fluorophore**	**Clone**
CD3	APC	HIT3a
Vα24	PE-Cy7	6B11
Vβ11	PE	REA559
CD4	APC-Cy7	RPA-T4
CD8	eF450	SK1
Live/dead	BV510 (ghost 510®)	–

2.2 Flow Cytometry and Cell Sorting

1. Cell sorter.
2. Cell analyzer.
3. Antibodies (*see* Tables 1 and 2).
4. FACS buffer: 1× PBS (Ca^{2+}, Mg^{2+} free), 1% human AB serum (*see* **Note 2**), 0.5 mM EDTA, 0.1% NaN_3.
5. Sort buffer: 1× PBS (Ca^{2+}, Mg^{2+} free), 2% human AB serum (*see* **Note 2**).
6. 2% Paraformaldehyde (PFA).
7. Round-bottom polystyrene FACS tubes.
8. 15 mL sterile conical polypropylene tube.

2.3 Functional Assay: Antitumor Cytotoxicity

1. Jurkat cell line.
2. Jurkat growth media: RPMI 1640® w/ L-glutamine, 10% FBS (*see* **Note 2**), 1% penicillin–streptomycin. Store at 4 °C and warm to 37 °C prior to use.
3. Day 21 expanded, sorted human iNKT cells.

4. iNKT media: RPMI 1640® w/ L-glutamine, 10 mM HEPES, 0.02 mg/mL gentamicin, 10% human AB serum (*see* **Note 2**). Store at 4 °C and warm to 37 °C prior to use.

5. 50 ng/mL α-galactosylceramide, α-GalCer.

6. Chromium-51 radionuclide, ^{51}Cr (0.1 mCi) (PerkinElmer).

7. Anti-CD2/3/28 T Cell Activation/Expansion Bead Kit (Miltenyi Biotec).

8. 96-well round bottom plate.

9. LumaPlate™ (Thermo Fisher Scientific).

10. Liquid scintillation counter.

11. Triton-X (SIGMA).

3 Methods

Carry out all procedures at room temperature in a sterile BSL2 biosafety cabinet, and follow standard sterile cell culture technique unless otherwise specified.

3.1 iNKT Expansion

1. On day 0, plate single-donor human PBMCs in T-75 flasks at a concentration of 2×10^6 cells/mL in iNKT media. (iNKT media should be filtered, warmed to 37 °C, and supplemented with 100 U/mL rhIL-2, 0.4 ng/mL rhIL-7 and 100 ng/mL α-GalCer prior to use.) Incubate T-75 flasks for 7 days in 37 °C, 5% CO_2 (*see* **Notes 3** and **7**).

2. On day 7, stain cells and sort for live CD3$^+$, Vα24$^+$ (clone 6B11, eBioscience 50-112-3387) iNKT cells using the sort panel shown in Table 1. Collect sorted cells in chilled iNKT media in a 15 mL conical polypropylene tube. *See representative day 7 pre-sort and post-sort flow plots*, Fig. 1.

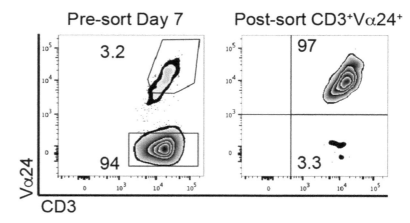

Fig. 1 Representative flow plots showing CD3 and Vα24 expression pre- and post-sort on gated CD3$^+$ cells on day 7. (Reprinted with permission from [17])

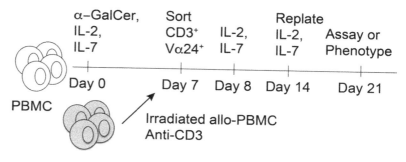

Fig. 2 Human iNKT ex vivo expansion timeline. (Reprinted with permission from [17])

3. Count sorted day 7 $CD3^+V\alpha24^+$ iNKT cells using trypan blue exclusion, and replate in a T-75 (*see* **Note 6**) at a concentration of 1×10^3 to 5×10^4 iNKT cells/mL of iNKT media with allogeneic PBMC a ratio of sorted iNKT cells to irradiated allogeneic PBMC of 1:50 (*see* **Note 8**). Supplement iNKT media with 1 µg/mL anti-CD3 MoAb, 100 U/mL rhIL-2 and 4 ng/mL rhIL-7 (*see* **Note 9**). Incubate culture flasks, standing flasks upright to enhance cell-cell contact, for an additional 14 days (through day 21), replacing fresh iNKT media supplemented with 100 U/mL rhIL-2 and 4 ng/mL rhIL-7 on days 14 and 21.

On day 21, iNKT + feeder cells may be cryopreserved for subsequent surface phenotyping and/or functional assays, or they can be stained with antibodies (*see* Table 2) and $CD3^+V\alpha24^+$ iNKT cells re-sorted for immediate use. Collect sorted cells in chilled iNKT media in a 15 mL conical polypropylene tube, and count using trypan blue exclusion. *See expansion protocol timeline in* Fig. 2.

3.2 iNKT Yield and Phenotype Assessment by Flow Cytometry

Harvested samples may be further handled under nonsterile conditions. Keep samples on ice at all times to preserve viability and function.

1. Assess and compare iNKT expansion yield and phenotypes by flow cytometry at days 0, 7 (pre-sort), 14, and 21, by harvesting at least 100,000 cells/sample at relevant time points.

2. Wash each sample with 1–2 mL of FACS buffer and centrifuge for 5 min at $400 \times g$. Carefully decant supernatant and repeat wash step.

3. Using the panel shown (*see* Table 2), stain samples and relevant compensation controls for 30 min in the dark, on ice.

4. Wash each sample using 100–200 µL of FACS buffer and centrifuge for 5 min at $400 \times g$. Carefully decant supernatant and repeat this wash step two times further.

5. Fix the stained cells with 100 μL of 2% PFA for 10 min in the dark, on ice. Wash with 100–200 μL of ice cold FACS buffer and centrifuge for 5 min at 800 × *g*. Carefully decant supernatant and repeat this wash step two times further.

6. For immediate flow cytometry analyses, resuspend cell pellets in 200–300 μL of fresh, ice-cold FACS buffer, and transfer to round-bottom FACS tubes to run samples. For future analysis, store cell pellets in the dark at 4 °C until time of analysis (*see* **Note 10**).

7. Analyze data using FlowJo® v10. *See iNKT expansion yield comparisons between days 0, 7, 14, and 21 in Fig. 3 and CD4/CD8 phenotypic comparisons between days 0, 7, and 21 in Fig. 4.*

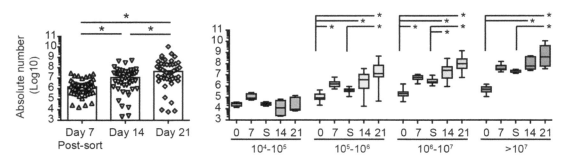

Fig. 3 *Left panel:* median absolute number CD3+Vα24+ iNKT cells at day 7, day 14, and day 21 stratified by day 7 sort yield categories 10^4 to 10^5 (orange, $N = 4$), 105-106 (yellow, $N = 16$), 10^6 to 10^7 (cyan, $N = 21$), and $> 10^7$ (magenta, $N = 6$). *Right panel:* sub-analysis of expansion data by day 7 sort categories showing median and IQR ± range absolute number CD3+Vα24+ iNKT cells at specified time points in the expansion protocol (S, day 7 post-sort). (Reprinted with permission from [17])

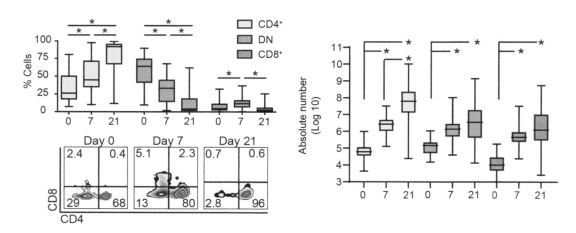

Fig. 4 *Left panel:* Median and IQR ± range percentage *(top)* with representative flow plots *(bottom)* of CD4 and CD8 expression in gated CD3+Vα24+ cells on days 0, 7, and 21 ($N = 36$). *Right panel:* Median and IQR ± range absolute number of CD4+, DN, and CD8+ CD3+Vα24+ iNKT cells on days 0, 7, and 21 (left panel; $N = 36$). $P < 0.05$ is represented by *. (Reprinted with permission from [17])

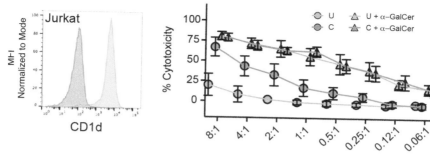

Fig. 5 *Left Panel:* Representative histogram showing CD1d expression, normalized to mode, on Jurkat cells. *Red*, isotype control; *blue*, anti-CD1d. *Right Panel:* Mean percent cytotoxicity $\pm$ SEM of day 21 sorted iNKT effectors (E) against Jurkat targets (T) at the indicated E:T target ratios (*x* axis) via ^{51}Cr release assay ($N = 4$). *Blue circles*, iNKT + unloaded beads; *blue triangles*, iNKT + unloaded beads + 50 ng/mL α-GalCer; *red circles*, iNKT + anti-CD2/3/28 loaded beads; *red triangles*, iNKT + anti-CD2/3/28 loaded beads + 50 ng/mL α-GalCer. (Reprinted with permission from [17])

3.3 iNKT Functional Assay: 51Cr Release Antitumor Cytotoxicity Assay

1. In a 24-well plate, stimulate day 21 iNKT cells (effectors, *E*) (either freshly sorted or previously sorted, cryopreserved and re-thawed) using anti-CD2/CD3/CD28 loaded beads, control beads, or media only (*see* **Note 11**). Incubate for 24 h at 37 °C, 5% CO_2.

2. Label Jurkat T-ALL human cell line (targets, *T*) with 0.1 mCi ^{51}Cr in 200 μL of pre-warmed Jurkat media. Incubate for 24 h at 37 °C, 5% CO_2 (*see* **Notes 12** and **13**).

3. After 24 h, wash ^{51}Cr-labeled Jurkat cells three times with Jurkat media (*see* **Note 13**), and plate in triplicate in 96-well round-bottom plate at 10^5 cells/well, either with or without 50 ng/mL α-GalCer.

4. After 24 h, add stimulated iNKT cell effectors (*E*) over ^{51}Cr-labeled Jurkat targets (*T*) in the 96-well plate holding the target cell number constant and varying the effector numbers to achieve **E:T ratios** of 8:1 to 0.0625:1. Incubate plates for 18 h at 37 °C in 5% CO_2.

5. After 18 h of co-culture, centrifuge the 96-well plate at $400 \times g$ for 5 min and transfer the supernatant to a LumaPlate™.

6. Place the LumaPlate™ in a liquid scintillation counter and quantitate beta-emission (*see* **Note 14**). *See Fig. 5 for representative cytotoxicity data across varying E:T ratios.*

4 Notes

1. Two allogeneic donors are needed per single-donor expansion (one is the iNKT expansion product and the other is the allogeneic feeder source, co-cultured with sorted iNKT cells from day 7 onward). Autologous PBMCs may also be used as

feeders in place of allogeneic PBMCs. PBMCs may be either freshly isolated prior to expansion or previously cryopreserved and thawed for expansion.

2. Human AB serum and fetal bovine serum (FBS) must have complement heat-inactivated for 30 min at 56 °C.

3. We recommend filtering formulated iNKT media through a 0.45 μm CA membrane filtration unit before using for culture.

4. 0.4 ng/mL rhIL-7 (1×) is used for the first 7 days of expansion, prior to the first sort. 4 ng/mL rhIL-7 (10×) is used for the remainder of the expansion period, i.e., on day 7/8 post-sort and day 14.

5. For feeder irradiation, either a standard orthovoltage source irradiator or a ^{137}Cs (cesium-137) radioisotope source irradiator may be used.

6. Depending on donor-specific iNKT yield variations on day 7 post-sort, T-25 flasks, 6-well, 12-well, 24-well, or 48-well plates may be needed to accommodate lower iNKT yields. For example, if day 7 post-sort yield is ~8000 total iNKT cells ($<10^4$), then the number of irradiated allo-PBMCs needed is 50×8000 cells = 400,000 irradiated allo-PBMCs. Thus, the total number of cells to plate is 400,000 allo-PBMCs + 8000 day 7 iNKTs = 408,000 total cells. Plate these cells in a 48-well plate (1 well), in ~400–500 μL media.

7. Our data shows that higher iNKT day 7 yields correlate with higher iNKT yields at the end of 21 days expansion (*see* Fig. 3). Therefore, it is advised to start with at least 2×10^8 PBMCs per donor. Given the recommended PBMC culture concentration of 2×10^6 PBMCs/mL iNKT media, 10 mL/flask of PBMC-iNKT media suspension and a total of 10 T-75 flasks are required for 2×10^8 starting PBMCs.

8. Irradiate the required number of allogeneic or autologous feeder human PBMCs at 5000 cGy. Feeder cells may be either fresh or previously cryopreserved and thawed.

9. 100 U/mL rhIL-2 and 4 ng/mL rhIL-7 may be added as early as day 7, immediately after sorting, or as late as day 10.

10. It is highly recommended to analyze samples within 1 week of staining and fixing.

11. Prepare stimulation beads (loaded with antibodies or unloaded beads) as per manufacturer's instructions. Stimulate iNKT cells using a 1:2, bead:iNKT cell ratio in 1 mL of iNKT media.

12. Harvest Jurkat cell line at 80–90% confluence for use in cytoxicity assay.

13. ^{51}Cr presents an external dose hazard via its gamma emissions. Users must minimally follow the "*Safe Handling Guide: Chromium-51 Handling Precautions*" provided by the

manufacturer and are encouraged to consult their institutional radiation safety specialist to tailor safety precautions to the user's specific needs and/or applications.

14. Use the following formula to calculate % cytotoxicity from counts per minute (CPM) data collected from liquid scintillation counter:

$$\frac{\left(CPM_{experimental} - CPM_{spontaneous}\right)}{\left(CPM_{maximum} - CPM_{spontaneous}\right)} \times 100 = \%Cytotoxicity$$

Acknowledgments

We thank Patricia Guevara and Natasha Ward of the Sylvester Comprehensive Cancer Center (SCCC) Flow Cytometry Shared Resource for assistance in cell sorting. We thank Jim Houston of the Department of BMTCT and the St. Jude Shared FACS Facility for FACS sorting and instrument support, Dr. Mark Exley for early discussions on reagents, and Drs. Helen Heslop, Nelson Chao, Randy Brutkiewicz, and John Koreth for their critiques. This work was funded by grants 5P30CA021765-36 (A.B.P.), R12/94-000 (Assisi Foundation) (A.B.P., K.A.), the V Scholar Award of the V Foundation for Cancer Research (A.B.P.), the Hyundai Scholar Award (A.B.P), the American Lebanese Syrian Associated Charities (ALSAC) (A.B.P., K.A.), and the Batchelor Foundation for Pediatric Research (A.B.P., K.A.). This research was conducted in collaboration with and using the Biostatistics and Bioinformatics Shared Resource of the Sylvester Comprehensive Cancer Center, University of Miami. This study was supported by the National Institutes of Health, National Cancer Institute (NIH/NCI) Cancer Center Support Grant P30CA240139 at the Sylvester Comprehensive Cancer Center. The content is solely the responsibility of the authors and does not necessarily represent the official views of the National Institutes of Health. Natasha K. Khatwani and Kelly J. Andrews contributed equally to this work.

References

1. Lantz O, Bendelac A (1994) An invariant T cell receptor alpha chain is used by a unique subset of major histocompatibility complex class I-specific CD4+ and CD4-8- T cells in mice and humans. J Exp Med 180:1097–1106

2. Prussin C, Foster B (1997) TCR V alpha 24 and V beta 11 coexpression defines a human NK1 T cell analog containing a unique Th0 subpopulation. J Immunol 159:5862–5870

3. Bendelac A, Savage P, Teyton L (2007) The biology of NKT cells. Annu Rev Immunol 25:297–336

4. Brossay L, Chioda M, Burdin N et al (1998) CD1d-mediated recognition of an α-Galactosylceramide by natural killer T cells is highly conserved through mammalian evolution. J Exp Med 188:1521–1528

5. Kawano T, Cui J, Koezuka Y et al (1997) CD1d-restricted and TCR-mediated activation

of valpha14 NKT cells by glycosylceramides. Science 5343:1626–1629

6. Borg N, Wun K, Kjer-Nielsen L et al (2007) CD1d–lipid-antigen recognition by the semi-invariant NKT T-cell receptor. Nature 448:44–49

7. Rossjohn J, Pellicci D, Patel O et al (2012) Recognition of CD1d-restricted antigens by natural killer T cells. Nat Rev Immunol 12:845–857

8. Matsuda J, Naidenko O, Gapin L et al (2000) Tracking the response of natural killer T cells to a glycolipid antigen using CD1d tetramers. J Exp Med 192(5):741–754

9. Godfrey DI, Kronenberg M (2004) Going both ways: immune regulation via CD1d-dependent NKT cells. J Clin Invest 114 (10):1379–1388

10. Sakuishi K, Oki S, Araki M et al (2007) Invariant NKT cells biased for IL-5 production act as crucial regulators of inflammation. J Immunol 179(6):3452–3462

11. Coquet J, Kyparissoudis K, Pellicci D et al (2007) IL-21 is produced by NKT cells and modulates NKT cell activation and cytokine production. J Immunol 178(5):2827–2834

12. Pillai AB, George T, Dutt S et al (2007) Host NKT cells can prevent graft-versus-host disease and permit graft antitumor activity after bone marrow transplantation. J Immunol 178 (10):6242–6251

13. Kuns R, Morris E, MacDonald K et al (2009) Invariant natural killer T cell–natural killer cell interactions dictate transplantation outcome after α-galactosylceramide administration. Blood 113(23):5999–6010

14. Chaidos A, Patterson S, Szydlo R et al (2012) Graft invariant natural killer T-cell dose predicts risk of acute graft-versus-host disease in allogeneic hematopoietic stem cell transplantation. Blood 119(21):5030–5036

15. Fereidouni M, Derakhshani A, Exley M et al (2019) iNKT cells and hematopoietic stem cell transplantation: two-phase activation of iNKT cells may improve outcome. Clin Immunol 207:1521–6616

16. Etxeberria I, Olivera I, Bolaños E et al (2020) Engineering bionic T cells: signal 1, signal 2, signal 3, reprogramming and the removal of inhibitory mechanisms. Cell Mol Immunol 17:576–586

17. Andrews K, Hamers A, Sun X et al (2020) Expansion and CD2/CD3/CD28 stimulation enhance Th2 cytokine secretion of human invariant NKT cells with retained anti-tumor cytotoxicity. Cytotherapy 22(5):276–290. https://doi.org/10.1016/j.jcyt.2020.01.011

Chapter 14

Intravital Microscopy Imaging of Invariant Natural Killer T-Cell Dynamics in the Liver Using CXCR6-eGFP Transgenic Mice

Zhou Hong, Zeng Zhutian, and Wang Fei

Abstract

The immune response in the liver is a highly dynamic process involving the recruitment of many types of immune cells. As a powerful imaging technique, intravital microscopy has been widely used for real-time observation and quantification of cell movements in living animals. Here we describe the use of an in vivo half-dissociated preparation method combined with intravital confocal microscopy to observe the dynamic activities of invariant natural killer T cells in the liver of CXCR6$^{GFP/+}$ transgenic mice. We believe that this method will enable researchers to explore the dynamics of many other types of immune cells in the liver.

Key words Intravital microscopy, Live cell imaging, Invariant natural killer T cells, Liver, CXCR6$^{GFP/+}$ transgenic mice

1 Introduction

Natural killer T (NKT) cells are a heterogeneous group of T cells that share properties of both T cells and natural killer cells. These cells can efficiently recognize the self and foreign lipid and glycolipid antigens presented by the major histocompatibility complex class I-like molecule CD1d [1, 2]. NKT cells constitute approximately 1% of all peripheral blood T cells. These cells are involved in removing pathogens or tumor cells from the body, as well as in the development of allergic reactions and autoimmune diseases. Invariant NKT (iNKT) cells represent a major population of NKT cells expressing a unique invariant TCRα chain (Vα14Jα18 in mice or Vα24Jα18 in humans) and a limited number of variable TCRβ chains. iNKT cells are mainly distributed in the liver, thymus, adipose tissue, spleen, lymph nodes, and peripheral blood [3, 4]. iNKT cells are particularly enriched in the murine liver and form a nexus between innate and adaptive immunities; therefore,

Chaohong Liu (ed.), *Invariant Natural Killer T-Cells: Methods and Protocols*, Methods in Molecular Biology, vol. 2388, https://doi.org/10.1007/978-1-0716-1775-5_14,
© The Author(s), under exclusive license to Springer Science+Business Media, LLC, part of Springer Nature 2021

these cells play an important role in mediating immune responses under inflammatory conditions in the liver [5, 6].

Intravital microscopy (IVM) imaging has become a cutting-edge technique for tracking the behaviors of living cells in real time while providing remarkable insight into cellular dynamics and pathophysiological processes within tissues. Liver half-dissociated fixation is a process in which the mouse's liver is partially separated from the body and stabilized onto an observation board without damaging the hilar structure (Fig. 1). With this method, cellular activity of iNKT cells in the liver could be examined in real time by confocal microscopy.

In CXCR6$^{GFP/+}$ transgenic mice, one allele of the murine *CXCR6* gene is replaced with the gene encoding green fluorescent

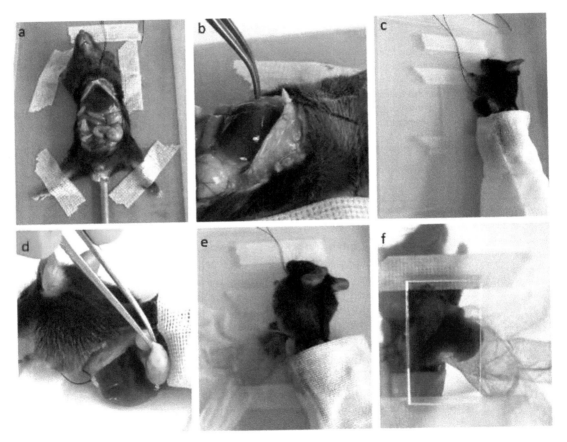

Fig. 1 (a) Expose the abdominal cavity of the experimental mouse, tie the free end of the sternum stem with surgical thread, and pull it upward and fix it; (**b**) use forceps to lift the cholecyst, and carefully dissect the falciform ligament; (**c**) transfer the mouse to the observation board, fix the traction line, remove other organs in the abdominal cavity, and wrap them with moist gauze; (**d**) lift the stomach and carefully dissect the patogastric ligament; (**e**) use multiple air-laid papers to pull the liver out of the abdominal cavity, and fix it on the transparent glass area of the observation board; (**f**) after the surgery, the size and position of the free liver can be viewed from the bottom of the observation board

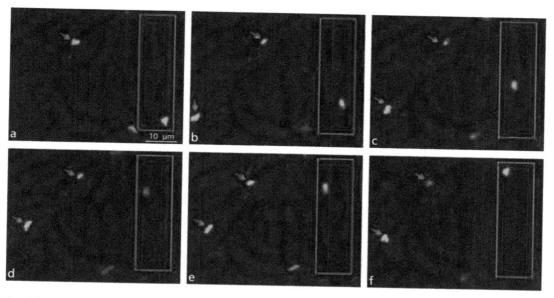

Fig. 2 Migratory trajectories of iNKT cells in murine liver using IVM. The recording time was 20 min, with an interval of 2 min for each capture (**a–f**). The fields of view show the movement track of green iNKT cells in the liver tissue of CXCR6$^{GFP/+}$ transgenic mice

protein (GFP), enabling GFP to be specifically expressed by CXCR6-expressing cells that are mainly found in the liver and spleen. These transgenic mice can be used as an ideal model to visualize the cellular behaviors of hepatic iNKT cells, as more than 70% of GFP-expressing cells in the liver are iNKT cells. Here we established a gentle preparation and stable fixation method for observing the migratory trajectories of iNKT cells in the liver of anesthetized CXCR6$^{GFP/+}$ transgenic mice using intravital microscopy (Fig. 2).

2   Materials

2.1   Mice

CXCR6$^{-/GFP}$ transgenic mice were purchased from Jackson Laboratories (Bar Harbor, ME, USA). Mice between 8 and 10 weeks of age were preferred for this procedure. All animal experimental protocols were performed in accordance with the requirements of experimental animal ethics and national animal care guidelines.

2.2   Reagents

1. 0.9% sodium chloride, normal saline.
2. 75% ethyl alcohol solution.
3. 1.25% avertin solution.

2.3 Equipment	1. Confocal microscope.
	2. Pet electric clipper.
	3. Chemical hair removal cream.
	4. Sterile cotton swabs.
	5. Microscope cover slips, 24 × 50 mm.
	6. Sterile cotton gauze, 8.5 × 5 cm.
	7. 1 mL and 20 mL syringes.
	8. Dissecting scissors (straight), length 9 cm.
	9. Dissecting scissors (curved), length 9 cm.
	10. Graefe serrated forceps (straight), length 10 cm.
	11. Graefe serrated forceps (curved), length 10 cm.
	12. Microdissecting scissors.
	13. Graefe tissue forceps.
	14. Gemini cautery system (*see* **Note 1**).
	15. Millex GS filter unit, 0.22 μm.
	16. Sterile surgical gloves.
	17. Imaging board.
	18. Medical tape.
	19. Air-laid paper.
	20. 4-0 Nonresorbable polypropylene sutures.
	21. Autoclave.
	22. Heating pad.

2.4 Reagent and Equipment Setup

1.25% avertin solution: Dissolve 2.5 g of tribromoethanol in 5 mL of *tert*-Amyl alcohol, add 200 mL of normal saline in it, mix thoroughly, and then filter-sterilize the solution through a 0.22 μm filter. This solution should be stored at 4 °C, which remains stable up to a month.

Custom-made imaging board: Position the 24 × 50 cover slip on a viewing window and fix it with a tape.

3   Methods

Disinfect the working space using 75% ethanol and all surgical instruments by autoclaving for 1.5 h. Prepare all the reagents at room temperature (20–24 °C) in the laboratory and perform filter sterilization.

3.1 Preoperative Preparation of Mouse

Timing ~20–30 min

1. Weigh the mouse and intraperitoneally inject an appropriate dose of 1.25% avertin using a 1 mL syringe (*see* **Note 2**).

2. Place the anesthetized mouse in dorsal recumbency, and fix all the four legs with medical tape on a heating pad to maintain its body temperature during the surgery (*see* **Note 3**).

3. Thoroughly shear the hair over the ventral side of the mouse using an electric clipper. Apply a layer of chemical hair removal cream over the shaved region with a cotton swab. Next, use a sterile gauze to wipe off the cream toward the head (opposing the direction of the fur) after 1–2 min (*see* **Note 4**).

4. Sterilize the shaved area with 75% ethanol, which also helps remove residual hair and the chemical hair removal cream.

3.2 Surgery for Liver IVM

Timing ~30–50 min

1. Hold the skin of the mouse's abdomen with serrated forceps, and make a 1.5 cm single midline incision through the skin using sterile scissors, extending down from the xiphoid process. Carefully incise the linea alba to separate the fascia located between the skin and underlying muscle and open the abdomen. Make a 1 cm lateral incision from the end of the midline incision to the left and right sides while carefully exposing and avoiding the large vessels in the abdominal wall. Cauterize all visible vessels on one side and remove the skin. Repeat the same procedure on the other side (*see* **Note 5**).

2. Lift the peritoneal wall with smooth forceps, make an incision longitudinally using sterile scissors, and separate the peritoneum from the both sides by cautery system, thereby exposing the proximal liver to the mid-axillary line (*see* **Note 6**).

3. Tie the xiphoid process at the end of the sternum stem with a surgical suture, pull this suture up to the top of the mouse's head, and tape it down to the heating plate. Grab the cholecyst with smooth forceps with maximum precaution. The falciform ligament can be observed between the diaphragm, cholecyst, and liver wall. Cut the ligament downward to the suprahepatic inferior vena cava to dissociate the liver from the diaphragm (*see* **Note 7**).

4. Clean the visible glass area in the center of the observation board using an air-laid paper. Thereafter, place a sterile gauze on the right side of the observation board, and drip normal saline onto the gauze to moisten the gauze on the left side.

5. Move the mouse to the observation board. Tape the xiphoid traction thread on the front of the mouse's head. The large and small intestine, spleen, and stomach should be sequentially removed from the abdominal cavity with two cotton swabs

and then were placed on the lower limbs. Lift the stomach with forceps and carefully dissect the hepatogastric ligament. Wrap all the exposed organs of the mice with a gauze (*see* **Note 8**).

6. By moving and squeezing other tissues or organs of the mouse, the liver viscera can be exposed to the field of vision facing upward, and the largest lobe of the liver is attached to the optical window made of glass. Cover the surface of the liver lobe with air-laid paper, and slowly pull the paper to move the liver lobe out of the abdominal cavity. Use additional air-laid paper to cover and move the liver as described above if necessary (*see* **Note 9**).

7. Adjust the position of the liver by pulling two pieces of air-laid paper to ensure that a large area of the liver is firmly attached to the visible glass area of the heating plate. Next, fix the position of the air-laid paper with tape (*see* **Note 10**) (Fig. 1).

3.3 IVM Observation

Timing ~40 min to several hours

Turn on the confocal microscope and apply appropriate laser and filter settings. The exposed liver lobe should be firmly attached onto the glass area of the heating plate and be visible through the microscope slot (*see* **Note 11**). The excitation light should be focused directly on the exposed area of the liver (*see* **Note 12**). Use acquisition software for tracking and recording, and set the time interval for time-lapse imaging (*see* **Note 13**) (Fig. 2).

4 Notes

1. During cauterization, do not always maintain constant heating. Heat the knife, release the switch, and quickly perform electro-coagulation of the blood vessels or cut the tissues.

2. The dosage of 1.25% avertin working solution is calculated according to the body weight of the mouse at 400 μL/20 g. During injection into the abdominal cavity, fix the mouse upside down with the head of the animal facing downward. This prevents mouse organs, particularly the liver, getting damaged by injection. After waiting for 5–10 min after anesthetization, the mouse can be lightly clamped with ophthalmic forceps to determine the anesthesia state. If the anesthesia is effective, fix the mouse's limbs with tape, and then proceed further.

3. Do not overheat the mouse and keep the heating pad at 36–37 °C, as this enhances the depth of the anesthetic and may be lethal to mice by causing respiratory failure.

4. Hair is strongly autofluorescent; therefore, it is essential to remove as much hair as possible or use mineral oil to prevent it from sticking to the abdominal cavity or liver surface and hampering imaging.

5. For blunt separation, it is best to use Graefe tissue forceps. If bleeding occurs, quickly cauterize the vessels to stop bleeding.

6. As the peritoneum layer is thin and blood vessels are abundant, the procedure starting from infliction of the wound should be performed with an electrocoagulation knife. Expose the lower edge of the chest cavity and xiphoid process on both sides of the mid-axillary line and down to the lower abdominal area.

7. Do not touch the liver during surgery. While lifting the gall-bladder, precautions should be taken to avoid puncturing of the gallbladder and bile outflow, as this can obscure the visible area under the microscope. While dissecting the falciform ligament, precautions should be taken to avoid damage to the diaphragm (including diaphragmatic veins), abdominal aorta, or inferior vena cava.

8. The gauze used to wrap the exposed organs of the mouse must first be wetted with normal saline and wrapped around the lower body of the mouse. During the experiment, ensure that the gauze is moistened with normal saline to avoid dehydration and death of the mouse.

9. Observe the diaphragm surface of mouse's liver under a confocal microscope.

10. Do not touch the liver with instruments or cotton swab throughout the procedure except while using air-laid paper.

11. Procedures involving movement and handling of the mouse should be performed with caution.

12. Because the excitation light of the inverted confocal microscope is emitted from the bottom, when the liver is placed in the best observation area, it nearly blocks the beam of excitation light.

13. After debugging under an eyepiece, the shooting mode can be selected on a computer to capture the live images of the liver. Sequentially recorded images from the same field of view can be exported as a time-lapse video.

Acknowledgments

This work was supported by the National Natural Science Foundation of China [grant numbers 81871241 and 81571614].

References

1. Bendelac A, Lantz O, Quimby ME, Yewdell JW, Bennink JR, Brutkiewicz RR (1995) CD1 recognition by mice NK1+ T lymphocytes. Science 268:863–865

2. Gapin L (2016) Development of invariant natural killer T cells. Curr Opin Immunol 39:68–74

3. Matsuda JL, Mallevaey T, Scott-Browne J et al (2008) CD1d-restricted iNKT cells, the "Swiss-Army knife" of the immune system. Curr Opin Immunol 20:358–368

4. Bendelac A, Savage PB, Teyton L (2007) The biology of NKT cells. Annu Rev Immunol 25:297–336

5. Chawla A, Nguyen KD, Goh YP (2011) Macrophage-mediated inflammation in metabolic disease. Nat Rev Immunol 11:738–749

6. Kohlgruber AC, Donado CA, LaMarche NM et al (2016) Activation strategies for invariant natural killer Tcells. Immunogenetics 68:649–663

Chapter 15

In Vivo Cytotoxicity by α-GalCer-transactivated NK Cells

Patrick T. Rudak and S. M. Mansour Haeryfar ⓘ

Abstract

Invariant natural killer T (*i*NKT) cells are innate-like, lipid-reactive T lymphocytes known for their potent immunomodulatory properties. In addition to expressing and utilizing cytolytic effector molecules of their own against certain target cells, *i*NKT cells can be stimulated with α-galactosylceramide (α-GalCer) to augment the cytotoxic capacity of natural killer (NK) cells. Herein, we describe a flow cytometry-based in vivo killing assay that enables examination of α-GalCer-promoted cytotoxicity against β2 microglobulin knockout ($\beta 2M^{-/-}$) target cells, which mimic tumor and virus-infected cells displaying little to no MHC class I molecules on their surface. Using an anti-asialo GM1 antibody, which depletes NK cells but not *i*NKT cells, we confirmed that the increased clearance of $\beta 2M^{-/-}$ cells in α-GalCer-primed recipients was mediated by NK cells. The protocol detailed here can be leveraged to assess the functional fitness of *i*NKT cells and their crosstalk with NK cells and to further our understanding of α-GalCer-promoted cytotoxicity in preclinical immunotherapeutic applications.

Key words *i*NKT cells, NK cells, α-galactosylceramide, Cell-mediated cytotoxicity, In vivo killing assays, Flow cytometry, CFSE, Anticancer immunity, Antiviral immunity, Immunotherapy

1 Introduction

Invariant natural killer T (*i*NKT) cells are innate-like T lymphocytes harboring a canonical Vα14-Jα18 gene rearrangement in their T cell receptor (TCR) α chain that is paired with a limited number of Vβ chain options [1, 2]. *i*NKT cells recognize and respond rapidly to glycolipid molecules typified by α-galactosylceramide (α-GalCer) [3]. Upon activation, *i*NKT cells release T helper (T_H)1-, T_H2-, or T_H17-type cytokines, thus shaping the nature of immune responses in various contexts [4], including in cancer immune surveillance and antimicrobial host defense.

α-GalCer-stimulated mouse *i*NKT cells are known to transactivate and augment the cytotoxic function of natural killer (NK) cells [5]. This functional axis relies largely on *i*NKT cells' ability to secrete mediators such as IFN-γ [6] and on reciprocal interactions

Chaohong Liu (ed.), *Invariant Natural Killer T-Cells: Methods and Protocols*, Methods in Molecular Biology, vol. 2388,
https://doi.org/10.1007/978-1-0716-1775-5_15,

between iNKT cells and dendritic cells (DCs), which lead to DC maturation and their upregulated expression of NK cell-activating ligands [5]. α-GalCer-transactivated NK cells are indispensable for the antimetastatic effects of α-GalCer in B16 melanoma, EL4 lymphoma, and other mouse tumor models [7, 8], as well as for the resolution of infections with hepatitis B virus and murine cytomegalovirus [9, 10].

α-GalCer-based immunotherapies have been tested in clinical trials for malignancies and viral diseases [11, 12]. Once optimized, they will offer tempting modalities that should work in genetically diverse patient populations since α-GalCer and similar glycolipid antigens are presented to iNKT cells by a non-polymorphic molecule called CD1d [13, 14]. Furthermore, iNKT cells' recognition mode is evolutionarily conserved [15]. This is to the extent that human iNKT cells bind mouse glycolipid-loaded CD1d and vice versa [16]. Therefore, experimental methods that enable examination of mouse iNKT cell activation by α-GalCer and its downstream effects should be informative for understanding iNKT cell functions and therapeutic potentials in clinical settings.

In vivo killing assays offer a sensitive and well-controlled approach to studying cell-mediated cytotoxicity within the intact architecture of lymphoid tissues [17]. Therefore, they are superior to traditional in vitro cytotoxicity assays in which the effector phase takes place in test tubes. In vivo killing assays can be employed to assess the cytolytic effector function of tumor-specific CD8+ T cells [17–19], virus-specific CD8+ T cells [20, 21], NK cells [22], iNKT cells [23], and alloantibodies [24]. We recently optimized and used a version of these assays for the measurement of α-GalCer-transactivated NK cells [25, 26]. This method was adapted from a previous report describing the clearance of β2 microglobulin knockout (β2M$^{-/-}$) target splenocytes, which simulate MHC class I$^{nil/low}$ tumor or virus-infected cells [27], in wild-type (WT) mice [22]. Syngeneic naïve WT splenocytes, which are co-injected into the recipient, serve as control and should remain viable. Labeling control and β2M$^{-/-}$ target cells with different concentrations of 5-(and-6)-carboxyfluorescein diacetate N-succinimidyl ester (CFSE) before their co-transfer, in equal numbers, into α-GalCer- or vehicle-primed recipients allows for their accurate detection by flow cytometry in multiple locations, including the spleen, liver, and lungs. Percent in vivo killing of β2M$^{-/-}$ target cells can be taken as a measure of NK cell-mediated cytotoxicity. By pre-treating the recipients with an anti-asialo GM1 antibody, which depletes NK cells but not iNKT cells [28], we have confirmed the enhancement of β2M$^{-/-}$ target cell lysis in α-GalCer-primed animals to be largely NK cell-dependent.

The method described here can be employed to assess the crosstalk established between iNKT and NK cells following in vivo treatment with α-GalCer or its analogs [11, 12]. When combined with other tools, such as gene knockout mice, neutralizing or blocking monoclonal antibodies (mAbs), and pharmacological agents, it can shed light on pathways that govern the above crosstalk and the ultimate act of killing. Moreover, this assay should help in testing the preclinical efficacy of new or modified *i*NKT cell-based treatments for cancer and viral diseases. Among information that cannot be deduced from the data are the exact number of killing cycles before the effector cells rest and recycle and a global picture of all tissue sites in which target cells are detected and destroyed.

In this chapter, we provide a step-by-step assay protocol, covering treatment procedures, tissue processing, target cell labeling and injection, data acquisition and analysis, and the formula we use to calculate percent in vivo cytotoxicity. We offer several technical points to ensure assay precision and the high quality of data to be generated.

2   Materials

2.1 General Instruments, Plasticware, and Buffers

1. Certified class II biological safety cabinet (BSC).
2. Centrifuge.
3. Vortex mixer.
4. Water bath.
5. Ice bucket.
6. Hemocytometer or an automated cell counter.
7. Flow cytometer with data acquisition software. The panels described in this chapter are compatible with a two-laser (488 nm and 633 nm), eight-color BD FACSCanto II flow cytometer equipped with BD FACSDiva software.
8. 15-mL and 50-mL conical centrifuge tubes.
9. 1.5-mL microcentrifuge tubes.
10. 5-mL polystyrene round-bottom tubes for flow cytometry.
11. 1× phosphate-buffered saline (PBS), pH 7.4.
12. Staining buffer for flow cytometry: 1× PBS supplemented with 2% heat-inactivated fetal bovine serum (FBS).

2.2 Mice

1. Target cell donors: Adult WT C57BL/6 mice and adult β2M$^{-/-}$ mice on a C57BL/6 background (*see* **Notes 1** and **2**).
2. Target cell recipients: Adult WT C57BL/6 mice (*see* **Note 3**).

2.3 Materials and Reagents for Treatment Procedures

1. 1-mL syringes with 28-gauge needles (*see* **Note 4**).
2. KRN7000/α-GalCer (Funakoshi Co., Ltd.): to be dissolved in ultrapure water containing 5.6% sucrose, 0.75% L-histidine, and 0.5% Tween-20, heated for 10 min in an 80 °C water bath, and subsequently stored in 4–8 μg aliquots at −80 °C.

3. Vehicle for KRN7000 containing 5.6% sucrose, 0.75% L-histidine, and 0.5% Tween-20 in ultrapure water to be heated for 10 min at 80 °C and then stored in small aliquots at −80 °C.

4. Rabbit anti-mouse asialo GM1 polyclonal antibody (Cedarlane), if applicable: to be reconstituted in ultrapure water following the manufacturer's instructions and stored in aliquots of desired quantity at 4 °C until use.

5. Normal rabbit serum (NRS), if applicable: to be reconstituted in ultrapure water according to the manufacturer's instructions and stored in aliquots of desired volume at −20 °C until use.

2.4 Instruments and Materials for Tissue Processing

1. Autoclaved surgical instruments: scissors and tweezers.

2. Single-edge razor blades.

3. 15-mL Wheaton Dounce glass homogenizer.

4. 37 °C humidified incubator containing 6% CO_2.

5. MACSMix tube rotator (Miltenyi Biotec).

6. 100 mm × 15 mm polystyrene Petri dishes.

7. 10-mL syringe plungers.

8. 70-μm nylon mesh cell strainers compatible with 50-mL conical centrifuge tubes.

9. Parafilm.

10. 70% ethanol in a spray bottle.

11. Type IV collagenase from *Clostridium histolyticum* (MilliporeSigma).

12. Percoll PLUS density gradient media (GE Healthcare).

13. RPMI 1640 medium.

14. 10× Dulbecco's PBS.

15. Filter-sterilized water suitable for cell culture.

16. ACK (ammonium-chloride-potassium) lysis buffer containing 150 mM ammonium chloride, 10 mM potassium bicarbonate, and 0.1 mM ethylenediaminetetraacetic acid (EDTA) in ultrapure water.

2.5 Labeling and Injection of Target Cells

1. 1-mL syringes with 29-gauge needles (*see* **Note 4**).

2. CFSE reconstituted to a concentration of 5 mM in dimethyl sulfoxide, aliquoted and stored at −80 °C until use.

3. Heat-inactivated FBS.

2.6 Immunophenotyping (If Applicable)

1. Fc γ receptor blocking reagent: unconjugated rat anti-mouse CD16/CD32 mAb (clone 2.4G2).

2. Fluorescent dyes, fluorochrome-conjugated CD1d tetramers, and fluorochrome-conjugated mAbs (Table 1).

Table 1
Reagents and cytofluorimetric settings used to confirm the efficacy of anti-asialo GM1 Ab treatment in C57BL/6 mice

Marker	Reagent or mAb clone	Fluorochrome[a]	Excitation laser (nm)	Emission filter (nm)	Source
Live/dead	Fixable viability dye	eFluor 780	633[b]	780/60	Thermo Fisher Scientific
iNKT cell TCR	PBS-57-loaded CD1d tetramer	APC	633[b]	660/20	NIH Tetramer Core Facility
iNKT cell TCR (negative control)	Unloaded CD1d tetramer	APC	633[b]	660/20	NIH Tetramer Core Facility
TCR-β	H57-597	FITC	488[c]	530/30	Thermo Fisher Scientific
NK1.1	PK136	PE-Cy7	488[c]	780/60	Thermo Fisher Scientific

[a]If necessary or desired, alternative fluorochromes for each reagent are available from the sources listed (or other sources)
[b]Red laser
[c]Blue laser

3   Methods

3.1   General Considerations

1. Prior to commencing mouse experiments, ensure that the procedures have been approved by your institutional animal ethics committee (*see* **Note 5**).

2. During donor tissue processing, use sterile instruments and materials and perform all procedures inside a certified class II BSC.

3. During tissue processing, keep tissues/cell suspensions on ice whenever possible, use ice-cold buffers, and perform all centrifugation steps at 4 °C unless otherwise indicated.

3.2   Treatment of Recipient Mice

1. Thaw α-GalCer (2 μg for each mouse to be injected) and the corresponding vehicle at room temperature (*see* **Note 6**).

2. Dilute α-GalCer or vehicle with PBS to a final volume of 200 μL per injection. Prepare each mixture in 1.5-mL microcentrifuge tubes. Keep tubes on ice until injection.

3. Draw up each dose of α-GalCer or vehicle into a syringe with a 28-gauge needle. Avoid drawing air into the syringe as much as possible.

4. With the needle pointing upward, gently flick the top of the syringe and depress the plunger slightly to allow any air bubbles to escape.

5. Inject WT mice intraperitoneally (i.p.) with α-GalCer or vehicle (see **Notes 7** and **8**).

6. Return all mice to home cages for 24 h.

3.3 Isolation of Splenocytes from Donor Mice

1. Euthanize the required number of naïve WT and $\beta 2M^{-/-}$ donor mice (see Subheading 3.3, **step 15**, and Subheading 3.4, **steps 26–27**) following your approved animal use protocol.

2. Spray the abdominal area of each carcass liberally with 70% ethanol.

3. For each carcass, use tweezers to pull a portion of skin around the center of the abdomen upward, and use scissors to make a small incision in the area. Avoid deep cuts not to puncture or pierce the peritoneum.

4. Pull gently on either end of the incision to peel the skin away from the abdominal region and fully expose the peritoneum.

5. Cut the peritoneum with scissors to access the peritoneal cavity.

6. Locate the spleen toward the left side of the mouse. Gently pull the spleen upward with tweezers while removing as much surrounding connective tissue and fat as possible with scissors.

7. Place WT and $\beta 2M^{-/-}$ spleens into separate 50-mL conical centrifuge tubes containing 10 mL PBS. Transfer the content into a 15-mL glass homogenizer.

8. Grind the spleen several times until it is disrupted into a single-cell suspension (see **Note 9**). Transfer the homogenate into separate 50-mL conical tubes. Fill the remainder of each tube with PBS.

9. Centrifuge tubes at $400 \times g$ for 5 min.

10. Discard the supernatant and wash cells once more in PBS.

11. Remove erythrocytes by resuspending cells in 4 mL of ACK lysis buffer for 3 min at room temperature. Immediately afterward, dilute the ACK lysis buffer with 10 mL of PBS.

12. If multiple WT and $\beta 2M^{-/-}$ mice are needed to obtain adequate cell yields, pool cell suspensions together in separate tubes designated for WT and $\beta 2M^{-/-}$ target splenocytes.

13. Filter each cell suspension through a 70-μm cell strainer into a new 50-mL conical tube.

14. Centrifuge tubes at $400 \times g$ for 5 min, discard the supernatant, and resuspend cells in 5 mL of PBS.

15. Using a hemocytometer or an automated cell counter, count splenocytes and confirm their viability (of at least 95%) by

trypan blue dye exclusion. Be as accurate as possible. We typically obtain $5–10 \times 10^7$ cells/spleen with $\geq$99% viability depending on the donor's age.

16. Isolated splenocytes from WT and $\beta 2M^{-/-}$ mice are to be used as control target cells and NK target cells, respectively (*see* **Note 10**).

3.4 Labeling and Injection of Target Cells

1. Transfer all the splenocytes from the preparation containing the lower number of cells (either WT or $\beta 2M^{-/-}$ cell preparation) into a 15-mL conical centrifuge tube. Transfer an equal number of cells from the other preparation to a separate 15-mL conical tube (*see* **Note 11**). Be as precise as possible while pipetting.

2. Fill the remainder of both tubes with PBS.

3. Spin the tubes at $400 \times g$ for 5 min.

4. During the centrifugation step above, prepare 7 mL of a 2 μM solution of CFSE in PBS. Upon adding the stock solution of CFSE to PBS, vortex thoroughly. Next, in a separate tube, add 1 mL of the above solution (2 μM CFSE) to 9 mL of PBS to prepare a 0.2 μM solution of CFSE. Vortex thoroughly.

5. Discard most of the supernatant from each tube containing splenocyte suspensions, leaving behind approximately 50–100 μL of PBS on top of the pelleted cells (*see* **Note 12**). Be as consistent as possible with the amount of PBS left in each tube. Make sure both tubes contain visually similar PBS levels.

6. Resuspend cells thoroughly in the remaining PBS in each tube by gently pipetting up and down several times. Ensure that the resulting suspension is completely homogenous.

7. Add 5 mL of 0.2-μM and 2-μM CFSE solutions to WT and $\beta 2M^{-/-}$ splenocyte suspensions, respectively, while shaking the tubes by hand at a moderate pace (*see* **Note 13**).

8. Incubate samples in a 37 °C water bath for 15 min. At 5-min intervals, mix tubes gently by hand to ensure that the cells remain in suspension.

9. Immediately afterward, add 3 mL of FBS to each tube. Mix well by inversion and/or gentle shaking by hand.

10. Fill the remainder of each tube with PBS.

11. Centrifuge tubes at $400 \times g$ for 5 min.

12. Discard the supernatant and wash cells once more in PBS.

13. Resuspend cells thoroughly in 3 mL of PBS.

14. Into a single 5-mL polystyrene tube containing 500 μL of PBS, carefully pipet 10 μL, each, of WT and $\beta 2M^{-/-}$ splenocyte suspensions (*see* **Note 14**).

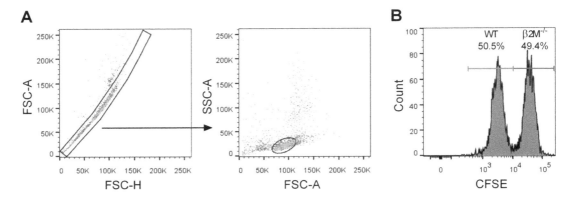

Fig. 1 Confirming equal numbers of WT and $\beta 2M^{-/-}$ splenocytes present in cell mixtures. (**a**) Gating strategy used to define singlets (left panel) followed by lymphocytes (right panel) during cytofluorometric analyses. (**b**) After applying the pre-gate described in (**a**), the frequencies of CFSE^{low} and CFSE^{high} cells after being mixed at a 1:1 ratio are determined as shown in the representative histogram

15. With the CFSE channel open (488 nm excitation laser, 530/30 nm emission filter), acquire 5,000–10,000 events from the preliminary cell mixture using a flow cytometer.

16. After excluding doublets based on FSC-A and FSC-H properties, gate on lymphocytes using FSC-A and SSC-A characteristics (Fig. 1a).

17. Using histograms, draw CFSE^{low} and CFSE^{high} gates corresponding to WT and $\beta 2M^{-/-}$ target cells, respectively.

18. Calculating the frequencies of CFSE^{low} and CFSE^{high} events will allow for subtle volume adjustments to cell suspensions to be made, if necessary, before they will be mixed again for injection into the recipients. The final cell mixture should contain equal or near-equal numbers of CFSE^{low} and CFSE^{high} cells (*see* **Note 15**).

19. Into a new 5-mL polystyrene tube containing 500 μL of PBS, carefully add adjusted volumes of WT and $\beta 2M^{-/-}$ splenocyte suspensions, no more than 10 μL each, based on the above frequency ratio calculation.

20. Confirm by flow cytometry that the new cell mixture contains the desired CFSE^{low} and CFSE^{high} cell frequencies (50 ± 2% of total CFSE$^+$ cells for each population).

21. Once the required volume of each cell suspension to prepare a target cell mixture with a ~1:1 ratio of WT to $\beta 2M^{-/-}$ splenocytes is known, transfer the highest possible volume of each splenocyte preparation into a single 15-mL conical tube.

22. Pipet 10 μL of the above cell mixture into a 5-mL polystyrene tube containing 500 μL of PBS.

23. Set the CFSE^{low} population as the "stopping gate" and record 2,000 events by flow cytometry (Fig. 1b).

24. Fill the remainder of the 15-mL conical tube containing the cell mixture with PBS.

25. Centrifuge the tube at 400 × *g* for 5 min, discard the supernatant, and resuspend cells in 1 mL of PBS.

26. Count the number of cells in the mixture and assess their viability by trypan blue dye exclusion. Use PBS to adjust the mixture to a concentration of 4–6 × 10^7 cells/mL (*see* **Note 16**).

27. Inject each recipient mouse that had received either α-GalCer or vehicle 24 h earlier (*see* Subheading 3.2) with 200 μL of the above target cell mixture intravenously (i.v.).

3.5 Processing of Recipient Mouse Tissues

1. Euthanize recipient mice 2 h after being injected with donor cell suspensions (*see* **Note 17**).

2. For each recipient, access the peritoneal cavity according to Subheading 3.3, **steps 2–5**.

3. Excise the liver by gently pulling the organ upward with tweezers while using scissors to detach it from the diaphragm, intestines, and other surrounding tissues (*see* **Note 18**). Ensure that all hepatic lobes are collected. Non-parenchymal liver mononuclear cell (MNC) isolation is described in Subheading 3.5.1.

4. Remove the spleen and prepare a splenocyte suspension as described for donor mice in Subheading 3.3, **steps 6–14**. During the final step, resuspend splenocytes in staining buffer.

5. Cut into the thoracic cavity with scissors to locate the lungs. Harvest the lungs by grasping them firmly with tweezers while cutting away the trachea and connective tissue with scissors. Once outside the carcass, separate the lungs from unwanted surrounding organs including the heart and the thymus. Lung MNC isolation is described in Subheading 3.5.2.

3.5.1 Liver MNC Isolation

1. Place each liver in a Petri dish containing PBS and shake it with tweezers to wash away any excess blood.

2. Transfer each liver to a new Petri dish containing PBS. Use a razor blade to chop each liver into fine pieces.

3. Pour each sample in PBS into a 15-mL glass homogenizer. Grind the pieces several times until they are disrupted into a single-cell suspension (*see* **Note 19**).

4. Transfer each homogenate into a separate 50-mL conical tube. Fill the remainder of each tube with PBS.

5. Centrifuge tubes at 400 × *g* for 5 min.

6. Discard the supernatant before washing cells once more with PBS.

7. During the centrifugation step above, prepare 12.5 mL of 33.75% Percoll in PBS per liver by mixing 14.06 mL of filter-sterilized water, 2.5 mL of 10X PBS, and 8.44 mL of Percoll PLUS. Use reagents stored at room temperature for mixing.

8. Resuspend cells in 12.5 mL of 33.75% Percoll solution.

9. With the brake off, centrifuge tubes at 700 × g for 12 min at room temperature.

10. Carefully siphon off the top layer containing the hepatic parenchymal cell fraction before aspirating the remainder of the supernatant.

11. Resuspend cells in 3 mL of ACK lysis buffer for 3 min at room temperature. Immediately afterward, dilute the ACK lysis buffer with 10 mL of PBS.

12. Filter each cell suspension through a 70-μm cell strainer and into a new 50-mL conical tube.

13. Centrifuge tubes at 400 × g for 5 min, discard the supernatant, and resuspend cells in 1 mL of staining buffer.

3.5.2   Lung MNC Isolation

1. Place each set of lungs into a 1.5-mL microcentrifuge tube containing 750 mL of PBS.

2. Within each tube, cut the lungs into fine pieces with small scissors. Between lungs, clean the scissors extensively with 70% ethanol.

3. Transfer each lung sample into a separate 15-mL conical tube containing 4 mL of RPMI medium supplemented with 0.5 mg/mL collagenase IV.

4. Wrap parafilm around the cap of each tube to prevent leakage and incubate samples at 37 °C in a MACSMix tube rotator (or a similar instrument) for 1 h.

5. Filter each lung sample through a 70-μm cell strainer and into a 50-mL conical tube.

6. With the cell strainer still attached to the 50-mL conical tube, gently break apart the unfiltered lung tissue into finer fragments using the rubber end of a 10-mL syringe plunger.

7. Wash the cell strainer extensively with PBS to let the remaining cells into the tube underneath.

8. Centrifuge tubes at 400 × g for 5 min.

9. Discard the supernatant and wash cells once more with PBS.

10. Resuspend cells in 3 mL of ACK lysis buffer for 3 min at room temperature. Immediately afterward, dilute the ACK lysis buffer with 10 mL of PBS.

11. Centrifuge tubes at 400 × g for 5 min, discard the supernatant, and resuspend cells in 3 mL of staining buffer.

3.6 Data Acquisition and Analysis

1. Transfer 500 μL of recipient liver MNC, lung MNC, and splenocyte suspensions to separate 5-mL polystyrene tubes for cytofluorometric analysis (*see* **Note 20**). Keep cells at 4 °C or on ice until their cytofluorometric interrogation.

2. Define the gates for singlets, lymphocytes, CFSE^{low} donor cells, and CFSE^{high} donor cells as described in Subheading 3.4, **steps 15–17** (*see* **Note 21**).

3. With the CFSE^{low} population set as the stopping gate, record 2,000 events from each sample.

4. Export all of the recorded data from the experiment as Flow Cytometry Standard (FCS) files.

5. Import all of the FCS files into FlowJo (BD Biosciences) or similar software for data analysis.

6. After applying the same gating strategy utilized during data acquisition, use histograms for CFSE to visualize the differences in the frequencies of remaining CFSE^{high} ($\beta2M^{-/-}$) cells between recipients (*see* **Note 22**). A maximum *y*-axis value, which entails a count of typically between 80 and 120, will need to be applied manually to adequately visualize CFSE$^+$ populations (Fig. 2a).

7. Export the number of events recorded for CFSE^{low} and CFSE^{high} populations from every recipient and the initial donor cell mixture to a spreadsheet software such as Microsoft Excel.

8. For each recipient, calculate cytotoxicity against target cells using the following formula: percent specific killing = {1 − [(# of CFSE^{high} events in recipient ÷ # of CFSE^{low} events in recipient) ÷ (# of CFSE^{high} events pre-injection ÷ # of CFSE^{low} events pre-injection)]} × 100. The events recorded during Subheading 3.4, **step 23** serve as "pre-injection" data.

9. Plot the summary data for each group using GraphPad Prism (La Jolla, CA) or a similar graphing software (Fig. 2b).

3.7 Verifying the Contribution of NK Cells to Enhanced $\beta2M^{-/-}$ Target Cell Clearance in α-GalCer-Treated Recipients

1. Dilute the recommended, lot-specific dose of NK cell-depleting anti-asialo GM1 polyclonal antibody in PBS to a total volume of 200 μL. Dilute an equivalent volume of NRS with PBS.

2. Draw up each solution into a syringe with a 28-gauge needle.

3. Inject WT mice with diluted anti-asialo GM1 antibody or NRS i.p.

4. Three days later, sacrifice mice for their splenocytes (*see* Subheading 3.3, **steps 6–14**), liver MNCs (*see* Subheading 3.5.1), and lung MNCs (*see* Subheading 3.5.2).

5. Seed 1–10 × 10^5 cells from each sample into a separate 5-mL polystyrene tube. Include one additional tube per sample for negative control staining of *i*NKT cells.

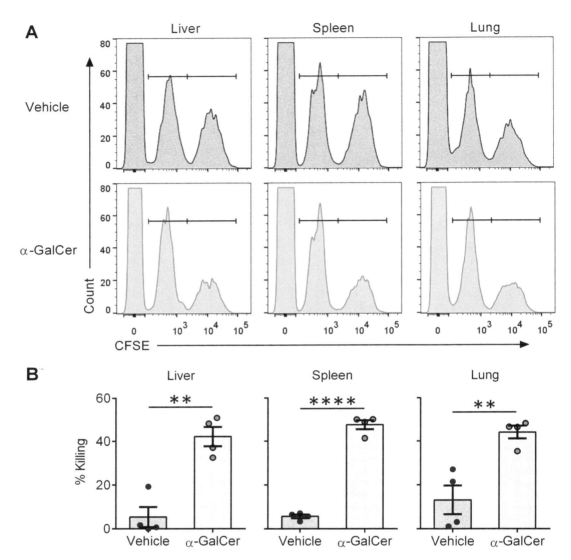

Fig. 2 α-GalCer treatment augments cytotoxicity against β2M$^{-/-}$ target cells. WT C57BL/6 mice received 2 μg α-GalCer or vehicle 24 h before they were injected with equal numbers of CFSE^{low} WT and CFSE^{high} β2M$^{-/-}$ splenocytes. Representative histograms (**a**) and summary data (**b**) illustrate the magnitude of cytotoxicity toward β2M$^{-/-}$ cells in indicated tissues after 2 h. ** and **** denote statistically significant differences with $p < 0.01$ and $p < 0.0001$, respectively, using unpaired Student's t-tests

6. Stain cells with Fixable Viability Dye (Thermo Fisher Scientific) and wash according to the supplier's instructions.

7. Resuspend cells at a concentration of 1–10 × 10^6 cells/mL in cold staining buffer.

8. Prepare 5 μg/mL of an Fcγ receptor blocking reagent. Add 20 μL directly to each cell suspension. Incubate cells on ice for 10 min.

9. Stain cells with the fluorochrome-conjugated tetramers/antibodies listed in Table 1 (except for unloaded CD1d tetramer), each at a 1:200 dilution, for 30 min at 4 °C. In separate tubes, include negative control staining for *i*NKT cells using cells stained with unloaded CD1d tetramer instead of PBS-57-loaded CD1d tetramer.

10. Wash cells with 3 mL of cold staining buffer.

11. Centrifuge tubes at $400 \times g$ for 5 min at 4 °C.

12. Wash cells twice more with 3 mL of cold staining buffer.

13. Resuspend cells in 100–200 µL of cold staining buffer. Keep cells at 4 °C or on ice until their cytofluorimetric interrogation.

14. To account for spectral overlap between fluorochromes, calculate and apply a compensation matrix on the cytometer using cells stained with each of the reagents listed in Table 1 alone (except for unloaded CD1d tetramer).

15. Record $1–5 \times 10^5$ total events from each sample on the cytometer.

16. Export the data as raw FCS files into FlowJo (or similar software). For each tissue in each mouse, analyze the frequencies of NK cells and *i*NKT cells among lymphocytes after excluding nonviable cells and doublets (Fig. 3a, b).

17. Once NK cell depletion has been confirmed, use the effective dose of anti-asialo GM1 antibody and an equal volume of NRS as per Subheading 3.7, **step 1**.

18. Inject separate cohorts of WT mice i.p. with anti-asialo GM1 antibody or NRS.

19. Two days later, inject mice with α-GalCer or vehicle i.p. (*see* Subheading 3.2).

20. After 24 h, perform in vivo killing assays and analyze their results as described in Subheadings 3.3–3.6 (Fig. 3c, d).

4 Notes

1. The $\beta 2M^{-/-}$ mice used to generate data for this chapter were provided by Dr. Anthony Jevnikar (Western University, London, ON) and bred in-house. They are commercially available for purchase, for example, from the Jackson Laboratory (catalog #002087).

2. WT and $\beta 2M^{-/-}$ mice on other genetic backgrounds (e.g., on a BALB/c background) can be used as applicable.

3. Donor and recipient mice should be sex-matched and closely age-matched.

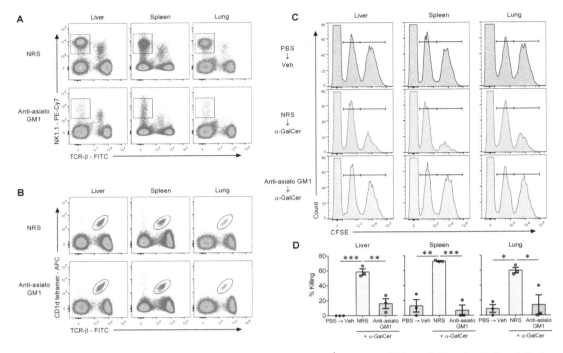

Fig. 3 NK cells are required for the enhanced clearance of β2M$^{-/-}$ target cells in α-GalCer-treated recipients. (**a** and **b**) WT C57BL/6 mice were injected with 50 μL of anti-asialo GM1 antibody or an equivalent volume of normal rabbit serum (NRS). Three days later, the presence or absence of NK1.1$^+$TCR-β$^-$ NK cells (**a**) and PBS-57-loaded CD1d tetramer$^+$TCR-β$^+$ *i*NKT cells (**b**) in indicated tissues was assessed. Data from representative samples (two mice per group) are illustrated. (**c**, **d**) Separate cohorts of mice were injected with anti-asialo GM1 antibody or NRS 2 days before they were given 2 μg α-GalCer. A control cohort received PBS followed by vehicle (for α-GalCer) instead. Twenty-four hours later, mice received equal numbers of CFSE^{low} WT (control) and CFSE^{high} β2M$^{-/-}$ splenocytes. Percent specific killing of CFSE^{high} β2M$^{-/-}$ cells in recipient mice was calculated using a formula described in the text under Data Acquisition and Analysis. Representative histograms (**c**) and summarized data (**d**) are depicted. *, **, and *** denote differences with $p < 0.05$, $p < 0.01$, and $p < 0.001$, respectively, using one-way ANOVA

4. We routinely use insulin syringes for i.v. and i.p. injections. This minimizes the amount of leftover suspensions or reagents after the plunger is depressed.

5. The data presented in this chapter were collected in compliance with Animal Use Protocol #2018-093 approved by the Animal Care Committee of Animal Care and Veterinary Services at Western University.

6. Out of an abundance of caution and to dissolve precipitates possibly forming during the freezing process, heat each thawed aliquot of α-GalCer in an 80 °C water bath for 10 min before preparing the solution to be injected.

7. Ideally, group comparisons should be made between cagemates.

8. Other glycolipid agonists of *i*NKT cells, such as a T_H1-polarizing α-GalCer analog called α-C-GalCer [29, 30], can be tested for NK cell transactivation using in vivo killing assays.

9. The presence of some connective tissue during homogenization may be inevitable. However, removing non-lymphoid tissue pieces as much and as early as possible will reduce clumping in subsequent steps and will ultimately improve cell yield.

10. Splenocytes are often chosen as ideal target cells due to their abundance in adult mice and the relative simplicity of their isolation. As potential alternatives, numerous other types of hematopoietic cells can be found in the lungs, thymus, and bone marrow of donor mice. Of note, the activation and maturation states of target cells may impact the rate of killing in recipients [22].

11. As an example, if the total number of WT splenocytes recovered is 5×10^7 and the total number of $\beta2M^{-/-}$ splenocytes recovered is $>5 \times 10^7$, use only 5×10^7 cells from each sample.

12. For smaller pellet sizes (i.e., splenocytes obtained from one donor), leave ~50 μL behind. For larger pellets (i.e., splenocytes obtained from more than one donor) leave closer to ~100 μL behind.

13. While adding CFSE, concurrent shaking of splenocyte suspensions will prevent cells from clumping and/or settling. Failure to do so may result in cell populations that will generate a wider distribution of $CFSE^+$ events in flow cytometry, which could hinder the interpretation of assay results.

14. After drawing each sample into a pipette tip, clean the external surface of the tip before transferring the content in order to minimize pipetting errors.

15. As an example, if $CFSE^{low}$ and $CFSE^{high}$ events represent 55% and 45% of splenocytes, dividing 45 by 55 computes a WT-to-β $2M^{-/-}$ cell sample ratio of 0.818:1. Therefore, mix 8.18 μL of the WT cell suspension with 10 μL of the $\beta2M^{-/-}$ suspension.

16. This concentration range accounts for $8–12 \times 10^6$ cells being injected per mouse. If cell yield is limited, injecting a lower number of cells is possible but not ideal. Doing so will necessitate the acquisition of more total events from recipient mice (*see* Subheading 3.6), which may lead to overwhelming background interference when attempting to visualize distinct $CFSE^+$ populations.

17. Longer assay times may be required to observe greater cytotoxicity.

18. To maintain optimal hepatic MNC viability, we recommend removing the gall bladder with scissors before harvesting the liver.

19. If a glass homogenizer is used to grind the liver, a "loose" pestle is recommended.

20. Whether NK cell-mediated cytotoxicity can be observed in other vascularized tissues that could conceivably be accessed by donor cells (e.g., lymph nodes, gut associated lymphoid tissue) remains to be validated in our laboratory.

21. A large CFSE⁻ population corresponding to recipient splenocytes should be easily distinguishable from injected donor cells during data acquisition.

22. Minor gating adjustments may be required between samples obtained from different tissue locations. However, always apply identical gates to samples obtained from the same tissue, which will be compared directly.

Acknowledgments

Our ongoing studies on invariant T cells are supported through operating grants provided to SMMH by the Canadian Institutes of Health Research (PJT-156295), the Natural Sciences and Engineering Research Council of Canada (NSERC) (04706-2019 RGPIN), and the Canadian Cancer Society (706396). PTR was an NSERC Alexander Graham Bell Canada Graduate Scholar (CGS—Doctoral).

References

1. Lantz O, Bendelac A (1994) An invariant T cell receptor alpha chain is used by a unique subset of major histocompatibility complex class I-specific CD4+ and CD4-8- T cells in mice and humans. J Exp Med 180(3):1097–1106. https://doi.org/10.1084/jem.180.3.1097

2. Bendelac A, Lantz O, Quimby ME et al (1995) CD1 recognition by mouse NK1+ T lymphocytes. Science 268(5212):863–865. https://doi.org/10.1126/science.7538697

3. Kawano T, Cui J, Koezuka Y et al (1997) CD1d-restricted and TCR-mediated activation of valpha14 NKT cells by glycosylceramides. Science 278(5343):1626–1629. https://doi.org/10.1126/science.278.5343.1626

4. Matsuda JL, Mallevaey T, Scott-Browne J et al (2008) CD1d-restricted iNKT cells, the "Swiss-Army knife" of the immune system. Curr Opin Immunol 20(3):358–368. https://doi.org/10.1016/j.coi.2008.03.018

5. Arora P, Baena A, Yu KO et al (2014) A single subset of dendritic cells controls the cytokine bias of natural killer T cell responses to diverse glycolipid antigens. Immunity 40(1):105–116. https://doi.org/10.1016/j.immuni.2013.12.004

6. Carnaud C, Lee D, Donnars O et al (1999) Cutting edge: cross-talk between cells of the innate immune system: NKT cells rapidly activate NK cells. J Immunol 163(9):4647–4650

7. Hayakawa Y, Takeda K, Yagita H et al (2001) Critical contribution of IFN-gamma and NK cells, but not perforin-mediated cytotoxicity, to anti-metastatic effect of alpha-galactosylceramide. Eur J Immunol 31(6):1720–1727

8. Smyth MJ, Crowe NY, Pellicci DG et al (2002) Sequential production of interferon-gamma by NK1.1(+) T cells and natural killer cells is essential for the antimetastatic effect of alpha-galactosylceramide. Blood 99(4):1259–1266. https://doi.org/10.1182/blood.v99.4.1259

9. Kakimi K, Guidotti LG, Koezuka Y et al (2000) Natural killer T cell activation inhibits hepatitis

B virus replication in vivo. J Exp Med 192 (7):921–930. https://doi.org/10.1084/jem. 192.7.921

10. van Dommelen SL, Tabarias HA, Smyth MJ et al (2003) Activation of natural killer (NK) T cells during murine cytomegalovirus infection enhances the antiviral response mediated by NK cells. J Virol 77 (3):1877–1884. https://doi.org/10.1128/ jvi.77.3.1877-1884.2003

11. van den Heuvel MJ, Garg N, Van Kaer L et al (2011) NKT cell costimulation: experimental progress and therapeutic promise. Trends Mol Med 17(2):65–77. https://doi.org/10.1016/ j.molmed.2010.10.007

12. Fujii SI, Shimizu K (2019) Immune networks and therapeutic targeting of iNKT cells in cancer. Trends Immunol 40(11):984–997. https://doi.org/10.1016/j.it.2019.09.008

13. Haeryfar SM, Mallevaey T (2015) Editorial: CD1- and MR1-restricted T cells in antimicrobial immunity. Front Immunol 6:611. https:// doi.org/10.3389/fimmu.2015.00611

14. Dascher CC (2007) Evolutionary biology of CD1. Curr Top Microbiol Immunol 314:3–26. https://doi.org/10.1007/978-3-540-69511-0_1

15. Kjer-Nielsen L, Borg NA, Pellicci DG et al (2006) A structural basis for selection and cross-species reactivity of the semi-invariant NKT cell receptor in CD1d/glycolipid recognition. J Exp Med 203(3):661–673. https:// doi.org/10.1084/jem.20051777

16. Brossay L, Chioda M, Burdin N et al (1998) CD1d-mediated recognition of an alpha-galactosylceramide by natural killer T cells is highly conserved through mammalian evolution. J Exp Med 188(8):1521–1528. https:// doi.org/10.1084/jem.188.8.1521

17. Choi J, Meilleur CE, Haeryfar SMM (2019) Tailoring in vivo cytotoxicity assays to study Immunodominance in tumor-specific CD8+ T cell responses. J Vis Exp 147. https://doi. org/10.3791/59531

18. Haeryfar SM, DiPaolo RJ, Tscharke DC et al (2005) Regulatory T cells suppress CD8+ T cell responses induced by direct priming and cross-priming and moderate immunodominance disparities. J Immunol 174 (6):3344–3351. https://doi.org/10.4049/ jimmunol.174.6.3344

19. Memarnejadian A, Meilleur CE, Shaler CR et al (2017) PD-1 blockade promotes epitope spreading in anticancer CD8(+) T cell responses by preventing fratricidal death of subdominant clones to relieve Immunodomination. J Immunol 199(9):3348–3359. https://doi.org/10.4049/jimmunol. 1700643

20. Meilleur CE, Wardell CM, Mele TS et al (2019) Bacterial Superantigens expand and activate, rather than delete or incapacitate, pre-existing antigen-specific memory CD8+ T cells. J Infect Dis 219(8):1307–1317. https://doi. org/10.1093/infdis/jiy647

21. Meilleur CE, Memarnejadian A, Shivji AN et al (2020) Discordant rearrangement of primary and anamnestic CD8+ T cell responses to influenza a viral epitopes upon exposure to bacterial superantigens: implications for prophylactic vaccination, heterosubtypic immunity and superinfections. PLoS Pathog 16(5): e1008393. https://doi.org/10.1371/journal. ppat.1008393

22. Oberg L, Johansson S, Michaëlsson J et al (2004) Loss or mismatch of MHC class I is sufficient to trigger NK cell-mediated rejection of resting lymphocytes in vivo - role of KARAP/DAP12-dependent and -independent pathways. Eur J Immunol 34(6):1646–1653. https://doi.org/10.1002/eji.200424913

23. Wingender G, Krebs P, Beutler B et al (2010) Antigen-specific cytotoxicity by invariant NKT cells in vivo is CD95/CD178-dependent and is correlated with antigenic potency. J Immunol 185(5):2721–2729. https://doi.org/10. 4049/jimmunol.1001018

24. Memarnejadian A, Meilleur CE, Mazzuca DM et al (2016) Quantification of alloantibody-mediated cytotoxicity in vivo. Transplantation 100(5):1041–1051. https://doi.org/10. 1097/tp.0000000000001154

25. Choi J, Rudak PT, Lesage S et al (2019) Glycolipid stimulation of invariant NKT cells expands a unique tissue-resident population of precursors to mature NK cells endowed with oncolytic and Antimetastatic properties. J Immunol 203(7):1808–1819. https://doi. org/10.4049/jimmunol.1900487

26. Rudak PT, Choi J, Parkins KM et al (2021) Chronic stress physically spares but functionally impairs innate-like invariant T cells. Cell Rep 35(2):108979. https://doi.org/10.1016/j.cel rep.2021.108979

27. Vivier E, Tomasello E, Baratin M et al (2008) Functions of natural killer cells. Nat Immunol 9(5):503–510. https://doi.org/10.1038/ ni1582

28. Nakagawa R, Nagafune I, Tazunoki Y et al (2001) Mechanisms of the antimetastatic effect in the liver and of the hepatocyte injury induced by alpha-galactosylceramide in mice. J Immunol 166(11):6578–6584. https://doi.org/10.4049/jimmunol.166.11.6578

29. Schmieg J, Yang G, Franck RW et al (2003) Superior protection against malaria and melanoma metastases by a C-glycoside analogue of the natural killer T cell ligand alpha-Galactosylceramide. J Exp Med 198 (11):1631–1641. https://doi.org/10.1084/jem.20031192

30. Fujii S, Shimizu K, Hemmi H et al (2006) Glycolipid alpha-C-galactosylceramide is a distinct inducer of dendritic cell function during innate and adaptive immune responses of mice. Proc Natl Acad Sci U S A 103 (30):11252–11257. https://doi.org/10.1073/pnas.0604812103

Chapter 16

Redirecting iNKT Cell Antitumor Immunity with α-GalCer/CD1d-scFv Fusion Proteins

Lianjun Zhang and Alena Donda

Abstract

Invariant natural killer T (iNKT) cells display important properties that could bridge the innate and adaptive immunity, and they have been shown to play key roles in cancer immunotherapy. However, administration of iNKT cell agonist αGalCer fails to induce sustained antitumor immunity due to the rapid anergy induction after an initial strong activation. To this end, we have designed a recombinant CD1d protein that is fused to an anti-TAA scFv, which is able to recruit iNKT cells to the tumor site and induce tumor regression. Importantly, recombinant CD1d fusion proteins loaded with α-GalCer demonstrated sustained activation of iNKT cells upon repeated injections and superior tumor control, as compared to α-GalCer treatment.

Key words iNKT cell, CD1d-antitumor scFv, α-Galactosylceramide (αGalCer), Tumor-associated antigen, Anergy

1 Introduction

Invariant natural killer T (iNKT) cells represent a unique lineage of innate T cells which recognize glycolipid antigens presented on MHC like molecule CD1d [1, 2]. Interestingly, iNKT cells usually express certain NK-specific receptors and demonstrate strong cytotoxicity [1]. Importantly, iNKT cells have been well shown to promote antitumor immunity, at least in part via crosstalk with dendritic cells and transactivation of NK cells, or even killing of tumor-associated macrophages in the tumor microenvironment [3–5]. Recently, iNKT cells are used to carry chimeric antigen receptor (CAR) against ganglioside GD2 for immunotherapy of neuroblastoma [6].

The iNKT/CD1d agonist α-galactosylceramide (αGalCer) triggers a very strong iNKT cell activation associated with antitumor effects [3]. However, this initial massive iNKT cell activation is followed by a hyporesponsive state to subsequent free α-GalCer

Chaohong Liu (ed.), *Invariant Natural Killer T-Cells: Methods and Protocols*, Methods in Molecular Biology, vol. 2388, https://doi.org/10.1007/978-1-0716-1775-5_16,

treatments [7]. Therefore, iNKT cell anergy is a hurdle for efficient iNKT cell-mediated immunotherapy [3, 4, 8]. To this end, we have generated CD1d-antitumor fusion proteins to induce sustained iNKT cell activation by fusing CD1d with antitumor-associated antigen (TAA) scFv [8–11] (Fig. 1). In this regard, the recombinant αGalCer-loaded CD1d-scFv fusion protein will allow specific tumor targeting, and we previously showed that repeated treatments also lead to prolonged antitumor immunity [8, 9, 11]. Of note, iNKT cells activated by the α-GalCer/CD1d-scFv fusion showed similar PD-1 up-regulation, but they still produced IFNγ upon repeated injections, suggesting that PD-1 is not sufficient to mediate the iNKT cell anergy [9, 11]. We also noticed that, in contrast to free α-GalCer ligand, recombinant α-GalCer/CD1d-scFv fusion protein induce more rapid production of IFNγ and TNFα, indicating a mechanistic difference in the activation of iNKT cells depending on whether it occurs via endogenous CD1d expressed by antigen-presenting cells or via the recombinant α-GalCer/CD1d-scFv fusion protein. Another advantage of the α-GalCer/CD1d-scFv fusion proteins resides in the tumor targeting via its anti-TAA scFv, which allows redirecting the immune response to the tumor [9–11]. We have shown that the specific tumor targeting of the CD1d fusion, as compared to the non-targeted CD1d fusion protein, resulted in a higher reactivity of iNKT cells upon several stimulations, as shown by the increased cytokine production associated with better antitumor effects in mice. Yet, development of more stable covalent conjugates of αGalCer-CD1d-scFv may represent more effective cancer immunotherapeutic approaches [12].

2 Materials

2.1 Recombinant CD1d Fusion Proteins

The α-GalCer analog KRN7000 (Alexis Biochemicals Corp.) is dissolved in PBS-0.5% Tween-20. Genetic fusion of mouse β2-microglobulin (β2m) with the soluble part of mouse CD1d (sCD1d) and the anti-TAA scFv are performed by overlapping PCR, and a His Tag is added at the C-term for purification. Recombinant CD1d fusion proteins are produced by transient transfection of the HEK293-EBNA (Cellular Biotechnology Laboratory, EPFL, Switzerland), and supernatants are affinity purified on the Sartobind His-Tag membrane adsorbers for exchange chromatography (Sartorius AG, Germany). The recombinant fusion proteins are loaded with α-GalCer before administration in vivo.

2.2 CD1d Tetramer

The CD1d tetramer is developed by engineering a BirA consensus sequence at the C-terminus of the soluble mouse CD1d protein. The CD1d monomer is biotinylated by the BirA enzyme (Avidity, Denver, CO), and after loading with αGalCer, it is tetramerized on streptavidin-PE (Invitrogen) using a molar ratio of 4:1.

2.3 Antibodies Used for Flow Cytometry Analysis

The following antibodies are used to characterize iNKT cells: Fixable Viability Dye eFluor™ 506 (eBioscience 65-0866-14), α-GalCer/CD1d tetramer-PE (home-made), anti-mouse CD3-Alexa 700 (17A2, BioLegend 100216), anti-mouse CD4-FITC (RM4-5, BioLegend 100510), anti-mouse NK1.1-PerCPCy5.5 (PK136, BioLegend 108728), anti-mouse CD8a-PE-Texas Red (Ly2, Thermo Fisher Scientific MCD0817), and anti-mouse B220 FITC (RA3-6B2, BioLegend 103206), anti-mouse IFN-γ-PerCP/Cy5.5 (XMG1.2, BioLegend 505821), and anti-mouse TNFα-Pacific Blue (MP6-XT22, BioLegend 506318).

2.4 Buffers

T cell complete media: RPMI 1640 basal medium (Gibco No. 11875-093) supplemented with 10% fetal bovine serum (FBS), non-essential amino acids, penicillin-streptomycin (10,000 U/ml, Gibco No. 15140-114), L-glutamine (Gibco No. 25030-024), non-essential amino acids (NEAA, Gibco No. 11140-035), sodium pyruvate (Gibco No. 11360-039), and 50 μM β-mercaptoethanol (Sigma No. M-7522).

Fixation buffer (BioLegend Cat. No. 420801).

Intracellular staining perm wash buffer (BioLegend Cat. No. 421002).

RBC lysis buffer (BioLegend Cat. No. 420301).

FACS buffer: Phosphate-buffered saline (PBS) with 2% FBS plus 1 mM EDTA and 0.05% sodium azide.

3 Methods

3.1 Administration of α-GalCer/CD1d-scFv Fusion Proteins

1. Inject i.v. with 0.4 μg αGalCer or equimolar amounts of α-GalCer/CD1d-scFv fusion proteins (40 μg) (Fig. 1).
2. Sacrifice the animals 2 h after the last injections of α-GalCer or α-GalCer/CD1d-scFv fusion proteins.

3.2 Preparation of Single-Cell Suspension

1. Harvest the spleens and smash through a 70 μm filter.
2. Add 2 ml 1× Red Blood Cell Lysis Buffer (*see* **Note 1**) and incubate for 5 min at room temperature.

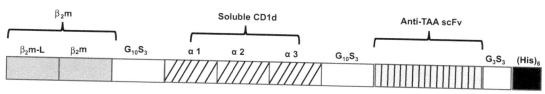

Fig. 1 Schematic representation of the design of CD1d/anti-TAA scfv fusion protein

3. Stop the RBS lysing by adding 10 ml T cell complete media and centrifuge at $400 \times g$ for 5 min and discard the supernatant.

4. Resuspend the cell pellet in 5 ml T cell complete media and keep on ice.

3.3 Surface Staining

1. Transfer 3–5 million splenocytes/well to a round-bottom 96-well plate.

2. Centrifuge the plate at $400 \times g$ and discard the supernatant.

3. Wash once in and then resuspend in 100 µl of 1:250 dilution of Aqua Dead (*see* **Note 2**) and incubate for 20 min at room temperature in the dark.

4. Centrifuge the plate at $400 \times g$ and discard the supernatant.

5. Block the Fc receptors with 50 µl of rat anti-mouse CD16/32 2.4G2 hybridoma supernatant for 15 min.

6. Add 150 µl FACS buffer to each well, centrifuge the plate at $400 \times g$, and discard the supernatant.

7. Add 50 µl of αGalCer/CD1d-PE tetramer to each well and incubate for 25 min on ice.

8. Add 150 µl FACS buffer to each well, centrifuge the plate at $400 \times g$, and discard the supernatant.

9. Add 50 µl surface antibody cocktails (*see* **Note 3**) or isotype controls (*see* **Note 4**) at recommended concentrations and further incubate for 25 min on ice (Fig. 2).

10. Add 150 µl FACS buffer to each well, centrifuge the plate at $400 \times g$, and discard the supernatant.

3.4 Fixation and Permeabilization

1. Resuspend the cell pellet in 100 µl fixation buffer. Incubate for 20 min on ice.

2. Add 100 µl 1× Intracellular Staining Permeabilization Wash Buffer (dilute 10× stock solution with ddH$_2$O), and centrifuge for 5 min at $400 \times g$. Discard the supernatant.

3. Wash again with 200 µl 1× Intracellular Staining Permeabilization Wash Buffer, and centrifuge for 5 min at $400 \times g$. Discard the supernatant.

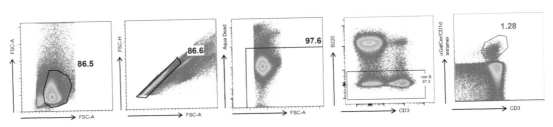

Fig. 2 Gating strategy of iNKT cells from mouse spleen

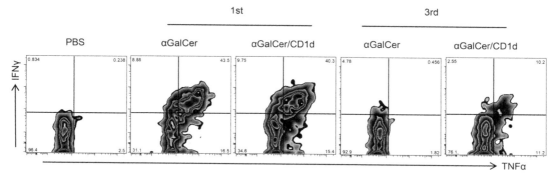

Fig. 3 Flow cytometric analysis of IFNγ and TNFα production by spleen iNKT cells upon the first or third injection of free α-GalCer or α-GalCer-loaded CD1d-scFv fusion protein

3.5 Intracellular Staining

1. Stain the cell pellet with the appropriate amounts of antibodies IFNγ-PerCP/Cy5.5 and TNFα-Pacific Blue diluted in 1× Intracellular Staining Permeabilization Wash Buffer (Fig. 3).

2. Incubate for 30 min on ice.

3. Wash 1× with 200 μl 1× Intracellular Staining Permeabilization Wash Buffer (*see* **Note 5**) and centrifuge at 400 × *g* for 5 min.

4. Repeat **step 3**.

5. Resuspend the cell pellet in 200 μl FACS buffer prior to acquisition.

4   Notes

1. Dilute the 10× Red Blood Cell Lysis Buffer to 1× working concentration with ultrapure water.

2. Aqua Dead should be diluted with PBS.

3. It is important to gate out B cells with anti-mouse B220 antibody to exclude nonspecific staining of α-GalCer/CD1d tetramer.

4. Appropriate isotype controls are needed to carry out flow cytometric analysis.

5. Dilute 10× Intracellular Staining Permeabilization Wash Buffer to 1× with ultrapure water.

References

1. Salio M, Silk JD, Jones EY, Cerundolo V (2014) Biology of CD1- and MR1-restricted T cells. Annu Rev Immunol 32:323–366. https://doi.org/10.1146/annurev-immunol-032713-120243

2. Zhang L, Tschumi BO, Corgnac S, Ruegg MA, Hall MN, Mach JP, Romero P, Donda A (2014) Mammalian target of rapamycin complex 1 orchestrates invariant NKT cell differentiation and effector function. J Immunol 193 (4):1759–1765. https://doi.org/10.4049/jimmunol.1400769

3. Fujii SI, Shimizu K (2019) Immune networks and therapeutic targeting of iNKT cells in

cancer. Trends Immunol 40(11):984–997. https://doi.org/10.1016/j.it.2019.09.008

4. Nair S, Dhodapkar MV (2017) Natural killer T cells in cancer immunotherapy. Front Immunol 8:1178. https://doi.org/10.3389/fimmu.2017.01178

5. Song L, Asgharzadeh S, Salo J, Engell K, Wu HW, Sposto R, Ara T, Silverman AM, DeClerck YA, Seeger RC, Metelitsa LS (2009) Valpha24-invariant NKT cells mediate antitumor activity via killing of tumor-associated macrophages. J Clin Invest 119 (6):1524–1536. https://doi.org/10.1172/JCI37869

6. Heczey A, Courtney AN, Montalbano A, Robinson S, Liu K, Li M, Ghatwai N, Dakhova O, Liu B, Raveh-Sadka T, Chauvin-Fleurence CN, Xu X, Ngai H, Di Pierro EJ, Savoldo B, Dotti G, Metelitsa LS (2020) Anti-GD2 CAR-NKT cells in patients with relapsed or refractory neuroblastoma: an interim analysis. Nat Med 26(11):1686–1690. https://doi.org/10.1038/s41591-020-1074-2

7. Parekh VV, Wilson MT, Olivares-Villagomez D, Singh AK, Wu L, Wang CR, Joyce S, Van Kaer L (2005) Glycolipid antigen induces long-term natural killer T cell anergy in mice. J Clin Invest 115(9):2572–2583. https://doi.org/10.1172/JCI24762

8. Stirnemann K, Romero JF, Baldi L, Robert B, Cesson V, Besra GS, Zauderer M, Wurm F, Corradin G, Mach JP, Macdonald HR, Donda A (2008) Sustained activation and tumor targeting of NKT cells using a CD1d-anti-HER2-scFv fusion protein induce antitumor effects in

mice. J Clin Invest 118(3):994–1005. https://doi.org/10.1172/JCI33249

9. Corgnac S, Perret R, Derre L, Zhang L, Stirnemann K, Zauderer M, Speiser DE, Mach JP, Romero P, Donda A (2013) CD1d-antibody fusion proteins target iNKT cells to the tumor and trigger long-term therapeutic responses. Cancer Immunol Immunother 62 (4):747–760. https://doi.org/10.1007/s00262-012-1381-7

10. Corgnac S, Perret R, Zhang L, Mach JP, Romero P, Donda A (2014) iNKT/CD1d-antibody immunotherapy significantly increases the efficacy of therapeutic CpG/peptide-based cancer vaccine. J Immunother Cancer 2(1):39. https://doi.org/10.1186/s40425-014-0039-8

11. Zhang L, Donda A (2017) Alpha-Galactosyl-ceramide/CD1d-antibody fusion proteins redirect invariant natural killer T cell immunity to solid tumors and promote prolonged therapeutic responses. Front Immunol 8:1417. https://doi.org/10.3389/fimmu.2017.01417

12. Veerapen N, Kharkwal SS, Jervis P, Bhowruth V, Besra AK, North SJ, Haslam SM, Dell A, Hobrath J, Quaid PJ, Moynihan PJ, Cox LR, Kharkwal H, Zauderer M, Besra GS, Porcelli SA (2018) Photoactivable glycolipid antigens generate stable conjugates with CD1d for invariant natural killer T cell activation. Bioconjug Chem 29(9):3161–3173. https://doi.org/10.1021/acs.bioconjchem.8b00484

Chapter 17

Investigating the Dynamic Changes in iNKT Cell Metabolic Profiles During Development

Jana L. Raynor and Hongbo Chi

Abstract

Emerging research has highlighted the importance of metabolic pathways and metabolites in dictating immune cell lineage decisions during thymocyte development. Here, we discuss several complementary approaches, including flow cytometry, metabolic flux, and transcriptome analyses, to characterize the dynamic changes in metabolic profiles associated with invariant natural killer T cell development.

Key words Metabolism, iNKT cell, Glycolysis, Oxidative phosphorylation, Flow cytometry, Seahorse, Bioinformatics

1 Introduction

Cellular metabolic processes are broadly categorized as anabolic or catabolic, characterized by the building up or breaking down of macromolecules that either use or generate energy, respectively. It is now well established that peripheral T cell homeostasis, activation, differentiation, and function are associated with dynamic changes in cellular metabolism [1, 2]. However, emerging studies highlight that these alterations in cellular metabolism are not limited to peripheral immune cells. We recently showed that metabolic signals driven by mechanistic target of rapamycin (mTOR) complex 1-dependent glycolysis regulate the lineage decisions of $\alpha\beta$ and $\gamma\delta$ T cells during development in the thymus [3]. Further, invariant natural killer T (iNKT) cells, a specialized subset of innate-like $\alpha\beta$ T cells, dynamically remodel glycolysis and mitochondrial homeostasis and oxidative phosphorylation (OXPHOS) during thymic development, and these changes correlate with quiescence entry [4]. Metabolic pathways may also direct the emergence of iNKT effector subsets during thymocyte development [5], as these subsets have varied metabolism-associated transcriptional profiles and

Chaohong Liu (ed.), *Invariant Natural Killer T-Cells: Methods and Protocols*, Methods in Molecular Biology, vol. 2388,
https://doi.org/10.1007/978-1-0716-1775-5_17,

requirements for Opa1-driven mitochondrial fusion [4]. These recent studies highlight the important role of immunometabolism in dictating T cell developmental fate and function.

There are several unique challenges of studying immunometabolic processes during thymocyte development. First, while several in vitro and emerging in vivo systems are available to study the metabolic state of peripheral T cell populations [6–8], the thymic microenvironment provides unique signals that cannot be fully recapitulated in vitro. Thus, there is a need to establish integrative approaches that reliably assess the metabolic state of thymic cell populations in vivo. Second, thymic populations, including iNKT cells, are relatively more rare than conventional T cell subsets, which makes it difficult to perform conventional profiling assays, such as metabolomics or CRISPR-based screening approaches, to assess the metabolic requirements of these cells in vivo. In this chapter, we provide an overview of a recently established comprehensive approach to profile the metabolic state of developing iNKT cells [4], which can be applied to both developmental and effector subsets. First, we describe a flow cytometry-based approach for profiling of mitochondrial parameters and glucose uptake as a surrogate for glycolysis. Next, we discuss how to apply Seahorse metabolic flux analysis on these cells. Finally, we detail how to perform transcriptome-based predictions of metabolic state using gene set enrichment analysis (GSEA).

2   Materials

2.1   Preparation of an Enriched Single-Cell Suspension from the Mouse Thymus

1. Hanks' balanced salt solution (HBSS) (Gibco, #14170–112). Add 2% heat inactivated fetal bovine serum (FBS). Store at 4 °C.

2. 10 cm polystyrene petri dish (Kord-Valmark, #2900).

3. 155 μm nylon mesh (Component Supply).

4. 3 ml syringe (BD, #309657).

5. 15 ml conical tube (available from multiple vendors).

6. Centrifuge (e.g., Thermo Fisher Scientific Sorvall ST Plus Series).

7. CD8+ T Cell Isolation Kit (Milteyni Biotec, #130-117-044).

8. LS columns (Milteyni Biotec, #130-042-401) and magnet (Milteyni Biotec, #130-091-051).

9. Hemocytometer and microscope for cell counting.

2.2   Flow Cytometric Assessment of iNKT Cell Metabolism

1. Flat-bottom 96-well plate (Falcon, #353072).

2. FACS buffer. Prepare using 1× PBS (Gibco, #14190-144) with the addition of 2% FBS. Store at 4 °C.

3. Metabolic dyes to assess mitochondrial quantity, membrane potential, cellular or mitochondrial reactive oxygen species (ROS), and glucose uptake. Prepare the dyes in FACS buffer immediately prior to use according to the below final working concentrations.

   (a) MitoTracker™ Deep Red or Green (Invitrogen, #M22426 or #M7514). Working concentration = 10 nM.

   (b) TMRM (ImmunoChemistry Technologies, #9105). Working concentration = 10 nM.

   (c) CellROX™ Deep Red (total cellular ROS indicator) (Invitrogen, #C10422). Working concentration = 2.5 µM.

   (d) MitoSOX™ Red (mitochondrial superoxide indicator) (Invitrogen, #M36008). Working concentration = 5 µM.

   (e) CM-H2DCFDA (general ROS indicator) (Invitrogen # C6827). Working concentration = 1 µM.

   (f) 2-NBDG (Thermo Fisher Scientific, # N13195). Working concentration = 30 µM.

4. 37 °C incubator. Either a 5% CO_2 or a non-CO_2 incubator can be used.

5. Mouse CD1d tetramer loaded with the glycolipid PBS-57 and conjugated to the R-phycoerythrin (PE) or Allophycocyanin (APC) fluorophore (mCD1d-PBS-57-PE or mCD1d-PBS-57-APC) (NIH Tetramer Core Facility).

6. Anti-TCRβ antibody conjugated to the Pacific Blue (PB) fluorophore (anti-TCRβ-PB; clone H57-597, available from multiple vendors).

7. Flow cytometer (e.g., BD LSRFortessa).

2.3 Agilent Seahorse Metabolic Flux Analysis of iNKT Cells

1. HBSS containing 2% FBS.

2. mCD1d-PBS-57-PE tetramer and anti-TCRβ-PB.

3. 5 ml polypropylene tube (Falcon, #352063).

4. 50 µm cell strainers (Sysmex CellTrics, #04-004-2327).

5. Complete Click's medium (FUJIFILM Irvine Scientific, #9195) containing 10% FBS, 1× penicillin/streptomycin/glutamine (Gibco, #10378-016), and 63 µM β-mercaptoethanol (Sigma-Aldrich M6250).

6. Agilent Seahorse Dulbecco's modified essential medium (DMEM; Gibco, #103575-100). The morning of the Seahorse assay, aliquot 48 ml of DMEM and supplement with the below reagents and adjust the pH of the medium to 7.4 (*see* **Note 1**).

   (a) 1 ml of d-(+)-glucose (Sigma-Aldrich, #G8644). Working concentration = 10 mM.

(b) 0.5 ml of 100 mM sodium pyruvate (Gibco, #11360–070). Working concentration = 1 mM.

(c) 0.5 ml of 200 mM L-glutamine (Gibco, #25030-149). Working concentration = 2 mM.

7. Agilent Seahorse XFe 96 instrument.

8. Agilent Seahorse FluxPak including 96-well cartridge plate, cell culture plate, and XF calibrant (#102601-100).

9. Ultrapure water (Invitrogen, #10977-015).

10. Poly-L-lysine (Sigma, #P8920).

11. Drugs for the Agilent Seahorse mitochondrial stress test (*see* **Note 1**). Stock solutions of these drugs should be prepared in supplemented DMEM Seahorse medium immediately prior to running the Seahorse assay. Working concentrations listed below are the final drug concentrations after injection.
(a) Oligomycin (Tocris Bioscience, #4110). Working concentration = 1 μM.

(b) Carbonyl cyanide 4-(trifluoromethoxy)phenylhydrazone (FCCP) (Sigma-Aldrich, #C2920). Working concentration = 1.5 μM.

(c) Rotenone (Sigma-Aldrich #R8875) (*see* **Note 2**). Working concentration = 0.5 μM.

12. 37 °C dry, non-CO_2 incubator (e.g., Labnet mini incubator).

2.4 Transcriptome-Based Bioinformatics to Assess iNKT Cell Metabolism

1. Gene expression data from microarray (e.g., Affymetrix Mouse Gene 2.0 ST Array) or RNA-sequencing generated in-house or downloaded from a public data repository [e.g., NCBI Gene Expression Omnibus (GEO)].

2. GSEA software from Broad Institute. This software is free to download from https://www.gsea-msigdb.org/gsea/index.jsp.

3. Data files necessary to input into GSEA (*see* **Note 3**).
(a) annotation.chip—File contains the annotation of each probe set for each gene based on the microarray expression chip used and is typically provided by the manufacturer. If it is not available within the GSEA software, it can be uploaded manually.

(b) phenotypelabels.cls—The purpose of this file is to inform the GSEA software how to annotate the samples in the expression.gct file. The file can be prepared in Excel and saved as a tab deliminated text file with the extension .cls.

(c) expression.gct—This is the expression dataset file and contains the gene identifiers and sample expression data. It can be prepared in Excel and saved as a tab deliminated text file with the extension .gct or .txt.

3 Methods

3.1 Preparation of iNKT Cells from the Thymus for Flow Cytometry and Cell Sorting

1. Harvest the thymus from one mouse into 1 ml of HBSS containing 2% FBS in a 10 cm petri dish (*see* **Note 4**).
2. Set a piece of 155 µM nylon mesh over the thymus, and crush the tissue with the flat end of a 3 ml syringe (*see* **Note 5**).
3. Transfer the single-cell suspension into a 15 ml conical tube.
4. Wash the petri dish with 3 ml of HBSS containing 2% FBS and transfer into the 15 ml tube.
5. Centrifuge the cells at $600 \times g$ for 5 min.
6. Resuspend the cell pellet in 500 µl of HBSS containing 2% FBS (*see* **Note 6**).
7. Enrich the iNKT cells by depleting $CD8^+$ T cells using Milteyni Biotec $CD8^+$ T Cell Isolation Kit per the manufacturer's instructions (*see* **Note 7**).
8. Centrifuge the cells at $600 \times g$ for 5 min.
9. Resuspend the cell pellet in HBSS containing 2% FBS at a concentration of 20×10^6 cells/ml. The cells are now ready to stain with fluorophore-conjugated antibodies and mouse CD1d tetramer to identify the iNKT cells by flow cytometry. The protocols for staining for flow cytometric analysis and cell sorting are described in the following sections.

3.2 Flow Cytometric Assessment of iNKT Cell Metabolism

1. Aliquot 2×10^6 cells isolated from the thymus into one well of a flat-bottom 96-well plate (*see* **Note 8**).
2. Centrifuge the cells at $600 \times g$ for 5 min and then remove the supernatant.
3. Dilute metabolic dyes in FACS buffer (*see* **Note 9**).
4. Add 50 µl of diluted metabolic dye to 2×10^6 cells.
5. Incubate the cells in a 37 °C incubator for 45 min for 2-NBDG or 30 min for other dyes.
6. Wash the cells by adding 100 µl of FACS buffer.
7. Centrifuge the cells at $600 \times g$ for 5 min and then remove the supernatant.
8. For surface staining, add 20 µl of FACS buffer containing mCD1d-PBS-57-PE and anti-TCRβ-PB at a 1:200 dilution (i.e., 0.1 µl of tetramer or antibody stock into 20 µl of FACS buffer) (*see* **Note 10**).
9. Incubate the cells at room temperature (RT) for 40 min.
10. Wash the cells with 100 µl of FACS buffer.
11. Centrifuge the cells at $600 \times g$ for 5 min and then remove the supernatant.

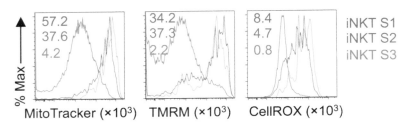

Fig. 1 Flow cytometric analysis of MitoTracker™ (left), TMRM (middle), and CellROX™ (right) in thymic iNKT developmental stage 1 (S1), stage 2 (S2), and stage 3 (S3). These data indicate a reduction in mitochondrial mass (Mito-Tracker™) and membrane potential (TMRM), as well as reduced cellular ROS (CellROX™), in S3 iNKT cells. Numbers indicate the mean fluorescence intensity (MFI). (Similar observations have previously been published [4, 10, 11])

12. For flow cytometry analysis, resuspend 2×10^6 cells in 50–100 μl of FACS buffer.

13. Analyze the iNKT cells on a flow cytometer (*see* **Note 11**). *See* Fig. 1 for representative MitoTracker™, TMRM, and Cell-ROX™ staining from thymic iNKT developmental stages.

3.3 Agilent Seahorse Analysis of iNKT Cell Glycolysis and OXPHOS

The evening prior to the Seahorse assay:

1. Coat the wells of the 96-well cell culture plate with poly-L-lysine. To do so, add 50 μl of poly-L-lysine diluted 1:10 in ultrapure water per well. Incubate the plate overnight at 4 °C.

2. Hydrate the calibrant plate by adding 200 μl of ultrapure water per well, and place the plate in the non-CO_2 37 °C incubator overnight.

*The day of the Seahorse assay (see **Note 12**):*

In the morning, prepare the DMEM Seahorse medium. Place the medium and cell culture plate coated with poly-L-lysine in a 37 °C non-CO_2 incubator to warm. Seahorse analysis requires >95% pure population of live thymic iNKT cells; therefore, cells should be sorted the morning of the Seahorse assay.

1. Isolate and enrich cells from the thymus for iNKT cell sorting (*see* **steps 1–7** in Subheading 3.1).

2. Stain the enriched cells from one thymus in 500 μl of HBSS containing 2% FBS, mCD1d-PBS-57-PE (1:200 dilution) and anti-TCRβ-PB (1:200 dilution) (*see* **Note 13**).

3. Incubate the cells at RT for 40 min.

4. Wash the cells with 2 ml of HBSS containing 2% FBS.

5. Centrifuge the cells at $600 \times g$ for 5 min and then remove the supernatant.

6. Resuspend the cell pellet at a concentration of 15–20×10^6 cells/ml in HBSS containing 2% FBS.

7. Filter the cells through a 50 μm cell strainer to remove any remaining cell clumps and transfer the cells into a 5 ml polypropylene tube for cell sorting. Sort cells into collection tubes containing complete Click's medium.

8. While cells are sorting, remove the water from the calibrant plate and replace with 200 μl of XF calibrant per well. Place the plate back into the non-CO$_2$ 37 °C incubator. This step should be done at least 1 h prior to running the Seahorse assay.

9. Count the cell number obtained from the sort (*see* **Note 14**).

10. Wash cells into 37 °C pre-warmed DMEM Seahorse medium supplemented with glucose, sodium pyruvate, and L-glutamine.

11. Resuspend cells in DMEM Seahorse medium at a concentration of 5 × 10^6 cells/ml.

12. Count the cells a second time to confirm the cells are at a concentration of 5 × 10^6 cells/ml (*see* **Note 15**).

13. Wash the Agilent Seahorse cell plate to remove the poly-L-lysine with 200 μl/well of 1× PBS. Dump the 1× PBS from the plate into the sink, and blot the plate onto a paper towel to remove excess liquid. Repeat this step one more time.

14. Immediately plate the cells by adding 50 μl of 5 × 10^6 cells/ml single cell suspension per well of an Agilent Seahorse 96-well cell culture plate (=250,000 iNKT cells into each well). Be sure to add the cells slowly to obtain an even cell distribution on the bottom of the well. It is best to have enough cells to plate 4 technical replicate wells per sample (*see* **Note 16**).

15. Centrifuge the plate at 200 × g for 10 s, with the centrifuge acceleration and deacceleration set at medium speed. Rotate plate 180° and spin again at 200 × g for 10 s. Check the cells under a microscope to confirm that the cells adhered as a single monolayer and are 90–95% confluent.

16. Incubate the cell plate in a 37 °C non-CO$_2$ incubator for 0.5–1 h. After the incubation is complete, add the remaining DMEM Seahorse medium to bring the final volume per well equal to 175 μl.

17. While the cell plate is incubating, prepare the drugs (oligomycin, FCCP, and rotenone) for the mitochondrial stress test.

18. Add 25 μl of the drugs into the appropriate port of the Seahorse cartridge:
    (a) Oligomycin (8× stock solution)—Port A.
    (b) FCCP (9× stock solution)—Port B.
    (c) Rotenone (10× stock solution)—Port C.

19. After the drugs are added, load the cartridge into the Agilent Seahorse XFe 96 instrument and initiate the run. Set up the

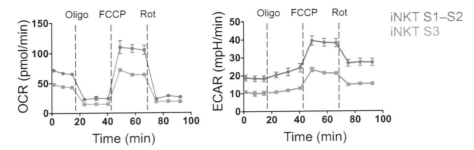

Fig. 2 iNKT developmental stages 1–2 (S1–S2) and stage 3 (S3) were sorted from the thymus of C57BL/6 mice and analyzed by Seahorse. Oxygen consumption rates (OCR, left) and extracellular acidification rates (ECAR, right) were measured before and after the sequential addition of mitochondrial inhibitors (Oligo, oligomycin; FCCP, carbonyl cyanide 4-(trifluoromethoxy)phenylhydrazone; and Rot, Rotenone). These data demonstrate that S3 iNKT cells have reduced OCR, an indicator of OXPHOS, and ECAR, an indicator of glycolysis, compared to S1–S2 iNKT cells. (Similar observations have previously been published [4])

template for the run, including the drugs and ports being used and the cell plate map. Parameters should be as follows: cycles, 3; mix, 3 min; wait, 2 min; and measure, 3 min. Select run assay to begin. **Critical**: Be sure to remove the lid of the cartridge plate before loading into the instrument.

20. After the Agilent Seahorse XFe 96 instrument completes the initiation (~15–20 min), it will prompt you to add the cell plate. Follow the prompts provided by the instrument. **Critical**: Be sure to remove the lid of the cell plate before loading into the instrument.

21. The Agilent Seahorse XFe 96 instrument will indicate when the run is complete. Unload the cell plate and export the data for analysis. *See* Fig. 2 for representative oxygen consumption rates (OCR), an indicator of OXPHOS, and extracellular acidification rates (ECAR), an indicator of glycolysis, from thymic iNKT developmental stages.

22. Before discarding the cell plate, confirm that the cell monolayer is still intact by examining under a microscope. Inconsistent cell adherence during the Seahorse assay may account for variability in the OCR and ECAR data.

3.4 Transcriptome-Based Bioinformatic Assessment of iNKT Cell Metabolism

1. Open the GSEA analysis software.

2. Under the "Load data" tab, add the annotation.chip, phenotypelabels.cls, and expression.gct files, and then select "Load these files."

3. After the files are loaded, go to the "Run Gsea" tab and fill out the following boxes under "Required fields":
   (a) Expression dataset—Select the expression dataset. If the dataset is not listed, it has not been loaded properly under the "Load data" tab.

(b) Gene set database—Select the curated gene sets of interest available in Molecular Signatures Database (MSigDB) (*see* **Note 17**).

(c) Number of permutations—Specify the number of permutations to assess the statistical significance of the enrichment score. GSEA recommends 1000 permutations.

(d) Phenotype labels—Select the directionality of comparison (e.g., knockout_versus_wild-type).

(e) Collapse dataset to gene symbols—Select "true."

(f) Permutation type—Select "gene_set." The "gene_set" option is recommended when there are fewer than seven samples within one group. "Phenotype" is the recommended method when there are seven or more samples in each group.

(g) Chip platform—From the pop-up window, click on the "Chips (local chip)" tab and select the annotation.chip file uploaded. Alternatively, click on the "Chips (from website)" tab and select the chip file used to generate your data. If the chip file is not available within the software, it is necessary to upload an annotation.chip file obtained from the manufacturer.

4. Select the "Show" button next to "Basic fields." Here you can change the name of the analysis and select the directory where the analysis will be saved.

5. Select the "Show" button next to "Advanced fields." Here you can modify the number of plots you want GSEA to generate under the "Plot graphs for the top sets of each phenotype" field.

6. Select "Run" to execute the GSEA analysis. *See* Fig. 3 for an example of the enrichment plots generated by GSEA.

4   Notes

1. Supplements for Seahorse DMEM medium (glucose, sodium pyruvate, L-glutamine), and drugs (oligomycin, FCCP, rotenone) can also be purchased from Agilent.

2. 1 µM Antimycin A can be used in addition to rotenone.

3. For more information on how to format the phenotypelabels. cls and expression.gct files, refer to the User Guide provided by GSEA (https://www.gsea-msigdb.org/gsea/doc/GSEAUserGuideFrame.html).

4. This protocol can be applied for secondary lymphoid tissues, such as the spleen and peripheral lymph nodes.

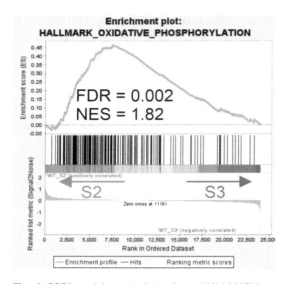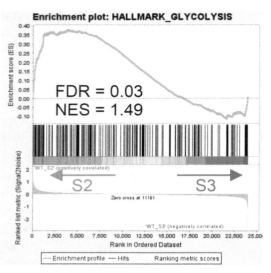

Fig. 3 GSEA enrichment plots of two HALLMARK gene sets, oxidative phosphorylation (OXPHOS) (left), and glycolysis (right), from the pairwise comparison of thymic iNKT developmental stage 2 (S2) and stage 3 (S3). Results show increased expression of genes related to OXPHOS and glycolysis in S2 relative to S3 iNKT cells. Gene expressions in iNKT developmental stages were determined using the Affymetrix Mouse Gene 2.0 ST Array. FDR, false discovery rate. NES, normalized enrichment score. (Similar observations have previously been published [4])

5. Grind the tissues gently in order to reduce mechanical damage and maintain viability of the lymphocytes. It is also important to keep tissues and cells on ice during processing.

6. If isolating cells from the spleen, an additional red blood cell lysis step is required. To do so, centrifuge the splenic cells ($600 \times g$ for 5 min) and remove the supernatant. Add 1 ml of ACK lysis buffer (Gibco, #A1049201) per spleen for 1 min at RT. Add 9 ml of HBSS containing 2% FBS, centrifuge ($600 \times g$ for 5 min), remove the supernatant, and resuspend cells in HBSS containing 2% FBS.

7. This step is optional, but it will decrease the amount of time needed for sorting and sample acquisition on the flow cytometer.

8. If more than 2×10^6 cells are required for flow cytometry analysis, scale up the number of cells and volumes for metabolic dyes and antibody mixes accordingly (e.g., 10×10^6 cells can be stained in 250 μl of metabolic dye mix and 100 μl of antibody mix).

9. Two dyes can be combined to minimize the number of staining sets. We typically combine MitoTracker™ Green (FITC channel) with CellROX™ Deep Red (APC channel) and TMRM (PE channel) with 2-NBDG (FITC channel).

10. If analysis of iNKT development stages is required, include the following antibodies in the staining set at this step: anti-CD24 (M1/69), NK1.1 (PK136), and CD44 (1M7). Stage 1 iNKT thymocytes are CD24$^-$NK1.1$^-$CD44$^-$. Stage 2 iNKT thymocytes are CD24$^-$NK1.1$^-$CD44$^+$. Stage 3 iNKT thymocytes are CD24$^-$NK1.1$^+$CD44$^+$.

11. Cells should be collected on a flow cytometer within 1–3 h of staining with metabolic dyes.

12. General tips for Seahorse:
    (a) Only use a non-CO_2 37 °C incubator for warming cell plates and medium.
    (b) Maintain reagents at 37 °C as much as possible to minimize temperature fluctuations.

13. To sort the iNKT developmental stages, also stain the cells with anti-CD24, NK1.1, and CD44 antibodies and sort the subsets as outlined in **Note 10**. If iNKT effector subsets need to be sorted, reporter mice are the best tools [5], although combinations of surface markers have been described to faithfully subset iNKT effector cell populations [9].

14. Typical iNKT cell yield from the thymus of one 5–6-week-old C57BL/6 mouse: 150,000–250,00 cells.

15. If the cell concentration has changed between the first and second count, adjust the volume added per well to plate 250,000 cells/well.

16. 200,000 cells/well is the lower limit for iNKT cells.

17. We have found the following molecular signature database collections available in MSigDB (https://www.gsea-msigdb.org/gsea/msigdb) to contain informative metabolic gene signatures:
    (a) H: HALLMARK gene sets.
    (b) C2: curated gene sets (including the KEGG and BIO-CARTA subsets).
    (c) C5: ontology gene sets, specifically the Gene Ontology (GO) gene sets.

Acknowledgments

The authors thank Dr. Hao Shi for edits and Dr. Nicole Chapman for contributing edits and writing for this manuscript. This work was supported by NIH AI105887, AI131703, AI140761, AI150241, AI150514, CA221290, and CA250533 (to H.C.).

References

1. Geltink RIK, Kyle RL, Pearce EL (2018) Unraveling the complex interplay between T cell metabolism and function. Annu Rev Immunol 36:461–488. https://doi.org/10.1146/annurev-immunol-042617-053019

2. Chapman NM, Boothby MR, Chi H (2020) Metabolic coordination of T cell quiescence and activation. Nat Rev Immunol 20 (1):55–70. https://doi.org/10.1038/s41577-019-0203-y

3. Yang K, Blanco DB, Chen X, Dash P, Neale G, Rosencrance C, Easton J, Chen W, Cheng C, Dhungana Y, Kc A, Awad W, Guo XJ, Thomas PG, Chi H (2018) Metabolic signaling directs the reciprocal lineage decisions of alphabeta and gammadelta T cells. Sci Immunol 3(25): eaas9818. https://doi.org/10.1126/sciimmunol.aas9818

4. Raynor JL, Liu C, Dhungana Y, Guy C, Chapman NM, Shi H, Neale G, Sesaki H, Chi H (2020) Hippo/Mst signaling coordinates cellular quiescence with terminal maturation in iNKT cell development and fate decisions. J Exp Med 217(6):e20191157. https://doi.org/10.1084/jem.20191157

5. Lee YJ, Holzapfel KL, Zhu J, Jameson SC, Hogquist KA (2013) Steady-state production of IL-4 modulates immunity in mouse strains and is determined by lineage diversity of iNKT cells. Nat Immunol 14(11):1146–1154. https://doi.org/10.1038/ni.2731

6. Ma EH, Verway MJ, Johnson RM, Roy DG, Steadman M, Hayes S, Williams KS, Sheldon RD, Samborska B, Kosinski PA, Kim H, Griss T, Faubert B, Condotta SA, Krawczyk CM, DeBerardinis RJ, Stewart KM, Richer MJ, Chubukov V, Roddy TP, Jones RG (2019) Metabolic profiling using stable isotope tracing reveals distinct patterns of glucose utilization by physiologically activated CD8(+) T cells. Immunity 51(5):856–870. https://doi.org/10.1016/j.immuni.2019.09.003

7. Johnson MO, Wolf MM, Madden MZ, Andrejeva G, Sugiura A, Contreras DC, Maseda D, Liberti MV, Paz K, Kishton RJ, Johnson ME, de Cubas AA, Wu P, Li G, Zhang Y, Newcomb DC, Wells AD, Restifo NP, Rathmell WK, Locasale JW, Davila ML, Blazar BR, Rathmell JC (2018) Distinct regulation of Th17 and Th1 cell differentiation by Glutaminase-dependent metabolism. Cell 175(7):1780–1795. https://doi.org/10.1016/j.cell.2018.10.001

8. Artyomov MN, Van den Bossche J (2020) Immunometabolism in the single-cell era. Cell Metab 32(5):710–725. https://doi.org/10.1016/j.cmet.2020.09.013

9. Engel I, Seumois G, Chavez L, Samaniego-Castruita D, White B, Chawla A, Mock D, Vijayanand P, Kronenberg M (2016) Innate-like functions of natural killer T cell subsets result from highly divergent gene programs. Nat Immunol 17(6):728–739. https://doi.org/10.1038/ni.3437

10. Salio M, Puleston DJ, Mathan TS, Shepherd D, Stranks AJ, Adamopoulou E, Veerapen N, Besra GS, Hollander GA, Simon AK, Cerundolo V (2014) Essential role for autophagy during invariant NKT cell development. Proc Natl Acad Sci U S A 111(52):E5678–E5687. https://doi.org/10.1073/pnas.1413935112

11. Park H, Tsang M, Iritani BM, Bevan MJ (2014) Metabolic regulator Fnip1 is crucial for iNKT lymphocyte development. Proc Natl Acad Sci U S A 111(19):7066–7071. https://doi.org/10.1073/pnas.1406473111

INDEX

Chaohong Liu (ed.), *Invariant Natural Killer T-Cells: Methods and Protocols*, Methods in Molecular Biology, vol. 2388,
https://doi.org/10.1007/978-1-0716-1775-5,
© The Author(s), under exclusive license to Springer Science+Business Media, LLC, part of Springer Nature 2021

CPSIA information can be obtained
at www.ICGtesting.com
Printed in the USA
LVHW061918230922
728951LV00008B/323